BEHIND THE CRYSTAL BALL

BEHIND THE CRYSTAL BALL

MAGIC, SCIENCE, AND THE OCCULT
FROM ANTIQUITY THROUGH
THE NEW AGE

ANTHONY AVENI

TIMES BOOKS

RANDOM HOUSE

All rights reserved under International and Pan-American Copyright Conven-
tions. Published in the United States by Times Books, a division
of Random House, Inc., New York, and simultaneously in Canada
by Random House of Canada Limited, Toronto.

Library of Congress Cataloging-in-Publication Data
Aveni, Anthony F.
Behind the crystal ball : magic, science, and the occult from antiquity
through the New Age / Anthony Aveni. —1st ed.
p.   cm.
Includes bibliographical references and index.
ISBN 0-8129-2415-0
1. Magic—History.   2. Occultism and science.   I. Title.
BF1589.A9   1996
133'.09—dc20   96-2592

BOOK DESIGN BY FEARN CUTLER

Random House website address: http://www.randomhouse.com/

Printed in the United States of America on acid-free paper
9 8 7 6 5 4 3 2
FIRST EDITION

To Carlyle Aveni—whose life is filled with magic

Beavers build dams, birds build nests,
ants excavate, but they have no magic, just as
they have no science or religion.

Lynn Thorndike,
A History of Magic and Experimental Science

PREFACE

". . . there are hidden powers in man, which are capable of making a *God* of him on earth."[1] When mystic Helena Blavatsky so concisely penned magic's credo a little over one hundred years ago, she also offered me a guideline for this book. Magic as open deception—the world of rabbits and hats, saws and ladies, hocus and pocus—is only the tiniest remnant of what history has bequeathed us; the telltale appendage of an epic story of humanity's quest for knowledge of the truth, and for what is real.

There was a time when science and the occult happily coexisted under the same roof, one scarcely discernible from the other in method and practice. How they parted company and why one was relegated to the darker side of history while the other came to bask in the limelight of mainstream belief is our subject matter. Treating both magic and science as belief systems about how the real world works, I will explore the tangled territory between these two, oft-retreating, sometimes converging, oppositely charged accounts of reality. If we draw science and magic closer together by tracing their courses through history, we learn how social forces over the ages have slowly altered our common sense about the natural world and its relation to the human spirit—what we term religion. Along with magic and science, religion makes up the third point of an eternal triangle of ideological warfare.

As I peek through the cracks between science and magic, my goal will not be to attack alternative ways of perceiving reality. I have no desire to pronounce all magic superstitious flotsam—science gone awry. Nor do I wish to demystify magic and reduce it to a set of explanations that are inferior to my own scientifically trained way of understanding the world. This has been done before. No one ought to lift thoughtways like astrology and alchemy out of time and culture and place them on the examining table for postmortem dissection. On the other hand, I have no desire to grind the heretical axe of discrediting scientific thinking. I would be a hypocrite if I did so.

Instead my goal is to give a balanced account of how and why people in the Western tradition have changed the way they think about the real world and to understand why most of us who do not believe in the ghosts and spirits that haunt mystical and paranormal experience nevertheless can accept the unseen cold dark cosmic matter and evaporating black holes modern scientific explanation offers us.

Today's occult arts are barely recognizable offsprings of complex imaginative cosmologies that once were a part of the establishment—commonsense ways of thinking in the mainstream of their time—not a source of simple answers to complicated questions that many critics perceive them to be today. Whether they know it or not, both participant and practitioner of the contemporary occult acquire their directions from the past. That's why a knowledge of our magic-oriented forebears is important.

Why do people cling to ideas society judges to be outdated? I offer two answers, which I think are correct whether spirits really exist or whether there's nobody down here but us: Either we long for an imagined, more beneficent world that we feel has been lost to us or we shun the invasive and personally threatening philosophies that gave rise to our scientific way of explaining nature, or both. Can the rational element in all of us still wholeheartedly accept a universe out of which one can create symbols and interrelate them in a way that can tell us something about ourselves? Are we too strongly shackled to belief in a world that science determines for us? Have we for too long been nonparticipatory residents of an indifferent world that has lost its use for magic?

Throughout history the wise always have seemed to say: What we do is legitimate; what everybody else does is pretending. This is what a scientist like Albert Einstein or Richard Feynman might have said of a conjurer like Harry Houdini or David Copperfield. The difference between long ago and here and now is that then there was much more to magic than pretending.

Anthony Aveni

ACKNOWLEDGMENTS

I am indebted to my colleagues Robert Garland, Joscelyn Godwin, Robert Goodwin, and Michael Peletz for helpful discussions on a number of subjects dear to their hearts and mine that appear in this text. Thank you also to my extraordinary students Lorren Hotaling, Steven Morandi, and Polly Peterson for their valuable input (my students have always been my most demanding audience); to Ruth Hartshorne for providing material once used by her late husband Steve, a professor at Colgate who taught an outstanding course on Occult Philosophy; to indefatigable library sleuths David Hughes, Debbie Huerta, and Julia Meyerson; once again to Betsy Rapoport and her expert editorial staff at Times Books (especially John Rambow, Martha Trachtenberg, and Ginny Carroll), and to Faith Hamlin for ten enjoyable years of book publishing; and lastly to the best up-front production team who have been on word trips with me before—Lorraine Aveni, Jackie D'Amore, Wanda Kelly, and Patricia Ryan.

CONTENTS

PREFACE   XI

ACKNOWLEDGMENTS   XIII

LIST OF ILLUSTRATIONS   XVII

INTRODUCTION: Above the Ordinary   3

PART I: MAGIC IN ANTIQUITY:
HOW MAGIC WORKS AND WHY WE MISUNDERSTAND IT   13

CHAPTER 1:   Middle East Exotica:
Ancient Egypt and Magical Mesopotamia   15
CHAPTER 2:   The Ancient Art of Hepatoscopy   20
CHAPTER 3:   The Greek Paradox: Magic Confronts Science   24
CHAPTER 4:   Magic in the Roman Empire   42
CHAPTER 5:   The New Outcasts: The Rise of Secret Doctrines   52
CHAPTER 6:   Knowledge through Number and the Word   60

PART II: FROM LIGHT TO LIGHT:
MAGIC FROM THE DARK AGES TO THE ENLIGHTENMENT   73

CHAPTER 7:   Pathways to Knowledge   75
CHAPTER 8:   Resurrection of the Kabbalah   78
CHAPTER 9:   Music of the Spheres   91
CHAPTER 10: Two Sides of the Coin of Alchemy   98
CHAPTER 11: Rise of the Clear Seer   112
CHAPTER 12: Medieval Astrology   117
CHAPTER 13: The Devil and the Proliferation of Good and Evil 123
CHAPTER 14: It's Witchcraft   133
CHAPTER 15: Summary: Who Turned on the Lights?   141

PART III: RAISING SPIRITS:
NINETEENTH-CENTURY OCCULTISM   149

CHAPTER 16: Rochester Rap: The First Haunted House   151
CHAPTER 17: Before Hydesville: Strange Forces, New Experiments 163

CHAPTER 18:   "Mr. Sludge"   179
CHAPTER 19:   DDH to HPB: Pipelines to the Past   191
CHAPTER 20:   After the Foxes: From Parlor to Stage   201
CHAPTER 21:   My Body, My Map: "Bumpology"   212
CHAPTER 22:   Summary: A Light That Failed?   224

PART IV: A MODERN KALEIDOSCOPE OF MAGIC   229

CHAPTER 23:   Who's a Magician?: The Houdini Legend   231
CHAPTER 24:   Who's a Magician?: Trickster from Far Rockaway   238
CHAPTER 25:   Magic in the Twentieth Century:
              What the Pollsters Say   245
CHAPTER 26:   Different Time, Same Channel   252
CHAPTER 27:   PK Wars: Psychics vs. Physics   256
CHAPTER 28:   The Personalized Magic of Healing:
              Mending the Cartesian Split   264
CHAPTER 29:   You Are What You Eat   274
CHAPTER 30:   Come Fly with Me: UFO Abductions   279
CHAPTER 31:   Life After Life   288
CHAPTER 32:   Crystals: Who's Scrying Now?   291
CHAPTER 33:   Geomancy: From Saws to Sausages   295
CHAPTER 34:   Summary: On Shifting Ground   303

PART V: GOD, DICK, AND HARRY:
           MAGIC AT THE MILLENNIUM   305

CHAPTER 35:   Is Magic a Religion?   307
CHAPTER 36:   Magic and Science:
              J.Z. and the Ramsters Meet Arch Debunker   313
CHAPTER 37:   Anthropologists Encounter the Occult   324
CHAPTER 38:   Summary:
              Crossing Curves in an Age of Interconnectedness   339

EPILOGUE: Of Bacon and Black Holes   349

NOTES   351
BIBLIOGRAPHY   377
INDEX   391

LIST OF ILLUSTRATIONS

PAGE

1. "As Above, So Below." The Zodiac and the Human Body   33

2. "I'll Nail Him." A Greek *Defixion* from an Aegean Gravesite   37

3. Plants with Animal- and Human-like Characteristics   46

4. Magic Numbers and Words   62

5. Adam and the Ten Sephiroth   80

6. The *Sephiroth*, the Kabbalah's Tree of Life   81

7. The Outstretched Human Body   86

8. Music of the Spheres   92

9. The Astrologer at Work   96

10. The Philosopher's Egg   106

11. Hell and the Devil Have Taken on Many Forms   124, 125

12. A Mesmerist and His Patient   171

13. The "Stammering" Century's Table Tipping and Levitation   181

14. The Odd Couple: H. P. Blavatsky and H. S. Olcott   193

15. A Spaghetti–faced Spiritualist   206

16. A Catalog of Foreheads: Metoposcopy   214, 215

17. Phrenological Diagram and Palmistry   218, 219

18. Debunking "Pseudopods"   228

19. Conjurer Harry Houdini   233

20. *Kundalini*—The Body Serpent   272

BEHIND THE CRYSTAL BALL

INTRODUCTION:

ABOVE THE ORDINARY

$\sim$

One man's religion is another man's superstition.
Gustav Jahoda, *The Psychology of Superstition*

Texas Ranger baseball pitcher Mike Griffin says he always ate bacon the day before he took to the mound. Leo Durocher, colorful manager of the Giants and Dodgers in the post-World War II era, always wore the same clothes outside the clubhouse whenever his teams went on a winning streak. When the Dodgers drove to a pennant in 1941, Durocher lived in the same black shoes, gray slacks, and blue tie for three consecutive weeks. Hall of Fame hurler Rube Waddell always carried a lucky coin, a lucky bobby pin, and lucky covers torn from old baseballs when he pitched. Al Hrabosky refused to cut his hair and beard for the entire baseball season; his coiffure earned him the title "the Mad Hungarian." Old Cincinnati Reds manager Sparky Anderson always jumped over the foul line on the way to and from the mound to visit with a pitcher.[1]

These magical paraphernalia, charms, fetishes, and superstitious rites—all prescribed to ward off bad luck—are the same tools and techniques we will find in Harry Houdini's act, in Merlin the Magician's spells, in accounts of exorcism inscribed on three-thousand-year-old clay tablets from Babylonia, performed by high priests whose real personae are lost in the sands of time. Though our rational side denies it, magic is everywhere. It has always been with us and it always will be. Its sinister terminology be damned, its effectiveness disclaimed by the scientifically minded from the Roman Empire to the Renaissance, the spark of magic still lives.

Remember the little half-truths we acquired from our playmates when we were kids—beliefs in the extraordinary powers of knocking on wood, brandishing horseshoes and rabbits' feet, avoiding walking under a ladder or breaking a mirror? Most of us outgrew our childish beliefs. But how many of us still carry a lucky charm on our keychain or above the dashboard of our car—just in case? "Step on a crack and break your back (or your mother's back)" is an oldie that can be traced at least as far back as nineteenth-century England where there were many variations of the fate that resulted from doing so. If you stepped on a crack in Norfolk, for example, snakes would chase you. Do it in Manchester and they'd marry you. Bears will bite you, squeeze you, eat you, writes A. A. Milne, author of *Winnie the Pooh*.[2] You'll marry someone not of your ethnic group, says an old Scottish legend.

When was the last time you witnessed someone knocking on wood? The likelihood is that it was only a matter of a few weeks or months ago; the custom is very common. We usually knock wood to avoid bad luck. Wood knocking goes all the way back to primitive tree worship. Though we urban dwellers might not get it, anyone who lives in nature's world understands the way trees protect the toiling farmer from rain and sun, nurture his family with their fruit, drop their leaves for a resting place. By living on for generations, the tree becomes nature's role model for the immortality we all desire yet for which none of us is destined. A tree's branches were once thought to connect all earthly creatures with the heavenly abode of the gods. Might the gods look down favorably upon us if we touch and embrace this umbilicus that binds us physically to them? Little wonder trees play a major role in stories of creation all over the world.[3]

Finger crossing is as common as wood knocking. It may emanate simply from the unity symbolized by two things that join together, like the junction we also discover in the chicken wishbone or a handshake. An old English version of this custom has a friend making a special secret wish for you and then crossing his/her index finger with yours to make it come true. Later the custom became an individual act accompanied by a verbal gesture.

Horseshoes and rabbit's feet certainly belong on the solid gold lucky charm list. A friend in rural New York state has an old horseshoe hanging over the doorway to his barn. He tells me it protects his chickens from predators, especially if it's hung with the ends pointing up, to keep in the luck. Why a horseshoe? What's unusual about it is its semicircular shape—a variation of Medieval lore's magic circle, the protective perimeter of confinement you draw around yourself to ward off the Devil. A horseshoe's practical function was protective. Horseshoes were invented by the Greeks over two thousand years ago to shield the feet of their horses; in fact, many older versions of equine footwear still carry the lucky seven holes the Greeks used to drill to fasten the nails to the horses' hooves.

A rabbit's foot brings good luck because the glassy eye of the rabbit was believed to ward off the evil eye. And what is more menacing than a gaze? Many people still believe emanations of ill fortune can be transmitted by eye-to-eye contact with foxes, snakes, and certain humans such as hunchbacks, who were alleged to possess the requisite power. As we shall learn later, our theory of vision has since changed drastically but the custom of warding off the evil eye still survives, as witnessed on key chains all over the world that carry a rabbit's foot (more practical to tote than a rabbit's eyeball).

The list of popular contemporary lucky charms both good and bad is interminable. Own some shark's teeth or mistletoe, find a button or a pin, see a white horse or an ambulance, carry the right stone or wear it on your neck or finger, or get a mascot—if you're a member of a team: any way to improve your chances against bad luck or an evil encounter. On the dark side, walk under a ladder, or even look at a black cat and you could undo the efficacy of all the positive paraphernalia you might care to cart around.

Then there's the "God bless you" gesture after a sneeze. It can be traced back to ancient Greece when sneezing was believed to expel ghosts, demons, or fairies from one's body. But blasting out these unwanted tenants at high velocity endangered those around the sneezer—one generation's evil spirits are another's germs. Once the cataclysmic respiratory quake ensued, a short prayer or invocation to the gods seemed in order: "Long may you live!" or "Jupiter preserve you!" said the onlookers, not just as a means of self-protection, but also to appeal to the gods that the victim be rid of evil possession. Another version suggests that when you sneeze you temporarily lose your soul. Aristotle called the sneeze an emotion in the brain. And isn't the actual instant of a sneeze almost an ecstatic experience?

All these amusing little appendages of past ways of thinking that have managed to survive the ravages of change fit the definition of the term superstition. Superstition literally means to "stand above cause." By their presence or occurrence, things magic were said to suspend people in wonder and amazement—sometimes in fear, often in veneration—as in that rare case of dangling disbelief known as the miracle. Today's dictionaries label these ancient superstitions as beliefs in which religious veneration is shown where none is deserved, or as faith—based on insufficient causal evidence or no evidence at all—worshipping false gods through fear.

But who decides what *is* rational, what unknown there is to fear, what lies within the realm of causal explanation? Only common sense. And what is common sense but a culturally shared belief—a manner of viewing and relating to the world we all agree upon and out of habit adopt as part of our way of life? What makes superstition a pejorative or insidious term is the implied deep-seated connection with belief in a direct connection between you and me and the powers of evil. That's where generally negative words like "witchcraft" and "omen" plug into the definition. In turn, these terms are often associated with religious forms of worship.

Now, common sense for most of us is based on the firm conviction that the material world that consists of any-leaved clovers, the full range of colors of cats, and the podiatric protector of any quadruped has no direct link with or power over the human condition. Maybe the Old Testament connection with the evils associated with idol worship still strikes fear in our hearts. The very thought of someone who would believe in the efficacy of material objects in dealing with matters human is very bothersome to our rational minds, even if playful versions of such old customs still survive. Yet we don't find praying to saints silly; if slugger Rocky Colavito makes the sign of the cross before batting a baseball, you might say to yourself: "That's religion, not superstition" or "What's wrong with praying to the one true God?"

But praying to God is the norm even in our secular world. It is part of our "common sense" to believe that prayer works. It is culturally acceptable. We do it out of habit. Those who perform a little ritual to court lady luck will reason: "I know it's silly, but what if I don't do it; what if there's something in it?"

If we all lived in a world like that of Middle Age Europe, where belief in witches was part of organized common sense, then the skeptics would be the deviants and rational scientists the heretics. My discussion of wood knocking and horseshoes isn't intended purely to amuse my readers with the recitation of odd quirks and trivia. I want to use these little stories as a jumping-off point to penetrate to the very heart of taking other ways, other times, other people very seriously. In this book I want readers to discover, as I did, that all the amusing half-truths that survive (and many that are lost from our daily activities) were not always considered whimsical or irrational.

"God bless you!" and "knock on wood" are just two examples of word formulas that descend from a time before there were pages of history, a time when words alone, like vows or oral promises, were thought to carry power. Like words of protection, objects of ownership—horseshoes and rabbits' feet—manifested the embodiment of spiritual attachment between people and animate higher powers that were very real. Today we call them charms (a positive term) or fetishes (a negative term), conduits of power through which one might dare to influence the gods. When writers of dictionaries define a fetish as an object of irrational reverence or devotion they demonstrate their unwillingness to employ the term "reasonable" to describe the behaviors and actions of any culture other than their own living in any time other than the present. In my view this is just one dangerous short step away from presupposing that there can be no validity in any cultural context to harboring such a belief. What an unfortunate position to take, for it works against human understanding. Such a definition encourages us to rule out exploring what sounded reasonable in the place and time of the believer who worshipped the object. It discourages us from trying to know our predecessors. And if we care less about how *they* got changed into *us,* we might believe falsely that we can forget the past and need think only about the present.

Yes, rational human beings like you and me subconsciously practice divination. When Mike Griffin eats bacon the day before he pitches he isn't just following a custom or habit. He is conducting a rite. "Would you ever deliberately not step on third base?" a superstitious baseball player once was asked. "Never! I wouldn't dare. It would destroy my confidence to hit."[4] He knows what he's doing and specifically why he is doing it. And that is quite different from my daily custom of pouring my juice before I start making the coffee. The coffee will taste the same regardless of when I brew it.

Whether we realize it or not, we still invoke gods, exhort them to amplify their power, seek their protection to intervene in our behalf. We beg them to tell us what the future will bring. Wishing on a star or getting kissed under mistletoe is amusing enough, but attach these desiccated appendages of belief to terms like fetish, charm, apparition, omen, occult, and magic—the stuff our progressive world is supposed to have outgrown—and we all become a bit uneasy, for we see in them that shadowy side of human nature, which can occasionally erupt in irrational, often violent forms of expression, such as drug-induced out-of-body experiences, devil worship, and human sacrifice.

If superstition is belief in suprasensible powers (powers that lie beyond the senses), and in the connections between mind and matter, and spirit and substance, then magic, a more potent term, is the operative word that puts that connection into play. We can think of magic as the means, the action that launches the power of the spirits. It is the learned art that produces the marvelous effects of superhuman beings or departed spirits that believers witness and talk about. To its detractors magic is sorcery, enchantment, black art, the occult—that which is hidden from the eye. Magic is secret; it is undercover and therefore suspect. But to believers it is a pathway to "alternate realities," and there is value in defining its vocabulary and exploring its range of subject matter for both believer and skeptic alike as a way of understanding the diversity of human experience.[5]

You make magic by invoking superrational powers (deities, indefinable impersonal beings, or forces of nature), provided you know how to do it. And here is what makes magic even more suspect to contemporary common sense: You learn it only by being initiated into its art and craft through secrecy. That's because magic's subject matter is said to be arcane, its practice mysterious and cryptic. Legend has it that this is because the way to the supernatural once was revealed to people in very ancient times by the gods themselves.

Today science writers seem content to teach *their* truths; the real world is the strictly tangible one. A host of New Age books are just as dogmatic about preaching that mind and matter *do* meet and that comprehending and controlling the nonmaterial side of the coin of reality is a valid and legitimate human goal. Content to grow in their own gardens, few are concerned with exploring the soil where these now diametrically opposed ideas about mind and matter developed.

Putting science and magic under the same cover can be dangerous and misleading. Magic has been around far longer than the rational, seeing-is-believing way of life most of us live today. As we trace Western magic all the way back to its ancient Middle Eastern roots in Part I, we will find it becomes ever more mainstream in character, closer to the norms of its day—an amalgam of science, religion, and metaphysics, if we insist on labeling it in contemporary terms.

We also will find that, like ancient science, magic had its own technology: amulets, precious stones, and magic wands. And magical words emerge as the archaic counterparts of computers, mathematical formulas, and linear accelerators. Effective magic is different from science that works, as is learned by exploring the subjective, persuasive element of magic that evolved from believing in a world that connected like with like, mind with matter, people with things; a world in which knowledge acquired from pagan antiquity takes precedence over modern progressive learning.

We derive all of these magical trappings from the same ancestors who gave us our gods, our calendar, our science, our politics, and our economics: the people of ancient Egypt and Mesopotamia via Classical Greece—who established science as a category separate from magic—and the Roman Empire. At the Empire's end religion begins to figure heavily into the debate. And so we will explore one of antiquity's great gifts to civilization, one which would drive a wedge between magic and religion as well as magic and science, molding what we today call magic. That gift was Christianity.

In Part II, "From Light to Light," I'll trace the principal developments of what are considered to be the *occult* arts and practices from the Dark Ages to the eighteenth-century Enlightenment. If you dealt with magic during most of that thousand-year-plus period, then you were tampering with something that belonged in the realm of the sacred and untouchable. Such arts in their most malicious form became confined to the shadow of history. They include Kabbalistic mysticism, astrology, alchemy, telling the future, devil worship, and witchcraft, the most common forms that magic took.

Reason and scientific fact were simply not a part of the accepted way of thinking a thousand years ago. Even though it existed in the Latin vocabulary, the word "magic" as a label didn't really take hold until the sixteenth century. It was then that the foundations of modern science were laid down by the rapid advance in instrumentation and the art of measurement, along with the proliferation of scientific experimentation—testing the behavior of nature for cause and effect. It was also then that a great religious reformation—away from idolatry and toward more abstract forms of supernatural belief—took hold. Both of these developments led to a bear market for the art of conjuring.

What a surprise it is to discover (in Part III) that the nineteenth century, called by many the Century of Spiritualism, was an unanticipated wild time for magic. It flourished on the American frontier, home of the first haunted house to attain international recognition. Why, in that age of science and reason, would spiritualism blossom into esotericism, the belief in secret doctrines? Some of the occult world's most fascinating characters come alive during this period. The Fox sisters, also known as the Rochester rappers, claimed to have contacted the dead via a kind of "spiritual wireless"; Daniel Dunglas Home, a master of deception,

•

claimed he could elevate himself from floor to ceiling as well as in one window and out the other, with a record of never having been caught in a single act of deception. We will meet Helena Petrovna Blavatsky, who carried her spiritualism to more contemplative ends and founded the theosophical movement, which claimed that all religions stem from the same ancient myths and symbols. Today she enjoys a New Age revival.

The roots of the Gilded Age's occult revolution actually began a century earlier in Europe with two characters who would have been called fringe scientists in their day. Franz Mesmer experimented with magnets and Emanuel Swedenborg precisely described out-of-body experiences featuring a dialogue with angels and demons from the hereafter. What began as a revolt against reason ended, circa the 1920s, with a backlash of condemnation against all things occult as the roller-coaster ride of magic hit bottom and the lights were nearly extinguished.

Down the narrow aisles of musty antiquarian bookstores we can still find the recognizable grandparents of New Age literary works—nineteenth-century books on animal magnetism, emanations of the astral spirit, theosophy, and esotericism: *Isis Unveiled, The Marvels Beyond Science,* and *Tertium Organum: A Key to the Enigmas of the World.* Like the mainstream scientists of that day, those who practiced the occult seemed to be seeking the laws governing the behavior of a vibrating universe that resonates with our very soul. But their laws were heavily laden with a moral force notably absent from the impartial mathematical statements that ruled the science of the times: wave theory, magnetism, and radioactivity. Science and magic, like science and religion, were destined to conflict.

What does eating granola have to do with demonic cults? The grist for the mill of modern days' "Kaleidoscope of Magic" (Part IV) needs to be thinned and sampled, lest the reader (and writer) suffer from indigestion. And so I have tried to cull out and interrelate the most influential aspects of the occult arts that comprise the New Age today, as well as its earlier twentieth-century antecedents from the '60s, '70s, and beyond: crystals, geomancy, channeling, psi phenomena, the healing arts, UFOs, and near-death experiences among them.

We end with "Magic at the Millennium" (Part V), an exploration of the present state of binding of the eternal triangle: religion, science, and magic. What, after all, *is* magic? Is it a movement or a religion—or both? Is it science gone awry, a dead appendage of a once respectable art? All of these are answers supplied by our past. My answer is that magic is culturally self-defining. As our views of the real world are influenced by what happens in society (i.e., revolution, contact with other people, whatever happens among us to affect our beliefs), what we call magic, like everything else, changes with the times. Two former mainstays of the discipline, the studies of herbs and meteorites, have escaped to the camp of science, for they have tested positive and their labels have been changed. What does and doesn't belong at any given time depends on who does the testing. My answer to "what is magic?" on another level is that magic is part and parcel of religious practice, a disclosure that becomes apparent only when we examine what magic is like in cultures other than our own. By exploring the details of magic's cross-cultural kingdom through stories that describe a diverse selection of contemporary magical rites—from the Azande witch of Central Africa to the Bogang healer of Western Malaysia—we discover that in all cultures, powerful magic, like any good scientific experiment, has an organized set of methods and an impressive body of knowledge that needs to be learned diligently and practiced rigorously in order to be effective. Above all, we learn that magic is normal behavior.

There are many layers of ideas and beliefs that define human culture and (as we learn in Part V) magic has penetrated every level of society in every culture of the world. It is as universal as religion, with which it has been contrasted, and more widespread than science, its traditional archenemy. Why is magic such a universal transcultural art?

Today's postmodern brand of magic as practiced on the streets of our cities and in the suburban rec room is slowly being diluted into the mainstream of mass culture by an imagined principle of interconnectedness. Magic's more frivolous appendages are indulged in with a playful attitude (e.g., newspaper astrology or seeking the poltergeist in a haunted castle). That the branches of minimalist Zen-yoga healing and dieting grow higher on the tree of respectability than either UFO visitations or channeling only demonstrates what has held true in all ages: that the true magician, whose magic has been adopted by both adept and apostle alike, always has his counterpart—the conjurer (called a juggler in days of old) who playfully deceives strictly for entertainment, the Houdini of the soul.

PART I

MAGIC IN ANTIQUITY

HOW MAGIC WORKS AND WHY WE MISUNDERSTAND IT

CHAPTER I

MIDDLE EAST EXOTICA: ANCIENT EGYPT AND MAGICAL MESOPOTAMIA

The word "magic" is out of fashion though its spirit was never more widely diffused than at the present time. Thanks to the gradual debasement of the verbal currency, it suggests to the ordinary reader the production of optical illusions and other parlour tricks. It has dragged with it in its fall the terrific verb to "conjure," which, forgetting that it once undertook to compel the spirits of men and angels, is now content to produce rabbits from top hats.

Evelyn Underhill, *Mysticism*

Evelyn Underhill reminds us that what is now entertainment for the gullible is traceable to a well-established tradition. Since recorded Western history began in the great civilizations of the Mediterranean Middle East about five thousand years ago, the search for magic's beginnings need go no further than Egypt and Mesopotamia.

The Nile Valley of 3000 B.C. was another major spawning ground of magic. When we think of Egypt we think of bandaged mummies, boxed in their painted coffins and stashed away inside dark, dusty tombs. Nowhere in the world of antiquity did any civilization develop such a preoccupation with the dead and the afterlife as these early Middle Eastern ancestors of ours. Why? We will never know. Perhaps belief in the hereafter is a logical extension of the periodic recurrence of the rising and setting of the sun or of the ebb and flow of the waters of the Nile which they experienced generation after generation. The archaeological record suggests that once Egyptian mortuary practice—safekeeping the dead for their journey into the eternal afterlife and providing them with all they needed once they got there—became established, it grew into the paraphernalia archaeologists have dug out of the tombs: vases to hold the individually linen-wrapped internal organs of the deceased; resin-

and perfume-soaked bandages covering the body; gilded finger and toe-
nail holders; jeweled masks over the face of the royal mummy; and
amulets tucked between the wrappings over the thorax, arms, hands, legs,
and genitals.[1] These magical objects, found by the hundreds in tombs
dating to before 2000 B.C., were designed to protect the pilgrim on his
or her voyage toward eternity each in its own specific way.

The scarab or dung beetle (*scarabaeus sacer*) was the amulet par excellence of ancient Egypt. Its Egyptian name is *kheprer,* the same as the verb
"to come into existence." To dismiss the custom of placing a beetle next
to the dead as superstitious nonsense would be to deny access to the
mind of the ancient Egyptian; for him there was deep hidden meaning
in the beetle's symbolism. Just as a Roman Catholic might think nothing of wearing a St. Christopher medal for protection when traveling,
so too the Egyptian wore the beetle for protection on the journey to
the hereafter.

What's so extraordinary about a dung beetle? If you watch the weird
way this metallic-colored fecal feeder gets around, you'll see why it
might attract attention. The odd placement of its rear legs helps it roll
protective balls of excrement around its eggs. The dung balls also serve as
food for newly hatched larvae. The beetle performs its act in the heat of
the day, when the sun rolls about the sky, by standing on its head and
hunching up its legs so that it is turned away from the spheres it pedals
around. Once the beetle secures the balls in its underground nest it proceeds to help roll another's.

Offer me the gift of a scarab beetle for Father's Day and I'll think
you've lost your senses. But if you can free your imagination from logic's
dictates, you may just pick up on some of the connections the ancient
Egyptians made between the lowly beetle, the higher realm, and the
essence of Dad. To them, the scarab connotes fatherliness because it is engendered by a father. It defines the world, for it generates the form of the
world. Egyptians called the sun "the roller" for it rolls around heaven like
the scarab's ball. Chepera (after *kheprer*), the god representing the insect,
is the father of the gods, creator of heaven and earth, the one who makes
himself out of the matter he produced. Funerary scarabs composed of
jasper, carnelian, ruby, or amethyst, often monogrammed with the names
of gods or people, were placed in the forms of rings on a dead person's
fingers or tucked in the linen bandages of the mummy, usually over the
heart. These amulets would revivify the deceased the same way the sun
is reborn after it dies in the west.

The oft-bejewelled beetle as an amulet was so placed because it was believed to bring the gods under the power of the dead person. The words of the chant that accompanied the placement of the charm (words archaeologists have discovered written on the mummy bandages) suggest an empowerment of their own. Mind over matter, script over matter, spoken word over matter, all serve the purpose of setting into play the interaction of the body of the deceased and the forces of the supernatural.

But for the non-believer—the enemy of ancient Egypt—the scarab symbolized something quite the opposite. A Syrian natural historian once wrote that the scarab conceives through the mouth and gives birth through the ears. It is a gadfly that steals gold and silver and hides it in its hole. Like the cheating shopkeeper it mixes cheaper ingredients with more precious ones (lentils, rice, millet, and wheat) to cheat the customer. They are heretics polluted by filth (these backward rollers). And they roll up nothing but wickedness and sin against all mankind. But does this Syrian speak of an Egyptian rather than an arthropod? Is he saying: "My amulet is authentic, yours is fraudulent"?

Magic was not confined to the Nile Valley, however. It was emerging concurrently in the plain between the Tigris and Euphrates stretching from Baghdad to the Persian Gulf, where one of the first great dynamic urban civilizations of the world sprang up. Led first by the Sumerians, the societies that grew in this area successfully irrigated the flat desert between the two rivers and created an extensive trade network. They also developed a unique system of writing with a stylus on clay tablets. Mesopotamia produced brilliant astronomers capable of predicting celestial events well in advance; they created the foundations of arithmetic that we still use today. By 2000 B.C., the Sumerians had been overrun from the north by the Semites, who developed the culturally distinct group known as Babylonia and its famous capital city that boasted brilliant civic architecture and inspiring temples of worship. While cities like Nippur, Kish, and Babylon flourished in the south, Nineveh, Ashur, and Nimrod began to develop on the upper Tigris in the northern part of the Assyrian empire.

The story the Babylonians tell about their own creation is as filled with magic as is our own Big Bang theory of the origin of the universe with logical mathematical laws. For example, when Marduk, king of the gods, is sent forth by a council of the gods to conquer the unruly forces of nature, his powers are put to the test.

They placed a garment in their midst
And said to Marduk their firstborn:
'O Lord, thy lot is truly highest among gods.
Command annihilation and existence, and may both come true.[2]

To prove his worth as a leader, Marduk must demonstrate that he is a magician by destroying and recreating a material article, through word power alone, in this case a mantle or garment.

May thy spoken word destroy the garment,
Then speak again and may it be intact.'
He spoke—and at his word the garment was destroyed.
He spoke again, the garment reappeared.
The gods, his fathers, seeing (the power of) his word,
Rejoiced, paid homage: 'Marduk is king.'[3]

In an earlier episode, Ea the earth god conquers Apsu, god of the fresh underground water, by reciting a magical spell. He literally pours poisonous words into the ear of his rival. Of course, we tend to read these statements metaphorically. If a spell describes "taming the sweet water," we claim it is just a way of saying civilized man harnessed its power by developing a system of irrigation. But the ancient Mesopotamians did not make these statements figuratively. Any misinterpretation lies in our failure to perceive how close these people really were to nature and how powerful was the spoken word of authority in their way of life.

The power of the spell was often employed in the art of exorcism. The exorcist of ancient Nineveh was as highly regarded as a modern surgeon. The only difference is that his world was filled with living forces both good and evil that manifested themselves by giving rise to symptoms in a sick person's body. The exorcist alone held the power to get to the root of the malady—to carve it with words out of the diseased person using his tongue as an implement the way a surgeon removes a tumor with a knife. His tool kit contained amulet and incense rather than scalpel and laser beam. The technology, methods, and procedures associated with the craft of exorcism would have been as legitimate and benevolent in his day as those of today's doctor.

A vast literature on ancient Mesopotamian magical practice—formulas, incantations, rites, medical prescriptions—comes down to us from as early as the 1st millennium B.C. Texts speak of two kinds of therapeutist:

the physician—a harmless practitioner who used potions, bandages, herbals, suppositories, etc., to relieve symptoms; and the exorcist—who dealt with demons that inhabit the body. The latter specialized in oral incantations and laid hands on his clients. An exorcist could talk to forces both good and evil directly or he could address them through objects like amulets or charms. For example, he might talk to water as the water god or to fire as the fire god. Above all he was a legitimate practitioner of magic, professionally trained to liberate his patient from evil forces and to protect him or her from future harm.

That the Babylonian exorcist stood as elevated above the street sorcerer as our contemporary surgeon rises above a quack is not hard to believe provided we are aware that the ancient Babylonians did not think of the world as a machine that operated under the dictates of mathematical principles and the body as a mechanism subject to biological laws. They lived instead in a world governed by beings like themselves, just as fickle and compromising as they were—nature personified in the form of male and female deities who could be cajoled and threatened, appeased and flattered.

Ancient exorcists practiced a form of *involuntary divination*. They interpreted signs and indications of the presence of demons that just happened to thrust themselves upon an unwitting victim: bulging eyes, exhaustion, skin rash.

Astrologers of old also were involuntary diviners. They interpreted celestial phenomena—the sudden appearance of a comet, a total eclipse of the sun, or any other unusual combination of sightings: "When a halo surrounds the Moon and Mars stands within it, there will be a destruction of cattle—[the city of] Abarru will be diminished," reads an omen on a Babylonian tablet.[4] In addition, there also were *voluntary* diviners, those who deliberately sought out some object or means of penetrating the unknown future. Reading entrails (loosely, internal parts) is a good example worth exploring, so widespread was the belief that your future is in your guts.

CHAPTER 2

THE ANCIENT ART
OF HEPATOSCOPY

The science of the augur and the haruspex [seer or diviner] was not so foolish as our modern science of political economy. If the hot liver of the victim cleared the soul of the haruspex, and made him capable of that ultimate inward attention which alone tells us the last thing we need to know, then why quarrel with the haruspex? To him, the universe was alive, and in quivering *rapport*. To him, the blood was conscious: he thought with his heart. To him, the blood was the red and shining stream of consciousness itself. Hence, to him, the liver, that great organ where the blood struggles and "overcomes death," was an object of profound mystery and significance. It stirred his soul and purified his consciousness; and it was also his victim. So he gazed into the hot liver, that was mapped out in fields and regions like the sky of stars, but these fields and regions were those of the red, shining consciousness that runs through the whole animal creation. And therefore it must contain the answer to his own blood's question. (*Brackets mine*)

D. H. Lawrence, *Etruscan Places*

D. H. Lawrence knew what he was talking about. He so aptly captured why our Middle Eastern ancestors once believed the liver, rather than the heart, was the place where the soul resided; the center of human vitality. Hepatoscopy—divining by inspection of the liver—was the pop-science of the past. So skilled and persistent were the Babylonians in this art that the ancient Etruscans who then lived in northern Italy adopted the technique from them. When we look at examples of the way these divinatory arts were practiced, we are left with the impression that, far from being wayward and uninformed versions of their modern day descendants, each method and mode had a complexity and symbolism all its own.

You didn't have to give up your liver to find how things would turn out. To learn the will of the gods in ancient Babylon, a *baru* or seer (a haruspex for the Etruscans) would cut out the liver of a sacrificed animal, usually a sheep. He would hold it in his hand and, gazing into that "red, shining consciousness," he would look for signs so that he might anticipate the intention of the gods of nature, the arbiters of our fate. He who could read the soul would penetrate the gods' very being. The liver became a map of life, the conduit for communicating with the gods, and the one who could interpret it would enter the workshop of the gods.

Hepatoscopy took years of study. It developed out of careful observation accompanied by the need to organize and classify knowledge. The diviner sought a set of laws for how to communicate with the gods—a reasoning quite different from that of today's natural scientist. Yet, in its organization, and its attempts to observe and classify, the process and conduct of this sort of magic was not so different from, and indeed gave rise to, what today we call science. Omen texts that survive on clay tablets give just a hint of how complex liver-watching became. Every zone of the liver had its portent that corresponded to a different sphere of human life. For example, the right and left lower lobes were favorable and unfavorable, respectively. The former was the king's side, the latter that of his enemy. A swollen gall bladder (it lies atop the liver) meant an increase of power. A long cystic duct signified a lengthy reign. Every tangible part of the organ—hepatic duct, bile duct, hepatic vein, gall bladder, pyramidal process, papillary process—was thought to resonate with a particular quality in the transcendent world.

Traces or markings on the liver were dealt with in much the same way a palmist interprets lines and creases on the hands or a phrenologist interprets bumps on the head. The "presence," for example, is a vertical groove on the left lobe. Its appearance determines whether a communication with the divine has been established. "If the head of the 'view' is wide: the god will raise the man's head," reads an inscription on a tablet over twenty-five hundred years old.

Another highly specialized text gives a lengthy list of how to interpret only holes in the liver. For example, "If a hole is situated in the . . . of the Presence: the fully loaded boat will sink or the pregnant woman will die in her labor."[1] (There seem to be a host of instances in which pregnant women and loaded ships are associated with one another.)

To judge from these old clay texts the learned *baru,* who used them in his library as procedural manuals, seems to have addressed his inquiries directly to the liver and would get an answer by inspecting the appropriate part. We have reason to think that extispicists—a general term for those who foretold the future by inspecting entrails—were members of a respectable profession something like chiropractic today. (They differed from hepatoscopists the way an internist differs from a heart specialist.) The typical *baru* came from a fairly well-off family of diviners. It must have been a tough profession to crack. To succeed you might start by divining at the city gate, taking on all comers who could afford to pay a fee, then slowly climbing the ladder of success to a district job. Finally, if you were lucky (and skilled) enough you might accompany the rare few who moved all the way up to the palace staff.

Divining by liver inspection is one form of magic that has almost completely vanished today. It was carried along for more than a thousand years and spread out from the Middle East in all directions. The fourth-century B.C. Etruscans were so attuned to it they set up special temple training schools. A bronze life-sized model of a liver—probably a teaching device—survives in a museum in Piacenza, Italy.[2] When the Etruscans founded a city they always sacrificed a sheep and called in a haruspex to read the liver just to be sure the site was right. I think a connection is not so farfetched. We can well imagine that a skilled examiner could tell something about the ecology of the place—good drainage free of poisonous waste, no history of disease, etc.—by inspecting the innards of an animal that had grazed on the local hillside.

Like many early forms of magic we've been discussing, hepatoscopy was clearly not a game you played by making up the rules as you went along. There were specific indications and regulations. But this craft, like all magic, had both objective and subjective elements—a fact often misunderstood. Evidently it did not always work, because texts also divulge that if unfavorable signs dominated, the *baru* might sacrifice another sheep, perhaps even a third until the right signs were found. This doesn't mean a *baru* was dishonest, only that his first requisite was to please the king. As in politics, more than any inherently possessed power, his importance and the influence he wielded was achieved both by public opinion and by that of his employer.

Reading internal organs seems to be a habit practiced worldwide. Five hundred years ago, the Inca chronicler of Peru, Garcilaso de la Vega, wrote about llama sacrifices. The Aztecs of Mexico peered into the innards of the pelican, the ruler of all the water birds in their lacustrine capital city, to seek their future in objects they found there. And when the Kodi (of the Lesser Dunda Islands in modern Indonesia) roast a chicken to honor the dead, they first examine its entrails to read auspices for the coming year.[3]

Why this pervasive belief that the vital organs should hold the keys to the future? The seat of the vital principle, the residence of the soul linking all living things with god, is the logical place to seek out answers. The hepatoscopist once probed the liver with the same fervor with which a modern physicist uses an accelerator to penetrate the microcosmic structure of the nucleus or an astronomer employs a large telescope to seek out the first nanosecond of creation billions of light years away. The places and times where we happen to believe all things come together differ significantly from those of an Inca or a Babylonian.

CHAPTER 3

THE GREEK PARADOX:
MAGIC CONFRONTS SCIENCE

⟨⟩

When in the beginning the universe was being formed, both heaven and earth were indistinguishable in appearance, since their elements were intermingled: then, when their bodies separated from one another, the universe took on in all its parts the ordered form in which it is now seen; the air set up a continual motion, and the fiery element in it gathered into the highest regions, since anything of such a nature moves upward by reason of its lightness . . . while all that was mud-like and thick and contained an admixture of moisture sank because of its weight into one place; and as this continually turned about upon itself and became compressed, out of the wet it formed the sea, and out of what was firmer, the land, which was like potter's clay and entirely soft. But as the sun's fire shone upon the land, it first of all became firm, and then, since its surface was in a ferment because of the warmth, portions of the wet swelled up in masses in many places, and in these pustules covered with delicate membranes made their appearance . . . and finally, when the embryos had attained their full development and the membranes had been thoroughly heated and broken open, there was produced every form of animal life.

Charles Henry Oldfather, ed.,
Diodorus of Sicily

So goes the story of the origin of life in the universe according to Diodorus of Sicily, a philosopher/scientist who lived in the Greek colonies of South Italy in the sixth-century B.C. Historians of science recognize it as one of the earliest statements to suggest that nature runs all by itself, independent of whimsical godly interference.

While the earth is characterized as a living organism in this description (doesn't she resemble a woman giving birth?) the process of creation seems mechanical. (By the way, modern commentators wonder whether the bubblelike membranes are genuine forerunners of the atoms of the atomic theory of matter that would flourish centuries later.) Diodorus' creation even begins to sound like a theory of evolution where things develop by themselves, unaffected by any dialogue between humans and the gods of nature.

The Greeks have given us many gifts: the logic of philosophers—literally "wisdom lovers"—including Socrates and Plato, the spherical model of the world of Aristotle, the geometry of Euclid, and the style and sensibility of great art forms, such as sculpture and architecture. Such things give meaning to the word *Classical*. But above all, the Greeks changed, once and for all, the notion of a personal cosmos to an impersonal one; they handed down to us the first scientific way of understanding the world.

The process of developing an abstract universe whose workings were taken out of the hands of God begins with these so-called Ionian philosophers. They were all practical men who convinced themselves that the laws that guide all parts of the world we live in also function identically in the unseen portions of the world above and below.

Their Greece was, to put it simply, but one of a series of layered elements; a living organism immersed in a nurturing interactive sea. Three centuries later, Plato's logic and Aristotle's application of it to its natural processes would transform this idea into a working model, a hierarchically ordered spherical universe consisting of four basic elements arranged one upon another like the skins of an onion: earth, water, air, fire, and quintessence, a fifth element out of which all celestial bodies were made.

Aristotle employed a form of logic to account for everything that happened in this highly ordered world. Motion, for example, was caused by the tendency of all objects to acquire a state of rest, to go to their natural place: earth to earth, water to water and so on. This explains why a stone once removed from its earthly abode falls downward through air to get back to earth. It rains because water displaced to the air above it seeks to return to its natural place, an ocean or a pond on the surface of earth. Bubbles exhaled by a frog who dives off a lily pad on that pond naturally rise upward and break through the interface between water and air, returning air to the place where it belongs. Where does a piece of wood belong in this scenario? Compound elements, Aristotle reasons, must be separated before each component can return to its natural place. A burning wooden ship, therefore, is decomposed into ashes (earth), which fall to the bottom of the sea, and into flames (fire), which lick their way upward toward the domain above air where all fire naturally resides. Deity moves neither stone nor ash, neither air bubble nor flame; only the natural tendency, the natural law that brings about whatever we witness in the world through our senses. One needs no gods in this sort of universe.

Remember all those geometrical proofs from high school? They represent the most highly developed form of Greek logic (logic with a mathematical language that the Greek philosophers developed along with the gift of numerical quantification borrowed from the Babylonians and passed on to us). The paramount faith of these first philosopher/scientists is that the causes behind what we see in nature are physical and mechanical. All of nature is assumed to be regular in its behavior.

Yet there remains a paradox. What the science textbooks often forget to tell us is that Aristotle—even Plato—believed in magic. "Let us not boast, lest some evil eye should put to flight the word which I am going to speak," writes a wary Plato.[1] He even betrayed his belief against incantations and waxen images by proposing laws to outlaw sorcery. And though he discounted hepatoscopy, which was still widely practiced in fifth century B.C. Greece, Plato admitted that the liver was indeed like a mirror that reflected the soul and onto which the mind's thoughts fell. He spoke freely of the five elements loving one another. Aristotle, too, endowed the elements with personae by the desire he claimed each of them possesses to return to home base. And even though all the stars are composed of the same element, they are at the same time superintelligent gods and they are capable of exerting a rational influence on those of us who live life beneath them. To put it simply, Aristotle firmly believed in the "as above, so below" principle on which all astrology is founded.

If astronomers deal with the motion of the stars, then astrologers study the effects those motions have upon our lives. The astrologer thinks of parts of an animate universe in the same sense that we might regard the living red and white corpuscles that make up our blood to be a part of our bodies. According to this analogy, our bodies here below are the microcosm of a living intelligent universe—the macrocosm there above.

Though the Greeks developed the system of astrology whose remains still touch us through tabloid and telephone, the basic idea behind it can be traced all the way back to an old Chaldean scheme. It says that celestial destiny is the result of the complex interaction of sky spirits, whose influence touches us through the energy their rays give off. We mortals of the lower world vibrate sympathetically in response to these celestial emanations. The strength of this radiation depends on where the celestial luminary or source lies in the sky and the time of year or night the emanator rises and sets. The zodiac, along which these influential emitters travel, is divided into twelve zones that serve as compartments for every category of existence. All human attributes are placed under some dualistic influence or rule and, therefore, are subject to extremes of behavior—beneficent or tyrannical, strong or weak, positive or negative—of which transcendent gods, like ordinary mortals, are capable.

It is easy to see how the character traits and behavior of people came to be mirrored in qualities perceivable in nature. For example, the fast-moving, changeable planet, Mercury, which always lay close to earth, acquired a flighty lighthearted temperament because he is so hard to pin down. Why is Venus (Ishtar to the Chaldeans, Aphrodite to the Greeks) the love goddess? Because her extreme swings of position between evening and morning star led to her characterization as fickle woman—capable of the lowest, most reprehensible debauchery as well as the highest form of pure love. She carried the full spectrum of femininity as conceived in the male (sexist by our modern thinking) Chaldean mind; she became the celestially personified role model—good or bad—of femininity in the extreme. We still can feel the dull, heavy, gray tones of the "saturnine one" if we carefully watch his planet (the slowest moving of all) plod slowly along the highway of the stars, and we recognize the fiery red, warlike character of the "martial deity." These sky gods emerge as characters not unlike our modern movie, TV, or comic book heroes whose human qualities—sexuality, goodness and evil, strength and prowess—are magnified to extremes. Like the superintellects and super-egos our cartoonists create, they populate an imaginary plane of reality, a medium in which it becomes safe to raise questions about our own existence that we do not ordinarily discuss: Where does the power of human life originate? Do we survive and continue after death? What is real love?

As the living luminaries shifted their position along the fixed screen of the twelve constellations of the zodiac, the astrologer alone had the magical power to analyze the sky map at any place or moment in the future and give an assessment of the situation. Thus, he would create a *horoscope*. We owe our word to the Greek *horoskopus*. It means "I observe the hour," or colloquially, "I watch what rises," and it refers specifically to the art of predicting the general patterns that are preprogrammed in a person's future life based on an examination of the celestial bodies that were coming over the horizon in the east at the time and in the place he or she was born. Unlike the Babylonians, whose astrology was concerned with what might befall an entire state depending on what was happening in the sky, the Greeks—reared in a more democratic system—believed that everyone should have his or her own personal horoscope.

The bible of astrology in the Classical world was the *Tetrabiblos,* written by Claudius Ptolemaeus (Ptolemy) of Alexandria at the beginning of the second century A.D. We know nothing about Ptolemy except that he was alive between about A.D. 85 and 115 and that his name ties him to the dynasty that ruled in Egypt at the turn of the first century A.D. His "Four Books" explains the doctrine and goals of astrology as they have been passed down to us. It advocates the careful determination of the appearance of the course of heavenly bodies and the codification of mathematical laws to describe, delineate, and predict where all the sky objects will be at any future time, a goal modern astronomy still shares with its ancient sister discipline. At the same time, and with equal commitment, Ptolemy also sought to predict the events that took place in society and the lives of individuals. He believed—for sound scientific reasons at the time—that the celestial spheres were superior to the world below because they were perfect and immutable, the divine source of all heat, light, and motion.

The Ptolemaic mathematical scheme for reducing the errant motions of the planets to a component of regular orderly movement is rooted in geometry and based specifically upon the principle that the planets move on circular orbits, the centers of which move about other circular orbits around the earth, which is fixed at the center of all motion. Another modern astronomical legacy of the Ptolemaic system is that the universe operates like a series of mechanical wheels perfectly fitted together, each planet being driven along its course through space and making its place in the sky known in advance, at least to one who is appropriately initiated in the geometrical method of determining it.

How did our Old World ancestors believe the celestial forces were arranged? When you seek the answer to a question about magic, you look to the behavior of the people to whom it applies. And invariably you find an explanation rooted in their culture. Ancient societies were hierarchically structured from Pharaoh all the way down to the lowliest peasant. What happened in nature usually took place in recognizable patterns that oscillated from one extreme to another—rain to drought, cold to hot, elation to tragedy, good times to bad times and back to good times again. So, too, did the ancients read the messages written in the stars.

This familiar way of ordering things—by hierarchy and by alternation between extremes—was applied to the planets to create the astrology we know today. The system is as complex as hepatoscopy (except that the sky replaces the liver as text), but its rudiments can be placed in the context of related kinds of ancient magic. In Greek–Babylonian astrology, the intensity of the influence of a planet upon terrestrial matters was thought to depend on the *magnitude of its sphere;* that is, the higher in heaven the planet rolled about the fixed earth, the more power it held. As you passed down the heavenly hierarchy, like moving down the political stepladder from high nobility to common bureaucrat, the influence became weaker. The alternation principle added the elements of good and evil to the hierarchy. These qualities switched back and forth as you moved from the highest to the lowest sphere.

Accordingly, Saturn, which lumbers along slowly and ominously on the outermost orbital lane of the zodiacal roadway, was termed the Greater Ill-fortune. It was universally acknowledged to be the most potent, evil, and malignant of all the planets. On the contrary, Jupiter, Saturn's next-door neighbor down the orbital ladder in the earth-centered universe, was the most propitious of planets (they called it the Greater Fortune), although his influence was somewhat weaker than Saturn's Next came Mars (the Lesser Ill-fortune), who was inferior only to Saturn in malefic influence. The Sun came next in power, and it had generally a good influence. Venus, the next, bore the same relation to the Greater Fortune, Jupiter, that Mars bore to Saturn. She was the Lesser Fortune, and her influence was in nearly all respects benevolent. Then came Mercury, a cold, dry, and melancholy star with a weak general tendency toward the unfortunate and, finally, the fast-moving Moon, lowest in the planetary hierarchy. As the one nearest the earth, she was the least influential of all celestial bodies, being regarded by astrologers as a cold, moist, watery planet, like the Sun partaking of a bit of good or evil. And so the qualities of absolute good and evil seem to blend together as they diminish—in effect to cancel each other out—as you move down the heavenly hierarchy toward earth.

The signs of the zodiac constituted another celestial list, which survives as a scheme almost as familiar to nonbelievers as to practicing astrologers. Unlike the planets, the signs remain fixed with respect to the stars, but they move together as the sphere of stars appears to rotate daily about the earth.[2] Each zodiacal sign carried with it a list of associated properties capable of articulating the full range of qualities or phases of human mental and emotional experience. Every one of these properties had its antithesis somewhere in the composite list. For instance, the adjectives said to describe a person whose sun sign is Aries are vernal, dry, fiery, masculine, cardinal, equinoctial, diurnal, movable, commanding, eastern, choleric, violet, and quadrupedal![3]

As the planets pass among the zodiacal signs, each exercises its motivating power, which, too, alternates between opposing states: good and evil as well as strong and weak. Moreover, the influences of the planets may be canceled or enhanced by their relationships to one another. For the Greeks, the interrelations were explained, as we might expect, through geometry. For example, if you connect every third constellation (Aries, Leo, and Sagittarius; Taurus, Virgo, and Capricorn; Gemini, Libra, and Aquarius; Cancer, Scorpio, and Pisces), you end up with four equilateral triangles called Trines. You can also make three squares by tying together Aries, Cancer, Libra, and Capricorn, and so on, as well as a pair of hexagons (Aries, Gemini, etc.; and Taurus, Cancer, etc.), one of which holds the masculine and the other the feminine signs.

A modern astrologer reads your birth chart or "nativity horoscope" using a local system in which the place of the planets and the zodiac are charted (usually with a computer), with respect to where they lay over your cradle; that is, in the time and space framework associated with your birth. This "house" system comes straight out of the Greeks and Ptolemy.[4] We can think of it as a set of allotments. The first house is the first 30° segment beneath the eastern horizon (called the ascendant),[5] and it contains the celestial objects that are just about to cross the local skyline and come into view. Called the House of the Ascendant, it is most influential of all, and will affect your appearance, your self, and your beginnings. Planets residing there at the time of your birth will have the most potent outcome on your life and destiny. The second house, the House of Riches, is the 30° to 60° zone below the eastern horizon. Kindred and short journeys in the third house combine foreordained knowledge of contracts and communications; inheritances reside in the fourth house, children in the fifth, health as well as your service and employment tendencies in the sixth. The House of Love and Marriage is seventh, Death is eighth. To the ninth house belong long journeys and foreign affairs. Tenth is the House of Honor, and it affects your public standing and inclinations in professional life; eleventh is the House of Friends, and twelfth that of enemies.[6]

We are forced to admit that the rules of astrology are clear and organized, even if they do not make sense to us. The ancients arranged their
knowledge in a different way. Would you think to look in an anatomy
text if you wanted to know where to go to view the next eclipse of the
sun? Ptolemy's *Tetrabiblos* relates astrology to such disparate considera-
tions as the nature of disease and the body, for in the Greek mind all
natural phenomena were related. Greek medicine taught that, just as
the universe was composed of four basic elements so, too, does the
body consist of four basic fluids: blood, which is warm and moist; yellow bile, which is warm and dry; black bile, which is cold and dry; and
phlegm, which is cold and wet. These basic fluids—called humors—were
aligned with the seasons of the year: spring, summer, autumn, and winter, respectively, and were paralleled with stages of life: childhood, youth,
maturity, and senescence. Is not the quick pulsing of hot blood
in the veins like spring and youth, the slow lethargy of phlegm like winter and old age? In the Greek view of nature, aspects of one domain
automatically take on a relationship with those from another. In these
acquired likenesses there is no need of the kind of causal connection
between things our modern minds require.

Magically (and conveniently), the planets fit into the logic of hierarchy by assignment of ages and humors to them. Saturn, for example,
being in the highest orb (in other words the one farthest from earth),
would govern old age because it moved slowest of all. It would dominate
the phlegm, which is the most viscous and slow-moving of the body's
fluids. Being farthest from the sun's warmth, Saturn would be inclined to
make us cold-bellied and fill us with phlegm to make us cough. Sometimes the planetary associations were so complex and detailed that their
meaning, at least for us, has become totally obscure. For example, Saturn
governed the right ear, spleen, bladder, and bones; Jupiter the sense of
touch, lungs, arteries, and male semen (being between cold Saturn and
fiery hot Mars, he was lukewarm). Mars covered the left ear, kidneys,
veins, and genitals. As his red color and nearness to the sun indicate, he
emitted a parching heat. In his lower orbit he governed black bile, which
is why he could make us feel melancholic. Venus warmed less than Jupiter
but moistened more, for her large surface caught Earth's vapors. She governed the nose, liver, and muscles while Mercury ruled the tongue and
thought, bile and buttocks. Because of his high velocity, he could be a
potent cause of change. The Moon completed the list, accounting for the
sense of taste, the womb, and the belly. By proximity to Earth, the Moon,

too, was affected by the rising vapors. This is why she made bodies soft, causing them to putrefy. Finally, the Sun governed eyes, brain, and heart. He warmed and dried, and the nearer he came to our part of the world, the more heat he produced.

Not a single aspect of human existence was excluded: metals, herbs, body parts, individual organs, types of discharge. All entities were compartmentalized among the bodily humors and thus among the planets. Humorous[7] to us (in the modern corrupted sense of the word), the theory of humors quite simply and boldly states that when your juices are all in balance you function well,[8] which makes sense. This means you need to be aware when things are not in proper influence so that you can act accordingly.

The basic logic connecting astrology with medicine that I have outlined, though hinted at in the fifth-century B.C. writings of Hippocrates, seems not to have developed fully until second-century B.C. Alexandria. The correspondence principle goes something like this: Different parts of the body are "in sympathy" with particular signs of the zodiac (Fig. 1). When a given sign is, say, malevolently aspected by a planet, the part of your body allied with that sign can get sick. To get better you must make the sign stronger by administering the herb, medicine, or amulet made of a substance that is naturally sympathetic to that sign. This intimate connection forged by the Greeks between medicine and astrology endured well into the Middle Ages. By then, the old Greek herbarium had grown to vast proportions. For example, lunatics were treated by tying a certain herb about the neck with red cloth when the moon was waxing either in the sign of Scorpio or Taurus. The herb Monaster, bound in linen and placed, together with a loaf of whole wheat bread, under your pillow would help give you a sign of which star influenced your humors.[9]

Along with "as above, so below," "like cures like" is another remarkably consistent eternal law of magic that we will discover in force around the world. Greek medicine bequeathed us the Hippocratic oath, the byword of modern medicine, yet its corpus and practice, like that of astrology, sounds more like miracle than medicine. Curing epilepsy is a good example. An anonymous fifth-century B.C. author calls it "The Sacred Disease" because the muscular agitation, spasms, and alternations of conscious and unconscious states once were thought to manifest direct contact with the world beyond ordinary experience. The ancient Greeks believed as we do that the logical explanation for the cause of the disease lay in the brain. Following along practical Ionian lines, any competent

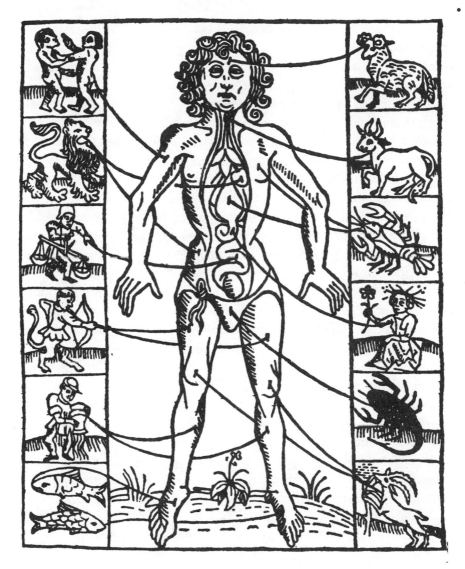

Fig. 1: "As above, so below." The zodiac and the human body: a place for everything and everything in its place. From a late 15th century medical astrology text. (Martyrologium der Heiligen nach dem Kalender.)

Greek doctor would have conceived the arteries to carry not blood, but air to and from the brain. As air is responsible for consciousness, obstruct its passage and you cut off the air supply from all your vital organs. This produces the symptoms of loss of voice, choking, and vomiting. So far this explanation sounds objectively rational even if the venal function remains incorrect by our standards. But here the account takes a quirky turn. Because blockage happens more on the *right side* of the body than on the left (there are more veins on that side) and because attacks seem to occur more often when the wind blows from the south (empirical if unsubstantiated data observed outside the body?), you cure the disease by performing a series of treatments that link the body with the outside world (i.e., you cure by employing a tactic closely related to the cause). For epilepsy, one physician writes, apply the proper hot and cold, wet and dry poultices to the exterior of the body at the appropriate times and with the appropriate diet to restore the balance of the bodily fluids to normal. The fluid or offending substance that blocked the normal flow of air to the brain is in this case an excess of phlegm, a perfectly legitimate bodily fluid in the classical anatomy devoid of the negative quality we might assign to it today.

For the Greek physician, the sacred disease was not caused by divine intervention; it happened when nature, which usually behaves quite uniformly, suddenly deviates from the norm—when things become imbalanced. His medicaments were necessary to restore the balance. Besides all this, the divine surely existed. It pervaded everything; therefore you could neither invoke it to cause a specific ailment nor appeal to it as a means of cure.

The Persian name of Zoroaster (also called Zarathustra) is commonly linked in Middle Eastern antiquity to the practice of magic. He lived sometime around the reign of Ashurbanipal (a ninth-century B.C. king of Assyria) and seems to have been the first to preach about the dualistic nature of forces in the universe. Life is a struggle and just as darkness opposes light, evil exists alongside good—thus spoke Zoroaster. He and Ashurbanipal were personified in the form of the male deities Ormazd and Ahriman, each with his retinue of angel or demon helpers, battling one another like black and white figures on a chessboard for control of the world they had created.

Zoroaster's cosmology predicted that even though the war between the forces of light and darkness will be waged for a long time, ultimately it will come to an end, with the forces of light winning. When this happens, the day of redemption, like Christianity's Judgment Day, will be at hand. Then all wicked people will be flooded by rivers of molten metal that will erupt from inside the earth; all good people will be spared. Ormazd, the one true god, will rule forever over all mankind. Given this philosophy, so similar to Christianity, why is Zoroaster held in such negative light by later organized religions? Maybe it's because there is a dark side to his dogma, for along with his story of creation comes a whole retinue of rituals that advocate dealing with angels and demons through magic. Zoroaster's teachings include using secret words and transformations and employing personal effects as a way of communicating with the higher powers.

In the beginning the magician was an outsider, a descendant of the Magi, a tribe of the Middle East, according to Herodotus, the Greek historian. While Greek philosophers carried on their discussions in the agora, or marketplace, of ancient Athens, these naturalists, many of them foreigners, were becoming the quack doctors of antiquity. They practiced so-called low magic, offering spells and potions at a price. Outside the surrounding temples, each dedicated to a specialized cult of worship in Polytheistic Greece, they peddled their wares, claiming to cure all ills from love sickness to scabies. Low magicians had a fairly widespread public following, despite being part of society's fringe element.

Far more dangerous to the established order were those who dealt in high magic. Their claims of calling forth the spirits of the dead were vastly more powerful than the simple pleading to and cajoling of higher powers practiced by their lower brethren. They conducted elaborate rites and often organized religious groups. Like science in the hands of the mad scientist, the evil or good magic creates is affected by the mind and heart of the one who practices it. High magicians evolved into the unwanted cult leaders of the day—Charles Mansons and David Koreshes—for with their practice came attempts to organize believers, to institutionalize their philosophy into a countercultural movement.

To be sure, Greek scientific writers left plenty of room in their treatises to attack these magicians. They dubbed them cunning men who are ignorant, deceitful, fraudulent, inconsistent, and impious for proposing meaningless purifications, incantations, and abstinence from bathing and restricting certain foods in the diet. Those who said that wearing a goatskin could cure epilepsy are wrong, for why do not all people who don't wear goatskins die from epilepsy?, reasoned one critic.

So deeply entrenched in magic were the Greeks that they bequeathed us a fair portion of the technology still associated with modern versions of occult practice. The touch or thrust every sorcerer used to make magic happen resides in the end of his or her pointing stick (the magic wand, which finds its origin in ancient Greece). As an agent of transformation, the wand literally aimed the magic, drawing its power from one source

and passing it on to another. It lives on in forms ranging from the royal
scepter held by a monarch at the time of coronation to a baton in the
hands of the conductor of a symphony orchestra.

When the hero Odysseus encounters Circe, the wicked sorceress who
had changed his men into pigs, he is momentarily made powerless by her
magic wand (and by a magic potion):

> She made a potion for me to drink and gave it in a golden
> cup, and with evil thoughts in her heart added the drug to
> it. Then when she had given it and I drank it off, without
> being enchanted, she struck me with her wand and spoke
> and named me: "Go to your sty now and lie down with your
> other friends there."[10]

Make an image out of wax, wood, or clay and strike it blows in the
heart or the head with a magic stick and you can inflict pain at that very
site in the victim. We have all heard of the famous parallel of the voodoo
doll stuck with pins. Similar habits among the Ojibwas and Australian
aborigines reveal just how widespread magic wands really are. Who has
the power, I wonder. Is it the person wielding the stick or is it the god
whose power the magician summons to enter the stick—the way the
modern faith healer calls forth the deity to act upon the wounded or
through the agency of pure touch? Today, if it's the person, we call it
magic; if it's the god, we call it religion—fringe religion at that.

One magical custom I think unique to the Greeks consists of "nailing"
an opponent or adversary (Fig. 2). Archaeologists have recovered hosts of
tablets with proper names written on them through which nails have been
driven. Sometimes an added inscription reads "I nail his name, that is himself."[11] As with the voodoo doll, the name is identical to the person and
like the magic wand's action, the penetration of the name by the nail is a
curse leveled directly at the enemy, completely bypassing the gods in this
instance. Interestingly, the words "I'll nail him" survive colloquially today.

In the field of magical divining—learning about what awaits us
around the corner—the Greeks are justly famous. The Oracle of Delphi,
which emanates from a Mycenaean earth goddess cult, is probably the
most well-known of all the ancient conduits to the future. There a resident priestess acted as a medium between people and the gods. She lived
in a cave and consorted with snakes, symbols of her wisdom. Once paid
her fee and asked a question by selected inquirers—the queue could

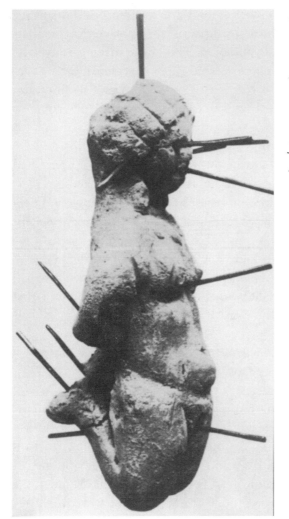

Fig. 2: "I'll nail him."
Like sticking pins in a
voodoo doll ancient Greeks
pierced images of their ene-
mies, like this female figur-
ine, with needles and pins
This defixion *is from a*
fourth-century Alexandrian
gravesite. (© Maurice et
Pierre Chuzeville/Museé du
Louvre.)

be quite long by midday, one historian tells us—she would retire to her chamber and induce a trance by inhaling smoke or chewing laurel leaves. Then she would wail, moan, and speak in tongues her garbled response. The message would be interpreted by her priestly assistants and cast into verse form, the results relayed back to the questioner.

Recently, Classicist Simon Price has challenged the mediumistic image of a smoke-inhaling, ranting hag, full of drugs, holding helpless questioners hostage to her irrational prognostications; he regards all of this as so much undocumented imaging of nineteenth-century romanticism. Organized consultations certainly did take place, but the efficacy of the oracle probably had more to do with the interpretive prophets than with the mental state of the priestess. The oracle may have involved the manipulation of earthly substances and there is evidence most operations were accompanied by preparatory rites such as goat sacrifice, but the oracle certainly existed—a part of Greek life, a place for people to project their thoughts onto, a medium to motivate ordinary people to decide a future course of action.

The oracle, then, was not a malicious magical device that controlled the lives of otherwise intelligent people; rather it kick-started believers into making their own decisions on serious political, religious, and personal problems in their lives. Price recounts the story that the Athenians, under the threat of the Persian invasion, sent representatives to the oracle. The Delphic interpreters advised them to flee the city. Being dissatisfied with this opinion, the emissaries sought a different oracle which offered another lengthy prophecy that spoke of a wooden wall that would save them, ending in the words:

> Divine Salamis, you will bring death to women's sons
> when the corn is scattered, or the harvest gathered in.[12]

When the envoys returned to Athens a huge debate about the two interpretations ensued. Should they build a wooden wall around the Acropolis (i.e., defend their city), or had the prophecy stated the Athenians could save themselves only with a wooden wall of ships? And did the last line refer to their defeat at Salamis? If so, perhaps they should abandon the whole of Greece. Or was a Persian defeat implied? Today we might resolve these uncertainties by appealing to oracle tests and ratings. Which ones work for what percent of the time? Let's test it and look at the facts. But belief in the oracle was a part of Greek common sense. It would have been impious of them to make scientific tests to determine which oracles were best at predicting the future. As it turned out, the Greeks undertook one of their greatest maritime offenses and, under the leadership of Themistocles, won the day in the Battle of Salamis (479 B.C.)

Alchemy was another popular form of magic in the Aegean world (its origin compliments of the Greeks). The word *alchemy* is Greek, probably from *kême*, "the black (soil)" of Egypt where the Alexandrian Greeks of the first few centuries A.D. first practiced the art, and *chyma*, "to fuse or smelt" together.

Not surprisingly, the idea of transmuting one element into another comes right out of Aristotle's notion that all tangible matter is made out of the basic four elements. As in the cure for epilepsy, balance is the key. You only need to get the right proportions together to effect the change. Sounds rational enough. After all, modern physics has enabled one chemical element to be transformed into another. But in the Greek version you needed an agent—the Philosopher's Stone—to carry out the work, and this incorporated the universal soul, the highest spirit or power in the universe.

Seeing is believing; the proof of the pudding is in the eating; see no evil, speak no evil, hear no evil. We take it for granted, but there have been times in the past when we didn't put much faith in the senses. It was once quite normal to believe that there are realities that lie beneath or above and beyond what the senses tell us, realities we possessed before birth and continue to possess after death and of which we are reminded every time we use our sensory apparatus. The idea of the soul, as the later Roman Christian and Medieval worlds would come to understand it, originates in a very different kind of common sense, one we will find difficult to grasp precisely because of our sensory pragmatism, but grasp it we must if we hope to understand Greek magic.

Reflecting the precious regard accorded the soul by the Greeks, Plato wrote:

> . . . a certain organ in every student's soul is cleansed and rekindled, which has been blinded and destroyed by his other pursuits, yet it is more worth saving than a thousand eyes, for by this organ alone is the truth perceived.[13]

The things we see, feel, and touch, argued Plato, are but imperfect, corrupt aspects of the true versions of things that underlie them; Forms, he called them. At the risk of oversimplifying, take the chair you're (likely) sitting in as you read this chapter. According to Plato, your chair is a concrete manifestation of the idea (or Form) of a chair which we all share by perceiving it in our mind's eye in various ways. When I wrote what you are now reading I happened to have been sitting in a comfortable brown swivel with padded metallic arms. Perhaps you now repose on a hardback, or a rocker. Should you describe it, I can imagine your chair just as you get a picture of my swivel in your mind's eye. Plato would say that all of these images share the element of "chairness" that binds all such sitting devices together as a category. The same can be said for Love, a Form which we all express and share in the tangible world in various ways: romantically, carnally, brotherly, motherly. Each instance represents a worldly aspect of the Form Love (love perceived and experienced through our sensual apparati). But the archetype of all our shared experiences is the one true Love—the emotion that lies above all experience and can be imaged imperfectly only through our mundane behavior. As Plato put it, "Each of the Forms exist(s) and other things acquired their name by having a share in them."[14]

Now we know where the expression "our love is purely Platonic" comes from. The correct implication would be that this particular love is so far above and beyond love in all its practical and applied manifestations that it resides on a plane of its own. It aspires to the perfect meaning of that word, a meaning that can be found only in pure thought, in the mind, and not in one's experience. The gist of Platonic Forms is just about as remote as we can get from today's practical-minded materiality. Despite my attempts to explain it, it really loses practically all meaning for us.

What has the Soul to do with Forms? It is, Plato argues, that Form present in all of our bodies that renders us alive and it is the ultimate idealized state we all attain when we die, for then our being consists of pure Soul,[15] which alone is capable of apprehending the true and ultimate reality of the Form of things. Do not be deceived by your senses, says Plato. Seeing is believing, say we.

Whether modern culture has done as much with the Greek gift of Soul as it has with logic and mathematics might depend on whom you ask. For most of us the word has become a mere adjective denoting one's degree of "hipness." But Christianity would mold the Platonic Soul into the seat of all redemption, a premium vied for by the polarized forces of good and evil. Still later, philosophers called Neoplatonists (see p. 69) would accord great importance to the World Soul, a state that one could attain through training and contemplation.

In Greece, matter and soul coexisted. We have seen that for all of its rational, objective aspects, magical thinking was not so distant from science in ancient Greece two thousand or more years ago, where it resided more or less comfortably alongside nascent science, a new, more abstract, impersonal strategy of universal management. The examples I've chosen from physics and medicine suggest that what the Ionians and Aristotle believed about the nature of things would have a lot of appeal in an elementary science classroom even today. Aside from the fact that the Sun is "he" and the Moon "she," the interaction among all of heaven's and Earth's parts is basically mechanical, the way we still imagine most organizations from the solar system to the human brain. Though we owe the Greeks the foundation of our logical, rational, abstract way of thinking that makes up the bulwark of science today, we must realize that science didn't arrive on our contemporary doorstep fully clothed in mathematics and controlled experimentation. But in its earliest form, as best exemplified by the way the Ionian philosophers practiced it, we can already anticipate science's role in setting up a stage on which a battle would take place, one of many in a war of the future that would be waged by abstract materialists seeking to reorient society's perspective and ideology of the outside world. Their opponents: conservatives who supported a more animistic, human-centered philosophy of nature. It would take twenty more centuries, including the sweeping wave of a new religion and an intellectual Renaissance, before the tide of battle would turn in the invaders' favor, toward a way of knowing the world that has become quite common sense at least for most educated classes.

CHAPTER 4

MAGIC IN THE ROMAN EMPIRE

In days of old it was from Athens of high renown that the knowledge of cereal crops was first disseminated among suffering mankind. It was Athens that built life on a new plan and promulgated laws. It was Athens no less that first gave to life a message of good cheer through the birth of that man, gifted with no ordinary mind, whose unerring lips gave utterance to the whole of truth.

Lucretius, *On the Nature of the Universe*
R. E. Latham, translator

The Romans seemed proud of all that the Greeks had created and bequeathed them. They proceeded to alter some Greek gifts and they left others intact. The Romans were practical-minded; for example, they made enormous changes in the civic calendar (the twelve-month version with a shortened February that comes down to us today is essentially Roman). On the other hand, they did little more with art and sculpture than imitate what they saw, sometimes rather poorly judging by our modern tastes. They seem to have taken little interest in Aristotle's high-minded ideas and Plato's abstract ideals. But curiously for pragmatic people, in the realm of magic they had more to say than all their historical forebears combined. Initially their actions widened the gap between science and magic, but toward the end of Roman rule (the third and fourth centuries A.D.), as the empire began to dissolve and its power center shifted eastward across the map of Europe from Rome to Constantinople, their ossified pagan philosophy clashed explosively with Christianity, a new religion spawned at the periphery of the empire. As we will see in the next section, out of this clash crystallized an alternative way of interacting with the outside world called Gnosticism, which in its ideas and actions begins to appear several shades closer to what we now term "occult."

I think one reason why the Romans seem to have written so much about popular conceptions of magic is that a much larger share of all of their writings has survived when compared to the meager trickle emanating from the chronologically more distant Greeks, Babylonians, and Egyptians. And so much of what they have to say strongly impacts our imagination.

In the first century A.D., Pliny, an amateur historian,[1] wrote a thirty-seven-volume work on nature. The contents of Pliny's vast encyclopedia of knowledge, insofar as they relate to magic, are well worth a brief tour, not simply for the sense of amusement modern rationalists like us might acquire from hearing about ridiculous remedies and potions of antiquity, but also—and this is far more important—to understand the way a fairly learned individual of one of the great civilizations of the ancient world classified and organized magic's general principles and operations.

There is this rather precise cure relating to the power of herbs: For boils rub nine grains of barley on the mass three times each with the left hand, then burn the barley. You can anoint yourself with vervain (genus *verbena*) to cure a fever but only if you pick the plant when Sirius, the Dog Star, is rising and no moon lights the night sky. Pulverized animal parts were a hot prescription for toothache: Grind up the ashes of an owl's head, mix it with honeyed wine and lily root, then pack it into the ear on the side with the affected tooth. Under some circumstances the salted liver of a cat, consumed with wine, will do as well as vervain for fever—provided you slay the cat when the moon is waning. For incontinence, drink the ashes of a boar's genitals in sweet wine. Then urinate in a dog house and say, "That I may not urinate like a dog in its kennel."

The catalog of cures, each recipe sounding more absurd than the last, runs to hundreds of pages and Pliny is careful not to miss a detail. For nightmares, try a lizard's tail wrapped in gazelle skin and bound with deer sinews, or a mixture of lizard's tongue, eyes, gallbladder, and intestines—all boiled in oil (it won't work unless it is cooled out of doors at night and rubbed on the body before retiring). To cure warts: On the twentieth day after a new moon rub dirt on them while you lie in the road and gaze at the moon. For headache: Pour vinegar on your door hinges. To dislodge a bone in your throat: Put the same kind of bone on the top of your head. If bread gets stuck in your throat: Stuff bread in your ears.

Keep in mind that Pliny was not an expert. He was a navy admiral by profession and he compiled his oddball mixture of folk wisdom and establishment science in his spare time. Nonetheless, from what his nephew, Pliny the Younger, tells us, we can only imagine what this prodigious encyclopedist could have done with a research staff and a word processor. Modern Roman historians have dubbed him a monomaniac with a morbid appetite for hard work.[2] He spent every spare moment prowling in libraries rooting out factoids. He worked late into the night and arose early in the morning, snatching only a bit of lunch as he made meticulous notes on species of birds, insects, and animals, trees and herbs, metals and minerals, meteorology, tides, and earthquakes. When he took his weekly bath he would have his secretary read his notes to him; in cold weather he would don a pair of gloves and write. His nephew tells us that when he died at fifty-six, devoured by his lust for knowledge, Pliny left 160 notebooks filled with tiny scrawl on both sides of every page. His motivation? He found it lamentable and shameful that in an empire so great as Rome there was too much interest in making money and pitiful little concern with taking up learning where the Greeks had left off in their study of nature.

When? Which way? How many? What to say and how to say it? These are the basic elements of Plinian magical instruction. But those who have read carefully will note a common denominator in many of the medicinal cures Pliny reports. You must use particular materials, suspensions, ligatures under certain ambient astronomical/meteorological conditions, and you must accompany your treatment with specific actions that involve position, direction, handedness, number, spoken words, etc. All his instructions seem grounded in the basic notion that cause and cure are directly tied together. "Like cures like" glares out at us in the bone-on-head and bread-in-ears cures, which exemplify this universal principle of magic in a fairly straightforward way.

Why do we moderns fail to see the point in these odd concoctions Uncle Pliny dishes up for us? Suppose I gave you the following list of natural phenomena: earthquake, volcanic eruption, comet, and asked which one doesn't belong? Even an elementary school child will discern that the first two are catastrophic events that result from geologic processes which can be particularly disastrous to anyone situated close by when they occur. The third, which belongs with other astronomical categories like supernovae and shooting stars, is beautiful to behold yet totally unthreatening (unless you happen to have lived among the dinosaurs sixty million years ago). The point is that the ancient Roman taxonomy of nature is not necessarily the same as ours. In Roman eyes, all three phenomena would have been closely linked in cause—all as bad omens conjured up by deities. The really interesting question then becomes not: Why did these ignorant people fail to see the truth?, but in-

Contemporary American restorative folk remedies follow the "like-cures-like" principle. Some of them might as well have fallen directly out of Pliny's *Natural History:* relieve thighs chafed from horseback riding by rubbing them with foam from the horse's mouth. Break up painful gallstones by eating herbs whose flowers look like pearls. Touch a scorpion with heliotrope and you will kill it.* Modern botanists still describe the floral sprouts of this plant as scorpioid in shape (see Fig. 3). You can stop a nosebleed by wearing a red handkerchief; hang a carrot in your basement to cure jaundice. Cure frostbite by rubbing snow on the affected area, and a dog bite with the hair of the dog that bit you—or eat the snake that bit you. Sometimes the affected area is the opposite of that treated, as in rubbing Vicks Vaporub in your rectum to cure a sore throat. These last amusing examples teach us that folk medicine isn't just a quaint practice we read about in ancient history books or in modern anthropology texts on aborigines, but a deeply entrenched part of modern life, its habits practiced automatically and without question.

While simple restorative remedies like these were believed to be the direct work of nature, the curing process could be enhanced in the Roman apothecary with appropriate additives like human hair, urine, ear wax, saliva, powdered tooth, and gemstone. Pills and plasters, mixtures and melanges were fashioned to help nature along the way, just as the French vintner creates a better wine by adding sugar and yeast to pure grape juice to assist the process of fermentation.

* For a vast collection of American folk remedies, see W. Hand, "Folk Medical Magic and Symbolism in the West."

stead: What principles of association had the ancient mind devised that caused these phenomena to bear a significant relationship to one another? This is a much more difficult question. In Pliny's magic we must ask what would be peculiar, extraordinary, or paranormal *to him*—or, better, to the practicing source he reports on. Would it be a hot spring, a chunk of lodestone, a five-legged calf, a dream, a sneeze?

Why grind up plant and animal parts to cure your ills? Because, as Pliny tells us, animals have moral standards. Lions are courageous, ele-

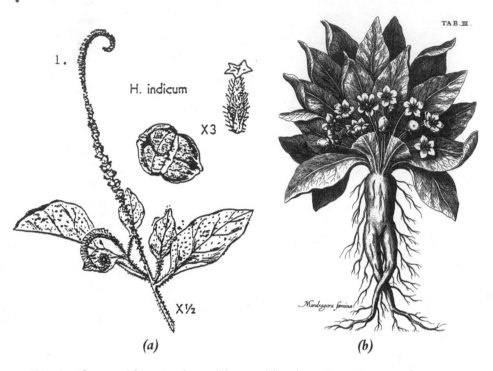

Fig. 3: Plants with animal- and humanlike characteristics were often a part of ancient magic: (a) Heliotrope (Heliotropium Indicum), *a weed famous for its scorpion tail appearance. (b) One of Medieval witchcraft's most famous hexing herbs was the mandrake* (Mandragora officinarum). *Note the likeness between the (exaggerated) shape of its root and the female torso. Pulling the root from the earth meant severe consequences for the Collector, who would be driven mad from the screams and howls uttered by the plant. Engraving by Matthäus Merian, in M. Valentini,* Viridarium Reformatum, seu Regnum Vegetabile.

phants just. Animals have their own wisdom. Have you ever seen a hippo cure itself of bleeding when sharp reeds have torn its leg open by plastering the wound with mud? And have you witnessed a hawk rubbing hawkweed on its eyes to make it see better? Or a sick dog or cat cure itself by eating grass?

In addition to the idea of like-to-like association, Greco-Roman magic also operated on the principle of transfer. If you can't cure it, get rid of it by passing it on to another animal or object. For example, to relieve cough, spit into a frog's mouth or kiss a mule. For gas pains, press a duck against your stomach. The transfer principle often was carried out

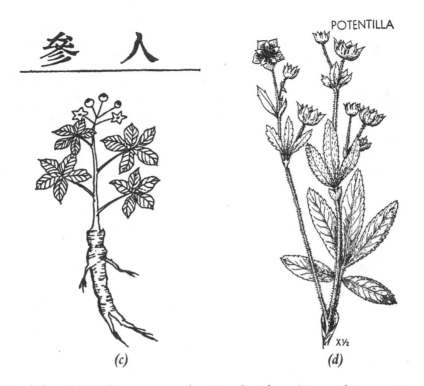

Fig. 3 (cont.): (c) Ginseng, a psychoactive plant from Asia, used to promote sexual potency. (Pen Tsao Kang Mu Chinese Herbals.) (d) Among the many members of the Potentilla *family is this* P. palustris. *Pentafoil flowers like these were used in rites to raise the Devil. Note also the five-pointed flower on the ginseng plant. ((a) and (d) from H. Gleason (ed.),* The New Britton and Brown Illustrated Flora of the Northeast United States and Adjacent Canada. © The New York Botanical Garden.)

through a secondary principle called "action at a distance"—the same idea that lies behind Newton's explanation of the force of gravitational attraction of all objects in the universe, which he devised seventeen centuries after Pliny compiled his encyclopedia! But the action principle by which objects interact in magic has nothing to do with abstract and impersonal inventions of the mind such as our fields and plasmas; rather it is concerned with personified forces of attraction or repulsion—like love and hatred, concord and discord that exist between all things as a matter of course. We will discover in later chapters that the mediating principle between culture and nature changes with the times and very much reflects the aberrations of the scientific principles of a particular age. For example, the Roman deer and snake are associated with one another not through magnetic forces but via a natural hatred they possess for one another. A stag can follow a snake to its hole and extract it by breathing into the opening, we are told. That's why ground-up fawn embryo is a good remedy for snakebite. If you want to avoid snakes completely, try wearing a deer's tooth around your neck. In ancient Rome, amulets were believed to work by the transfer principle: Two bed bugs tied to the left arm in a woolen band stolen from a shepherd will keep out nocturnal fever. Fox blood smeared on a starfish and nailed to the threshold of your house will ward off bad drugs. . . .

Oddly enough, after trotting out and meticulously describing cure after cure in his *Natural History,* Pliny, well-imbued in the ways of Greek science, condemns it all with the swipe of a pen. For example, he tells about an elaborate mixture called *theriaca:*

> . . . which is compounded of countless ingredients, although Nature has given as many remedies, anyone of which would be enough by itself. The Mithridatic antidote is composed of fifty-four ingredients, no two of them having the same weight, while of some is prescribed one sixtieth part of one denarius. Which of the gods, in the name of Truth, fixed these absurd proportions? No human brain could have been sharp enough. It is plainly a showy parade of the art, a colossal boast of science. And not even the physicians know their facts; I have discovered that instead of Indian cinnabar there is commonly added to medicines, through a confusion of names, red lead, which, as I shall point out when I discuss pigments, is a poison.[3]

(The last sentence is particularly amusing in that Pliny replaces one toxin with another.)

Later Pliny condemns all magic by adding the opinion that nonsense is what they believe in, these quacks who import their art from Persia and Zoroaster via the Greeks. How could anybody believe in a mass of dogma attributable to a single founder anyway? Still the moderate, Pliny complains that while there may be some truth in the herbal cures he dutifully reports, decadent Roman society has allowed things to be carried too far. (An almost identical complaint has been voiced about certain

New Age practices by members of our own society.) There are now magicians, Pliny tells us, who dare to propose that herbs can dry up rivers, open locked doors, and scare away the enemy. Even though the Roman government had finally abolished the open practice of magical rites, he tells us, many people still believe in magical absurdities like the popular notion that a loaded ship can be made to move along more slowly and safely if the captain brings the right foot of a tortoise on board!

So Pliny ends up drawing the conclusion that anybody who really believes in what he describes is a fool. All magi are impostors, he declares. The Roman emperor for whom he composed his work would have agreed with him, for magic officially was deemed dangerous to the state if not in the public eye. Would magicians discover dangerous secrets about the future? he might wonder. A typical emperor's family would likely have had its own household astrologer and diviner, but even if an emperor listened to the soothsayers, it was inappropriate for the public to do so.

For every skeptic like Pliny, there is a believer like Tacitus (first century A.D.), a historian who fully defended the practice of magic. His position was that magic could foment revolt, but on the other hand, if it works and we really can see into the future, then why not study it?—a position advocated by some respectable researchers in the paranormal sciences today. Was the employment of amulets any different from the established Roman practice of worshipping idols in temples? What, he wondered, is the difference between a magician and a priest? The same difference that endowed the statue of Venus with the powers of love and rendered any other carved piece of stone powerless: the sanction of the state.

The Romans had their expert healers, too. Galen (A.D. 129–200) was a Roman doctor who followed Pliny the Elder by about two generations. If Pliny was an amateur who wrote about magic, Galen was a pro who practiced it, though he never would have admitted it in his day. He led as exciting and creative a life as any superstar surgeon of our day. Born in Pergamum on the coast of Asia Minor, he served in the demanding post of team doctor for the Roman gladiators before entering practice in Rome during one of the great plagues. Later he worked as a military surgeon on the northern front where the Romans were just beginning to fight off the Germanic invaders who would eventually overrun the empire. Ultimately he won fame thanks to an incredibly high cure rate—so high that jealous colleagues accused him of practicing the black arts, a charge we will return to time and time again when we discuss celebrated magical healers of later generations.

Galen also wrote as voluminously as Pliny but with considerably more authority because of his high position in society as a medical expert.[4] Still, the imaginative treatments he offered sound almost as silly to our ears as Pliny's. Fortunately, Galen wrote up many of his cases in his notebooks for us to ponder in hindsight. For example, he explains how he successfully treated a gout patient by mixing extra sharp cheese with boiled salt pork and rubbing it on the man's aching joints. To one woman who came to him afflicted with a cough so violent that she threw up blood, Galen administered the following complex treatment: He first gave her a good enema, then rubbed her hands and feet with a drug (he does not say what it contained), and then bandaged them. Next he shaved her head and rubbed it with bird droppings. After a light supper consisting of cereal, the patient was fed unripe fruit for dessert; then followed a rubdown with a compound of ground-up snake. On successive mornings a large dose of honey preceded another serpentine slather, each time administered with an older and therefore stronger version of snake oil. Galen writes in his journal that he continued this rubbing and dieting accompanied by bathing for days. It worked!

What could have been the rationale for such a regimen? I see it as a combination of magic and science. The effect of the increasingly toxic rubdown, Galen tells us, was to promote strongly alternating heating and drying, which seems sensible in light of the acceptable scientific theory of the day that all illness happens when the bodily humors get out of whack. Like much of the drug therapy our physicians apply today to restore acid, sugar, or blood pressure balance, the treatment is also restorative in nature. The substances administered—from avian excrement to the nectar of the gods—have less to do with causative and more to do with associative principles lost to us in the sands of time.

What drove Galen? His writings are filled with references to the Creator. Galen believed that seeking to know His power and wisdom so that he can effect a cure is far more an act of reverence than offering sacrifice or burning incense on an altar. And while Galen believed everything that transpired in the flesh and humors he manipulated was governed by a higher intelligence, he seems to have distinguished himself by keeping his belief in God out of his procedures and diagnoses. In this respect perhaps Galen is not so different from some of our modern surgeons.

I think the Roman uncertainty about the place of what we call magic in their world view is vividly reflected in both Pliny's *Natural History* and Galen's *On the Greek Medical Corpus*. After reading both authors, you get the sense that Galen and Pliny inhabit a world *halfway* between science and mysticism. As we become absorbed in reading about those superstitious cures, we must remind ourselves over and over that Roman and Greek alike shared an absolute faith in an animate universe imbued with forces of nature personified by gods and goddesses. The principles of transfer and like-to-like were their natural by-laws. The assumption that trickery or deceit operate in these collective procedures offers us a convenient label for "magic" and the "occult arts" that resemble them today. Any evil lay in the heart and mind of the practitioner and not in the practice. Condemning a Roman healer in historical hindsight is a little like damning a modern scientist because among the fruits of his or her craft are toxic chemicals and a terrifying nuclear arsenal.

All of the cures Galen and Pliny—two among many Roman authors I might have chosen—describe also can be categorized as sympathetic or imitative magic.[5] Imitate the desired result and it will happen. What I find so remarkable about this way of curing is that it, too, was universal. It seems to have been and still is practiced by people all over the world—cultures that could not possibly have acquired it from contact with the Mediterranean area. Does this suggest something very deep in human nature about how people think they are tied to the natural world? The similarity of the laws by which diverse cultures operate upon the natural world is so striking that I have decided to deal with some of them in a separate chapter in Part V rather than detouring the reader into some of these exotic foreign practices. For now let's continue with the flow of the stream of Western history where big things were about to happen in the world of magic as the Roman Empire came to an end.

CHAPTER 5

THE NEW OUTCASTS: THE RISE OF SECRET DOCTRINES

If a prophet arises among you, or a dreamer of dreams, and gives you a sign or a wonder, and the sign or wonder which he tells you comes to pass, and if he says, "Let us go after other gods," which you have not known "and let us serve them," you shall not listen to the words of that prophet or to that dreamer of dreams; for the Lord your God is testing you.

Deuteronomy 13: 1–3

. . . therefore you shall no more see delusive visions nor practice divination . . .

Ezekiel 13:23

Imagine living in a hotbed of competition among a flock of mystery religions—beliefs and secret cults all purporting to disclose mysteries about the supernatural. To belong to one of these clubs you needed to be initiated—into the cult of Dionysus if you were a member of upper crust society, the cult of Mithras if you belonged to the military, or the cult of Eleusis if you were a world leader. There would be a wide latitude of beliefs to suit your individual tastes and upbringing. All of these were successors of local cults, many of them imported from abroad and cultivated for immigrants who chose to worship old godly allegiances. Many carried out missionary work to spread their rites among other members of cosmopolitan society. When you live in a diverse expanding society you need to develop special ways to retain and maintain your religious group identity and with all that competition you need to do it carefully. This is what life in the Roman world had become by the first century A.D.

When Caesar came to power two generations before the birth of Christ, the Roman Empire encompassed the countries we now call Italy,

France, and Greece plus parts of Spain, the Dalmatian coast, Western Tunisia, and Egypt. By the time the Emperor Trajan ruled, six generations later, the State had doubled in size, extending itself to include all of Western Europe (with the exception of today's Scotland, Ireland, and Germany), all of Turkey, Iraq, and Armenia, and the whole of the territory from Lebanon south and west to Gibraltar, extending hundreds of miles inland on the Iberian peninsula. In the midst of this explosive expansion and the consequent attempts to consolidate authority over so many disparate ethnic enclaves into a single social and economic structure, a new force—a new covenant with the deity—was unleashed that would alter the concept of magic ever thereafter.

The coming of Christianity spelled the decline of paganism and the philosophy of Classical Greece expressed through Plato and Aristotle. Magic, as it would come to be known in the Dark Ages and Medieval and Renaissance Europe, was shaped here, out of the remnants of Greek ideas filtered through the new Christian religion. It is no coincidence that this molding and forming process becomes more recognizable to our modern senses just at the height of the Roman Empire when Christian ideas were becoming firmly rooted. We are already aware that divination and natural magic were widely practiced before and during the time of the Roman Empire. What Christian doctrine offered that was so profound is the idea that there is only one true God, manifested in his Son, and not the multitude of personified forces advocated by all those nature-worshipping cults with which Christianity competed.

I chose a couple of verses from the Bible that express the uncompromising Old Testament view that endured in the new Christian revelation. For no God—neither idol nor amulet—in any form shall stand before Him. And the soul with which He endows us, bound by the new covenant, must strive to return to Him through Christ after death; for the soul, like all things, was created in God's image. In this sort of spiritual New Deal, there isn't much room for human action to manipulate the course of things, no gods to be cajoled or convinced via magical powers. And this is why when the Emperor Constantine (A.D. 272–337)—the first to adopt Christianity officially as his true faith and therefore that of the Eastern [Holy] Roman Empire he ruled—came to power, he rooted out and banned all magical practice. Constantine wrote: "There shall be no more divination, no curious inquiry, for evermore. Whoever dares disobey shall lose his head by the avenging sword of the executioner."[1]

How can we explain these paranoid persecutions? Only by understanding what religion was like in those times. Christianity today comes in a variety of forms, cultivated over changing times to suit the moral tastes of a wide variety of practitioners. Rich in ritual and imagery, the Roman Catholic faith represents the most traditional line. Its believers follow the set of teachings headed by the Pope and descended from the Orthodox Roman Church. Reformation sects labeled Protestant were created as a result of Martin Luther's protest against a religious decree by Emperor Charles V in 1529. Today all mainstream Protestant sects follow the word of the Bible alone, eschewing decrees of any dignitary in a spiritual hierarchy, such as a pope. Justification by faith and the right to worship according to one's own conscience are fundamental to their creed. There the faith subdivides into sects or followings according to a particular teacher's philosophy. For example, Lutherans believe that they most closely follow the doctrines of church reformer Martin Luther; Methodists follow John Wesley, who prided himself on the strictness of the observation of certain religious duties; Baptists hold that baptism through immersion in water ought to be administered to all believers upon their acceptance of Christ, and so on. The Episcopalian is often considered to live in a religious halfway house between Catholic and Protestant. For him or her the supreme authority of the Pope is supplemented by a hierarchical government of the church headed by bishops, who are distinct from and superior to priests who, in turn, are situated above deacons.

Then there are the sects that lie on the fringe of Christian orthodoxy, if measured only by the number in their membership. Adventists believe in the second personal coming of Christ, while Mormons follow a doctrine based upon truths and miracles said to have been revealed through a particular nineteenth-century American, Joseph Smith, who claimed to have found sacred truths written on Golden Plates. I find it interesting that in common parlance many fringe sects are referred to as cults, a term often taken to imply excessive, obsessive devotion—extremes that often draw harsh social judgment, as did the Branch Davidian cult viewed through contemporary middle class American eyes, or the New World Aztec cult of sacrifice as perceived by colonial Spaniards.

If I run the risk of oversimplifying, it's only to make a point: That as many and varied are the sects that make up major branches of organized religion today, there were far more in number engaged in far more fierce competition at the time of Christ's teachings. His view was one among the many in contention to ignite the popular imagination in the first few centuries A.D. The sudden contact and communication of ideas across the Mediterranean Sea via Roman conquest was bound to breed ideological conflict. Local variations of religious beliefs developed in different cities from Antioch (today in Lebanon) to Alexandria were now embraced by Rome; and missionaries carried their specific teachings from place to place.

Also in the thick of the competitive fray were those we call the Gnostics, who represented a class of sects most closely allied with magical practice. Today we are familiar with this term through its negative or absented popular form "agnostic," by which most of us mean someone who has not decided, or can never deem it possible to decide, in belief in a deity. But the true Gnostics sought the same union with God advocated by more mainstream Christians. They felt, however, that it was not sin that cut us off from our creator, but ignorance. Gnostic life consisted of the search for true knowledge. They believed that revelation could be found among all civilized nations and that every faith contained a germ of truth that culminated in Christ. So Gnosticism was a form of religious internationalism.

To early church fathers, the magic of Gnosticism was dangerous and they took great pains to discredit it. Simon the Magician, a Gnostic of the first century A.D. was baptized Christian after witnessing miracles of healing conducted by the apostles John and Peter. So desirous was Simon to acquire these powers, he even offered money for them. In New Testament *Acts,* the apostle Peter tells the story:

> But there was a man named Simon who had previously practiced magic in the city and amazed the nation of Samaria, saying that he himself was somebody great. They all gave heed to him, from the least to the greatest, saying, "This man is that power of God which is called Great." And they gave heed to him, because for a long time he had amazed them with his magic. Acts 8: 9–11

When he saw God's true miracles, Simon himself was amazed. And so, he appealed to Christ's apostles:

> Give me also this power, that any one on whom I lay my hands may receive the Holy Spirit. (19)

But Peter rebukes him:

> You have neither part nor lot in this matter for your heart
> is not right before God. Repent therefore of this wickedness
> of yours and pray to the Lord that, if possible, the intent of
> your heart may be forgiven you.   (21–2)

Simon thus became the symbolic founder of Christian heresy and his
crime (simony) came to be regarded as one of the most despicable sins
against the Christian Church. The lesson, of course, is that there is only
one way to make miracles happen: through Christian faith.

So why did the Gnostics practice magic? They reasoned that God
who created everything also was responsible for the evil in the world.
There is a whole world of spirits between us and Him and it is out of
their sin—not ours—that the world arrived in its present corrupt condition. The only way to seek salvation is through the "psychic," the one
with that latent capacity for true knowledge. Only he can redeem those
among us who by our very nature can be saved. The rest—the purely
material people of the world—are doomed. Only an adept can know the
magical password needed to ascend the ladder of the demon-filled planetary spheres toward heaven and redemption.

Rome ruled in an age of limited and slow transportation and communication, when people had long lived in relative isolation, and we can
scarcely imagine the intensity with which religious ideologies chafed
against one another. As diverse customs and folkways entered into confrontation, they blended together and changed in the wake of Rome's attempt to control so many widespread, diverse cultures. Persian and other
Oriental religions entered from the East and collided with Christian ideology head-on to produce the odd combination of Christian scripture
read by the Magi. It told of direct contact of the human spirit and the
real universe, a union superior to the normal mode of perceiving the
world. Tools of the ideological trade, including symbols, numbers, formulas, and names, accompanied the widespread belief acquired from ancient Babylonia and Greece that the powers of nature created our
inferior world here below and they still rule over it.

Historian R. M. Grant calls Gnosticism a mixture of Eastern religions
couched in the language of Greek philosophy and originating in "an atmosphere of intense otherworldliness and imaginative myth making."[2]
One Gnostic sect, for example, held that its believers were tied directly

to the real world by the fact that John the Baptist's disciples, being thirty in number (one for each year of the life of Christ up to the time he began his ministry) also equaled the number of days of the moon's phase cycle as well as the number of eons of Gnostic teaching that had elapsed in the world. The seven (then-discovered) planets[3] are the gods of astrological theory who mediate between the mundane and the world of divine light, claimed another group. Yet a third sect advocated that when the Lord cast the serpent down into the mundane world, the serpent had six sons who together with himself made up seven demons who are alien to all people.

Of all the mystical wisdom of early Christian Gnosticism that floated about the Empire, the two traditions that would exert the greatest influence on Western occultism of the future were housed in the so-called Hermetic doctrine and in the mysticism of classical Judaism known as the *Kabbalah* (Cabbala). I will sketch out their fundamentals in forthcoming chapters, because they will figure in our discussion of the magic of the Dark Ages and Medieval times.

Every culture has its myth about the sources of ancient wisdom. Our own honors the Greeks and Renaissance Europe. But if you were Greek and lived in Alexandria in the first few centuries A.D., you would likely have gleaned your ancient wisdom from the Egyptians. Imagine how awed you would have been by the past's relics that surrounded you in this magical land—its colossal pyramids and the bejeweled mummies interred within them. The Greeks knew the Egyptians had mined precious metals, like gold, eons before them and the knowledge of how to do it was said to have been a closely guarded secret passed down by priests.

Iamblichus, Stephanus, Clement of Alexandria—all the historians of those times—name the ancient Egyptian wise man Hermes Trismegistus the master of alchemical philosophy and one of the great founders and fonts of the ancient magical arts. He is called Hermes[4] after the god who founded alchemy; Trismegistus means "three times great," an Egyptian title that recognizes him as the greatest of kings, the greatest of philosophers, and the greatest of priests. They say the ancient Hermetic corpus, forty-two books in number,[5] was written by Trismegistus himself. Our derivative phrase "hermetically sealed" still means chemically or scientifically preserved.

Ten of the Hermetic books dealt with the basic laws and gods and instructions on how to train priests; ten were on prayers and rites, ten more on hymns. The others dealt with medicine, astrology, geography, and the tool kit that accompanied various secret rites embedded in these disciplines. All that survive, however, are eighteen fragments; the remainder were said to have been destroyed in the fire that leveled the great library of Alexandria. Later historians discovered that most of these were recopied and may in fact have originated in Medieval times. Authentic portions include fragments of prayers known to have existed in the early Christian centuries, Gnostic teachings such as the statement that stars are gods or the doctrine that the planets control the world and the signs of the zodiac, the human body, etc. The Chosen, these writings reveal, are the only ones capable of receiving divine knowledge; only they can escape the fate decreed by the stars and return to the spirit world by passing through the region of demons to the eighth heaven above the spheres of the seven planets.

Hermes' greatest bequest regarding the secrets of the past to mankind were the words inscribed on the Emerald Tablet[6]—the magician's credo. The tablet is said to have been discovered by Sarah, wife of Abraham, clasped in the hands of Hermes' mummy, which had been laid away in a secret passage in the Great Pyramid. Reproduced in its entirety it reads:

> Tis true, without falsehood, the most real: that which is above is like that which is below, to perpetrate the miracles of one thing. And as all things have been derived from one, by the thought of one, so all things are born from this thing, by adoption. The sun is its father, the moon is its mother. Wind has carried it in its belly, the earth is its nurse. Here is the father of every perfection in the world. His strength and power are absolute when changed into earth; thou wilt separate the earth from fire, the subtle from the grown, gently and with care. It ascends from earth to heaven, and descends again to earth to receive the power of the superior and the inferior things. By this means, thou wilt have the glory of the world. And because of this, all obscurity will flee from thee. Within this is the power, most powerful of all powers. For it will overcome all subtle things, and penetrate every solid thing. Thus the world was created. From this will be, and will emerge, admirable adaptations of which the means are here. And for this reason, I am called Hermes Trismegistus, having the three parts of the philosophy of the world. What I have said of the sun's operations is accomplished.[7]

Need I point out that from the opening foundation statement on astrology to the closing sentence on the power of the adept, the tablet's statement is loaded with numinous terminology accompanied by a license to control and manipulate the world—a far cry from the traditional scriptures?

CHAPTER 6

KNOWLEDGE THROUGH NUMBER AND THE WORD

⟿

From a seventh-century armorplate:
Protect my bladder, fat and all the innumerable rows of connecting parts. . . .

John Gager, *Curse Tablets and*
Binding Spells from the Ancient World

Kabbalah, the other great wellspring of so many forms of magic that would be continually breathed back to life later in history, means "received love." Today it is a general term for Jewish mysticism.[1] In contrast to Hermetism, Kabbalism has little to do with the withdrawal from humanity in order to pursue the union with God and enlightenment. Like many Gnostic sects, Kabbalists carried on a normal social and family life while practicing their art. Though it would be adopted and radically altered by later occult sects of the Middle Ages, the Renaissance, the eighteenth and nineteenth centuries—even the twentieth century—its original intent, when first appropriated by Christian Gnostics, was like that of so many progressive disciplinary programs: to elevate the practitioner to higher, more refined levels of achievement. Through fasting and recitation of hymns and prayers uttered in a trance state, one moved up the ladder of the seven heavenly houses to the *Merkabah,* or "God's throne chariot." To protect the soul from demons on the ascent, initiates employed special formulas, incantations, and amulets. Put in Christian terms, the idea of climbing the ladder corresponds to elevating your soul from the world after the Fall and back to unity with God, a notion not fully developed until the Renaissance (especially in Rosicrucianism and freemasonry). This concept of advancing through discipline to higher, more refined levels of achievement is still with us today in practices as diverse as Kundalini yoga on the one hand and diet and exercise on the other.

One of the earliest and most influential handbooks of Kabbalah is the *Sefer Yezira,* or "Book of Creation," dated to the first to third century A.D. Like most books of magic, it was said to have been revealed divinely. The

Sefer Yezira tells how God designed and created the world to have thirty-two secret paths to wisdom comprising the twenty-two letters of the Hebrew alphabet, the unique sound of each having its own special power, along with the ten *sephiroth* or intelligences attributable to Him. We will deal with the thirty-two paths in Part II because the scheme of ascending via pathways was not exploited to its fullest until the Middle Ages. But the idea of the staying power of numbers and words as advocated by Kabbalistic thinking is worth a short excursion here so that we can understand how it works in practice and what remains of it today.

We are all familiar with word puzzles. We use them to while away time in the dentist's office, or waiting for an oil change, or on a commute home when we're too burned out to think about summing up what happened in the office that day. The daily newspaper is an excellent source for brainteasers. There are games like Jumble©, where you unscramble the letters of four non-words to make real ones; then you unscramble a second time only those letters selected and circled among the deciphered quartet to make yet another word or phrase, the meaning of which is hinted at in a cartoon. Each entry is called an *anagram,*[2] because we need to transpose its letters to make another word. Another game consists of finding hidden words embedded in a square grid of letters by connecting certain of the letters via horizontal, vertical, and diagonal chains. Usually, these puzzles are made simpler by a clue that links all the words.

Magic squares substitute numbers for letters; they are close relatives of our early crosswords. For example, how do you arrange a four-by-four array of the numbers one to sixteen so that the horizontal, vertical, and diagonal sums are all equivalent? (Fig. 4, top) The ancient Chinese also were particularly fond of such puzzles. Puzzle pastimes like these had their place among leisurely interests in the ancient European world, too. Archaeologists in ancient Rome have recovered a marble game board remarkably like our Scrabble called "12 Writings." (Fig. 4, bottom)[3] It consisted of a dozen six-word, six-letter sentences laid out on a board in twelve lines, each split into six plus six letters. (Imagine a backgammon board on which the triangular spaces are six-letter words and you get the picture.) Opposing players read the dice and moved the counters the indicated amount over the letters in a specific sequence, capturing one another as they went. The first one to run his or her counters over the entire board won the game. The underlying sentences (nobody knows where they fit into the game either) often had a moral tone. One, for example, read ". . . I can't stand losers who lose their temper."

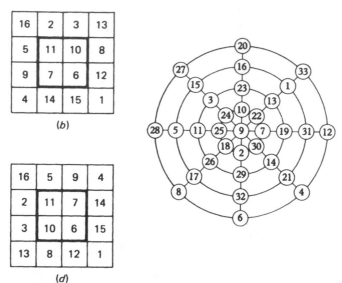

16	2	3	13
5	11	10	8
9	7	6	12
4	14	15	1

(b)

16	5	9	4
2	11	7	14
3	10	6	15
13	8	12	1

(d)

Fig. 4: Magic numbers and words. Top left: *The magic squares consist of the numbers 1 through 16 rearranged so that if you add the numbers horizontally, vertically, and diagonally (or even the four boxed in the center) you get the same total. During the Middle Ages there was one magic square for each planet that signified the way it affected each of us here below.* Top right: *In the magic circle, the numbers 1 to 33 are laid out along radial lines that sum to 78.* (T. Crump, The Anthropology of Numbers. *Reprinted with the permission of Cambridge University Press.*) Bottom: *A Roman game board made out of six six-letter word sentences. This one reads "circus full, terrific shouting, doors bursting." (After* O. A. W. Dilke, Mathematics and Measurement, © *British Museum.*)

A puzzle, literally from the word "opposing" or "opposite," opposes order. It is confusing, complex, disordered—until you discover the secret. The basic theory behind all puzzles from the *New York Times* crossword[4] to "Where's Waldo?" is to find what lies hidden beneath the tangled and confusing web of pictures, letters, or numbers. Only the clever person can crack a puzzle and solve the mystery. We enjoy doing puzzles because

---

Gematria tries to reveal the hidden meaning of things—objects, buildings, words—by analyzing numerical values assigned each of their parts. One version of Kabbalistic *gematria* popular with New Age numerologists goes like this. First I add the letters of my name as I usually write it:

1	14	20	8	15	14	25	1	22	5	14	9
A	N	T	H	O	N	Y	A	V	E	N	I

When I do I get 148. Next I reduce this number to one of the single digits (0 to 9) by adding together the digits that make up my sum; thus $1 + 4 + 8 = 13$ (sounds bad already!). If I sum once again: $1 + 3 = 4$, I get my "digital root." A chart in a modern book on numerology[*] tells me that digital root #4 connotes a solid, practical, uninspired, and uninspiring personality without any creative spark—an administrator. Another chart tells me further that it is also in my nature to be stern, grim, repressive, and plodding. To get my "heart number," I add only the vowels in my name. When I do I get 31, which reduces to $3 + 1 = 4$. This number tells me about my inner self, my deeper interests, ambitions, likes, and dislikes, regardless of what nature might intend. The chart suggests that at least I have a chance against the universal demons, for I seem to be a good talker and I am very sure of myself. Add the consonants in my name and I get my "personality number," which turns out to be 9 ($117 = 1 + 1 + 7 = 9$). This number connotes masculine qualities.[†] I am intuitive, loving, and desirous of being loved, but I can easily be hurt.

[*] K. Roquemore, *It's All in Your Numbers: The Secret of Numerology.*

[†] Even numbers are feminine because their geometrical arrangement, e.g., ∷, always has a receptive opening, a generational part of space within itself, while the odds are phallic, with a protrusion in the middle: ∴.

when we succeed we feel very wise. You may not realize it, but whether you're a sometime sleuth who does the crossword or Jumble in the daily newspaper or a puzzle fanatic who solves an entire monthly magazine full of acrostics, you share in a very old sort of magic once practiced by your ancestors.

In Scrabble we use our skills to create words out of letters, each of which is assigned a numerical value by order of the perceived difficulty in using that letter to make a word. Vowels are abundant and cheap (most of them count for one point). More difficult letters like J score big—eight points. Q and Z are each worth ten. Now suppose we change this rule slightly, to one in which the numbers assigned to a letter indicate not frequency of use but order in the alphabet (i.e., A = 1, O = 15, Z = 26). You are now set to play a game of magic called *gematria* (Hebrew) that originated directly out of Kabbalistic doctrine over two thousand years ago.

Now, as then, numerology enters the world of self-help and its applications go far beyond your name. For example, live in a place that adds up to a "positive" number (NEW YORK = 3) and you'll be surrounded by brilliance and glitter, but forget "drab" and "placid" PARIS, which totals a "negative" nine. Sixes should avoid all drugs because the word DRUGS adds up to six. If you're a three, eat peaches because P-E-A-C-H-E-S sums to $16 + 5 + 1 + 3 + 8 + 5 + 19 = 57 = 5 + 7 = 12 = 1 + 2 = 3$. But the singular PEACH adds up to six, so you'd better eat more than one. I can do *gematria* with my birth number too: $3/5/38 = 3 + 5 + 1 + 9 + 3 + 8 = 29 = 2 + 9 = 11 = 1 + 1 = 2$. This reveals the stamp that mysterious forces in the universe have placed upon me when I was born.

Now, I realize it is difficult for most modern readers to swallow this stuff. You ask: How can my birth number be affected if the calendar that led to it is a human invention—and has been reformed several times? Wouldn't that change the meaning? If divining by the calendar is legitimate, shouldn't all people born on the same day behave in the same way? What if my name was given by chance by parents who knew nothing about numerology? Nothing is left to chance, answer the number crunchers. Even before you are born your name and your destiny are placed upon you, subconsciously, by the forces of the universe; for the soul you inhabit has taken many journeys in the past and it surely knows its name. But whether you and I take it seriously is not important. The real questions are why has Kabbalistic Gnosticism been resurrected over and over again, persisting in one form or another for over two thousand years?

To answer those questions, we need to apply Kabbalah as a means of decoding words to arrive at ancient secret truths. The unutterable name of god, YHVH,[5] consists of four letters, each of which is assigned a numerical value given by the order of that letter in the alphabet. In the Hebrew alphabet the corresponding numbers would be 10, 5, 6, 5. Added together they make 26, the same value obtained by performing *gematria* on the Hebrew words for "love" and "unity" and adding the result. One form of the secret message, therefore, is that God is Love and Unity, another that God is Unity manifested as Love.

An equally famous numerical riddle is the "number of the beast," a mystery that seems to have attracted a hundred generations of puzzle fanatics since it was first written down nearly two thousand years ago. The puzzle is laid out in the New Testament Revelation of the Apocalypse to St. John, a book filled with symbols involving numbers, beasts, and vivid pictorial descriptions all centered round the sublime visions of God and Savior. In Chapter Thirteen, first the beast and then his actions are described:

> And I saw a beast rising out of the sea, with ten horns and seven heads, with ten diadems upon its horns and a blasphemous name upon its heads.   Revelations 13:1

> And the beast was given a mouth uttering haughty and blasphemous words . . . it opened its mouth to utter blasphemies against God, blaspheming his name and his dwelling, that is, those who dwell in heaven.   (5–7)

Later the text gives the cryptic clue and an accompanying challenge to decode it—a clue regarding the beast's identity that has occupied major puzzle-time:

> Also it causes all, both small and great, both rich and poor, both free and slave, to be marked on the right hand or the forehead, so that no one can buy or sell unless he has the mark, that is, *the name of the beast or the number of its name.* This calls for wisdom: let him who has understanding reckon the number of the beast, for it is a human number, its number is *six hundred and sixty-six.*[6]   13: 16–18

Who's the beast—this false prophet of pagan worship? One answer given was the Emperor Nero, first to persecute Christians. Why? Because 666 = DCLXVI in Roman numerals; this is taken to be a secret Latin code provided each number is read as the first letter of a word. The words make the sentence: *Domitius Caesar Legatos Xti Violenter Interfecit* or "Nero violently killed the envoys of Christ." At the inception of the European nation state in the early nineteenth century, one puzzle solver deduced the beast to be none other than Napoleon, because the letters that make up his name can be grouped NAPOLE–ONBUON–APARTE, each group consisting of six letters. Finally, a sarcastic twentieth-century British code buster identified the blasphemous horned one with the House of Commons, which consisted of 658 members, three clerks, a sergeant, a deputy, a chaplain, a door keeper, and a librarian, totaling 666.[7]

If 666 is the most famous of all magic numbers, then ABRACADABRA is surely the archetypal magic word. A Roman doctor of the second century is said to have given a sick patient an amulet on which there was inscribed the triangular anagram:

```
A B R A C A D A B R A
A B R A C A D A B R
A B R A C A D A B
A B R A C A D A
A B R A C A D
A B R A C A
A B R A C
A B R A
A B R
A B
A
```

The patient was instructed to place the charm over the area of pain and, performing an "Old MacDonald" in reverse, to recite the magical formula given by the first word, then recite the second, then the third, etc. As each repetition lost one letter from the formula, it was supposed to gradually draw out the disease *in like manner*. In other words, as the magic word disappeared, so too did the pain. Though nobody knows the meaning of history's most famous magic word for sure,[8] "Abracadabra" is just one example that illustrates the power of likeness associated with magic as well as the force associated with uttering a word. Wearing the charm diverts the disease from the patient forever. Today's charm bracelets—minus the magical utterances that once went with them—are all that is left of this ancient custom.[9]

Word power occupies a major place alongside the power of numbers in ancient history. Our habit of swearing during moments of anger and frustration descends from this practice.[10] Early Hittite curses often took the form "Just as . . . so also." A modern version of this formula laid on a wayward adolescent by her mother might go: "May you have as much trouble raising your kids as I have had rearing you." In ancient Greece, such *maledictions* were formally written down. Archaeologists have dug up many *defixions,* inscribed pieces of thin-sheeted lead intended to bring supernatural power against people or animals. Often they were deposited in graves so that the dead could deliver them to the underworld goddess Persephone when they arrived there. Defixions run the gamut from brief simple prayers for good health like the armorplate inscription that opens this chapter, to complicated lengthy ones involving legal and political disputes—even pleas for revenge and justice. Sports and sex are alluded to on some of the more amusing defixions. (Some people will go to any length to win a contest.)

The Bible is also loaded with curses and magical spells. For example, the like-to-like formula surfaces in a curse from the book of Jeremiah:

> When you finish reading this book, bend a stone to it and cast it into the midst of the Euphrates, and say, "Thus shall Babylon sink, to rise no more because of the evil that I am bringing upon her says the prophet Jeremiah in denouncing the evil of the ways of the ancient city."
>
> Jeremiah 51: 63–4

I think the desire to believe in order and simplicity accounts for the staying power of the Kabbalah. In both the ancient *gematria* of the Kabbalah and the modern pastime of the crossword, the basic idea behind all puzzles common to both science and magic is that deep down, the whole world is ordered in accordance with certain logical, mathematical principles. This idea was expressed in perhaps its purest form by the Greek philosopher Pythagoras (580–500 B.C.), the same wise man who deduced the well-known geometrical theorem named after him. But there's a major difference between Pythagoras and today's rocket scientist, for Pythagoras believed that the principles—the numbers and letters we use today only as grammatical components of a convenient language to describe the behavior of the perceptible world—were the real thing *themselves*. But if we recall Plato's teaching about Forms and Soul, this is not so strange for those times, for it would have been more natural for all educated Greeks to believe that our senses reveal only corrupted, imperfect aspects of the ideas that underlie them. And it is the ideas—not their material representations—that carry *real* meaning.

It is but a sidestep from the seeming mumbo-jumbo magic of Kabbalism to the proto-scientifically based writings of Pythagoras. In our eyes, Pythagoras' keen discoveries accord him the position of scientist of paramount rank. In mathematics he deduced a number of axioms and in terrestrial physics he was the first to propose that the earth is spherical and to devise the notion of climate zones; in astronomy he first identified evening and morning star Venus as a single planetary object and he recognized that the moon shines by reflected light and causes eclipses.[11]

Though Pythagoras correctly deduced that the underlying cause of musical harmony is attributed to a mathematical relationship between the lengths of strings we beat or pluck and tubes through which we blow, the harmony, like Plato's later Forms, lies in the numbers and not in the instruments. "There is geometry in the humming of the strings. There is music in the spacing of the spheres," he tells us.[12]

I find it curious that we label as "magic" Pythagoras' belief in the power of numbers, while his application of those principles to a description of the tangible world, we call "science." But there is another ideological coin worth flipping here. One side of it reads "magic," the other "religion." Christians think of pagans as heathens and idolators; like Simon the Magician, they worship images of false gods. In this view, if magic is false science, then it is also false religion.

The two-sided science-and-magic coin on early Gnostic writings pits the rational against the irrational. Most of it seems to defy all reason. But that is only because our modern outlook has conditioned us not to take these texts seriously and to regard them as unworthy of our concern. To us, the magic formulae, the secret words and numbers of the Gnostics, are mind-boggling, nonsensical concatenations that we rationally discredit with our inbred suspicion that they were all made up on the spot. We can glimpse Pythagorean thinking in their numerological exercises; Plato's concept of the Soul is there too—marbled with the Christian notion of the relationship between life and the hereafter via the Soul, as well as with mystical beliefs from the Middle East. To pan-Mediterranean hard-lifers of the first few centuries A.D., these exotic ways of thinking offered exciting alternatives to the rigid, rational schemes passed down to them by Aristotle and the Roman philosophers or to the pessimistic, drab, contemporary existence promised the ordinary man and woman who followed the traditional Christian way to fulfillment. Magical teachings were driven by a yearning for identification with things divine. They offered a way of taking off the "outer covering of things which hide their inner quality," to borrow the words of a modern rabbi.[13] And the climate in which they were applied in late Roman times was akin to the emotional, ecstatic, and reactive environment offered by today's Pentecostal movements, which seem to thrive in impoverished societies where human rights often are violated and people are terrorized.

Plotinus, born at the time Christianity was just beginning to gain a foothold (A.D. 205–270), perhaps best exemplifies the intellectual side of the halfway house between magic and religion, between paganism and Christianity—the spawning ground of a new transformed notion of magic. He probably came from Egypt, spoke Greek, and definitely resided in Alexandria—the intellectual hub of the world—to study when he was a young man. Plotinus gave further shape to his future course by traveling extensively in the Middle Eastern land of the Magis before finally coming to Rome to settle. There he acquired an outstanding reputation among upper class Romans as a teacher of philosophy, dedicated, as he put it, to trying to wake us up—to bring us back to the realization of the God within and to the "Divine in the All" (his last words).[14] He must have been a charismatic character, for Porphyry, Plotinus' best student, says that he witnessed his master obtain ecstatic union with God on at least four occasions. But first and foremost Plotinus was a philosopher—at least he used philosophy as a way of trying to prove that Christian revelation was true—though what he exemplified was really a cross between mystical philosophy and religious practice.

Plotinus drew heavily on seven-hundred-year-old Greek ideas about the hierarchy of the world order, but he applied his own particular Christian spin to them. He wrote about the natural sympathy between the objects of nature: things he saw as expressions of a World Soul not apprehendable either by written or oral exhortation. For example, while Plato believed the stars were divine, positive animate forces—eternal animals, as he calls them—"Neoplatonists" like Plotinus thought stars had souls and their intellect was much higher than our own. As to God himself, nothing more could be said other than that he is the *One,* the ground where the distinction between the objective and subjective blends together. From Him emanates the *Nous*—all that is spirit and intelligent—which in turn radiates the Soul, the Body, and finally the material world. Each is created after the pattern of the *One* in successively lower spheres—a progression of emanations. The meaning of life—true reality—comes only in the integration of these emanations and not in any single one of them.

We shouldn't be surprised to learn that Plotinus attacked magicians, who said they could influence God through writing incantations and cure diseases caused by demons by expelling them from the body by speaking in tongues. But he also wrote that charms and amulets can influence the way we interact with the supernatural sympathetically, for demons indeed do exist, but it is only our irrational side that is affected by them. The rational side of our mind keeps us safe from magic. What proves it, he says, is that evil emanations from the stars once directed at him by one of his enemies had backfired and turned on their manipulator.

The early Christian Neoplatonists practiced *theurgy,* the art of compelling or persuading supernatural powers to act or refrain from acting (such as the calling down of demons to do one's bidding), thus laying the foundations for Medieval demon dealing, which only later came to be perceived as an exclusively evil act. In early Christian times, demons weren't all necessarily bad. In fact, they were thought by the Neoplatonist philosophers to be divinities. The countless gods and heroes of antiquity thus became the servants of the one true universal God incomprehensible in form to all ordinary mortals. There is no question Plotinus and his followers believed themselves to be divinely inspired. One of his students tells the story that Plotinus once was asked to invoke a demon in Rome's temple of Isis, but when he made the invocation a god appeared instead.

Early on, Plotinus' brand of Greek philosophy and science mixed with the good-and-evil duality of the new Christian religion succeeded in satisfying a lot of people largely because it proffered the belief that nature had a soul and everything that happened in the natural world, from the daily rising of the sun to a disastrous flood, was attributable to the mysterious working of the soul of the world. (Oddly enough, this idea is less out of step with popular culture today than it was a century or two ago.) Plotinus' magic achieved temporary success, too, because consulting with the demons and spirits seemed a valid way of investigating nature. The whole of Neoplatonism was not so out of line with the Greek notion of a universe populated by good and evil gods who remained in constant struggle with one another over the natural forces they represented.

But as Rome declined and with it the once-revered tenets of Classical philosophy, the mainstream Neoplatonism that had risen on the tide of Christianity became engulfed by the flood. We tend to look at Gnosticism and Neoplatonism in hindsight as compromises between ancient polytheism and Christian monotheism, but an early mainline Christian would have categorized both of them as bizarre cults of superstitious conservatives who worshipped at oracles, mumbled incantations, and dared see in themselves the selfish power of demon conjuration. The Neoplatonists, however, saw themselves not as radical outsiders but as the real preservers and defenders of Divine Truth.

Like all things we label magic, Gnosticism gives license to the human will to penetrate and manipulate the sacred powers and it is in this sense that we differentiate theurgy from praying or petitioning the Divine with reverence and supplication. This optimistic but demanding faith operated illegally but was tolerated in the first four centuries A.D. until the Emperor Justinian shut down all the cultic temples in 529. This was an "anxious"[15] period, a time when material wealth declined and moral insecurity increased. As the Pax Romana crumbled under epidemic, civil war, and barbarian siege, new religious offerings and new outlooks on life proliferated. For a while, some of these bizarre sects ran neck-and-neck with various forms of the early Christian religion before falling back into the shadow of history.

What once had begun as an isolated Jewish sect in one corner of the Empire washed over the entire state and became the premier religious force to reckon with. Christianity would tolerate no other beliefs before it. Once its teachings gained a foothold it had a profound effect upon how one ought to perceive the natural world. Thus, it transformed both magical as well as scientific ways of comprehending the universe.

Playing on the historian's themes of life and light, progress and regress, in the next chapter we are going to look at just how magic was transformed after the "age of anxiety."

As we go forward, I want to explore those parts of our past where the bond between matter and spirit, between science and religion, though stressed, remained intact. Only then can we understand why the fetters were loosed and finally broken. My goal, then, to restate it now that we have cleared away the soil around magic's tap root, is to seek a clearer understanding of how the vestigial magic that is still with us remains a vital force, even if organized contemporary society's outlook on the natural world regards it as illegitimate.

For it is society that decides who's who in religion as well as in science. If the sanction to perform magical rites comes from an accepted and established tradition or even from God himself, then the operation is worthy of being described as religious, and one who performs it a priest. If not, then the rites are termed magical and said to be conducted by a magician. For those who believe in the rites, an extraordinarily positive outcome is called a miracle. To the outsider, it is a hoax or a projection at best. For those alien to it, magic seeks to conquer the universe. The believer only wishes to commune with it. What *we* do is religion. What *they* do is magic. In the next period we are going to consider, it was only when Christianity became fully entrenched and the embryo of modern science began to form, that magic began to take the shape we recognize today.

PART II

FROM LIGHT TO LIGHT:

MAGIC FROM THE DARK AGES
TO THE ENLIGHTENMENT

CHAPTER 7

PATHWAYS TO KNOWLEDGE

Paracelsus' answer when asked, "What is magic?": "It is that which can bring heavenly power into the medium and perform its operation in the same."

Heinrich Schipperges,
"Paracelsus and His Followers"

History comes in shades. We think of the Dark Ages as the period beginning after the fall of the Roman Empire and the Enlightenment as the period from which the Modern Age embarked. In between, appropriately enough, were the Middle Ages, arranged from lowest to middle to highest as if time were gauged by the twist of a dimmer switch on history's kitchen lamp. To carry the luminiferous metaphor further, historians also speak of a Renaissance—a reawakening of civilization to the light of a new dawn of reason built on borrowed wattage from the pre-Christian Classical era, when wise men were thought—as never before or since—to have used their mental faculties to explore the real world that vibrated about them.

The purpose of this history, built as it is around the incandescence of human understanding, is to point out the way our predecessors followed ever brighter pathways of knowledge as they slowly ascended the great ladder of human progress. Each of the arcane pursuits that our present century characterizes as magic and occult lays claim to legitimacy from the very remote past. Thrice-great Hermes Trismegistus was then thought to be a mythical Egyptian king who reigned 3,226 years, not the composite group of writers who likely put together his corpus well into the Christian era. Early Christian writers like Zosimus claimed the foundations of alchemy came directly from the fallen angels who taught it to the Egyptians. Even great alchemists and astrologers are said to have "lived for thousands of years"—that's tradition! Stretching time this way seems to enhance the legitimacy of these practices. Contrary to our progressive age, for most of history people have believed the highest forms of thought existed in the most distant past. In other words, the further back you extend the time line, the more revered the knowledge. As people who have largely lost their reverence for the past, we who believe little in the lessons of history have difficulty grasping this principle.

The term Middle Ages, for example, was devised during the Italian Renaissance, when scholars began rediscovering pagan manuscripts that had long been hidden away in church and civic archives. They believed they saw the same intellectual glow in the ideas contained within those tattered pages that they felt was illuminating their own minds. The Middle Ages simply characterized the thousand-year chasm between them. The Dark Ages (when the map of Europe showed barbaric kingdoms replacing the glory that was Rome) is a label assigned to the very earliest part of the post-antiquity period, when Western culture, in hindsight, was thought to have slipped to the bottom rungs of the ladder of civilization. The Dark Ages also was a time characterized by war, when Rome's Colosseum and Emperor Hadrian's tomb were converted to fortresses. Low-level agricultural activity engaged in by serfs and ruled over by ignorant landlords caused widespread famine. Plague devastated what was left of the healthy population.[1] So wrote the later historians who described Dark Age Barbarism as a social order of a lower and lesser type in relation to a godly being (an order that needed to be transformed from its squalid, insecure state by Christianity before Europe could become the great world community that it is). While historians nowadays are a little more sensitive about using these present-biased terms to depict what happened in Europe after the fall of the Roman Empire, the names nevertheless have stuck.

The foregoing story line bears an uncanny resemblance to the history of Christianity as told by the ardent believer. It begins with revealed truth (fifth-century B.C. Greece), a fall from grace (the Dark Ages), and culminates in a second coming—a revival of things past. This begins with the rediscovery of the verity of ancient wisdom by the backward-looking Renaissance mind and peaks in the great Enlightenment, when "true" knowledge is transformed into works and deeds resulting in the ascension of human culture to its most exalted state—heaven on earth.

We in the present who hold our rational scientific view of the material world in high esteem—and favor the use of the senses to comprehend it—tend to regard the Dark and Middle Ages as a time for assessing scientific "damage control." Those times seem too spiritually oriented, too moralistically subservient to the will of higher authority to suit contemporary tastes. Yet, paradoxically, most rational people today are tolerant of, even participate in, understanding the meaning of the world through spiritual pursuits—so long as science and religion, two alternative and opposing ways of understanding the world, are not set into operation simultaneously.

As they rewrite history, progressive Western historians seem willing to grant that during the Middle Ages some sort of preservation and continuity of Classical learning was taking place, but there remains a huge temporal bridge over muddy intellectual water between the two lighthouses of knowledge that brightened the natural world: Classical antiquity and the Renaissance.

So much has happened since the "Age of Anxiety," the first few centuries A.D. that followed the introduction of Christianity. An artistic (thirteenth to fifteenth centuries) followed by a scientific (fifteenth to seventeenth centuries) Renaissance swept across Europe a thousand years after the end of antiquity, a religious Reformation boiled up in sixteenth-century Northern Europe, and the Industrial or Mechanical Age of the seventeenth to eighteenth centuries exerted a drastic influence on how we think about the world of nature. The seeds that grew into the two very diverse species of thought we call science and the occult were planted at the beginning of that period.

What happened to the forces and ideas of magic already in play during the long transformative period between the establishment of Christianity as the dominant religion in Europe in the fourth and fifth centuries A.D. and the flowering of science in the fifteenth to eighteenth centuries was important because it is during this period that so many of the concepts we associate with magic as we recognize it today were developed and shaped: alchemy and astrology (from which the modern sciences of chemistry and astronomy were developed); the invention of the Devil as the prime object of magical conjuration; the fear of witches who practiced Black Magic; and magical formulas, diagrams, and arrangements that led to forms of divination such as the Tarot.

In this part of the book I want to follow the changes that took place in each of these theaters of magic by bringing onstage some of the curious practitioners of the occult arts. By following their lives and their activities, we can witness how they were gradually transformed through the ages into close cousins of today's modern magicians.

CHAPTER 8

RESURRECTION OF THE KABBALAH

All that which is found upon the earth, has its spiritual counterpart also to be found on high, and there does not exist the
smallest thing in this world, which is not attached to something
on high, and is not found in dependence upon it.

The Zohar, translated by Isaac Meyer:
*Qabbalah, the Philosophic Writings of Solomon
Ben Yehuda Ibn Gebirol or Avicebron*

Beginning in A.D. 312 the Roman emperor Constantine ruled
the Empire from Constantinople as a declared Christian. By
391, Christianity displaced paganism as the dominant religion in
Gaul. The Christian religion also absorbed a lot of pagan magical custom; for example, gathering herbs for good luck in the first month was
now accompanied by saying Christian prayers. Magical spells and potions
were now specifically directed toward combating the Devil. This left little room for the pagan philosophy of magic as a way of invoking an entire panoply of powers that could be used for good or for evil. Over the
next several hundred years, edict after edict issued by Constantine and his
successors effectively shut down the underground cults that continued
to practice the magical arts. What once were common occurrences—
soothsaying, divining by everything from animal innards to excrement,
and other forms of fortune-telling carried on in the oral tradition—
slowly began to be regarded by society as superstition.

Since pagan magical books were banned, they and anything else about
the pagan arts that appeared in written form automatically became sacred
to the believer. A ninth-century Carolingian priest was horrified when he
accidentally came across some contemporary manuscripts showing how
illness could be cured by rearranging the letters of your name with numbers associated with the day you were taken ill; the Kabbalah was still alive.
But exactly how did this philosophy get modified and refined by Medieval
and Renaissance thought and how was it made adaptable to the Gentiles?

Practically all Classical knowledge was passed on to the Islamic world, which transformed it considerably. Early Arabic writers like the ninth-century Yaqūb ibn Ishāq aṣ-Sabah al-Kindi (Alkindi for short) translated Aristotle and other Greek works into Arabic. If anyone, it was they who closed the widening gap between science and magic that the Greek rationalist philosophers had earlier pried open. For example, Alkindi speaks of a force of radiation from the stars, the collision of their rays moving them to new positions. Earthly objects need not be in contact to influence one another. Magnets, sound, and a fire's heat are good examples. You don't need to be *in* the fire to get burned! Likewise, words inscribed *on* the proper materials and uttered at the right time and place can affect external objects. And the rays emitted by our minds have more effective powers if we concentrate on the names of God.

Learned Arabs also translated and reinterpreted Pliny and Galen. Discussions of physiology by Arab theoreticians constitute an interesting mix of mysticism and the kind of mechanistic science that would flourish centuries later.

We are fairly sure the Jews brought Kabbalistic teachings to Italy in about the ninth century. It took root there and then spread to Spain, France, and Germany. Thirteenth-century Spanish mystics developed the *Zohar*, a book of Kabbalistic commentaries on the scriptures. Thus, the *sephiroth* lives on in the body of the king (Fig. 5). But because all Jews were thought to be sorcerers carrying the plague with them from the Middle East, the Kabbalah acquired a bad name. Still, some of the more enlightened Gentiles were curious about this exotic Jewish wisdom. They saw in the disciplined ascent up the tree of life a way toward spiritual union with their God. Thus was Christian Kabbalism born.

How does it work? The tree of life (the *sephiroth* I mentioned earlier) looks like a modern game board. Basically, it is a map that guides the ascent of the mortal soul upward as well as the descent of God downward via twenty-two different branches connected to ten spheres or branching points that represent God's attributes or emanations (Fig. 6). God and creation make up the uppermost sphere, while the tangible physical outcome of all things manifested in the material world represent the lowermost sphere.

The seven lower spheres, which are characterized by names like "endurance," "majesty," "judgment," and so on, are levels of attainment characterized by a system of associations that employs the physical body itself. Akin to the "energy centers" in some New Age schemes, in certain

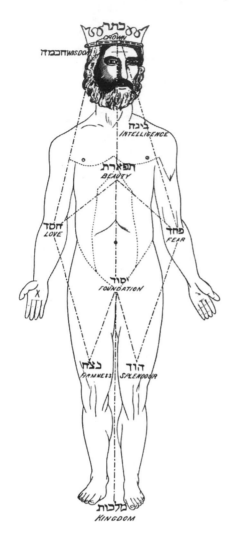

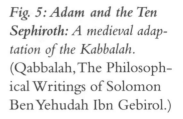

Fig. 5: Adam and the Ten Sephiroth: A medieval adaptation of the Kabbalah. (Qabbalah, The Philosophical Writings of Solomon Ben Yehudah Ibn Gebirol.)

doctrines these correspond to locations in the body along the backbone. (The similarity between the shape of the tree and that of the human body is no accident.) The Kabbalistic system of association is more complex yet, for it is further subdivided into female (left spheres numbered 3, 5, 8) and male (right spheres 2, 4, 7). The top triangle (1, 2, 3), characterized by understanding, wisdom, and humility (the crown or head), belongs to God. Other triangles connecting the spheres represent the evolution of life and the physical world.

When your soul comes down from God at birth it acquires different qualities from the different spheres—courage, love, intellect, etc.—taking

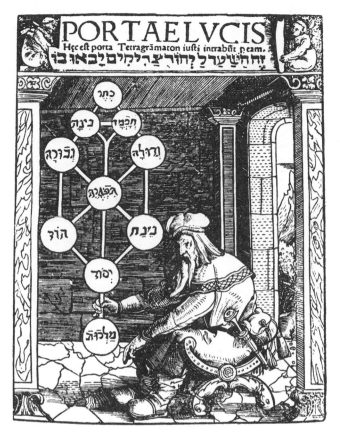

Fig. 6: The sephiroth, the Kabbalah's tree of life of Old Jewish wisdom. As in the kundalini *(Fig. 20) the key to higher reality comes via ascent through various levels of wisdom to God who, in effect, descends the tree of life to meet you. Originally numbering 22, after Christianity the highest branches of the tree were pruned to connect up with the World Soul. The hierarchical structure of the universe and its division into spheres that overlie one another like onionskin was common since the time of Aristotle. (Paulus Ricius,* Porta Lucis.*)*

on last the physical body at the moment it reaches the earth. When death arrives, the Soul ascends and sheds each of its skins, beginning with the body. But a skilled ascent requires discipline and practice, for sinister pitfalls can entrap the careless and itinerant Soul. You discipline yourself by separating your mind from your everyday worries. You learn mastery of your body, for example, by remaining stationary for long periods of time in awkward positions, such as standing on one foot and holding your other ankle while breathing in and out regularly. Or you impose rules on yourself for weeks at a time, like not raising your arms above the waist or crossing your legs for several weeks, or not using a word that has a particular letter of the alphabet in it. Only when you have cleared your mind of worldly thoughts by such discipline are you ready to concentrate on the *sephiroth.*

If we consider the multitude of ways of imagining how mysterious forces can converge to produce tangible outcomes,[1] we can understand why, with its many interconnecting houses and signs, the potential for geometrical and numerological flexibility inherent in the tree of life made it a safe haven for speculation among late Medieval and Renaissance scholars. They were trying to make sense of reconciling the state of the physical world with the promise of the hereafter. What is so appealing about the Christian Kabbalah is that it gives definite answers to age-old questions about good and evil. If God is good, then why did He create evil? Why is there pain and suffering in the world? The answer to the first question would be that God didn't "create" evil. He is the totality of things and you accept Him, contradictions and all, for every idea has its built-in contradictory opposite. The answer to the second question is that God's connection with the real world and with what we see, feel and touch is indirect.

The main selling point of Kabbalism—the one that appeals to the deprived, the poor, and the isolated, those with no outlets for the expression of their grief—is that the Soul can make its ascent to understanding God's wisdom ecstatically and emotionally *while you are still alive,* provided you are among the elect who are capable of practicing the discipline necessary to acquire the wisdom to do it. The Kabbalah says that there is a subsurface reality and the *sephiroth* tree is the key to the dynamic real world that underlies our illusory senses. (Sounds Platonic, doesn't it?) The Kabbalah is the vehicle for tapping into divine grace. The numbers and the geometry of remote antiquity are the language of creation. Word play, letter reversals, and punning make up its grammar. These are the vital juices that nurture the secret path up the tree.

Just how did the idea of the Christian God and theories of numeracy unite in the Middle Ages? Followers say that God gave the book of the Kabbalah to people in ancient times. It was revealed to Adam, who employed its wisdom to regain his sense of dignity after he ate the apple and fell from the grace of God. Another version has it that when Moses received the ten commandments, he also acquired additional knowledge, which God asked him to keep secret.

The question is, can we climb back up there or must we live a life of penitence and bank all our hopes on redemption in the hereafter? How to believe in the geometrical and numerological patterns descended from "pagan" wisdom without doing violence to the word of God in the Christian scriptures? One answer to these troubling questions on the minds of many Medieval Christians employed the multitude of mathematical possibilities to decode the hidden meaning in the sacred texts (i.e., the *pentagram,* to be discussed shortly).

As suggested earlier, the Kabbalah also came to Europe by way of Spain. This was the western borderland between Islam and Christianity, where Arabic teachings had a profound influence on both science and magic. The Spanish–Jewish philosopher Abraham ben Samuel Abulafia (born about 1240) was a prominent Kabbalist who delved deeply into the use of Hebrew letter permutations as a meditative device to elevate the mind to higher planes. The form of the *Zohar,* a crucial text on Kabbalah, that came to be read by Medieval and Renaissance philosophers was composed by one Moses de León (1250–1305), another Spanish Kabbalist Jew about whom little is known except that he was well aware of the concepts of the Godhead, his numbered emanations, and the complex upward pathway. He probably picked up his ideas from the writings of Plotinus set down close to the abolition of all pagan doctrine in the Eastern Holy Roman Empire early in the sixth century.

Nobody was more obsessed with uniting philosophy and Kabbalah than the fascinating German Heinrich Cornelius Agrippa von Nettesheim, who lived in the time of the Renaissance. Agrippa published the principle doctrine on the Kabbalah in 1531—fairly late in his relatively short life—only to recant every word of it before his death. It appears in his famous history of magic, *On the Occult Philosophy,*[2] done in three volumes, a work which has had a major influence on magical practice in the four-hundred-plus years since it was published. The first comprehensive survey of magic written in the Renaissance, Agrippa's books are based on ideas popular at the time: Man is made in the image of God; the whole universe taken together is God; therefore, Man is a miniature copy of the universe. We each have a soul, it has a soul—every portion of it has a soul: rocks, trees, stars—each is a part of the World Soul and each part relates to every other.

Heinrich Cornelius Agrippa von Nettesheim's life was touched by every extreme imaginable; from abbey to battlefield, he experienced both wealth and poverty as he moved from the houses of royalty to prison and back again, hounded from country to country along the way. Agrippa was said always to have been accompanied by a spirit figure in the form of a black dog. On his deathbed he took the collar, which was engraved with magical symbols, off the dog's neck and uttered the words of a man possessed: "Depart damned beast, who has wholly ruined me."★ The dog ran from the house, dove into the river, and disappeared forever.

Restless and erratic in temperament, Agrippa seems to have had a penchant for lost causes. After his ecclesiastical education in the University of Cologne, where he read both Plato and Plotinus, he was sent in his early twenties on a mission to France as a representative of the clergy by the Emperor Maximilian I of Austria. He fell in with a group of dissident free-thinking scholars and formed a secret society dedicated to reforming the world. His diverse activities centered on fighting with armed force for peasants dispossessed of their land and expounding as a part-time lecturer in a university in Holland on the superiority of the female sex and especially on the wisdom of the Jewish Kabbalah. This got him in trouble with the Dutch clerics, who sent him packing to England and Germany, then on to military adventures in Italy where he was knighted for heroism on the battlefield. Agrippa's carelessness in financial matters continually propelled him from sponsor to sponsor in his efforts to stay one step ahead of the debt collectors. Primarily a doctor, he practiced medicine in three different European cities and lectured on healing for very little compensation at a host of universities in places as far ranging as England and Italy. A born survivor, by his mid-forties he had managed to serve under five different royal houses (in England, Germany, Italy, Austria, and Holland). After a frenetic life the wandering scholar, finally, was accorded a few moments of peace. He went full circle and ended up as chief historian to the Emperor Charles V at Antwerp (1529–30).

★ M. Edwardes, *The Dark Side of History,* p. 51.

The *Occult Philosophy* treats every subject imaginable—from poisons and fumigations to ointments, light and color phenomena as portents, raising the dead, and dream analysis. There is even one divinatory skill for each of Aristotle's elements: geomancy for earth, aeromancy for air,[3] pyromancy for fire, and hydromancy for water,[4] but here I want to focus on what Agrippa had to say about numbers. Numbers, he believed, aren't arranged by accident; they were made in heaven and are infused into everything on earth via the World Soul. Moreover, they can reveal their divine virtues if we explore the world around us by means of seeking numerical resemblances among all things. What to look for? Coincidences in separations, sizes, openings and closings, and directions. Take the Hebrew alphabet. It has twelve simple letters, the same as the number of signs of the zodiac; seven double letters, the same as the number of planets; and three "parents," or sources which represent the three elements.

One of the most magical of all figures is the pentagram (Fig. 7). Agrippa tells us that every pentagram has the ideal qualities of the number five: five triangles, five obtuse angles, and five acute angles. It is an excellent force for counteracting demons. To make one is to understand its magic: First draw a circle over the human body spread-eagled with fingers outstretched, centered over the genital area; you will find that such a circle is tangent to the top of the head, the bottom of the feet, and the tips of the outstretched fingers. Connect each tangent point to its two opposites by straight lines and you have a pentagram. To each point of the pentagram corresponds one of the five planetary signs; the Moon and the Sun being assigned to the penis and the navel respectively. How can this be? Because, Agrippa explains, the form of the flesh was designed by God via number relations. Just how do you apply the magical principle of the pentagram? Take for example, the five-leafed herb known as pentafoil (Fig. 3). It is a cure for the five known types of fever. Take one of its leaves in wine to cure one type, two to cure another . . . and all five to cure the last.[5] The secret of curing resides in the natural proportion of numbers and things.

Legends about Agrippa's black magic abound. Once a man who boarded in his house was said to have rummaged through the magician's things, where he happened to have stumbled upon one such written magical phrase. When he made the mistake of uttering it, the prowler unwittingly conjured up the Devil, who instantly killed him, for he lay unprotected by the requisite magic circle. To absolve himself of any involvement in the incident and to keep his secrets intact, when Agrippa

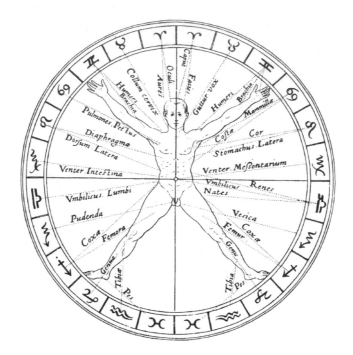

Fig. 7: The outstretched human body shows the division of the world into five parts, giving rise to the origin of the pentagram. Other astrological details show the authority of various planets over different parts of the body according to the law of association. (Tomus Secundanus De Supernaturali, Praeternaturali Et Contranaturali Microcosmi Historia, in Trautatus Tres Distributa.)

discovered the body he called back the Devil and embodied the cadaver with the diabolical one. Then he instructed him to go to the town square, walk around for a few hours, and then drop dead of a heart attack.[6]

Agrippa lived in a time of religious ferment. The year before he was lecturing in Metz, for example, only three hundred miles away Martin Luther had ushered in the Protestant Reformation by posting his ninety-five theses on a church door at Wittenberg (1517). And so, it is not surprising that the charismatic Agrippa attracted followers more than willing to join his secret societies because they were dissatisfied with their religion. Many of these doubters discovered in his work that they didn't have to reject Christianity completely. They could embrace a modified form of it that offered them some enlightenment; with it they could gain a measure of mastery over themselves as well as over nature, and an understanding of its power.

Even for its time, Agrippa's kind of reformation was a lot more radical than Luther's; for example, he preached that Adam and Eve had intercourse, that the Virgin Mary had been married three times, that
nunneries were often private brothels, and that many of the city's houses
of prostitution were located suspiciously close to the monasteries! There
may be more truth in some of these statements than in others; suffice to
say that Agrippa mightily offended the city's establishment for whom religion was the center of life.

In the Medieval–Renaissance mind, the magical way of thinking was
very holistic. What gives the pentagram and other tools such as the magic
square their meaning and effectiveness has nothing to do with our
chronological cause-and-effect explanations (for example, I turn on the
light switch; therefore, a surge of electricity is released which passes to
the light fixture; therefore, the filament in the light bulb is heated to incandescence; therefore, the light bulb glows), but rather with another set
of rules governed by what I call the Principle of Association.[7]

This associative way of thinking may have originated in archaic times
as a ready way to recall perceived patterns in the universe, and as a means
of fitting patterns and events into a scheme or system that would cover
all the mutual influences that might occur among things that make up
the universe. There is no need to look for a causal connection. I may say,
for example, that just as I list the parts of my body from my head to my
foot, so too may I organize the stages of my life from birth to old age by
passing along the continuum from top to bottom and by identifying each
stage in one list with a segment or joint in the other. Thus, I could say
that my head represents childhood and my foot old age. By arranging—
in a single list, table, or diagram—all the things and events that make up
my universe of existence, say the elements, the seasons, even the constellations of the zodiac, I can fashion a hierarchically ordered system whose
core is the Principle of Association. Often the properties will be found
to oscillate between extremes in like manner as I pass down the continuum; that they are extremes may be a motive for my fitting them together in the first place. Thus, the seasons and the winds can be said to
alternate—like one's temperament or disposition—just as the good and
evil properties of the astrologer's planets balance out one another as we
pass downward through their shell-like orbits from heaven to earth (Saturn being evil, Jupiter good, Mars evil, and so on).

Physical forces work automatically while spiritual forces can be prayed
to and influenced (another cardinal point that applies to the Principle of

Association). If this is one distinction we make in our own minds that differentiates science from religion, we can see that this certainly was not the case in the minds of magicians like Agrippa. The Sun may radiate heat and light which warms and illuminates the earth, but it is also one of the hierarchy of planetary deities, a conscious being that possesses its own specialized powers in a system of associations. Some modern psychologists explain the idea of reason by association to "projection"—when you endow everything around you with attributes you find in yourself.

Didn't we all talk to our toys when we were kids? Following the developmental psychologists, early cultural anthropologists attributed this sort of behavior to "undeveloped" cultures—so-called "savages." But these explanations are a bit too simple, for they are based on the assumption that you can equate whole undeveloped cultures with individual undeveloped minds. Also, they fall into the "progress trap": By looking backward, from adult to childhood or from high to low stages of civilization, we can account for the behavior of others who preceded us. Perhaps I "outgrew" the magical world I lived in as a child not because it was natural to do so but because cultural norms forced upon me a standard, acceptable way to understand the world—common sense. Likewise, perhaps civilizations that came into contact with the West shed their habits and customs not because they were undeveloped or inferior, but because we imprinted our accepted ways of knowing upon them.

When I was a kid I used to play the card game of War with my great-grandfather. We usually sat outside under a pear tree in the family backyard. As the cards were dealt I remember staring at the strange symbols; diamonds and hearts were straightforward enough, but what did spades and clubs mean? I remember being struck by the pleading look on the queen of spades and speculating on what mysterious evil lay in the mustachioed Jack of Hearts's heart as he gazed off to my left in profile. Was it his intention to steal a queen from her rightful husband? Why were these queens holding different flowers in their hands and what was that tangled bouquet of spaghetti the Jack of Spades seemed to be gripping? Why were there fifty-two cards in the deck; why four suits, and two colors? Without knowing much about what these symbols may mean, millions of us who confront them—from the friendly bridge table to those computerized poker machines in Las Vegas and Atlantic City that devour our cold hard cash—are touching the magical past. For an ordinary deck of cards, which descends from the Tarot, is one modern legacy of age-old Kabbalism filtered through Renaissance sensibilities. Possibly originating in China, the earliest deck of European playing cards dates to fourteenth-century Italy. Until the invention of the printing press, they were hand made and exclusively the property of the wealthy class.

Occult historian Richard Cavendish describes the Tarot deck as:

> . . . a sunlit Medieval landscape of tiny figures moving like marvelous toys—the Fool with cap and bells, the Emperor and Empress with a glittering cavalcade, Death at his reaping, the Hermit with staff and lamp, the Hanged Man swinging from his gibbet, the pale Tower falling.[8]

Is it really possible that if we could fully understand the mysterious figures that make up the Tarot deck, we would unlock secrets of the inner workings of the universe and tap into the "hidden rhythms of the Dance of Life," as Cavendish puts it? When we pick up a deck of cards we touch the Kabbalah directly: The royalty in a royal flush and the Joker (who is discarded in most games) are all thought to be vestiges of creation and pathways of the Soul up the *sephiroth* to God. A deck of Tarot cards: (Tarot is French, meaning "triumph") consists of seventy-eight cards, twenty-two of which are the Major Arcana or trumps that are related to the twenty-two *sephiroth:* The remaining fifty-six Minor Arcana are broken down into four suits representing the Medieval social classes: wands (farmers), swords (the military), cups (the church), and pentacles (the merchants), which later became the familiar clubs, spades, hearts, and diamonds, respectively. Drop one of the court cards (the obsolete knight or horseman) and you're down to our mundane deck of fifty-two made up of ace to ten plus picture cards.

We really don't know for sure how the Tarot deck was first used, but we can be sure the relationship between geometric form in the spread of cards on the table and association of specific meaning with each card was fundamental—like the positions of planets in astrological houses and signs. For example, in this simple five-card spread:

card one represents what is approaching (ascendent) and card two what is passing away (descendent). Card three is mid-heaven (now), four is the nadir (hidden in the future), and five is the synthesis that ties everything together. Each suit also has a meaning: swords (bad luck), pentacles (financial success), cups (love), wands (enterprise), and so on. The major twenty-two cards stand for the paths of the soul to union and wholeness. They are believed to have developed independently before having been attached to the others to create a bigger deck. Thus, like the twenty-two paths, they are probably intended for pure contemplation. The cards include all the personages who might figure in a Medieval romantic courtly drama: the Empress and Emperor, a Hermit, a Magician and a High Priestess, the Pope, Death, the Last Judgment, Temperance and Justice—and of course the Devil. Tarot, modern readers assert, is not achieved mechanically, for much of what happens rests on the psychic bond between the reader and the client who wishes to inquire about the future. We will deal with the subject of foreknowledge, called clairvoyance by the occultist, shortly; here I only wish to point out the historical tie between today's popular game and yesterday's Hebrew philosophy of number.

CHAPTER 9

MUSIC OF THE SPHERES

〜⌒

It is amazing! . . . Although I had as yet no clear idea of the
order in which the perfect solids had to be arranged, I nevertheless succeeded . . . in arranging them so happily that later
on, when I checked the matter over, I had nothing to alter.
Now I no longer regretted the lost time; I no longer tired of
my work; I shied from no computation, however difficult. Day
and night I spent with calculations to see whether the proposition that I had formulated fitted the Copernican orbits or
whether my joy would be carried away by the winds. . . .
Within a few days everything fell into its place. I saw one sym-
metrical solid after the other fit in so precisely between the appropriate orbits that if a peasant were to ask you on what kind
of hook the heavens are fastened so that they don't fall down,
it will be easy for thee to answer him. Farewell!

Arthur Koestler,
The Watershed: A Biography of Johannes Kepler

What started out in antiquity as a system of mediation became
a complex web of correspondences. Middle Age occultists
saw man and universe psychically bonded together in a multitude of ways that could be quantitatively and diagrammatically synthesized as in the *sephiroth* tree of the Kabbalah. Because all of God's
architecture—temples, houses, ships, the human body—is based on divine proportions, it makes good sense to circumscribe a human figure
and connect body and circle to come up with divine geometrical figures
like the pentagram. The spirit within the body is like an octave extending from God to Earth. Following this reasoning further, it would also
make sense to seek the divine proportions in our bodies that resonate
with the harmony derived from particular musical chords which are
based on plucked strings or air circulating in tubes whose fractional
length proportions are made up of small whole numbers (e.g., $1:2$, $4:5$,
$5:6$).

In the imaginative mind of the English mystic Sir Robert Fludd[1] (1574–1637), the *sephiroth* body tree could be depicted as a human figure. Using the Principle of Association, he compared the body's length to that of a stringed instrument, its pivotal points serving as stops that yielded harmonic musical chords equivalent to stages of the Soul's descent from heaven into the body and its reascent back toward heaven. If you rule off concentric spheres from the procreative organ connecting these body-stops—head to chest to knees, and so on—each will represent the God-given qualities of intellect, imagination, etc. (Fig. 8). For Fludd, all the world and heaven is God's instrument and its keyboard is made up of the houses of the heavenly hosts (angels), the stars, planets, and elements.

The body octave included all musical tones. To complete the associations, each bodily part is connected to one of the signs of the zodiac via the Principle of Association. Thus, Aries—the first in the parade of sky animals—represented by the place of the Sun in the zodiac on the first day of spring, is the head; Taurus is the neck, Gemini is the shoulders, Cancer is the chest, and so on down to Aquarius and Pisces, which are

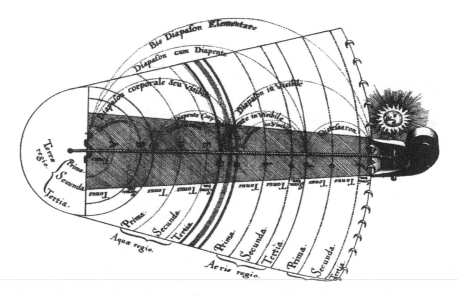

Fig. 8: Music of the spheres. Like the finely tuned strings of a cosmic violin the levels of heaven correspond to the lines of demarcation in the idealized human form. (Tomus Secundanus De Supernaturali, Praeternaturali Et Contranaturali Microcosmi Historia, in Trautatus Tres Distributa.)

associated with the lower limbs. These relationships were taken into account in astrological medicine. Fludd was noted for his musical Kabbalistic treatises. He even went so far as to graph out the sympathetic and antipathetic relationships among the elements on the pegs on the neck of a violin. When God tunes the celestial instrument, he turns the pegs to adjust the first octave, which ties God to the Sun, to be in perfect tune with the second, which covers the Sun and Earth, etc. In the human body, these chords are related to the intervals from head to heart, heart to hip, and so on.

Where do human emotions and feelings fit into the score? In Fludd's interpretation, the proportion of reason to concupiscence (sexual lust) is identified with an octave (consisting of sounds emanating from strings whose ratio of lengths is 1:2), that of reason to irascibility a fourth (3:4), of anger to concupiscence a fifth (2:3). He follows exactly the philosophy I explained earlier in Galen's medicine: that any human imbalance can be restored by the skilled practitioner—who in this case plays music, for music can appease wild animals and heal the infirm, says Fludd.

Absurd as these associations may sound to us, the idea of totally synthesizing macro- and microcosm was Fludd's sensible and ambitious goal in life. Connecting the structure of the body directly with that of the universe was as feasible an idea during the Renaissance as implanting a gene or bashing together a pair of nuclear particles is today. At a time when physicists are pursuing the "theory of everything," we cannot overstate the emphasis thoughtful people of the past once placed on synthesizing all of human knowledge. And don't we still speak of a Renaissance person as one who would still dare try to do so?

The life of Fludd, of whom most of my readers will scarcely have heard, neatly overlapped that of Johannes Kepler (1571–1630), the well-known German astronomer who discovered a set of laws on planetary motion that are still italicized in every textbook of modern astronomy, largely because they led to Newton's proposal of the universal laws of motion and the discovery of the "law of gravity." Though history might ridicule Fludd and lionize Kepler, the two actually never were very far apart in their mental outlook, for the science of the times was very heavily influenced by ideas like Fludd's that emanated straight out of Pythagorean Kabbalism.

Contemporary astronomy books often portray Kepler as one of the first true scientists, but if you read the opening lines of his autobiography you might shrink from that opinion:

I, Johannes Kepler, Keppler, Khepler, Kheppler, or Kep-
lerus was conceived on May 16, A.D. 1571, at 4:37 A.M., and
was born on December 27 at 2:30 P.M., after a pregnancy
lasting 224 days, 9 hours and 53 minutes.

Writes one biographer:

> The five different ways of spelling his name are all his
> own, and so are the figures relating to conception, preg-
> nancy, and birth, recorded in a horoscope which he cast for
> himself. The contrast between his carelessness about his
> name and his extreme precision about dates reflects, from
> the very outset, a mind to which all ultimate reality, the
> essence of religion, of truth and beauty, was contained in the
> language of numbers.[2]

If there is any doubt that Kepler was a mystic, one need only look further into his own account of how he took all the quantitative pretele-
scopic data available in his day about the motion of the planets and
crafted it into three simple statements that would pave the way for Newton and ultimately make both of them modern scientific heroes. Like
Fludd and other Kabbalists, Kepler was convinced that there was a real
Harmony of the Worlds—he even wrote a book with that title—and he
sought to tune in on that divine music with all the conviction and zeal
of today's particle physicists in search of the top quark or gravity waves.
What stand as basic building blocks of the mathematically abstract laws
of modern astronomy constituted for Kepler the crossbeams and merlons
of the grand architecture of the cosmos—the beats and measures of a
universal symphony composed by God.

The secret to God's musical score, thought Kepler, was manifested in
the spacing of the planetary spheres which he believed (like Fludd) had
been designed deliberately to create harmonic chords. Kepler spent years
of his workdays developing ideas and much of his salary building
wooden models that encased one geometrical construction inside another, like so many monkeys in a barrel. By serendipity he ended up with
his unanticipated third law of planetary motion (still called the Harmonic Law), which relates the time it takes a planet to complete an orbit
around the sun to the average distance of that planet from the sun.[3]

When we remove the cloak of mysticism from Kepler's important scientific discoveries, the process by which he revealed his findings vanishes from history. In this chapter's opening quote, Kepler expresses his love of geometry in the joy he communicates upon discovering that the celestial orbs fit perfectly with the geometrical figures ordained in heaven. What a pity it is that in our modern quest to comprehend the universe, too often what we read in textbooks about Kepler's Laws is pulled out of context; the content and substance of these mathematical statements seems to be the only creation of a lifetime of work that matters to us. Thus Kepler's attitude and approach to nature gleaned out of a different time and laden with life's alternative values and goals seems so completely lost to us—our loss.

In Fludd's *History of Both Worlds* (1617), there appears a picture of an astrologer contemplating the universe (Fig. 9). Fludd's picture shows no telescope, even though the "optic reed" (as it was then called) had been invented a decade earlier in Holland. Nor does the illustration reveal any other instruments, save for a celestial globe and a compass along with the obligatory pen and notebook. In other words, the astrologer is depicted as a wisdom seeker, one who studies texts, languages, and mathematics, not a charlatan who conjures up false images of the real world by looking though a spy glass.[4]

I find it somewhat ironic that the technology embodied in a telescope was once conceived as a destructive force (to the power of the mind) as opposed to an aid to the senses, the way we think of it today. But this is not surprising in an age when the use of the senses to comprehend the real world was still highly suspect. When first offered the opportunity, many of Galileo's colleagues refused to look through his telescope because they believed it would distort what the eye sees. About the time Kepler was working on his laws, Galileo's telescope (1610) was already beginning to introduce chords of dissonance into the harmony of the worlds. And what did Galileo himself think of the use of magic numbers to comprehend the structure of the world?

> I feel no compulsion to grant that the number three is a perfect number, nor that it has a faculty of conferring perfection upon its possessors; neither do I conceive the number four to be any imperfection in the elements, nor that they would be more perfect if they were three. These mys-

Fig. 9: The astrologer at work. *This early seventeenth-century depiction portrays an astrologer using his equipment and his direct gaze at the skies to advise his client. (Robert Fludd,* Alchemy Tomi Secundi Tractatus Primi Sectio Secunda, De Technica Microcosmi Historia in Portiones VII.*)*

teries which caused Pythagoras and his sect to have such veneration for the science of numbers are the follies that abound in the sayings and writings of the vulgar.[5]

Galileo utters this statement in one of his *Dialogues* against a pupil who argues the ancient Pythagorean position that says that numbers have value in and of themselves and they can tell us something about the world.

·

(Galileo's dialogues typify the Renaissance scientist's attitude of questioning and correcting the texts handed down from antiquity.) Despite Galileo's condemnation, there are many modern-day physicists and cosmologists who wonder in like manner about whether a hidden harmony might underlie the structure of the universe: Do the mathematical formulae they devise have an existence of their own, an intelligence quite apart from the functions to which we apply them to describe how things move, how change happens, how we arrive at the underlying uniformities and constancies in the world around us? Ask any mathematician!

CHAPTER 10

TWO SIDES OF THE COIN
OF ALCHEMY

Touch not the Philosophers Stone with your hands—you are
not of our race; you are not of the race of Abraham.
Attributed to Mary the Jewess by Henri Berthelot,
quoted in Lynn Thorndike's
A History of Magic and Experimental Science

W hat makes the sun shine? For the answers to macrocosmic
questions, scientists today look at what happens in the microcosm. An astrophysicist will tell you that billions of years
ago and tens of thousands of miles deep down in the sun's interior, the
pressure of the overlying weight of solar gases raised the ambient temperature to millions of degrees. This fired up the velocities of ionized hydrogen atoms or protons that make up the bulk of the sun's composition
to thousands of miles per hour—high enough for these positively
charged particles to overcome the natural electronic repulsive force they
exert on one another. Under these extraordinary conditions, significant
numbers of protons began to stick together to form more complex
atomic nuclei. By this process, called nuclear fusion, tiny amounts of matter were converted into rather significant[1] stores of energy (energy that
made its way upward through the foggy solar subsurface to the flaming
face of the sun) and then passed out into the universe.

The process continues today, and the one-two billionth of that continuous energy store received at the surface of the earth in the form of
light and heat is practically all that nurtures our planet. But the "ash"
residue that falls out of the clanging together of hydrogen atoms is something else again. The net result of the process of energy generation in the
sun—and in the stars, too—is that what once was the element hydrogen
becomes another element, helium.[2] There, our fascinating fairy tale does
not end, for at the even hotter internal temperatures found in stars much
older than the sun, helium and hydrogen nuclei bond together to form
heavier elements, such as carbon, nitrogen, and oxygen—the three atomic

building blocks of life—as well as magnesium, tin, and iron, which make up the bulk of metals found in the crust of the earth. What nature brings to life through a rise in temperature inside the stars, scientists have realized to a degree in nuclear accelerators, where they use powerful magnets instead of impossible-to-construct furnaces to get colliding protons up to speed.[3]

The key word to describe the process I've just outlined is *transmutation,* the change from one form of basic matter into another. What more ultimate power over nature can one exert than to make this happen? Like the achievement of today's particle physicist, the dream of the alchemist has always been to accomplish just such a feat. But there the dream ends and the resemblance ceases.

Making lead into gold and mixing up the elixir of life are two archetypal goals of alchemy familiar to all of us. There is much more than this locked within the secret heart of this fossil science. As astrology is the mother of astronomy, so too is chemistry the daughter of alchemy—a "tidied up," secular version of what once was a sacred art. Alchemy is anything but nuclear physics, either in its method or in its underlying philosophy. The practice, traceable via its name, may go all the way back to ancient Egypt,[4] where metallurgists experimented with gold and alloys. Their efforts went far beyond the practical, for they believed that many of the substances they created possessed marvelous virtues. The black powder made from Mercury, for example, was mystically identified with the form of the body of the God Osiris in the underworld and consequently was a source of life. In China, where making counterfeit metals can be clearly documented to the second century B.C., certain metals (gold especially) were placed in the body cavities of deceased Han princes in order to preserve them after death.

The alchemical literature is surprisingly sparse in Greek and Roman antiquity. The subject doesn't really begin to come alive until the turbulent early Christian era—those anxious times when magic and organized religion found themselves in a state of declared war.

Pliny mentions alchemy briefly. He records that the Emperor Caligula (A.D. 12–41) once made gold out of orpiment, an oxide of arsenic that looks like canary yellow paint (like-produces-like again!). A lot of this early "gold making" consisted of *multiplying* the substance, a process akin to making lots of sourdough bread out of a tiny bit of "starter." For example, one recipe from a third-century manuscript calls for mixing one part asemos (a silver-like alloy), three parts copper, and four parts gold.[5]

What modern metallurgists regard as changing twenty-four-carat to eighteen-carat gold alloy, a Roman alchemist likely would have understood as a seeding process in which the yield of gold grew because it had been nurtured by other basic substances. Even though these early alchemists were harmless scientific experimenters, because so many of their practices were divulged via magical papyri and conducted in secrecy, early Christian Roman emperors like Diocletian (A.D. 245–313) condemned them, just as they had denounced and ultimately forbidden Gnostic teachings.

In the Christian doctrine, mankind (through Adam) came to know good and evil when he ate the forbidden fruit of the tree of knowledge (Gen. 3:3). As punishment for aspiring to be godlike, man was cast into the fallen state in which we as his descendants now find ourselves; the best we can hold out for is a long shot at redemption when our final judgment is made. As far as the orthodox were concerned, alchemists, by proceeding with their investigations, were indulging in an improper moral diet by yet eating of that Biblical tree of forbidden knowledge. Gnostic teachings and practices such as alchemy fly in the face of Genesis and cannot be tolerated, they reasoned.

Early alchemists were powerful figures held in great reverence by their followers. Zosimus, the fourth-century mystic and alchemist, boasted that the whole world is upheld by the practice of exploiting metals and nobody does it like the alchemical priests. In his great works, *The Pneumatics* and *The Automatic Theater,* he shows himself to have been an ardent supplier of the temples with "pseudo-miracles." Fellow magician Hero of Alexandria tells how he devised marvelous contraptions like magic drinking horns that would dispense wine or water, bottomless water glasses, flying mechanical birds, and magic mirrors. Though these *automata* often were intended more to deceive the spectator than to convert one to occult beliefs, their technology would have made even our Kreskins and Copperfields proud.

Women figure prominently in some of these early references. Mary the Jewess, a (third-century A.D.) Greek alchemist noted for her innovative technical mind, is justly famous for the quotation about the exclusivity of magical practice opening this chapter—words that surely would have irritated any proper Roman. (Not so well known, by the way, is that Mary has left a legacy for every modern restaurant and cafeteria—she invented the first double boiler, today called the "bain-Marie.")[6]

What is the basic theory that underlies alchemy? As suggested in the title of this section, there are two sides to alchemy: the scientific and the allegorical. Where do the meat and milk of our cattle come from? How is it that water and dirt combine to create apples *and* oranges? Both questions inquire about how things get changed—transformed from one substance to another. The Medieval scientific theory of alchemy is based on a belief in the four Aristotelian elemental qualities: hot, cold, wet, and dry. Substances are transformed from one to another when these qualities are changed. In Medieval times, the alchemists' focus was on metallurgy, more specifically, the proposition that all metals are made up of sulphur and mercury, varying parts of which can be refined to make gold (which contains a high proportion of mercury). Less perfect mixtures of the two include copper, tin, and silver. This is not so fundamentally different from the idea that solids can be transformed to liquids and then to gas (e.g., ice to water to steam) except it begins with the idea that the old Greek elements (air, fire, water, and earth) can be reduced. Gnostics believed the four elements were created by a lesser god. They reasoned that if they could manipulate the primary qualities that underlie these elements, then they ought to be able to effect a change in them. Take away the hot from fire, for example, and it will become cold and dry; it will become ash or earth. Similarly, metals are nothing more than mixtures of the four elements in different proportions. By heating and cooling and wetting and drying, we ought to be able to change one into the other.

All cultures have their marvelous substances—the panacea or cure-all—that life-bearing, youth-giving remedy that helps us in our reach for immortality. Our ambrosia, our nectar of the gods, are the wonder drugs we all believe in—like aspirin. In Medieval times, when people believed practically all diseases had a common cause (imbalanced humors), the philosopher's stone was the marvelous substance *par excellence* that they all lusted after. Not only could it change metals into gold by mere touch, it could cure all illness and make you live longer. It was the universal medicine, the "elixir of life."[7] Legend has it that knowledge of the stone was taken from the Emerald Tablet clutched in the hand of Hermes Trismegistus and discovered by Sarah, the wife of Abraham. Every magi of the Middle Ages had an opinion on what it was and what it looked like, though rarely did they agree even on its color: solid and dark red, said one; bright yellow another; still others, poppy colored. One compromising Arab scholar declared that it was all of the above—it united all colors.

The basic idea behind the philosopher's stone is that confined within it was the World Soul or World Spirit; the essence of all substance—the "alkahest" or "burning water" as one alchemist describes it—sustains, fortifies, and preserves us from diseases within its reach. Its secret preparation is beyond human comprehension and God alone can reveal it to the chosen. It is the wonder medicine, says another,[8] the congealed essence of stellar radiation.

There were as many mystical descriptions in alchemical books about how to acquire the philosopher's stone as the variety of colors and cures it was thought to possess. Reads one riddle: It is found everywhere and yet it is universally valueless. It is vitriol, suggests an interpreter, for in the Kabbalistic style "*Visita Interiora Terrae; Rectificando Invenies Occultum Lapidem*" translated from the Latin, means "visit the interior of the earth and by purification you will find the stone."[9]

Stories of encounters with the stone are rife in the Middle Ages. A fourteenth-century alchemist writes in his notebook that at noon on Monday, January 17, 1382, he and his wife laid a mysterious piece of red stone on top of an equal quantity of mercury and by 5:00 P.M. all the mercury had been changed into gold, leaving the red stone intact. Helvetius, an avowed and knowledgeable Swiss seventeenth-century opponent of alchemy, tells the story of a man who came to his house one day and showed him three pieces of glassy pale yellow stone in a little ivory box. He claimed to be able to produce tons of gold out of tiny chips of the material. As he argued with the man, Helvetius managed to stealthily scrape off a bit of the substance with a fingernail. Later he tested it and found he could do no more than convert the substance into ordinary glass. When he saw the stranger later he was told, "That's because you didn't protect the stone with yellow wax." Helvetius then followed the visitor's instructions. He melted some lead and immersed the wax-coated piece of stone in it. It changed into the finest gold he had ever seen. "May the holy angels of God watch over him as a source of blessing to Christendom," he uttered after the unknown alchemist disappeared.[10]

Whatever the stone was, it was thought to have the power to perfect the imperfect elements—the baser ones like lead and iron, tin and copper, which nature strove to make into the nobler, more mature, and perfect elements of gold and silver. While the process of natural elemental growth was slow and enduring—hindered by negative forces and impeded by the existence of corrupt substances—the philosopher's stone accomplished transmutation rapidly, indeed almost instantaneously. The alchemists saw themselves as agents of action who only tried to help nature do what is normal for her.

Historian of religion Mircea Éliade has written that in taking on the responsibility of changing nature, the alchemist takes the place of time.[11] What would require eons to ripen, he can alter in minutes, days, or weeks. In this sense, the alchemist is really not so different from the chemist. Like our petri dish, the furnace takes the place of the earth's crust in the alchemical birthing process.

Alchemy is more about *us* than the substances that surround us, and if we briefly consider some of the detailed processes employed by the theories of generation we get a better understanding of the way scientific alchemy lends itself to allegorical interpretation. Collectively these alchemical processes—calcination, solution, separation, conjunction, putrefaction, congelation, cibation, fermentation, sublimation, exaltation, multiplication, and projection—have been given the name "great magistery" or "masterpiece"; whence our term "magnum opus."

As in man and woman, so too in matter! All these cyclic processes imitate the natural cycle of birth to growth to decay to death and back to rebirth again. Take *conjunction,* for example, one of the simpler alchemical processes to explain. A sixteenth-century tract says that it is "of dysseveryd qualytes a Copulaycon," as of the body with the purified soul; but it involves a union of earth, water, air, and fire. The "Woman" is to be impregnated by the "Man" after which the woman must be "stoppered up to lygg (lie) alone" for five months.[12] In other words, because metals grow in the belly of the earth, alchemists say it is as a child growing in the womb of its mother; in the sexual union of mercury and sulphur, the sulphur behaves like the female seed and the mercury like the male. Mercury and sulphur seemed to possess the perfect polar qualities necessary in the chemical reaction. Mercury is the metal, the malleable and lustrous element, sulphur, the changeable visible earthly property (mercury epitomizes the positive masculine, sulphur the negative feminine; mercury the soul, sulphur the body, and so on).

In the process of *cibation,* you feed the material with milk and meat moderately—meaning that you add nurturing material, such as blood, to an embryonic stone, which infuses life's energy into the stone, and honey for the sweetness of life. *Putrefaction,* on which many alchemists seem to dwell excessively, is variously described as being like causing a woman with all her children to go to purgatory to get rid of her original filth. There she will sit for a long time like liquid pitch bubbling and burping, settling and putrefying until she turns pure white (there's that sex-is-dirty element again). Putrefaction is immediately followed by *sublimation*. Sublimation means purifying by heating to vaporization, then cooling and condensing. This gets rid of the stone's body of original filth which accompanied its birth through putrefaction. Notice the way the chemical and psychological steps in the purification process always remain intertwined. From the putrid to the sublime: What is worthless at last becomes valuable—even precious. Thus are the esoteric doctrines of alchemy transmitted in veiled secrecy—as we well might expect of an art that had been persecuted for more than a thousand years.

There are some remarkable parallels both in goals and process in Chinese alchemy worthy of a brief detour. China's efforts with earthly substances seemed directed toward the idea of achieving human perfection. A Taoist tradition dating from the beginning of the Christian Era advocated withdrawal from society in order to keep oneself more attentive to experimentation with nature, which also included meditation and strenuous exercise. The key to immortality was the magic elixir called the "drug of deathlessness." Chinese alchemists pursued it with the same dogged determination that their western counterparts exhibited in seeking the philosopher's stone. Like the ancestors of the West, they vigorously explored every conceivable means to extend life. Associating the distant with the exotic, they undertook expeditions to faraway islands to look for immortals in hope of apprehending their diet and lifeways. Supplementing the diet with iron is one lasting ancient idea that emerged from Chinese experimentation. But the swallowing of addictive toxic substances, such as arsenic, led to large numbers of deaths among royal practitioners. Persistent doses of elixirs were recommended even in the face of symptoms that would strike the modern physician as merely troublesome. One two-thousand-year-old commercial assures the user there are signs of proof that the elixir he had been taking indeed was expelling his disorder:

> If after taking an elixir your skin feels as if insects are crawling all over it; if your hands and feet swell like blisters; if the smell of fine food nauseates you and you vomit after eating, and generally feel sick in the mouth; if your four limbs feel weak; if you have to go frequently to the latrine and there is always violent aching in your head and stomach . . . do not be alarmed.[13]

Not exactly an ad agent's dream today!

Slowing down and even reversing the decay process was also part of the Chinese alchemist's agenda. One prescription reads:

> To make white hair turn black and restore decayed teeth to normal, mix three pounds cinnabar with one pound honey. Make it into ten pills and take them over the course of one year.[14]

Adding metallic compounds to a corpse was said to revive it. Ambitious alchemists devised various effective compounds to toss into the sarcophagus. One second-century B.C. body unearthed from its tomb in the early 1970s was found to be in a rather excellent state of preservation, having been immersed in a liquid containing mercuric sulfide. As in ancient Egypt, gold and jade placed in the nine apertures of the corpse also were alleged to keep the body from putrefying.

It is the language along with the levels of meaning that baffle us most about alchemy. One early practitioner describes, in typical alchemical language, the theory behind the Philosopher's Egg, an appropriate term for the embryonic device that affected chemical transmutation (Fig. 10). This was the name given to the sealed egg-shaped glass flask containing salts of gold, silver, and mercury that were used in the minor magistery of transforming metals into silver—one step on the way to the magnum opus. The way to heat the Philosopher's Egg to just the right temperature via a series of stepped increases was so elaborate that we might better think of it today more like the religious ritual of high mass than a scientific laboratory experiment.

Decoding the Egg is like cutting the Gordian knot with a sword. In the words of alchemist Michael Majer (or Maier) (1568–1622):

> Learn about the egg and cut it with a flaming sword. In our world, there is a bird more sublime than all others. To search for his egg be thy only concern. Vile albumin surrounds its soft yolk; heat the egg according to custom, then with thy sword search for it cautiously; after Vulcan [five], Mars [one] will accelerate the work; and when thenceforth has come the chick, it will overcome fire and sword.

*Fig. 10: **The philosopher's egg,** a Medieval–Renaissance alchemical allegory. Veiled language and imagery hide the meaning—except for the initiated. (Michael Majer,* Scrutinium Chymicum.*)*

If you can find a bit of chemistry in this, what Majer recommends next is a little more obtuse: To make the 'noble medicine':

> Apply a toad to the woman's breast, that it may take milk from her; and the woman will die, when the toad is full of milk.[15]

What can this statement mean? To decode the message we must enter the world of allegory—another peculiarly Medieval concept and consequently very foreign to our way of thinking. In an allegory, the entire discourse deliberately veils the properties of one subject in the language and processes of another that resembles it.

The last portion of Majer's allegory, I think, bothers our rational minds most of all, because it brings together two acts—making a chemical mixture and a toad suckling a woman's breast—which simply do not belong together in our mind's eye. The egg, of course, is intended to be the crucible in which transformation of the embryo takes place. But what the alchemist is making we will never know, for his coded recipe is a far cry from anything we would expect to find in a chemistry book.

Philippus Aureolus Theophrastus Bombast von Hohenheim (1493–1541) is easily the most revered alchemist of the Hermetic Age (roughly the fifteenth and early sixteenth centuries). Nobody better embodies the Medieval striving for uniting all things and concepts under a single doctrine and practice than this philosopher-physician-theologian. Like so many of his scholarly contemporaries he lived the life of a wanderer. Born in Einseideln (near Zurich), first educated in Basel and Vienna, and equipped with a medical degree from the University of Ferrara, he consorted for more than a dozen years in far-flung places with diverse groups, including miners, astrologers, gypsies, and alchemists. (His biographers think he picked up his Hermetic wisdom in his travels to Constantinople.) He landed in Strasbourg where he opened a practice, then returned to Basel where he rubbed elbows with the Dutch philosopher Erasmus and the noted printer and publisher Froben(ius), whom he managed to cure of a serious illness.

Confident by this time of his own abilities as a doctor, he renamed himself Paracelsus, meaning "above Celsus" (the great Roman physician). Like Galen a millennium before him, his excellent cure rate got him appointed city physician. However, in that capacity he proceeded to offend everyone both with the unorthodox nature of his practice and his strong negative opinions on subjects ranging from orthodox medicine to womanhood. Paracelsus is described as a drinker, a braggart (reflecting one of his names), and very argumentative—a terrible mix if you are desirous of making your way in social circles. He was all too ready and willing to verbally attack anyone he felt disparaged him. Seeing himself as the only physician taught by nature, he even publicly burned the works of Galen. He characterized his fellow doctors as ". . . nothing but teachers and masters combing lice and scratching" and "not worthy that a dog should lift a hind leg against them." He once referred to a doctor he had accused of malpractice as a "wormy and lousy Sophist."[16] When a dissatisfied patient who refused to pay his bill took him to court and Paracelsus lost the case, he cursed and abused the bench. After being verbally threatened with contempt of court, he fled to Salzburg.

What surprises me about so repulsive a polemicist as Paracelsus is that his work attracted an immense following. In the ten volumes on alchemy he left behind, Paracelsus reveals his philosophy of holistic medicine, which later scholars have compared to some branches of natural medicine, such as modern homeopathy. The best doctor is God for He alone made our health, the mystic tells us. But because our bodies are houses for our souls, the good physician must treat both; he must study religion for the very meaning of that word (possibly from the Latin "religare") is to reunite man with God, body with soul. He must be an astrologer, too, because the harmony of the spheres influences the body, and above all an alchemist, so that he will know all the substances in nature that occur in harmonious mixtures everywhere and influence both body and soul.

Paracelsus' alchemical practice put less emphasis on cooking gold in a furnace and more on achieving perfection in oneself through the process of experimentation. You can make better gold by *psycho*-chemical rather than *physico*-chemical means, he believed. For Paracelsus, nature was the ultimate alchemist that brought about life and death, sickness and health. So a good doctor, in preparing medicines and administering cures, functions as the alchemist of nature. The active ingredient in all effective medicines was an *arcanum* or spiritual element that restores harmony in our *archeus,* another spiritual element that resides in the stomach. These remedies, he believed, could reach all the way out to the stars, which are inhabited by pagan deities. They emit a mortal light that affects our health and seeks to restore the balance between body and nature. Forget the complex herbals offered by those phony doctors, said Paracelsus in typical strong opinion, for their remedies shed about "as much light as a Spanish fly in a dysentery stool."[17] Raise your eyes instead to the stars and receive their beneficent light. Listen to the music of the spheres!

All this unorthodoxy couched in rude language by a drunkard who paid little attention to clothes and hygiene (he rarely bathed) was a bit too radical for contemporary high society ("philistine surgeons" as he called them), who failed to see him—as some later, more sympathetic historians did—as the last "Renaissance Man."

One day Paracelsus was found murdered on the bench of a tavern in Salzburg—either poisoned or beaten to death—allegedly by hired assassins. But his charisma lived on. After he was buried, followers dug up the

The treatments Paracelsus advocated were radically natural for their time. He collected midnight dew on glass plates for use in his medicaments. He left the wounds of leprosy and skin ulcers clean and open to the air to heal naturally rather than cauterizing them with boiling oil—the accepted treatment of the day. Plague victims he treated with minuscule amounts of their own excrement. Some of these cures worked and some didn't, but his batting average seems to have been relatively high. Parcelsus is given credit for having successfully dealt with cases of gout, syphilis, and ulcers; he even had some luck with the various plagues. He devised standards for purification and distillation that would later be employed by chemists. Our word for alcohol—*al-kohl,* or "black eyeshadow" from the Arabic synonym for "spirits"—was invented by Paracelsus. Followers of the eighteenth-century theory of magnetic healing were not unaffected by the exploration of the contact healing principles revealed in Paracelsus' ten volumes. Chemists credit him with the discovery of zinc★ and in the rebirth of Hermetism this century. Modern homeopaths claim many of the formulations of their discipline in his general attitude about the role of nature in treating ailments.

★ For a full account of Paracelsus' contributions to the science of chemistry, see, e.g., M. Graubard, *Astrology and Alchemy, Two Fossil Sciences.*

wizard's bones several times and moved them.[18] It was said that as late as 1830, when a cholera epidemic descended upon Salzburg, locals who went to pray at his grave were spared.

What does the life of Paracelsus teach us about the place of magic in history, about the ever-changing relationship between magic, science, and religion? Paracelsus' brand of Medieval alchemy stood at odds with both science and religion. At the root of Paracelsus' Renaissance Man philosophy lies one basic difference between chemistry and alchemy: The chemist investigates the composition of substances and the combinations and decompositions that result from their action on one another under the influence of natural chemical forces. As in physics, the emphasis is on the reduction of matter to the most fundamental substance perceived to be universal. Chemists destroy; they break things down. We build them up, said the alchemists. What they burn with fire, we burn with water (*alkahest*).

We can understand why scientists attacked alchemists like Paracelsus in the face of the new kind of experimentation they developed in the Renaissance. The emphasis was on matter and not on self. Interests had gradually turned away from gold making and toward concocting a wider range of substances. A variety of properties began to be noted and carefully described. The unity of matter began to be sought in the more microcosmic corpuscular structures. That ultimately would lead to mentally constructing impersonal atoms as the building blocks in which to seek chemical uniformity. As matter became separated from spirit, the evolutionary tie once thought to exist between organic and inorganic substances gradually broke down. Out of it two separate branches of chemistry would evolve, one positioned closer to the physics of inert material (inorganic chemistry), the other to the biology of living matter (organic chemistry). But modern chemistry still shares with ancient alchemy its devotion to a cryptic and symbolic language. Just open any science journal describing the biochemical structure of DNA and you will sense the connection between the wisdom of biochemists and their predecessors. There is something as secret and mysterious about the symbol for DNA's subunits as anything we find in Paracelsus' writings, even if we think it more correct.

Religion also attacked alchemy. The strongest volley emanated from the Protestants who, in the new age of secular common sense, accorded no more space to concrete idols, such as the philosopher's stone, than to statues of the Virgin Mary. When the printing press made many of the alchemical classics available to a now more literate public caught up in changing times, serious educated readers began to question the age-old dogmas as foolish and labeled their promulgators as tricksters and jugglers. If alchemy really worked, then how come Solomon couldn't make gold and had to send his assistants across the sea in search of it? complained rational objectors. Like modern illusionists, alchemists were accused of hiding gold in their stirring sticks during their experiments. Their magic wands could be skillfully manipulated to release the stuff into the heated solution in the crucible, critics suggested—they were nothing more than clever conjurors. To those like Paracelsus and his followers, who had dedicated their lives to the search for the unknown, still clinging in vain to the ancient wisdom that assured them body and soul

were one, chemistry connoted the real fall, for it had secularized and de-
based what once was sacred.

The alchemist's vision continues in our own dreams born in later
centuries—to improve the natural world through mastery of its parts. We
regard isolating new elements and adding them to the periodic table as
a way of perfecting both nature and ourselves. "Better living through
chemistry," reads the slogan of a prominent chemical company. Today we
transmute fossil fuels and atomic nuclei into energy. We increase the yield
in our gardens with the addition of chemical fertilizers and we enhance
our unfermented grape juice by adding sugar. Like ancient alchemists,
we speed nature along. Today we hold the power to fashion forms and
species nature wouldn't dream of creating, even given infinite time.
Though we have not yet synthesized our own transmutations into a
common good, the alchemists have given us the faith that, in Eliade's
words, "we might dare to become time in the first place." Are we the pot
calling the kettle black, I wonder? Caught up in pointing to the subjec-
tivity and self-delusion of the previous generations of custodians of matter—whose transmutations we now debunk—we don't seem to realize
we haven't *yet* adjusted to our own role as masters of the material world.

CHAPTER II

RISE OF THE CLEAR SEER

Hunger-maddened beasts will make the streams tremble;
Most of the land will be under Hister;
in a cage of iron the great one will be dragged,
when the child of Germany observes nothing. . . .

In a place not far from Venus
the two greatest ones of Asia and Africa,
of the Rhine and Hister will be said to come;
cries and tears at Malta and on the coast of Liguria. . . .

Liberty will not be recovered;
it will be occupied by one who is black, proud, low-born and
    iniquitous;
when the matter of the bridge is open,
of Hister, Venice is greatly annoyed at the republic. . . .

Nostradamus,
quoted in Colin Wilson's The Occult: A History

O pinions are sharply divided on whether these quatrains, written
nearly five hundred years ago, are amazingly accurate predictions foretelling the course of World War II or total gibberish
penned by a lunatic. According to one interpreter, Hister is Hitler and
"the child of Germany observes nothing" characterizes his amoral attitudes. The second stanza foretells the Axis pact between Hitler and Mussolini and the subsequent bombing of Malta and Genoa. Venus may be
Venice, which was then located near the border between the two Nazi
powers. The last stanza refers again to Hitler; the bridge symbolizes the
Pope (Pontifex = bridge) and refers to the uneasy peace Mussolini made
with him in 1928, an action disapproved of by the French Republic. A
quite different, more literal, geographic interpretation sees Hister as the
Danube River (also called the Ister) and not far from Venus means not

far from Venice. (The bridge is an actual one that crosses the Danube.) The Republic of Venice was annoyed when Charles V of Austria—who became King of Spain in the year 1500—interfered in Italy and Malta.

These controversial passages are among hundreds written by a man regarded by many as the most famous magician in history. His writings have experienced a sharp rise in popularity as the end of our millennium approaches. Nostradamus (1503–1566) was a clairvoyant—said by his followers to have foreseen the entire history of the British Monarchy, the Napoleonic Wars, the American Revolution and Civil War, the assassination of Lincoln and both Kennedys, space travel, and the development of nuclear weapons. During World War II—which he is said to have predicted—German planes once dropped printed leaflets containing his quotations over occupied France, quotations interpreted to foretell the impending Nazi victory. On the other side, the U.S. government featured the same prognostications in morale-boosting propaganda films, suggesting instead that Nostradamus had predicted that America would carry the torch of freedom 'round the world.[1]

Nostradamus is often pictured as the archetypal magician garbed in black cape and cone-shaped hat gazing into the future through his crystal ball. He started out normally enough, born Michel de Nostredame (Michael of Notre Dame) at Provence, the eldest son of a Jewish family that had converted to Catholicism. Like most people of means, young Michel learned all the Classical languages along with astrology and medicine. The first chance he had to ply his trade—which he performed with great success—came during awful plagues that broke out near his home in the south of France. This moved the doctor up the social ladder, on each rung of which he rubbed elbows with scholars and literati. But the unorthodox medicine he practiced got him into trouble with establishment medicos; he mixed his own medicinal brews and refused to bleed patients as was the custom. So he hit the road and spent the rest of his life wandering.

It was not until he was in his late forties that Nostradamus says he began to acquire glimpses of the future. First aural, then visual flashes of insight began to lead to more complicated previsions. Nostradamus says he would hear things through voices in his head but later he turned to *scrying* or "discerning," a process that consists of looking into a reflective surface under deep concentration—what later would come to be known as the principle underlying crystal-gazing. Geologist George Kunz has given a scientific explanation of just how scrying works: The gazing eye fixes points of light from a highly polished surface such as a sphere until the optic nerve becomes fatigued enough to shut down transmitting sensory impressions from the outside and begins to project images received from within the brain. Results vary with sensitivity of the given optic nerve; in some people, prolonged crystal gazing simply paralyzes the nerve and so it cannot respond to stimuli from within or without. But in others it is both deadened just enough to external impressions and active enough to react to stimuli from within.[2] For those so gifted, scrying appears to work.

Nostradamus describes his method of scrying with a bowl of water positioned on a brass tripod. He would first dip his wand into the bowl and then touch it to his robe. After gazing into the bowl for a long time, visions would come to him and he would write them down in French, Latin, or Greek—admitting that often he did not know what they meant. At first, his prophesies seemed mundane and insignificant. It's said that one day he predicted that his landlord would kill one of two piglets in the barnyard—a black one—and serve it for dinner. The white one would be devoured by a wolf. To disprove the prophesy, the landlord deliberately ordered the cook to kill the white one. But while the pig awaited roasting a pet wolf cub sneaked into the kitchen and made off with the carcass. The cook had no choice but to do the other little pig in and serve it up. When the boarders dined that night the master of the house informed Nostradamus of his trick only to have the cook admit what had actually taken place. At that meal one of Nostradamus' first skeptics was converted to a believer.

As the prophecies of Nostradamus became more earthshaking and far-reaching, the clairvoyant attracted more attention. He began to publish his forward-looking four-liners one hundred at a time, hence the name *Centuries* for the ten volumes that appeared by him, over a twenty-year period, until his death. The prophecies made Nostradamus as famous in his day as he has become in ours and for the same reasons. People have an insatiable curiosity about catastrophe, violence, and plague—the subjects of many of his futuristic missives. As the 1990s roll to a close, more and more books of Nostradamus' previsions have begun to appear in bookstores, their eager readers' appetites whetted in part by predictions about the impending end of the world he is said to have forecast. One of his most famous quatrains sounds particularly contemporary:

Like the great king of the Angolmois
The year 1999, seventh month,
The great king of terror will descend from the sky,
At this time, Mars will reign for the good cause.

A modern cryptographer has argued that in this prophecy, Nostradamus foresaw our doom by an invasion from space. Another suggested that the "great king of terror" is a nuclear device. If so, will China be responsible (Angolmois is a Nostradamian anagram for Mongolians)? Or does the message simply reflect that seven thousand years is the normal time cycle between creations and destructions of the world, according to ideas popular in the Middle Ages? In that case, the time elapsed from the fourth millennium B.C. starting date pegged by seventeenth-century Archbishop Ussher in his reading of Genesis to the end of the second Christian millennium would be six thousand years. Maybe the content of Nostradamus' message implies that July 1, 1999, marks the start of the last millennium of our existence—the beginning of the end. All clever magic is endowed with flexibility.

Nostradamus is even said to have prophesied his own death. After his return from Arles on a mission, he was found dead on the bench that he used to hoist himself into bed (he was a long-time gout sufferer and had difficulty walking). They buried him upright in the wall of a local church as he had requested. A quatrain reads:

On his return from his embassy, the king's gift put in its place,
he will do no more, being gone to God;
by close relations, friends, blood brothers,
he will be found near the bed and bench.[3]

Two hundred and fifty years after his death, superstitious soldiers in the French Revolution (which he is said to have foreseen in detail in dozens of quatrains) dug up his grave and moved his bones.

Nostradamus' art is familiar to us today as fortune-telling. "Clairvoyance"—from the French meaning "clear seeing"—is a type of psychic experience that became extraordinarily popular in the nineteenth century, when necromancy (communicating with the dead) lay at the root of the spiritualist movement. Under the more general rubric of parapsychology or paranormal phemonena, this sensing of images, either internally or externally by an adept, involves revelations about future time (precognition) and happenings both near and far in space (telepathy).

Our desire for foreknowledge is universal and timeless in extent, passionate in character. As we have learned, searching for omens or signs of future events is one form of natural divination that goes back to Greece and the Middle East, where diviners looked for signs of the future in substances as diverse as tea leaves and the innards of animals. At one time or another in history diviners have also looked at palms (chiromancy), dreams (oneiromancy), bird flights (augury), and moles on the body (metoposcopy). Other gateways to the temporal beyond include eating animal parts, sniffing herbs, ingesting or inhaling substances, casting lots, listening to sea shells, thunder, or wind, tying knots, gawking at fire, and gazing at the moon.

Distance makes for estrangement; one reason that prophecy and foretelling the future declined was that Western civilization began to change the very way it thought about time. By the early eighteenth century, when people became aware—through scientific investigations—of the vast spans of time that separated them from their ancient ancestors, they began to question the validity of much of the wisdom that underlay this sort of magic. This was also an era when historians began to identify periods and styles such as "ancient" and "medieval" and to use terms such as "epoch" and "era." Publishing valid ancient prophecies and styling new ones to look to the future began to appear a little silly as the linear, one-way conception of time we are all now so familiar with gradually replaced the old notion of cyclic time that portrayed the course of human events oscillating back and forth like an eternally swinging pendulum.

CHAPTER 12

MEDIEVAL ASTROLOGY

⟨⟩⟨⟩

Astrology now is the science of the stars of Christ.
Tertullian, quoted in Jean Seznec's
Survival of the Pagan Gods

I n an earlier chapter we traced the foundations of astrology, perhaps
the oldest of all the divinatory arts, back to the Middle East. During the Middle Ages, astronomy's half-sister was still alive and well,
having become firmly tied to other kinds of magic. A serious magician
needed to know as much about the stars as of medicine and alchemy. For
example, where did the energy come from that caused the transmutation
of the elements? It came from the stars of course. That meant that when
you prepared the various stages of the Philosopher's Egg, you needed to
perform each operation at the proper time—when the influence of each
planet was optimal—and for the appropriate duration, simulating the
hours and days over which various planets reigned. Even the color of the
appropriate planet needed to correspond with the color stage through
which the chemical embryo passed during its successive stages of controlled heating.[1]

Some opposition to astrology existed in the ancient world, but it
wasn't until the Christian religion took hold that opponents became
forceful in their attack. Why? Early Christian opponents of astrology saw
nothing inherently wrong with it; the problem was simply that the Greek
philosophers who had practiced it were pagans. If astrology was part of
pagan wisdom, then it must oppose God's will. How could God *and* the
stars rule human destiny? There were aspects of astrological doctrine,
such as truth by revelation and the dialogue between priest and client,
that appealed to certain early Christian sects. And so, as Tertullian, the
early Christian philosopher, implies above, when they took it over ideological compromises were made: In medical astrology, the stars would
rule the body while God guided the soul. The Christians were quick to

appropriate many of astrology's supportive aspects, along with the attending celestial imagery, where it fit with their teachings.

When an ideology as widespread and influential as the power of the stars takes hold, those who would change it must figure a way to adopt it. As believers were weaned away from pagan polytheism the planets still operated as ominous signs; they were simply rechristened as intermediaries who announced the intent of God. They were never allowed to act contrary to His will, although humanity's free will, with the grace of God, could act to overcome stellar influence. The celestial world, populated by both the angels of God and the sidereal demons of Lucifer, became a battleground on which to confront questions about the nature of sin, the qualities necessary to lead the good life, and above all, the nature of human free will.

In the Middle Ages, the planets spoke to our European ancestors through both God's word and His hidden natural laws—a kind of "natural theology." The language of these laws consisted of the Greek number symbolism and geometry we are already familiar with, combined with an even richer mathematical legacy endowed to Europe by the Arab world. Astrology revolved about the periphery of such proto-scientific concerns, but within many of its observations lay rational principles and ideas that we might regard as at least approaching correct scientific explanations of natural phenomena. An ingenious medieval philosopher, for example, once explained the tides by the production of vapors through the interaction of moonlight in the depth of the ocean. The differential upward pressure of such vapors caused tides to rise and fall when the Moon stood overhead. Just as the noonday Sun becomes hotter, the Moon could create more "virtue"[2] and consequently a higher tide, and while it lay nearer the horizon (at low water) its obliquity did not permit it to be as effective. Although this model fails to explain why there are *two* high and low tides a day, it does possess all the inherent qualities of mechanical explanations passed down to us by the Greeks that are still a vital part of science.

The Medieval courts of Europe were overrun with astrologers. One who was prominently involved in prefiguring planetary conjunctions was Cecco d'Ascoli, astrologer of the court of Florence, a member of the Franciscan Order, and special adviser to Florentine medical doctors. "A doctor must of necessity know and take into account the nature of the stars and their conjunctions," he tells his followers in his *Astrological Principles.*[3] He then goes on to list all the plants and herbs associated with each planet so that they might be administered at the proper time. Sadly, power and fame led Cecco to transcend the limits of his discipline. When he began to dabble in astrological predictions based on the birth of Christ, the coming of the Antichrist, and the end of the world, he landed in front of the inquisitor. In 1327 he was burned at the stake, whether for astrological malpractice or because of political intrigue we cannot say. One of his judges, the Bishop of the city of Aversa (also a Franciscan), regarded Cecco as a supporter of the rival city of Cesena, which in turn supported the breakaway faction of Franciscans to which Cecco belonged.

Like alchemy, astrology communicated its message via the disguised imagery of allegory, especially in the late Middle Ages and the Renaissance. For example, swift Mercury of pagan lore is turned into a scholar. And what is so scholarly about the image of Mercury? The reasoning differed little from that of the ancient Chaldeans: Swiftest of all the planets, Mercury would be the logical one to mediate between gods and mortals, for he skims low over the clouds, continuously probing the intellect. When he appears he seems to remove the low-lying clouds that dissipate after the storm. This godly function is an excellent parallel for one whose skill lies in exposing the soul. Thus by removing the clouds that veil the mind, Mercury enables us to penetrate closer to the soul, which, in the old Platonic tradition, harbors real truth and always lies out of reach of even the highest human intellect.

The allegorical imagery of the planet Venus as goddess of love is even more extensive. Philosophers of the fifteenth century seemed particularly adept at producing rather lengthy tracts on the nature of love. They classified and subclassified types of Venuses, the parts of the soul to which each corresponded and how the male libido was supposed to react to each form. They even produced a manual on the metaphysics of kissing. Debauchery was a disease, a kind of insanity ultimately traceable to an imbalance of humors in the heart. Like the self-awareness manuals that dot today's bestseller list, these dialogues on the nature of love influenced every courtier of the refined and enlightened societies of Renaissance Italy.[4]

The same society in which allegorical planetary imagery flowered also created the forces that ultimately killed astrology, or at least left it in its present lowly, unresurrectable state. Renaissance expressions of what the natural world was about echo from a tense time, when intellectuals who wanted to think and act more freely began to feel constrained by the demands of the cosmos bequeathed them by their predecessors—a

Even at the public level, planetary power remained pervasive and popular. Rely on the powers of Jupiter—the planet of prosperity—to bring good luck in gambling, says a recipe for making a Medieval talisman. On the first Thursday (Jupiter's Day) of the new moon at the last hour of Jupiter before sunrise, take a piece of unused parchment and write on it "your stake cannot be lost to the bank."* (Wear this when you go before your bookie and you can't miss.) Common questions addressed to a sixteenth-century British astrologer were no different from those we might pose to Ann Landers: Which profession is right for me? Will the man who conceived my child marry me? Is that child my servant girl bore really mine? Will our son keep running away from home? How long will my second wife live and will she leave all of her estate to me? Who else but an astrologer could give indication, direction, information to help the troubled inquirer? So, while it is easy for us to condemn them in hindsight, the astrologers of the Middle Ages helped clients through anxious moments by offering them confidence and bolstering their will to make decisions about the kinds of everyday affairs that still trouble us.

Today's astrology still provides a way to relieve financial stress. At a 1994 New York conference on "Astrology and the Stock Market," sponsored by the Astrologers' Fund, interpretive star-gazing techniques were showcased to identify turning points in the markets. Among the tidbits of portentous advice: Uranus and Neptune in Aquarius signal the need to look at information and technology and the Moon in the eighth house foretells a change in the interest rates on Wall Street.[†]

* R. Cavendish, *The Black Arts*, p. 243.
[†] Cf. *The New York Times Magazine*, 5 Jun 1994, p. 19.

universe that was animated, anthropomorphized—an environment in which matter and mind, body and spirit were one.

Joining these freethinking humanists in a new spirit of inquiry were empiricists like Sir Francis Bacon (1561–1626) and Galileo Galilei (1564–1642), who began to turn to the data acquired through their senses, to view nature close up, to dissect it, and to subdivide and separate celestial from terrestrial things. They began to ask different kinds of questions—*scientific* questions: If the planets can act on our humors, how do they control our bodies? Can we measure this activity? How can celestial influence apply both to individuals and societies? Over what time period does the influence function? Does it turn on and off or does it vary gradually? If the principle is not one of heat or light, then of what does it consist? How can we make it tangible? Is there a mechanism by which it works that is intelligible to us?

There were moral questions, too: If the demon in the stars chooses my fate, is it not also possible that I might be free on occasion to choose the demon star? Or even if I can predict the course of Mars, how can I account for the subtle disparities among individuals ruled by him? How can two people born under the same stars turn out so different? Radical thinkers of the age now felt the need to question assumptions and speculate anew upon celestial truths that had once been accepted as revealed.

Once astronomer Nicolaus Copernicus (1473–1543) knocked Earth off its hitherto immovable pivot with the radical proposition that the Sun instead is the center of all the planetary orbs, revolutionary implications in the ever-changing human relationship with the macrocosm followed. Copernicus reimaged the spheres, shattered old symmetries, and violated staid patterns of association between celestial and terrestrial entities. New ideas about the vast size of the universe and the movement of its parts were followed by empirical demonstrations with the telescope that showed these ideas make sense if the universe is viewed from a radically different, exterior perspective. Seeing the game played from a terrestrial box seat in the bleachers rather than from home plate out in space would have a devastating effect on astrology. Robbed of its perfection, a planet would be significant not because of where it stood in the signs and houses but by virtue of where it lay in its gravitational orbit about the sun. With Earth relegated to the status of a tiny speck in motion along with a host of others about one of myriad stars, the universe became too vast, too open-ended to be characterized as a tightly interlocked organism in which you and I figure prominently. How could what planets do have any bearing on the way we should act? Astrology would gradually evolve from the believable to the unbelievable. It would become unadaptable to the new common sense.

At first there were scientific attempts to standardize astrology—to make it "sane," as reformers put it. This meant isolating natural from personal astrology, testing out weather predictions against conjunctions, sea-

sonal variations against planetary appearances and disappearances, a patient's fever against the phases of the Moon. The very act of testing and
evaluating, then reformulating predictions already began to change astrology into a different discipline. The debate about astrology turned into
a war on the humanistic battlefield as the struggle between free will and
determinism was unleashed in all its fury. To what degree do individuals
and societies have the power to set their own course of action? Can the
shifting stars be entirely responsible for such devastation as we have witnessed in the world? We shall return to this confrontation between two
ideological powerhouses, but not before surveying some of the other
battlefields. We now turn our attention to other kinds of magic that were
resurrected before the dawn of the great Enlightenment—which is supposed to have evaporated all of them.

CHAPTER 13

THE DEVIL AND THE PROLIFERATION OF GOOD AND EVIL

Bagabi Iaca bachabe
Lamac cahi achababe
Karrelyos
Lamac Iamec Bachalyas
Cabahagy sabal yos
Baryolas
Lagoz atha cabyolas
Samac et famyolas
Harrahya
Kurt Seligmann, *The History of Magic and Experimental Science*

Sounds like pidgin Spanish mixed with Arabic and a little pig-Latin thrown in to bond it together. It is in fact a formula, written in Medieval times, to conjure up the unspeakable one. What does he look like? We have all seen him portrayed in film as a red demon with deep-set, flashing eyes. He may have horns[1] and a tail, claws, and hooved feet. He carries a pitchfork and tends the fires of Hell. He can also materialize as a dog, cat, or any other talking animal. His speech is throaty and gravelly, for one breathes a different air where he comes from. Like all filthy demons, the Devil smells bad. As "Lord of the Flies," he attracts all other unclean creatures who swarm around him. His foul breath of sulphur makes his odor as repulsive to the nose as is his image to the eye or the sounds he makes to the ear. The Devil is, quite simply, evil personified—a legacy of our tendency to search for the roots of all bad things in nonhuman influences and to express them in some knowable human form.

There are many demons—spirits that intermediate between men and gods are vouched for in the old Hermetic corpus—and the Devil is but one of them. There are many devils, too. Usually, they are other people's gods. The Hebrews said all the gods of Canaan were devils. Beelzebub

Fig. 11: Hell and the Devil have taken on many forms. Above left: *A German woodcut from the time of the Protestant Reformation shows hell in the jaws of a monster. (P. Carus,* History of the Devil and the Idea of Evil.*) Above right: A punishment that fits the crime. In this scene from Hell out of Dante's* Inferno, *painted on the ceiling of the Sistine Chapel, a serpent coils about the Pope's lecherous master of ceremonies (the snake symbolizes lechery), while demons look on from below and in the background. (© Victor R Boswell, Jr.,* National Geographic.*)*

(Lord of the Flies) was the god of the Phoenicians. During the Spanish conquest of the Americas, Roman Catholic missionaries characterized the gods of the ancient Aztecs and Mayas as devils. Describing a fifteenth-century sacrifice and impersonation rite to the Aztec black god Tezcatlipoca, alter ego of the white Quetzalcoatl in the dualistic pantheon, Spanish chronicler Father Diego Duran finishes with the words "Thus ended the feast of this idol and devil."

> ". . . one can say that the devil had persuaded and instructed them (teachers from an Aztec cult) . . . for everything (they taught) was a mixture of a thousand heathen beliefs, deceits, and imperfections; all was filled with stinking and abominable human blood, all consistent with [the ways of the devil] who had prevailed upon them!"[2]

Fig. 11 (cont.): Above left: *This sixteenth-century child of the devil took the form of a monster with eyes like fire, a nose like an ox, an elephant's trunk, monkey heads for breasts, a cat's face in its stomach and dog heads for elbows. He was seen in Cracow, Poland for just six hours. (W. Shumaker,* The Occult Sciences in the Renaissance.*) Above right:* Buer, the Devil, is shaped like a five-pointed star. (Collin de Plancy, *Dictionnaire Internal.)*

Demonologists say the Devil can take on any shape. In the Book of Isaiah he acquires the form of the dragon Leviathan. The collection of devils and demons in Fig. 11 gives us an idea of the limits to which Medieval and Renaissance imaginations could aspire. For example, one creature has eyes of fire, a nose like an ox, monkey heads for breasts, cat's eyes in his stomach, and dog's heads for elbows. He is said to have appeared on the occasion of the conversion of St. Paul in Poland—by coincidence close to the year of Copernicus' death—and to have materialized for just six hours. Another devil, called Buer, was described by a French informant as having the shape of a five-pointed star. He commanded fifty legions of devils. There is also Astaroth (not shown), one of God's fallen angels, who is not to be confused with a good angel because he is so ugly. He rides one of hell's bat-eared dragons and carries snakes with him. He can see into the past as well as the future.

Originally, the Devil was a good guy, one of God's angels. As early as the fifth century B.C., the Old Testament depicts him as a kind of District Attorney, that member of the staff who officially acted as God's prosecutor.[3] Like so many overzealous prosecutors he overstepped his office. Full of himself, he perversely enjoyed entrapment, torture, and revenge, and took to prosecuting just for the sake of it. Finally, he unjustly accused Job, a righteous man. "Skin for skin!," Satan answers the Lord in Job 2:4, when asked why he wishes to condemn a man without cause. Disregarding his superior, he afflicts the innocent man with sores. The Book of Zechariah tells a similar story of the self-interested prosecutor's treatment of Joshua—Satan again standing on the right hand of God just doing his job. The Devil becomes the "prince of darkness" when he falls from God's grace, along with other angels who become demons.[4] He is literally expelled from the court, rebuked for his mercilessness and defiance of God.

In most religions there's a bit of good and bad in every deity. Greek Zeus can be grandfatherly and downright mean at the same time. Babylonian Marduk is cruelly violent, yet entirely just. But under Christianity good and evil became highly polarized. As the positive and negative aspects of the Old Testament god Jehovah got sorted out, the negative qualities were all parceled out to the evil angel, so that the New Testament Christian version of Jehovah could be seen as entirely good.

Where then does evil come from? Says the Bible: from the fall of divine beings driven to sin, pride, and lust, condemned to hell as punishment. The Devil remains to this day[5] that force of temptation, ever present to prey on our weaknesses, to lead us down the many errant pathways of wrongdoing that branch out from life's straight highway. And if the Devil wins out, he gets us. If the evidence against us is strong enough on Judgment Day we get to spend the rest of eternity in his kingdom. When you fall, downward is the logical place to fall to and so the Devil's residence—appropriately enough in a dualistic religion—is as far below us as heaven is above.

The first mention of hell in Western history appears in the *Theogony* by the Greek oral poet Hesiod, about the eighth century B.C. They called it Tartaros, he says, the lower deck of a three-story structure that sounds difficult enough to get to much less to escape:

If an anvil of bronze should fall from the sky, it would travel nine days and nights before on the tenth day coming to earth;

and if an anvil of bronze should fall from the earth, it would travel
nine days and nights before on the tenth day coming to Tartaros.
A wall of bronze has been built around Tartaros, and over this wall,
surrounding its neck, Night is poured in three layers, above which
rise the roots of the earth and the springs of the exhaustless sea.
There, in Tartaros, the immortal Titans are hidden under
darkness invisible, as Zeus of the Storm Cloud wills them to be,
down in that place of decay at huge earth's outermost limits.
To them is left no escape, for Poseidon has set there a bronze door. . . .
There, farther on, stands the echoing house of the God of the
  Underworld,
and a frightening dog is on guard in front of its entrance,
one who is pitiless and knows a terrible trick: he welcomes
everyone entering by wagging his tail and putting his ears down,
but he allows no one to escape, but keeping a close watch
swallows whomever he catches emerging out of the gates.[6]

A gift from the Greeks, Medieval hell was amplified to a far worse
place than this. It was conceived as a macabre collection of dungeons.
One is a pit full of burning dirt, hence the pitchfork as a standard piece
of diabolic equipment. It is filled with sinners immersed up to their
chests. Women were hung by their braids above the pit and below them
those who had adulterated these women were immersed head first in the
seething dirt. In another demoniacal department, murderers were
squashed into a narrow crevice swarming with rats and snakes while the
souls of their victims hovered over the chasm tormenting them by uttering over and over the words: "God, your judgment is just." Women
who aborted a fetus were stuck up to the neck in a pool of blood fed by
a slow and stinking river of the claret-colored liquid. Those who falsely
accused others were continually given worms to digest—worms that
would eat out their insides. For too much blaspheming, your eyes were
burned out with a hot branding iron. For worshipping false gods during
life, residents of hell were whipped by attendants and forced to sculpt
statues of fake idols out of hard granite using only their broken, bare
hands. In hell the wealthy who neglected to help feed the poor could be
found walking on red hot razor-sharp flints. Those who had polluted
their bodies with drugs got pitchforked off a precipice. Bashed and bat-
tered by the fall they were driven up a sinuous pathway back to the top,
from where they were hurled again and again and again. . . .

Obviously influenced by the Greeks and the New Testament, Dante Alighieri (1265–1321), the Italian poet, tells of a hell that came equipped with nine decks, each of which offered inverse luxury accommodations. Reading Dante's description of the place, I am impressed by the way wrongdoing is redefined so profoundly with the times. The top-ten sin list for all time keeps on shifting ground. Capital sins in our criminology (i.e., rape and murder) are scarcely mentioned in Dante's time. In the Dantean hate parade gluttons, lustful, and slothful people sit near the top; murderers, blasphemers, and self-robbers (those who committed suicide) reside in the middle; and grafters, simonists (those who committed fraud), soothsayers, and a variety of traitors sit in the upside-down penthouse at the lowest level of hell.

Each punishment always seems to fit the sin perfectly. Thieves, who don't know the difference between what is theirs and somebody else's, are grotesquely metamorphosed by Dante into unidentifiable forms that bear no resemblance to themselves. Modern movie makers would have a hard time visually surpassing Dante's written description of this transformation from the twenty-fifth canto of the *Inferno* (it concerns the punishment for lechery [Fig. 11]):

> While I was watching them, all of a sudden
> > a serpent—and it had six feet—shot up and hooked
> > one of these wretches with all six.
>
> With the middle feet it hugged the sinner's stomach
> > and, with the front ones, grabbed him by the arms,
> > and bit him first through one cheek then the other;
>
> the serpent spread its hind feet round both thighs
> > then stuck its tail between the sinner's legs,
> > and up against his back the tail slid stiff.
>
> No ivy ever grew to any tree
> > so tight entwined, as the way that hideous beast
> > had woven in and out its limbs with his;
>
> and then both started melting like hot wax
> > and, fusing, they began to mix their colors
> > (so neither one seemed what he was before),

just as a brownish tint, ahead of flame,
    creeps up a burning page that is not black
    completely, even though the white is dying.

The other two who watched began to shout:
    "Oh Agnèl! If you could see how you are changing!
    You're not yourself, and you're not both of you!"

The two heads had already fused to one
    and features from each flowed and blended into
    one face where two were lost in one another. . . .[7]

The Medieval world especially was gripped by demons. All of society was engaged in a battle with the forces of darkness which constantly attacked the kingdom of God in this world. To banish demons from the face of the earth, you had to get rid of the black magicians who knew how to conjure them up. Magicians became the Antichrist and the popes sought to stamp them out. Thus began the first great witch scare.

If you are not fearful of horrible noises and terrible sights and if you are among the gifted, you can call the Devil up, so they say, via magical mutterings cast in strange and cryptic tongue (see this chapter's epigraph) accompanied by elaborate ritual acts. The black magician is capable not only of conjuring up the devil but also of commanding him, for he has studied the *grimoires* or "black books" that teach him how; thus he knows the correct formulas and how to draw the protective circle around himself to keep from being ripped to pieces, for the Devil is still reluctant to serve magicians even though he has contracted for their eternal souls.

The first mention of a pact with the Devil comes from a legend that dates from about the sixth century A.D. In the story, Theophilus, a simple clergyman, is introduced to the Devil himself through a Jewish magician. He sells his soul to the Devil via a formal contract in exchange for a higher position in the church. Later writers transformed this legend into the idea of a person becoming a servant of the Devil, doing his evil, bowing down to him, kissing his genitals and his buttocks, and so on—all ways of renouncing Christ.

The great Dr. Faustus seems to have been the archetypal medieval black wizard—an expert at devilish dealings. He even managed to obtain a spirit from the Devil to serve him. The guilty among us refer to our ultimate conscious wrongdoings for immediate personal gain—our sins of wealth, pleasure, pride, and worldly achievements—as "Faustian bargains."

> I adjure thee, O serpent of old, by the Judge of the living and the dead; by the Creator of the world who hath power to cast into hell, that thou depart forthwith from this house. He that commands thee, accursed demon, is He that commanded the winds and the sea and the storm. He that commands thee is He that ordered thee to be hurled down from the height of heaven into the lower parts of the earth. He that commands thee is He that bade thee depart from Him. Hearken, then, Satan, and fear. Get thee gone, vanquished and cowed, when thou art bidden in the name of our Lord Jesus Christ who will come to judge the living and the dead and all the world by fire. Amen.[8]

Thus reads a seventeenth-century rite of exorcism. And it sounds remarkably similar to Babylonian incantations that preceded it by two millennia.

Getting rid of the Devil can be as tedious an operation as conjuring him up. We have all seen films that make us frighteningly familiar with the violent fits, contortions, shrieks, and insults spoken in strange tongues exhibited by the possessed, especially when confronted by the professional exorcist. Magical elements in the rites of exorcism included charms and relics as well as curious combinations of prayers and apparent gibberish. The late sixteenth-century British exorcist William Weston specialized in taking the Devil out of possessed young maidservants. He would sit them in a chair and hold their heads over smoking brimstone; then he would force them to drink a glass of strong wine mixed with holy oil. All of this unfolded in a continuous torrent of babble.[9] Sometimes victims were instructed to fast and pray for months on end after being cleansed.

As recently as 1982, Pope John Paul II was said to have performed an exorcism. The account was given in the memoirs of a Vatican prefect. The woman was reported to have been rolling on the floor and shouting as the Pope began to pray and pronounce "various (words of) exorcism," all apparently in vain. But when he promised to say a mass for her she suddenly straightened up and became normal. A year later she and her husband had an audience with the Pope and she seemed perfectly healed.[10]

The exorcist was not the only one to possess the power of the word. In Renaissance Europe, using curse words developed into an effective, popular way of expelling evil. If you had the power of the Church behind you, your words could bestow God's malediction or curse directly against your offender. If you were robbed you could go to a cleric, report the theft, and have a mandate officially published and posted that would excommunicate the thief. A victim might publicly pronounce a malediction. In early sixteenth-century England, at the beginning of each of the four seasons, prime offenders were publicly and collectively cursed. Wishing evil on others by uttering expletives—particular profane words—began to become widespread and was believed in the popular realm to be effective if justified by the anger and vehemence of the curser. (I always feel better when I utter a choice epithet after being cut off in traffic.)

Poor people were among the most justified of all cursers. Beggars had their own special malediction they could lay on anyone who refused to give them alms. Cursing got so out of hand in sixteenth-century England that laws needed to be enacted to outlaw it. In one indictment, a woman from Shropshire was formally charged in court with cursing profanely sixty-seven times. One particularly effective "ranter" was said to be able to make the throat of his victim burn as if on fire. And a minister was stated to have cursed citizens who walked out on his sermon. Even little children took to cursing one another.[11] (Our construction sites and rowdy barrooms would seem tame by comparison!)

It is difficult for us to appreciate just how much time and energy the people of Medieval and Renaissance Europe spent contemplating the human forms that good and evil could take. The Medieval body politic proliferated in these times when religious devotion occupied a fair share of the *art-lit* scene. Visit any museum in Venice or Florence, check out the statuary on the outside of any French or German gothic cathedral, and you begin to appreciate the elaborate lengths to which artists and sculptors went to express the meaning of good and evil in concrete terms. Every kind of magic imaginable came to be associated with Devil worship. For example, the metallurgist, master of fire, was likened to the underworld devil who controls the fire in the belly of the earth. Anyone who fuels the fire in his belly—those who touch hot iron, swallow hot coals, walk on fire, or kindle the fires of passion in their sexual organs (the selfish heat from within)—goes against the ways of God. No wonder the village smithy makes such a good magician.[12] Other outstanding candidates by the nature of their profession include barbers, who are intimately involved with bodily waste, and gravediggers, who are always in close contact with the dead.

During the Reformation, when the clergy seemed supersensitive to sin, the Devil had his heyday. He came to symbolize everything on, as well as below, the surface of the earth. Like the UFO sightings and near-death experiences recounted on today's TV talk shows, devilish interventions were the graphic subject matter of preachers' sermons:

> Catherine Darea, in 1578, cut off the heads of her own child and that of another little girl. She explained this by saying that the Devil had appeared to her in the form of a large, dark man. This apparition had presented her with a sickle, and told her what to do.[13]

Little wonder the stereotypical images of the Devil that come down to us are as graphic as those of the Halloween witches—to whom he is related.

CHAPTER 14

IT'S WITCHCRAFT

Those who want to become witches go forth at night to the sabbat, and there they perform three somersaults, but first they call upon the devil, to whom they all give themselves; they re- nounce their faith in God three times, and then spit into their hands; after they have rubbed their hands together three times, they are carried off by the devil in spirit, and leave the body be- hind bloodless and dead, until the devil returns the spirit to it.

Carlo Ginzburg,
The Night Battles, Witchcraft and Agrarian Cults in the 16th and 17th Century

And it's all because of witches—those repulsive old hags. The typical witch *is* ugly. Her body is marked by unusual protuberances—a wart on the nose, and a telltale excres- cence somewhere on her body that won't bleed when pricked. She sheds no tears, casts no shadows, and her look can kill you at a glance. Like Oz's Wicked Witch of the West, she wears a black cape and hat and travels from place to place on a broom. She is a devil worshipper who afflicts people with curses and spells and demon forces fly all about her. What else can witches do? Listen to this impressive fifteenth-century list: They can raise storms, make men sterile, sacrifice unbaptized children to the Devil, make horses go mad and throw their riders, change an accusing judge's mind, see invisible things, pull down the moon from the sky, pen- etrate your liver with needles, make rivers run backward, wake the dead, tear snakes to pieces with mere words, and render anybody's generative desires null and void.[1]

The Devil and witches were not firmly linked until the late Middle Ages, when popular belief dictated that all witches acquired their magical powers from pacts made with the Devil. Before Christianity—when there was no Devil—the stereotypical witch was a bit different. In Mesopotamia the Kassapu (male)/Kassaptu (female)—most witches were women—

133

performed magic illegally, while the exorcist acted as a legitimate agent of the state. Both used the same skills, the only difference being that one was characterized as harming and the other as helping people. A witch would steal a person's possessions and use them to make likenesses of her victim, on whom she would then inflict pain by piercing the homemade statue with needles or violently contorting it. She would ply her victim's effigy with secret potions or place it in the arms of a dead person in a freshly dug grave. Thus would she send forth bad dreams and demons from the underworld.

"Eat thou not the bread of him that hath an evil eye," warns Proverbs 26:3. Eye contact with witches was particularly malevolent. In ancient Rome witches were said to possess the "evil eye." Even a wayward glance at them could lead to calamity and illness—"if looks could kill," we still say. In modern Italian communities one still wears a *corno*—a horn made of metal, often inlaid with precious stone—to ward off the wayward glance of the *strega* (witch), usually a barren woman or a widow dressed in black.[2] To get rid of her, make the sign of the fig by placing the thumb between index and third finger or the horn sign by extending index and little finger out of a clenched fist. The phallic symbol of creativity and birth evident in both fig and horn plays the role of an effective amulet to ward off the instant death perpetrated by the witches' glance. Or make a female circular symbol by touching thumb and index finger as a substitute. (The Irish use a shamrock and Native Americans, who also believe in the evil eye, use a whole range of amulets as protection against it.)

Having grown up in an Italian-American community, I can still remember my grandmother's rite for protecting all the children of the house from sickness she attributed to the passing glances of certain black-garbed neighborhood widows. She would pour droplets of olive oil on a saucer of water at the kitchen table and stir it around, being careful to note whether it clotted or stuck to the sides. Then she would make a sign of the cross over it and say "Dio Benedica" (God bless you), duplicating the hand gesture on all our little foreheads.

The belief that someone can harm you just by looking at you or your property has been traced all around the Mediterranean world, where it is primarily characterized as the action of an avenging deity, to Central America where it becomes the name of a sickness, to India where it is an emanation of the psychic power of the mind from behind the eye of a person.[3] The ancient Romans often placed a sexually obscene image in the fronts of their chariots to ward off evil eye. This figure became the

Roman god Fascinus, whence our word "fascinate"—literally to bewitch the bewitcher.

Very often paranoia and envy are connected with the evil eye. In many of these cultures, the eye has little to do with the Devil, but plays a role in how people interact with one another. Between dominant and subordinate ethnic categories, for instance, in Tunisia, "fear of the leer" is used as a rationalization scheme in the control of social relations among weaving communities.[4] Competitive weavers who have withdrawn from the shop and developed in-house looms say they were taken with the evil eye of fellow workers. There had been too many accidents and botched jobs in the former place of work. In turn, the communal weavers claim these greedy ones leer at them and bring them their misfortune. On the transmitting end, you cast aspersions on those who possess some thing or quality you wish you had. But you let the gods do your damage for you. Casting an evil eye is a step short of doing direct physical harm to a person (i.e., trying to harm a rival athlete you know is capable of beating you in a competition), another solution to the envy problem in contemporary society.

As we have seen, pagan competitors to the way of Christ were labeled Gnostic heretics; that is, they held beliefs that stood in contradiction to orthodox teachings and their gods, therefore, were demonized. The Christian concept of the Devil inflated the simple sorcerer, who concocted poisons, learned formulae, etc., to a full-blown witch—one who used her own innate powers and would think nothing of entering into a pact with the Devil. The Medieval witch embodied a catalog of nefarious habits: She repudiated Christ, desecrated the crucifix, killed babies, and indulged in cannibalism and orgy (at least these are the charges made by the clerics that survive in Church texts). The flight of the black witch silhouetted against a full moon can be traced to a ninth-century document that condemns wicked women who ride wildly at night across the sky with Diana, goddess of the moon, striking down anybody they encountered.[5] No wonder our ancestors developed a fear of witchcraft. No wonder there were witch hunts—bad press!

Why over the ages have most charges in the practice of witchcraft been leveled against women? That the "weaker sex" was thought more susceptible to the ways of evil is clear in the ecclesiastical writings of male prophets going all the way back to the role of Eve in Genesis. One theory has it that women herbalists who dared ease women's pain in childbirth were interfering with God's plan, for He had considered this just punishment for Eve's sin. Also, because the number of widowed women living alone was fairly high in the Middle Ages and because women had little empowerment or legal influence, they became the logical scapegoats during the witch craze.

In early Medieval times only women were believed to possess the secret of love that led ultimately to the generation of life; witches were famous for preparing love potions to control and disseminate it. The standard ingredients included tree sap (trees are worldwide symbols of procreation), animal testicles (like-cures-like), love apples (tomatoes), oysters (probably the resemblance to female genitalia), lizards (because a lizard is phallic looking), partridge (a male was said to be able to impregnate its mate by the sound of its voice alone), and huge helpings of bean soup (I haven't yet figured that one out!). Sexy veggies include artichokes, asparagus, leeks, parsnips, turnips, truffles, lettuce, and cabbage. Aphrodisiac plants consist of the mandrake root, which resembles the male or female body (see Fig. 3, page 46) and the satyricon, a double-rooted plant with smooth leaves (For the best results, dissolve it in goat's milk; it is allegedly good for seventy consecutive copulative acts!). More exotic preparations include powdered rhinoceros horn (again, look at its shape), ginseng root, and dried blistered beetles rubbed on the sexual organs ("Spanish fly").[6]

Witchhunting is an old profession. Exodus 22:18 says "you shall not permit a sorceress to live." But during the early Renaissance, when translations of the writings of Greek philosophers like Aristotle began to be absorbed into the teachings of the Church, popular witchcraft came to be viewed as even more demonic and it became highly polarized from the Church. For Aristotle, natural cause left no room for natural magic. It simply did not exist in the tangible world; therefore, any negative force or action that materialized in the real world would have to have resulted from demonic influence. This is why all forms of sorcery and witchcraft came to be allied with the Devil. No one can exploit God and his angels; so, if you're a witch you must be in consort with the Devil and serving him is the opposite of serving God. This sort of polarization gradually led to the European witch craze. Over two hundred years, from 1550 to 1750, an estimated 150,000 to 200,000 people were executed for practicing witchcraft—most of them women, most of them poor.

Decrees had been passed by the Pope condemning witchcraft as heresy as early as 1200 and papal inquisitions and tortures were conducted routinely in thirteenth-century Europe against Satan worship-

One Medieval recipe for an aphrodisiac calls for placing a fish in your vagina until it dies. Then you cook the fish (now charged with your generative powers) and feed it to your husband. Not only will this fill your spouse with amorous intentions but also it will keep him from straying. On the other hand, if you want to afflict a male with impotence you should strip, cover yourself with honey and roll around in a pile of wheat. Then scrape off the grains, grind them in a mill (by the way, you must turn the handle of the hand mill *clockwise* for this procedure to be effective) and bake a loaf of bread with the resulting flour. The theory goes that because the flour has been milled in the wrong direction the generative powers of nakedness and honey are negated and the man who consumes the bread is "desexed." Turn the crank in the other direction and—as you might anticipate—you get the opposite result. (For an extra strong dose of sexual power try kneading the dough between your thighs—the higher up the better.★) In a somewhat more romantic ritual, a witch sends her female apprentice to a barber shop to steal the hair cuttings of a young man on whom the apprentice has a crush; these are used to enchant him into having an affair with the novice witch.

Other love potions were made of female bodily effluvia such as menstrual blood and urine—a far cry from today's love potions. All these concoctions then and now seem based on the idea that women control the sacred power of generation; only they are able to capture the vital procreative forces that emanate from the natural world and the human body. All that remains of these archaic relics of love magic are the familiar daisy petal plucking litany ". . . she loves me, she loves me not," special vitamin pills, and the ubiquitous perfume ad.

★ P. Veyne (ed.), *A History of Private Life, I: From Pagan Rome to Byzantium,* pp. 523–4.

pers. Why were witches persecuted with particular vehemence in England during the latter part of this period? It hinges on the social climate of the times.[7]

When we think of Tudor England (late fifteenth–sixteenth century), we are reminded of Shakespeare and Newton. But few of us think of the underside of that society, which was borne on the backs of the working poor. Life was very tough and very short. Of one hundred children born in seventeenth-century London, thirty-six would die by the age of six and sixty before they reached ten. Average life expectancy was under thirty years. Threats to life lay everywhere; there was too little food in the world and what there was of it was very bad. If the AIDS epidemic makes our society feel threatened, imagine the fear and sense of insecurity stemming from waves of bubonic plague that occurred in all but a handful of years in the fifteenth and sixteenth centuries, killing tens of thousands in its peak years: twenty thousand in 1563; fifteen thousand in 1593; thirty-six thousand in 1603; forty-one thousand in 1625 (a sixth of the population) and sixty-eight thousand (about half) in 1665![8]

How to help the sick and the dying? Bloodletting and purging on the orthodox medical side, amulets and incantation on the magical side. When in doubt try anything. But nothing seemed to stem the inundating tide of misfortune. Victims, then caregivers, fell hopelessly and helplessly in the wake of ugly and virulent disease. Other maladies of the time included dementia, fire, and poverty. Continued misery led to social ills like alcoholism and narcotics addiction, robbery and assault, even gambling—any way to escape the adverse conditions, anything to transform oneself to escape the pervasive gloom.

In these desperate times the magic of the Church offered the greatest solace. People could pray to special saints, such as St. Christopher, whose magic had the power to heal them, or to St. Anthony to help them find a lost article. They could be blessed with holy water or touch relics—perhaps the finger and thighbone of a sanctified ancestor preserved in glass—to ward off ill fortune. Worshipping evil objects was scarcely distinguishable from worshipping the officially sanctioned good ones. The mechanisms and methods of razing malevolent forces that lay behind our misfortune—touching sacred objects, uttering magic words—were the same.

This blurred boundary line between magic and religion was hardened and focused eventually by the Reformists. With their own particular brand of hindsight, Protestant eyes reimaged the Middle Ages as a dark era, when spells and charms masqueraded in the name of religion—when even the clergy itself indulged in occult activities. They unleashed a vigorous campaign to take the magic out of religion. Like major media events, great public sermons preaching the evils of witchcraft were delivered from church pulpits all over Europe. River water is as good as holy water, they proclaimed. Bread and wine are mechanical religious symbols that have nothing to do with Christ's body and blood, nor can any magical incantation spoken over them change their nature. Church idols are meaningless chunks of stone and lumps of wax. Accept life as it is. What you believe in is a lot more important than all the rituals in which you participate. Life may be tough, but God's got it all worked out for you. Have faith in Him and you'll have a lot in the future to look forward to. He's taking care of you—even if it may not seem so at the moment.

In such unfortunate times we can understand why strong advocacy against ritual and against magic—blamed by many as the cause of much misfortune in the world—would lead to an all-out war against witchery. Witchcraft was more than an evil force that one could counteract by praying to God and his angels. It was the prime focus of antisocial, antireligious behavior and it needed to be eradicated. In what has been called one of the most delusional periods in the history of Western Europe, millions of people were persecuted.

If I had to choose a motto for the Reformation, I think I would adopt the title of the first chapter of anthropologist Mary Douglas' book *Natural Symbols,*[9] "Away from Ritual," for this is exactly what took place. Protestant churches in Britain passed one statute after another, finally (in 1542) making the ceremonies of witchcraft and the conjuring up of spirits a felony punishable by death. This law was fairly specific; it included a death penalty for enchantment to find buried treasure, even for provoking unlawful love. Curiously, no mention is made of the Devil; the law seemed to take on a more secular than religious tone. Professional witch-hunters brought thousands of charges against witches ranging from simple conjuration to making a formal contract with the Evil One. The conviction rate was better than 90 percent. America's Salem witch hunt—fairly late on the scene—was minor in comparison.

In the 1640s, Matthew Hopkins seems to have been the best witch-hunter in the field. He was personally responsible for rounding up several hundred victims—and he made a tidy profit for doing so. Hopkins had a special bias against Devil worship and, like New Testament Satan (the District Attorney who went awry), he was notorious for twisting and tampering with evidence to exact his charges. When questioning an afflicted person, he would usually begin with presumptive guilt. He would ask: "How did you come in contact with the Devil?" and "When did you cease in this activity?" In one deposition a woman described herself as particularly frightened at the sight of a beggar. Her husband forbade her to offer him any food. Several times she had violent nightmares in which the beggar came back to her door. In one of them he entered her bedroom while she slept and began to choke her. When this same beggar came aknocking a few weeks later, the frightened woman told him as instructed that she had no food to offer. Then as he turned to leave she suddenly fell into a violent fit. The beggar was tried for witchcraft and sent to jail."[10] Incidentally, Hopkins was so good at his job that he was eventually charged, tried (by his own methods), and hanged for witchcraft!

Today we might lay this sort of provocation of a fit to the woman's own nervous condition, but a seventeenth-century witch-fearing Briton would have been more inclined to look for a cause in exterior forces, like darts from an evil eye. The same for sudden death: He was working in his field when all of a sudden he fell down withering in pain and gripped his left arm. Then he turned blue and died—an obvious coronary case. But where we look to the overtaxed heart, the germ theory of disease, or the spread of malignant cell growth to account for death, those Britons would have been more inclined to attribute the event to the intervention of supernatural powers, often with a diabolical twist.

By mid-seventeenth century persecutions began to abate and by century's end they were practically unheard of. This is because European lifestyles drastically improved. As food production increased and population pressure eased, the plagues vanished. At the same time belief in an orderly clocklike universe not likely to be perturbed by the unpredictable intervention of Deity or Devil had begun to take root. Educated classes had begun to acquire the faith that even the most mysterious phenomena could be explained by causes inherent in nature itself.

Under the domain of science the attractive powers of the earth for the Moon and of the lodestone for iron were now explained by an inanimate secret virtue inbred by nature—far from a supernatural power with which you could bargain. The water witches' divining rod was turned into a kind of magnet, the heating of objects in an alchemist's furnace involved the exchange of a substance called phlogiston, and Devil possession was reduced to psychosomatic illness. What used to be magic gradually came to be known as only trickery, illusions of the senses, or, as we have come to characterize it today—stage magic.

CHAPTER 15

SUMMARY: WHO TURNED ON THE LIGHTS?

...there are no qualities which are so occult...that its
reason cannot be given by [the principles of the mechanical
philosophy].

René Descartes, *Principia Philosophiae*

Today we use the words *mystical* and *occult* to describe a general
perspective on how people thought about nature—people who
lived during the long period between the Roman Empire and
the Renaissance, when the Christian religion dominated Europe. By
Medieval times, the pagan intellectual qualities once conferred upon the
planets and the elements had been gradually refashioned to more ade-
quately represent a heaven and earth ruled by Christian principles.
Philosophers had slowly shifted their stance on how to express nature's
wonders. Less concerned with experiencing the natural world directly,
they now seemed more interested in mythologizing it abstractly.

To recap just how dramatic the shifting currents of thought about
magic that took place in the Renaissance had become, let me contrast
the fourteenth-century model of the universe Dante wrote about with
the image of the world Copernicus unveiled just two centuries later.
Dante's *geocentric* cosmos was as shell-like as Copernicus', though it made
no pretenses of being a fact-based map in our sense of the word. The
major difference between the two, I think, is not the one heralded in
most history books—that one is *Earth*-centered and incorrect and the
other *Sun*-centered and, therefore, correct. Rather it is that Dante's universe is imbued with life. In each of Dante's shells resided a hierarchy of
being from the corporeal here below to the spiritual and divine there
above—a quality that is decidedly absent in the later model of Copernicus. As our knowledge of the immense size of the universe began to expand, the reconceptualization of where life fits into the picture also
began to get squeezed out of it. In a world devoid of life, how could

mind have any effect on matter? All the charms, amulets, and incantations wouldn't mean a thing.

Traversing the boundary between Dante and Copernicus, our role changes from active agent to helpless bystander. When we crossed the Copernican barrier on our historical clocks we passed out of the realm of quasi-immaterial forces akin to the spirit—forces that exist in non-physical entities like number and name. We traversed the ideological line into the theater of physical causes governed by natural law where you and I are subject only to the mindless action of matter instead of being engaged in a conscious dialogue with it. The Earth-centered universe is inward directed, which we usually characterize as closed and negative, while the heliocentric universe is outward directed, open, and, therefore, positive. Having lived under its domain for so long, we cannot imagine what it must have been like to exist in a cosmos like Dante's—in a world that permits the human voice to penetrate to all levels of existence.

Despite these enormous differences between two radically different ways of thinking about time, space, and people, we must, nevertheless, beware of creating sharp historical boundary lines. Copernicus operated very much in the philosophical and religious framework of his own time. (He, like Kepler and Newton after him, appealed to Hermes Trismegistus as the ultimate source of scientific wisdom.) Copernicus' great achievement was one of mathematics, not physics. He contemplated his own theory of the organization of the solar system with the sun at the center as an act of God revealed through number manipulation, an attitude mirrored in the spirit of the Kabbalah and Hermes Trismegistus.

Leaning *toward* the senses rather than away from them as a way of validating reality is another factor that led to the great downslide experienced by magic after the Renaissance. When Galileo introduced his new telescope to academic colleagues, many of them declined the opportunity to see the moons of Jupiter and the phases of Venus for themselves. They believed, as had their ancestors, that the eyes can be deceived. Just look at the oar of a boat immersed in the water. It isn't *really* bent, is it? What we see is illusory—like those castles in the air we witness in a mirage floating at the edge of the sea. Our imperfect sensory organs distort reality; they keep truth from the mind. But nature's sleight-of-hand tricks, like natural magic, were unable to elude the new skeptics who sought explanations, not in the distortions of the imperfect human body, but instead in the veiled imperfections of the natural world—blemishes which, if peeled off one by one, would reveal pristine nature lying beneath them. Thus, the traversal of the electromagnetic disturbance that we call light through different media becomes a single process that is capable of accounting for both mirage and bent oar.

A famous example of how the experimental strategy was nurtured in the Renaissance goes like this: If you have faith in what you see, then it follows that you would be more willing to go out and create things worth seeing. You put the object of a particular belief to the test. If, for example, you'd been led to believe all fireflies are immune to fire, you should experiment by tossing huge numbers of them into the fire to find out what happens. Perception alone illuminates truth. But overturning common sense doesn't happen in a day. Like most systems of thought, once you accept the basic postulates, nothing can shake your faith. Thus a Renaissance magician who confronts your experimental data (a pile of singed, expired fireflies) might retort: Maybe the fire wasn't pure or maybe you used the wrong kind of firefly.

With the advent of new ideas and new technology—telescopes that reveal spots on the sun and blemishes on the moon and accurate clocks and compasses with which to chart both time and space—the seeds of a new kind of confrontation between culture and nature, the one we still experience today, were planted in late Medieval and Renaissance times. By the time of Kepler (the early seventeenth century), modern science's condemnation of all forms of magic was firmly taking root.

Much of the history we read today characterizes the dawn of science as having come after the passage of the long, dark night of occult mythology, a blind alleyway paved with a seductive doctrine and inconsistently applied methods—an age when humankind was held captive by superstition and magic until the great awakening, the rebirth, occurred.

Many contemporary historians now argue that this view is too simple and too polarized. Some historians credit magic and the Hermetic doctrine with playing a distinct role in the great transformation of human will from speculation to experimentation in sixteenth-century Europe.[1] There was great excitement in the discovery of the Hermetic writings, and the techniques of the Kabbalah aroused the imagination. The realization that magic could be an aid to acquiring knowledge gave new direction to the human spirit. For the first time it was all right for us to tinker with nature, to develop an applied science by suggesting that number was a master-key to manipulating nature and marshalling its forces to work for us.

René Descartes (1596–1650), the French philosopher, is generally regarded as the founding father of the idea of the mechanical universe, a concept that proved to be as devastating to magical ways of thinking as the sun-centered model of the universe. He wrote in his *Principles of Philosophy* (1644) that motion is nothing more than the act of going from being near one set of bodies to being near another—a situation that takes us about as far from the notion of a living universe as we can get. True, God did bequeath all motion to the universe, Descartes admits, but the business of the scientist is to measure and quantify that motion and to determine how it gets transferred from one body to another. The whole problem is like trying to figure the way the movement of the hands of a clock is accomplished through different motions of the wheels and gears that lie hidden beyond its face. In this sort of universe God does not meddle in your affairs. He is simply the realization of the principles of geometry and you come to understand him only through the natural laws he set up initially to run the universal machine. You can predict what will happen to matter in the future only by following the mathematical laws that govern the order of nature—nothing more.

Nature still harbors many secrets, but Descartes is confident that a mechanical account of all these occult qualities must emerge, for all things sensible, while not now yet explicable, ultimately will fall under the domain of science. Science historian Keith Hutchison, who has written on Descartes' attitude toward things sensible, offers this helpful historical parallel: We know aspirin relieves a headache, though we really cannot comprehend why in terms of accepted scientific explanation; that is, we cannot pinpoint what it is in aspirin that is effective and exactly how it works. Yet we are confident enough in our scientific methodology to believe that one day that hidden "occult" quality of aspirin will become intelligible to us.

We can understand why, under Descartes' materialism, the world became "disenchanted"—a most appropriate word. Physics offered a new process for searching out the simplest "natures," those that were irreducible to anything simpler: motion, size, shape—the arrangement of parts that make up all things. True Cartesian physicists banish all consideration of subjective qualities from their descriptions (e.g., hardness and color). These are regarded as illusory properties created by the bonding together of matter under the influence of motion; they are not fundamental to the understanding of matter.

If the universe is nothing more than a gigantic clock, then we might be able to wind it, oil it, maintain it, control it. Cartesian ideas about the nature of matter had the effect of relegating devils and witches to the world of the imagination—phantoms of the mind. The Devil became nothing more than any normal person's suppressed bad wishes—just a figure of speech. And Hell was no longer a localized place; but rather the torment that resides *within* a person. To be possessed by the Devil also acquired a metaphorical rather than literal meaning. It's all a state of mind. And so, it took a long time for the lights to go on—two hundred years or more—to alter the core of the establishment belief system from the magical one centered on personal wishes cast about an animate universe to one of rational skepticism pivoted on the senses and applied to inanimate surroundings—and many great thinkers had their hands on the light switch. In keeping with the metaphor of light, historians characterize the end of this period of transformation as the Great Enlightenment (circa the late seventeenth and early eighteenth century in Europe).

Notions about good and bad luck also fell before the march of Enlightenment science, which further promoted the development of mathematical concepts such as statistics. This in turn led to the phenomenon of coincidence: no need to blame supernatural spirits; two events *can* happen at the same time by laws of pure chance. During the Great Enlightenment, not only did religion and natural science change and begin to become separated, but also the social sciences were created. Now your misfortune could better be attributed to your upbringing or the economic class into which you were born instead of to some curse laid on you by a witch. Many of the outward manifestations of those said to be possessed by demons could be explained inwardly by a nervous condition brought about by anxiety and stress. Sudden death could better be accounted for by fear-induced shock, a natural condition of the body, rather than some force entering it from the outside.

Once the wise ceased deferring to antiquity, the lamps of the Enlightenment began to glow at full wattage. We have gradually grown accustomed to being part of a culture that believes itself to be progressive, one that finds greater wisdom in the present than in the past. Who today does not believe that humanity has advanced from primitiveness and will continue to advance, for it is in our very nature to do so? In this view, those who appeal to Hermes Trismegistus, even to the Bible to acquire revealed truth deceive themselves. Quite the contrary, belief in the superiority of the past goes hand-in-glove with the idea that, since the seventh day of Genesis, a world of accumulated sins has and will forever decline.

Auguste Comte (1798–1857), a French philosopher more closely allied with the idea of faith in scientific progress, believed the human mind evolved historically through three stages: from the theological, in which everything is explained by the action of deities, to the metaphysical, in which abstract, spiritual entities are called up, to the positive, genuinely scientific stage grounded in the empirical discovery of nature's true laws. This faith in scientific progress, which developed in the Enlightenment, is a lot like Christianity. Both are characterized by a pull that propels us forward in time and both strive toward perfecting the world and understanding God—the former through comprehension of His laws, the latter through the Second Coming. Indeed, it has been noted that when Comte devised his philosophy he was obsessed with the belief that Christianity had lost its position of authority and what was needed was a new outlook that would do for the present world what Christianity had done for the pagan one.[2]

If the changes engendered by the Renaissance and the Enlightenment were so revolutionary, then why does magic still exist? Why have occult practices flared up again and again out of the smoldering sparks our predecessors thought they had stamped out? Perhaps the ideas of high-minded experimental scientists like Galileo and Descartes really did not percolate down to the common people in the seventeenth and eighteenth centuries any more than those of working scientists do today, when a significant segment of the populace feels perfectly comfortable resorting to nonscientifically sanctioned healing practices such as homeopathy. If you take a look at the popular fiction and essay writing of the Enlightenment, you'll discover that magic was very much alive and that most people did not operate on the rational basis our historians of science trace in the work of their heroic figures. How many still pray to their god asking for direct intervention? Any intelligent person ought to know that such behavior runs counter to the laws of physics and probability. Does the expanding universe and the spherically shaped globe scientists depict us living on really have any impact on our everyday behavior?

So maybe the characterization of the dimming of the lights of magic in phase with the illumination of the rational view of the world is a little too simple, too elitist, and too progressive a model. Whatever historical explanation we may adopt, it will have serious difficulty accounting for the unexpected rise of magic in a new guise during the nineteenth century—in, of all places, the heartland of America. Here arose a new spiritualist movement that would impact the world and reverberate all the way to the present. As we trace its rise and temporary fall in the next section, we will discover what a mistake it would be to think of magic in all forms from astrology to numerology to crystals, etc., as a historical notion that can be assigned fixed definitions. All of these enduring beliefs and their operations were gradually shaped and modified to suit the common sense of the times. They never really died; they only hid out a while before being rediscovered and dressed up in brand-new clothing.

PART III

RAISING SPIRITS:
NINETEENTH-CENTURY
OCCULTISM

CHAPTER 16

ROCHESTER RAP:
THE FIRST HAUNTED HOUSE

$\smile\!$

> ". . . sounds on the wall, bureau, table, floor and other places,
> as loud as the striking with a hammer. The table was moved
> about the room, and turned over and turned back. Two men in
> the company undertook to hold a chair down, while, at their
> request, a spirit moved it, and notwithstanding they exerted all
> their strength, the chair could not be held still by them."
> Slater Brown, *The Heyday of Spiritualism*

I live in the "Burned-Over District"—a funnellike conduit of turf
spread out between the Catskills and Adirondacks connecting New
England and New York with the Great Lakes. In the early nineteenth century, restless adventurers, opportunists, and theologically disgruntled zealots trekked this way along the Mohawk River where the
Erie Canal—dotted by the cities of Utica, Rome, Syracuse, and
Rochester—soon would demarcate the economic pipeline between the
midwest and the Hudson River, directing the flow of commerce down
south to a little port city that would become and remain until this day
the business center of the Western world. Central New York State acquired the char in its dubious label from the fact that so many oddball
Yankee social and religious practices swept over it that, like an overused
cornfield, the land had reached spiritual burnout by the time more normal folks began to move in later in the century.

About five miles southeast of my house lies the tiny community of
Smyrna, a stopover residence of the family of Brigham Young, who had
migrated west from Vermont. Another seminal figure in Mormonism,
Joseph Smith would advance further west through the funnel of revivalism to Palmyra, New York, to pick up the Golden Tablets in 1827. He and
his followers would be driven farther out onto the fringes of establishment society, to found communities in Kirtland, Ohio, and Nauvoo, Illinois, finally coming to rest to grow roots in Salt Lake City, Utah. In
Seneca Falls, fifty miles west of my home, Elizabeth Cady Stanton au-

thored the first proclamation on women's rights in 1848. Fifteen miles north of where I sit, the utopian community of Oneida grew up. Founded in 1848 by pastor John Noyes, who had been booted out of his native Vermont on charges of adultery and fornication, these independent thinking "ultraists" conducted one of many experiments in total togetherness—a perfect communism under God with several families united in every level of intimacy under a single roof. The Shakers were here too; so were the Millerites, the Owenites, and so many other "ites."

Hydesville, New York, is a big dot on magic's map of the world, for here originated the modern notion of the haunted house. Today little more than a crossroad of scattered houses just south of Lake Ontario's shoreline, tiny Hydesville is the place where spiritualism—especially the raising of the spirits of the dead—first attracted attention. It would quickly become America's dominant garb of occultism in the nineteenth century.

Spirit mediums first came to light in the spring of 1848—the tenth anniversary of Samuel F. B. Morse's first message tapped out on the telegraph—in a cramped five-room farm house, one of a dozen or so in Hydesville, built about the turn of the century. The Fox family—a blacksmith said to be a good Methodist once he had quit drinking, his simple homespun wife, and their two youngest daughters—had moved in just the year before. It was these children, Maggie, fifteen (described as vivacious if not a raving beauty), and Kate, twelve (rather attractive and intellectual looking), who figure as the unlikely pivot of the spiritualist movement. The outcome of their actions would profoundly affect the magical beliefs that swept across America in the next decade in an unpredictable way, because members of this family were neither very widely read nor educated and none of them possessed the slightest interest in the occult.[1]

What actually happened at the Fox homestead on the snowy, cold night of Friday, March 31 is well documented by one E. Lewis, a curiosity-seeking intellectual from Canandaigua, just twenty miles down the pike to the southwest.[2] The Foxes' sleep had been disturbed for more than a week by pounding noises in the walls and floors of their little cabin—some so violent they rattled the furniture. On this evening, exhausted by their collective sleeplessness, all had retired early, but this time once the knockings began young Kate began to imitate them. She snapped her fingers and called out to the raps to answer. Amazingly, they did: snap, rap, snap, rap, snap-snap, rap-rap. Soon Mrs. Fox took over the inquisition by voice command: "Rap ten times,"[3] "Rap the ages of my children." The intelligent rapper responded correctly each time. The ghostly inquisition continued:

> I then asked if it was a human being that was making the noises? and if it was, to manifest it by two sounds. I heard two sounds as soon as the words were spoken. I then asked if it was an injured spirit? to give me the sound, and I heard the rapping distinctly. I then asked if it was injured in this house? and it manifested it by the noise. If the person was living that injured it? and got the same answer. I then ascertained by the same method that its remains were buried under the dwelling, and how old it was. When I asked how old it was? it rapped 31 times; that it was a male; that it had left a family of five children; that it had two sons and three daughters, all living. I asked if it left a wife? and it rapped. If its wife was then living? no rapping; if she was dead? and the rapping was distinctly heard. How long she had been dead and it rapped twice.[4]

As details of the rapping spirit's story emerged, a dozen or so neighbors were called in as witnesses and the rapping dialect about the previous occupants of the house continued. "I think no human being could have answered all the questions that were answered by this rapping," declared one witness.[5] Others present testified to hearing raps everywhere: the floor, the wall, the bedpost. Some neighbors claimed they heard knocks emanating from both the cellar below and the bedrooms above. By this method of questioning, now taken over by one of the more action-oriented neighbors, a Mr. Duesler, the awed and cramped enclave was able to learn in the next few hours that a peddler, the widowed father of three girls and two boys with the initials C.B. (determined by rapping out numbered letters of the alphabet), had been murdered—robbed then stabbed with a butcher knife—by a man who had occupied the Foxes' house four years before. The dead rapper identified his attacker as John Bell, a blacksmith then living in the nearby village of Lyons. When word finally got to Bell that he had been fingered by the disincarnate reverberating remains of his alleged victim, he promptly showed up with a testimonial attached to forty-four signatures that attested to his good standing in the community. But counter-testimony followed. A young woman in the Bells' employ claimed to have seen the peddler at their house. She said she also saw certain articles the man had pulled from his pack—a thimble and a pair of coats—items that later showed up in the Bell residence.

It wasn't long before the little haunted house of Hydesville became a stopover for curiosity seekers. The plot thickened as David Fox, the sisters' older brother, decided to excavate the cellar to seek further evidence. He claimed to have turned up some bones, hair, and teeth. Fifty years later the house's owner found still more bones when a wall caved in, but no one was able to document that they were not planted there after the fact to improve tourism.[6] Though no charges ever were brought, as the case gained popularity in the press, innuendo about Bell ran rife. Even Sir Arthur Conan Doyle, creator of Sherlock Holmes, who would himself become a devout spiritualist, proffered an opinion on Bell's guilt as the tale of the haunted Fox house became one of the many great frontier mystery yarns. Stories about it would not only enliven fireside conversation for many long, cold northeastern winters to come but also capture the imagination of the country and the world on a scale that exceeded even the UFO scares of the mid-twentieth century.

The Foxes soon became worn out and their landlord appalled by the incessant stream of oglers and curiosity seekers, along with investigative committee after committee who systematically dismantled and excavated the house out from under their feet. Finally, the family abandoned the place and moved in with one of their sons nearby—but the rapper moved with them. About this time somebody noticed that the sounds seemed to occur only in the presence of the two girls. Could it be they had perpetrated a hoax? Or maybe the spirits communicated only with them because of some special quality they possessed? And so the skeptical schism that dogs all stories about the paranormal was firmly lodged in place.

Enter the girls' thirty-four-year-old estranged and enterprising sister, Leah Fish. Ambitious, resourceful, and rather domineering, as soon as she heard of the Hydesville happenings, she promptly went, via packet boat, from her Rochester home down the Erie Canal to the town of Newark, two miles south of Hydesville. When she reached the house by stagecoach and found it abandoned she rerouted to her brother's place. Leah took control of the situation; she settled the disoriented, confused family and proposed to temporarily disperse the group as a way of dissolving the incessant rapping. Leaving Maggie with her brother, she

took young Kate and her mother back home via the Canal. No sooner
had they arrived and taken their places at Leah's dining room table, than
the rappings started up again—this time with an added frill: The table
rose above the floor a few inches at either end, knocking over water-
filled glasses and plates in the process. Leah writes in her autobiography
that once they arrived back in Rochester they were confronted with
other sounds—a liquid running. Could it be coagulated blood being
poured out onto the floor? Mother and younger daughter felt cold
hands touch them in the night and the rapping became louder and
louder.

They called in an exorcist, but his rantings could not dispel the ever-
more-daring spirits, who now seemed prone to violence—neither could
a whole congregation of Methodist extremists babbling in tongues dislodge the unwelcome guests. Leah used the same method her brother
had devised of employing an alphabet by numbers—a kind of spiritual
telegraph—to acquire specific messages from the spirits, now strangely
expanded in number and offering more pointed messages from beyond—directives that acquired a kind of personal, self-help quality. The
ghosts from the past had begun to take on a social worldliness of a decidedly liberal character:

> The Willets should get busy and help organize the anti-
> slavery movement. He should apply to the superintendent
> of the town of Auburn for a job and not leave the area and
> move to Michigan.[7]

Leah organized "séances"[8] in which a receptive, thirsty citizenry
could experience for themselves the now regionally recognized Rochester rappings. Word was if you were lucky you'd see the table move, maybe
even be touched by the hand of a spirit. Leah would accept a donation,
though she claims she never charged admission. (After all, in catering to
visitors from dawn until midnight how else was she to make a living?)
News of "God's telegraph" spread like a firestorm through the Burned-
Over District—where the appetite for phenomena outside society's
norms was as strong as the winter is long—and so did the commercial-
ism that would follow in the wake of spiritualism ever since.

Skeptics showed up at Leah's house too, for in this age of reason such
happenings ran against the grain of rational common sense. A proof was
needed. One doubter, E. W. Capron, a well-educated citizen of Auburn,

New York, who would write one of the few balanced, first-hand accounts of the whole affair, pondered the problem of how to investigate
the authenticity of the rappings. For one test he grabbed a number of
small seashells out of a basket, concealed them in his closed fist and then
asked the invisible rapper to toll out the number he held. It did so correctly. He isolated Kate and tested her. During rap sessions, he had her lie
on a feather bed with her arms and legs well off the floor—both with
and without her dress on (the latter in the company of ladies only, of
course). She was thoroughly frisked for hidden mechanical devices. He
even "mesmerized" her. Still he heard the rappings. It wasn't long before
floating guitars were twanging out melodies, papers and books were flying about the room, and ladies' hair combs were magically being exchanged. No way, concluded Capron, could a twelve-year-old manage
such trickery or deceit. These were psychic phenomena—completely supernatural in nature.

And so, Capron put Kate on a platform to perform public demonstrations. He accompanied her around the area and lectured on the subject. They played to a packed house in Rochester for two nights until a
threatening, unbelieving mob crashed the hall, shot off firecrackers, and
broke up the show. The public exposé did include a number of "official"
investigative committees consisting of doctors, legislators—even an army
general. None of them could uncover any trickery on the part of Kate,
her big sister Leah, or Capron.

Later, the reunited Fox sisters—Maggie and Kate—began to acquire
professional popular status and national recognition. Newspapermen
from New York City came up to witness the alleged spirit contact. Some,
like W. H. McDonald of the *Excelsior,* were completely convinced; on the
moving table, he opined: "We could not prevent it from vibrating." R. N.
Stimson, editor of the *Merchants Day Book,* was so astonished by the girls'
power to keep a table so firmly fixed to the floor, allowing it to be lifted
only by those they say the spirit designated, that he missed his train back
to the city. But a friend who accompanied him called the sitting he witnessed "the greatest humbug of this humbug age."[9]

Influential people like Judge John Edmonds of the New York Court
of Appeals and Horace Greeley, editor of the *Tribune,* were attracted to
the Foxes. Each had just lost a close relative, which might have given
them a special stake in communicating with the dearly departed. In the
spring of 1850, Greeley invited the sisters down to the city—all expenses
paid. On the way down the Canal they played Albany and Troy, before

floating down the Hudson to Broadway, where they stayed in Barnum's Hotel (owned by a distant relative of P.T.), holding séances and receiving important visitors at appointed hours.

Gotham's witnesses included poet William Cullen Bryant, writer James Fenimore Cooper, historian George Bancroft, and encyclopedist Charles Dana. Even city-wise folks were impressed. Wrote prominent lawyer George Templeton Strong in his diary:

> The production of the sounds is hard to explain, and still stranger is the accuracy with which the ghosts guess of whom one is thinking—his age, his residence, vocation and the like. They do this correctly nine times out of ten at least, where the inquirer is a stranger to the Exhibitors, where he is asking about people of whom they can know nothing . . . A systematic trick and deliberate legerdemain producing these results is . . . difficult to believe.[10]

Horace Greeley became so taken with the country girls (particularly with Kate), that he undertook to supervise their schooling. "Whatever may be the origin of the cause of the rappings, the ladies in whose presence they occur do not make them," he wrote confidently.[11]

In New York the girls entertained still more investigative committees. (The order of the day for people who did weird things was to be investigated.) The first members of the scientific community to examine the girls had consisted of three doctors from the School of Medicine of the University of Buffalo. They sat with Maggie for hours on end snatching at her knee joints and holding them still every time the raps started and otherwise trying to sense movement in any part of her skeletal structure by whatever empirical means they could devise. In one experiment:

> The two females were then seated upon two chairs placed near together, their heels resting on cushions, their lower limbs extended, with the toes elevated, and the feet separated from each other. The object in this experiment was to secure a position in which the ligaments of the knee-joint should be made tense, and no opportunity offered to make pressure with the foot. We were pretty well satisfied that the displacement of the bones requisite for the sound could not be effected unless a fulcrum were obtained by

resting one foot upon the other, or on some resisting body. The company, seated in a semicircle, quietly waited for the '*manifestations*' for more than half an hour, but the '*spirits,*' generally so noisy, were now dumb . . .[12]

After this intense examination, conducted in an air of suspicion and hostility (young Maggie broke down in tears several times), the Buffalo doctors offered the following (incomprehensible to most) scientific explanation:

> The displacement occasioning the knockings is sufficient to remove the ridge of bone which divides the two articular surfaces of the upper extremities of the tibia from its situation in the sulcus between condyles of the femur and to carry it, more or less, upon the surface of the outer condyle. This movement gives rise to the first sound, and the return of the bone to its place causes the second sound, which, in the Rochester knockings generally follows quickly on the first.[13]

In other words, there *was* a natural explanation for the raps: the girls were making the noises by deliberately dislocating their knee joints. To ice their case the Buffalo doctors produced a woman who had the capacity to do just what the Fox girls had done. But exactly how Maggie carried out this maneuver and how she could do it with such intensity and frequency the doctors couldn't say—evidently, she was young enough and her bones pliable enough to repeat the action without pain. Nor did the doctors' rational account explain either how witnesses could hear the crackings across a crowded room or how the raps could be produced in rapid sequence. But these were details. What mattered to them was that they had devised a physical explanation for the Fox sisters' sonorous knees; they were no mystery at all.

The press was quick to get on the docs' case. Mocked the *Cincinnati Commercial* in a lengthy parody:

> "The obtuseness of the abdominal indicator causes the cartaligenous compressor to coagulate into the diaphragm, and depresses the duodenum into the fandango."[14]

Another investigative group (the proponents of the big toe theory) suggested that particular phalange would be a better crack-producing candidate than the knee joint. After considerable experimentation, they asserted that a sizeable toe with strong muscular structure imprisoned in a tight, dry shoe was optimal for generating voluminous raps. One itinerant lecturer, a veritable nineteenth-century Amazing Randi who was dedicated to debugging unscientific theories, took to giving toe-snapping demonstrations to the public to prove the sisters were faking. Another scientifically-minded contingent held out for a concealed mechanical device; yet another for a combination of two theories: a piece of metal connected to the top of a snapping toe.

Religious responses to the Foxes' achievements were as skeptical as the scientific. Speeches made in pulpits drummed up dark, ominous figures from the past: Cornelius Agrippa and Paracelsus—phonies just like the Fox sisters. (In the religious community, feelings about psychic phenomena are still very strong!) A lot was at stake. After all, think of what communicating with the dead could mean. Imagine what it might assure us about the continuity of life in the hereafter. A whole new theology could be developed. But imagine how cruel it would be if our hopes and desires for a kind of immortality were dashed by a bunch of uncaring hucksters. Calvinists objected to communication with the dead because it implied that anyone could enjoy the privileges of the hereafter regardless of their belief. This meant there were no elect in the world. To think that a devout unbeliever could die unredeemed, then be announced by a medium to be saved, was not only anathema to Calvinists, who worked hard to develop their spirituality, but also seemed inconsistent with religious tenets of the time in general. On the other hand, some religious absolutists wondered: Could the raps be produced by the Devil himself, who was in possession of these girls? On her way to a séance in Troy, Maggie was even attacked by a gang of angry Irish Catholics, but assaults like this had little effect; in fact, they only increased the feedback process as media publicity resulted in still more converts to spiritualism in all forms.

As Maggie, the key rapper now turned medium, traveled under Leah's supervision from city to city, she led a very public life and acquired a respectable income. She broke through high society—even carried on an extended romance with the Philadelphia intellectual and polar explorer Dr. Elisha Kent Kane, but Kane's patrician family would have none of her

likes and strongly opposed their marriage. (She took his name and became his commonlaw wife.) Even the wife of President Franklin Pierce,
who had just lost a son in a railroad accident, invited Maggie to the
White House to conduct a session.

Nearly forty years after the first bumps in the night emanated from
the upstairs bedroom in Hydesville, Margaret Fox made a confession to
a New York newspaper. It was all a trick the mischievous girls had concocted to frighten their mother, she told a reporter:

> When we went up to bed at night we used to tie an
> apple on a string and move the string up and down, caus-
> ing the apple to bump on the floor, or we would drop the
> apple on the floor, making a strange noise every time it
> would rebound. . . . my sister Kate was the first to observe
> that by swishing her fingers she could produce certain
> noises with her nuckles [sic] and joints, and that the same
> effect could be made with her toes. Finding that we could
> make raps with our feet—first with one foot and then with
> both—we practiced until we could do this easily when the
> room was dark.[15]

Her younger sister denied the confession, but according to a Mrs. Culver, who assisted the sisters in some of their early Rochester sittings, Kate
had already confided some trade secrets to her:

> Catherine told me how to manage to answer the ques-
> tions. She said it was generally easy enough to answer right
> if the one who asked the questions called the alphabet. She
> said the reason why they ask people to write down several
> names on paper, and then point to them until the spirit
> rapped at the right one, was to give them a chance to watch
> the countenance and motions of the person, and that in that
> way they could nearly always guess right. She also explained
> how they held down and moved tables. She told me that all
> I should have to do to make the raps heard on the table
> would be to put my foot on the bottom of the table when
> I rapped, and that when I wished to make the raps sound
> distant on the wall, I must make them louder, and direct my
> own eyes earnestly to the spot where I wished them to be

heard. She said if I could put my foot against the bottom of
the door the raps would be heard on the top of the door.[16]

So, the sisters *did* make the noises with their toes—and by immersing
their feet in warm water before a session they had better luck. How to
explain sounds heard across the opposite side of the room? They could
suggest the direction of an apparent source to a distant point by looking
that way as they cracked their toes and by cracking them against the floor
or table they also could control both volume and tone. Maggie simply
practiced the technique until she got better and better at it. And the alphabetic communication? By watching the questioner's face when he or
she called the alphabet, they could detect facial muscular movements as
cues—a technique still employed by fortune-tellers.

But all of this was Mrs. Culver's hearsay and there are some inconsistencies in her testimony. For one thing, Kate never was in Rochester for
any investigations. And Mrs. Culver's description of rooms and furniture
in the environment where they worked together could not be corrobo-
rated by any other witnesses. The fact remains that the two girls were
never caught or directly exposed in the act of producing the raps by
using either a mechanical device or any part of their anatomy.

In the final analysis, maybe the Fox story isn't just a simple case of
fraud vs. real spirit manipulation. It has been suggested that enormous
social pressures and depravity forced Maggie to make a confession in
which she herself had little faith.[17] We are constantly driven to respect
authority, yet we hang on to powerful impulses generated by our own
experiences. Pressed by the Catholic clergy and the increasingly powerful anti-spiritualistic undercurrent of science, when Margaret Fox confessed and declared herself a fraud in 1888, she was a penniless alcoholic
whose children had been taken away from her. In fact, a year later she re-
canted, claiming she had been duped by the newspapers.

Perhaps the Fox sisters might better be labeled sensitives than spiritualists. Ernest Isaacs, a historian who has studied the case and weighed the
evidence from their many séances, thinks the sisters possessed an extraordinary capacity to sense and act upon their clients' desires and wishes.
While they may have practiced deception, they had no real control over
their gift and they didn't really understand what was happening to them
while they were entranced.

Whether occult forces had produced their spirit writings, or, as most
psychologists would argue the case today, they were simply echoing the

stresses and strains of their unconscious selves,[18] the damage had been done, as the unbeliever would say. Within twenty years of the rapping incident, eleven million people, or 30 percent of the American population, believed not only that there was life after death, but also that you could communicate with the dead via a variety of methods—and there were sixty thousand mediums around to help you! Methods of communicating with spirits included, in addition to alphabetic rapping and table tipping, spirit writing, clairvoyance (seeing objects, events, and people indiscernible through the normal senses), clairaudience (hearing same), clairsentience (detecting such presences through a sixth sense), spirit impersonation (being actuated by a spirit who enters the body of a medium—a form of possession). Dreams, déja vu, apparitions, and talking in tongues were additional techniques. Like scientists, the mediums of the enlightened scientific age could be assisted by all manner of automatisms. They used devices such as the ouija board (from the combined French and German words for "yes"). This was a board consisting of the alphabetic letters, numbers 0 to 9 and a yes/no space, together with a movable pointer controlled by the fingertips of one or more persons. The idea is to arrive at the answers to life's simplest or deepest questions by sensing the movement of the pointer. But, who controls the stick?[19] Is it the guiding spirit from beyond, the subconscious user, or the Devil?

So rampant had "rappomania" become that by April 1854—a mere six years after Hydesville—a bill to the U.S. Congress proposed organizing a national committee to investigate

> . . . certain physical and mental phenomena, of questionable origin and mysterious import, that have of late occurred in this country and in almost all parts of Europe, the same are now so prevalent, especially in the northern, middle, and western sections of the Union, as to engross a large share of the public attention.[20]

The goal was clear: to give an answer one way or the other to these phenomena. They must be determined by said commission to be "odylomagnetic"[21] or genuinely spiritualistic, the document went on. The legislation was tabled.

CHAPTER 17

BEFORE HYDESVILLE:
STRANGE FORCES,
NEW EXPERIMENTS

~~~~~~

> . . . I stepped and caught it by the upper end with one hand,
> with which I held it, and drew it through the other, but found
> nothing at all in it. There was nobody near to shake the bag, or
> if there had [been], no-one could make such a motion which
> seemed to be from within, as if a living creature had moved
> in it.
>
> Richard Cavendish, *Man, Myth and Magic*

hile we tend to explore more along psychological lines to explain what is unaccountable by physical laws, researchers of
the late nineteenth century, who were less likely than modern rationalists to dismiss all magical effects as humbug, searched for an
explanation of paranormal influences as some sort of unknown wave
phenomenon or forcefield-like magnetism, for this was the heyday of
classical physics, which proffered the belief that all phenomena we experience fall under the dictates of gravity and electromagnetism. Science
then was more tolerant of early spirit rapping than it is of, say, UFOs
today. There was a genuine curiosity about investigating its claims. In
1882 the Society for Psychic Research (SPR) was established in London.
Like the Air Force's Project Bluebook, set up to probe UFO reports in
the 1950s, it was an organized attempt, says its charter, to investigate
"without prejudice" "debatable phenomena" that involve "the influence
of one mind on another" and "the powers of perception beyond a higher
exalted sensibility of recognized sensory organs." Subject phenomena included experiences at death, hypnotism, and other spiritualistic phenomena. The president's address appealed to the search for "sufficient
evidence" regarding all reported phenomena of this sort "that would
convince the scientific world."[1] The SPR issued forty-nine annual volumes before suspending publication in 1949.

Some tended to view the automatisms of spiritualism as the products of phantom personalities that act within and interact with a person. These entities have information banks of their own, learned and stored subconsciously and processed "paranormally" (via skills that are not really tangible in physical and material terms). This is a long-winded way of saying we don't really understand how to account for spirit communications.

Incidentally, ghosts had roamed the world long before the Foxes had elicited messages from the dearly departed. We have all heard of poltergeist (noisy ghosts) of which the British always seem to have been fond. Take the case of the Drummer of Tedworth, so-called after the down-and-out veteran of the Cromwellian war who, when refused alms by a wealthy squire, snatched his drum. Then he returned (*in spiritu*) to the squire's manor for a period of five years to haunt him with incessant drum rolls which emanated from the attic, where the discarded instrument had been stored. Interestingly enough, firsthand experience with two young girls and the same general kind of rapping heard in Hydesville's haunted house also permeated the Tedworth case. In 1666, the Rev. Joseph Glanvill reported investigating noises in one of the squire's bedrooms occupied by two little girls—this time a scratching from behind the bedstead bolster. He thought he saw something moving, such as a mouse in a cloth bag (see the chapter epigraph). The scratching developed into raps which emanated from all over the house—on the roof as well as on pieces of furniture, which began to float about on their own.

More important than offering a blow-by-blow explanation of every reported case in history, I think, is the question of why different kinds of cases get witnessed and reported at different times and at different levels of intensity. Why the Fox phenomenon there and then?

Generically speaking, there are only two causes offered for such phenomena and they lie at opposite extremes. Either they are actual communication from spirits or they are a fraud. A third position, however, argues that we are dealing with natural forces—not magnetism, electricity, or gravitation—but forces of a different kind that can be activated by a sensitive or a medium. However, this hypothesis sheds no light on exactly what those unknown forces might be, so the more rational among us often are left in the uncomfortable position of being unwilling to opt for an incomplete and inconclusive explanation, simply because it is more in tune with our common sense to follow the lead of the obviously fraudulent cases by holding all the other examples suspect.[2]

Why would anybody in the afterwash of enlightened eighteenth-century scientific rationalism *really* care to raise the dead? How could educated, intelligent people, living in a progressive age when the scientific explanations of natural phenomena had come to be accepted, opt for a supernatural account of events that evidently were perpetrated by a couple of uneducated, unsophisticated country girls turned spiritualistic mediums? For most of us today, death is either a termination of all existence or it is the gateway to an eternity of being wherein we can have no influence on those who survive us. But it was different then.

Flip over a dollar bill. On it you'll see pictured the back side of the Great Seal of the United States. There, to the left of the big green "one" are written the words *Novus Ordo Seclorum,* "A New Order of the Ages Begins." (The words appear below a Gnostic-looking eye and pyramid.) By its own mandate, America was the natural spawning ground for new ideas and philosophies, for we all were entitled by our constitution to life, liberty, and the pursuit of happiness. And pursue it we did, both spiritualistically and materially in early nineteenth-century post-revolutionary America. The Fox girls lived during a time of accelerated social change. Mid-nineteenth-century America had witnessed an enormous immigrant flux on the heels of the great industrial revolution. Old Yankee ways of life were seriously threatened. And Darwin's theory of evolution was about to undermine the religious idea that all humans were immortal spirits. Restless New Englanders fled to the Burned-Over District primarily because they were dissatisfied with their lot and they felt inclined to support a wide variety of religious movements that challenged orthodox beliefs. They were radicals pure and simple.

The enthrallment with magic that flared up then in upstate New York was part of a deeper, more universal rebellious undercurrent known as the Romantic movement—a general rejection of reason as the key to acquiring true knowledge in all areas of thought. Emanating from a revival of interest in Medieval tales called romances, the movement combined a love of the macabre and occult alongside a kind of nature worship. The true Romantic appealed to the sentimental and the emotional rather than the tangible and the rational. In music, for example, the strength of feeling and passion in the strains of a symphony by Schubert seems a rejection of Haydn's sedate pieces of an earlier generation that valued strict adherence to laws of form. Artists in the Romantic period painted not just what they saw but also what they felt within themselves. Thus, the paintings of Delacroix and Turner place heroic tales, exotic and violent scenes, and emotional love stories all within a natural context portrayed by intense and contrasting colors that arrive on the canvas via quick and fluid brush strokes—a stark contrast to the hard-line objective and formal presentations offered by their more rule-bound predecessors. This rejection of classical form giving way to an exploration of colors and shapes—hidden inner feelings and emotions that deny the realities laid down by past masters—spread through the creative community.

Victor Hugo led the revolt in literature, Coleridge and Wordsworth in poetry, against the conventional form and pedantry of the established schools. Social doctrines espoused by William Miller,[3] philosophical and cosmological beliefs by Emmanuel Swedenborg rode the tide of Romanticism. In science, where such notions didn't really stick, the Romantic movement nevertheless had its proponents; for example, in the work of Anton Mesmer on animal magnetism. Fantastic, unusual, fanciful and weird are words receivers of the new knowledge applied to these liberal thinkers who claimed to acquire their knowledge by stretching, even breaking, accepted rules. They did so by violating the laws that bound together accepted ways of thinking. Whether they were all daring, creative geniuses or perverse madmen depended on one's attitude toward truth and how it was pursued.

In its earliest phases the spiritualist movement concerned itself more with religious rule breaking than with violation of scientific norms. Spiritualism is basically a philosophy, a movement rather than an organization. It advocates that the spirit is the ultimate reality, but in the nineteenth century it seemed to focus on belief in the survival of the human personality after death, together with the potential of communicating with the spirits of the dead. It is difficult for us to imagine how involved nineteenth-century frontier Americans were with their religious beliefs. The very institution in which I teach—like so many other small colleges in the northeast—was originally established for the express purpose of training those who would spread the word of God. Its theological curriculum once included homiletics (how to adapt the discourses of the pulpit to the spiritual benefit of the listener), devotional studies, and religious oratory. There were widespread campaigns to establish Sunday schools and Bible societies to distribute religious literature promoting temperance and the strict observation of the rules of the Sabbath.

Religion in America was in deep crisis by the mid-nineteenth century. Science had severely damaged the edifice of creation espoused in the Bible. Geologists had disproven the Genesis idea of a recent creation by laying out a time sequence for natural events on earth that extended millions of years into the past. On top of this, Darwin's ideas cast aside the notion that there was anything special about human development. Beside the scientific onslaught against Christian dogma, believers also began to question the moral precepts of their religion. Did eternal damnation in Hell really make sense? And what about the very existence of a vengeful God like that of the Old Testament who knows nothing of natural process? Why would He create a clockwork universe in seven days? Out of step with the knowledge of the times, the parish was ripe for change and the religious liberals would lead the way.

Spiritualism manifested a violent and exaggerated skewing away from religious orthodoxy, for it directly challenged the way people thought about the relationship between life and death—a topic that attracted a lot of social attention. The implications were clear and simple: If we can communicate with the dead, then there must be some form of consciousness about the tangible world that goes along with us after we die. A whole moral and social theory about the nature of human existence would need to be developed to accompany such a great revelation. What an exciting priority! Taken in this context, it is no surprise that such ideas could have wide popular appeal. And it was all proven by the rapid rise to stardom of the sisters of Rochester rap.

Settlers in the Burned-Over District were especially ripe for a new kind of spiritism. They were "enthusiastic" social and religious experimenters[4] by nature, adventurous fringe members of Yankee society from where they had migrated during a time of post-Revolutionary War economic depression. Searching for a new place and a new identity, they were religious rejects fleeing the newly created urban conditions of cities like New York, Boston, and Philadelphia. By settling in the rural areas of "upstate," they had opted for agriculture and a pastoral setting—a deliberate escape from the pressure of population and the pollution of industry. The deprived naturally turn more fervently, more emotionally toward God than those who are well-off and satisfied. They are likely to go to greater extremes to express and relieve their tensions. Take the Shakers, who developed a native religion founded on the shores of Lake Ontario. They believed in the Second Coming and their founder, Mother Ann Lee, was regarded as the embodiment of Christ (son of a bisexual God) in human form. They sought full equality of men and women and they practiced celibacy. Preferring to withdraw from society altogether, the Shakers lived by themselves and formulated and practiced their own code of ethics. As the popular name given to the sect implies, Shakers experimented with raising the spirits who manifested themselves through the rattling of furniture. They also said that spirits of the dead local Indians would knock on the door of the meeting house, enter, and with permission take possession of their bodies. In a state of *ecstasy* (literally an out-of-body experience) believers would shout and howl uncontrollably. Advocates of the conspiracy theory say that the Fox sisters got the idea of rapping from the Shakers in the first place.

Shakerism was just one of the "ultraist" sects that advocated direct divine intervention in human affairs and, like many of the other perfectionist groups on the religious edge, they seemed to be seeking to perfect society through human improvement based on a combination of individual effort and faith in progress. These people were optimistic about the potential of their human experimentation but deep down they were fearful that unless they could do something to make it better, the whole world would degenerate. Here, too, was an age that developed the power to harness nature—from horse power to the steam engine and the discovery of electricity. In the Foxes and their like, the power of mind over matter at last had been extended to the domain of the soul—like the canal, then the railroad, the spiritual telegraph had finally arrived. This was not an idle activity. Spiritualism, its believers predicted with confidence, was a new religion that would replace Christianity.

The new democratic heaven was accessible to everybody. No need to establish nebulous contact through a male priesthood that spoke religious jargon nobody could understand. We could all experiment for ourselves—defy the laws of authority. Romanticism had gone wild. The debate continued within establishment religion.

> It cannot be! This very low, vulgar, ludicrous, and at times, revolting manner of the alleged spirit manifestations, by means of knocks, rapping tables, and contorting the bodies of the Mediums, proves, at the very start, a fatal objection to, and repels the mind against, the idea that spiritual intelligences have any connection with the matter.[5]

On the other hand, wrote Thomas Wentworth Higginson, a well-known defender of mediums: "They say that the utterances through mediums are poor and weak. How should they be otherwise? The answers are as good as the questions."[6]

And so, the Fox sisters did not act alone and they certainly were not the originators of the spiritualistic explosion. They were merely the linchpin of the American movement. And like most ideas on this side of the Atlantic at the time, the sparks that ignited the flame had been kindled in Europe a generation before, where major developments were taking place on the experimental frontiers of science. A century earlier, Newton had established gravitation as the prime force that keeps Earth and the planets in motion. But there were other mysterious forces that exerted themselves in terrestrial laboratories, and we must back up just a bit to take their measure.

In 1831, English Physicist Michael Faraday (1791–1867) demonstrated how to produce "electromotive force" by the principle of magnetic induction. He passed a magnet through a fixed coil of wire to which a galvanometer was attached and recorded the electrical current thus induced into the coil. Few scientific discoveries have had such important results; the principle of magnetic induction would quickly lead to the invention of electric motors and generators.

Within thirty-three years of Faraday's experiments, Scot James Clerk Maxwell (1831–1879) would develop a theory to synthesize electricity and magnetism. He encoded the mathematical laws governing the interaction between electric and magnetic forces—laws that govern the behavior of radio waves, heat radiation, infrared, visible and ultra-violet light, X rays, and gamma rays. Now all of these energetic disturbances could be interpreted as wave forms that travel through the vacuum of interstellar and intergalactic space at the blazing speed of light and in one form or another penetrate all things. It was one of the greatest accomplishments of theoretical physics. Though the world of the early 1800s was a time of great scientific discovery, whatever percolated down to the public level was still thoroughly mixed with mysticism.

Picking up on these ideas, one popular scientific account of rapping suggested that the spinal column of the diviner is like a battery. The vertebrae are the metallic plates and the soft stuff in the spinal cord is analogous to battery acid. When the brain's right hemisphere gets overcharged the electrical force within it produces raps, flashing lights, movements, etc. As the whole environment gets disturbed by these electrical explosions, the medium acts as a draw on an external reservoir of energy.[7]

Into this pre-Romantic European age of establishing the experimental physical laws that run the universe, Franz Anton Mesmer (1734–1815)

was born. He was a flamboyant Swiss-German physician and healer
whose method of dealing with patients would ultimately give rise to
hypnotism as a form of therapy. Mesmer believed that Faraday's and
Maxwell's magnetic fluid that permeated all material things also affected
the human body, even the human psyche. All of us, he said, radiated this
magnetic fluid ("magnetisme animal," or animal magnetism he called it),
which can be used to influence the minds and bodies of those around us.
Now, this is just a logical extension of the aforementioned ancient principle of astrology. If the Moon can influence the tides in the ocean, then
could it not also create tides in the affairs of men? If the gravitational pull
of the planets could affect our behavior, why not a magnetic pull too?
Like the alchemists' elixir of life, Mesmer's invisible fluid offered the possibility of a cure-all, a panacea akin to the "snake oil" peddled by the bottle to a waiting public by the itinerant professor who traveled from town
to town in his pharmaceutical wagon.

Mesmer began to experiment with magnets to perform healing. One
of his scientific contraptions consisted of a half dozen jars full of water
with magnets submerged in them, all connected together with metallic
bands and set in a tub of water flavored with iron filings; he called it a *baquet*. He would treat patients by sitting them in the tub. Mesmer would
also spray his magnetic water all around his offices and treatment rooms.
He would carefully place magnets over and about the affected parts of a
sick person and observe the results. Then one day while bleeding a patient he noticed that as he approached the individual the flow of blood
increased and when he retreated it lessened. This convinced him that he
himself might be the real magnet (Fig. 12). He experimented further, dis-
carding his burdensome bathtub and using his own personal, animal energy, which he transmitted via the laying on of hands or with the help of
a metal wand to heal his patients. (Typically he would charge himself up
before a healing by putting magnets in his underclothing, pants, and shirt
pockets.)

Mesmer claimed to cure just about anything with this technique,
from the household variety of aches and pains to blindness and sexual in-
hibition—even boredom. His remedy for seasickness: grab hold of the
ship's mast, which acts as a magnetic pole to draw out the illness. The
magnetist seemed especially fond of treating attractive young women.
His hands-on method required prolonged kneading of body parts including thighs and breasts.[8] Investigated for this questionable practice by

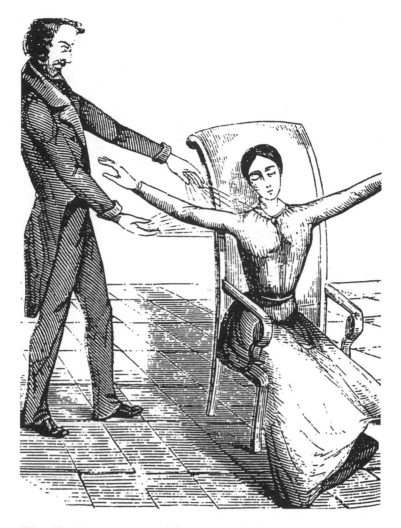

Fig. 12: A mesmerist and his patient. (The Mary Evans Picture Gallery.)

the Imperial Morality Police of Vienna, Mesmer was forced to flee to Paris in 1778; there he became an instant hit. In the late eighteenth century the "City of Lights" was indeed the European capital of Enlightenment, a place full of intellectuals and radical reformers ready for new ideas. They would soon overthrow the privileged patricians and attempt to establish the "liberty, equality, fraternity" for which the French would become so famous. As might be expected in such a tumultuous environment, a large share of occultists were in residence there too. As one baron

•

in the court of Louis XVI wrote: "Looking around, we see only sorcer-ers, initiates, necromancers, and prophets. Everyone has his own, on whom he relies."[9]

In Paris, Mesmer set up a combination hospital and séance parlor—low-lit, perfumed rooms decorated with mirrors, crystals, and fancy clocks. There he would appear in a flowing robe, wand in hand, stroking an assembly of patients who stood together, men alternating with women, pressed thigh against thigh. In the background a chamber or-chestra played classical music. Sometimes he would sashay over to his magnetized piano and play a few bars. Like so many evangelical believ-ers his following would go into convulsions, ranting and raving and falling on the floor as their diseases dramatically and at least momentar-ily seemed to be lifted out of their bodies.[10]

Mesmer's treatment became so celebrated that the Marquis de LaFayette wrote George Washington urging him to import Mesmerism into the United States. King Louis XVI offered Mesmer a pension for life, but only on condition that he provide proof establishing his method to a medical examining committee. Marie Antoinette begged him to sign a contract but the scientist refused. He left Paris in 1789 and headed for obscurity.

Mesmer was finally investigated by a commission consisting of four French university physicians who witnessed the Mesmeric healing process for themselves. Like the Buffalo doctors who would so method-ically explicate the phenomena of the Fox sisters, the committee wrote: "The convulsions are characterized by involuntary, spasmodic move-ments of limbs and of the whole body, by contraction of the throat, by spasms of the hypochondriac and epigastric regions . . ."[11]

The investigative commission blindfolded patients so that they didn't know when the magnetic juice was being turned on. Thus, when the magnetizer was hidden from view the passing of his stick or wand over a given area of the body usually had no effect. These experiments, they decided, "authorize us to conclude that the imagination is the true cause of the effects attributed to magnetism." How to explain it when it worked, then? Said the commissioners: "In these cases the imagination acts . . . by diffusing tranquility over the senses, [and calling into play] the genial influences of hope."[12] It's a psychic phenomenon and not a phys-ical or mechanical one. (Note that in this explanation the words "hope" and "tranquility" replace magnetic force, polarity, and physical cause—but only *some* other words for the effective terms "influence" and "diffusion" remain.) In other words, if you cannot subject the imagination to valid scientific tests, then any phenomenon induced by it is simply not science—which doesn't explain what really happened.

This was the verdict of the Age of Reason. There was no such thing as a magnetic fluid—only an over-extended imagination could have produced the effects. Mesmer made his quick exit at an opportune time, for the French Revolution was imminent. Though science casts him more in shadow than in light, he is credited at least by some with having established a link between hysterical illness and sexuality one hundred years before Freud. His "animal magnetism" is a precursor to the hypnotic trance—the altering of one's state of consciousness by the power of suggestion, which already was being employed as a surgical anesthetic with some success and eventually would open one of the gateways to modern psychic awareness. For Mesmer the universal life force was real—and if properly manipulated, it could restore the balance of wellness. Telepathy, clairvoyance, trance phenomena, communication with spirits of the dead—the mediumistic abilities many believe the Fox sisters possessed—are aspects of the basic idea behind animal magnetism: that there is a universal power in all of us to go beyond our normal sensory apparatus.

In their own time, Mesmer's ideas would not have seemed too terribly oddball to laypeople. A universal, all-pervading magnetic fluid was the medium for the transmission of mechanical forces and influences being explored in labs all over the world. What really did Mesmer in as far as the scientific establishment was concerned lay in his inability to drop the idea once he took the magnets out of his pants. Devoid of any material technology, the accepted form of scientific explanation in terms of mechanical causation became difficult. The effects that were produced in his treatment of patients—seizures of wild laughter, uncontrollable crying, hiccuping, and that prickly feeling on the skin everyone reported—might more sensibly be relegated to the patients' own imagination.

Franz Anton Mesmer, historian Robert Weyant suggests, tried to take old hermetic cures for hysterical disorders and modernize them—attune them to phenomena explicable by the science of his day. He failed. But in Mesmer's failure we glean something significant about the relationship between magic and science. Magic moved with the beat of time. Following the scientifically described workings of nature, so too the explanation of natural magic evolved from a basis in the sympathies and antipathies of its components during the Renaissance, to quite another foundation in the subtle, all-penetrating ethers of the eighteenth and nineteenth centuries and, as we shall see, finally to the more updated plasmas and energy fields of the twentieth century.

How exactly did Mesmer, a doctor working in Vienna and Paris, impact the Fox affair? The European practice of animal magnetism crossed over the Atlantic with French emigrés, many of whom became teachers of upper-class children. Their European ideas influenced a few physicians and inquisitive Harvard professors and other intellectuals in the big cities of the East. Word spread out of New England with the opportunists and eccentrics who funneled westward. Many contact healings are recorded in Salem, New Bedford, Nantucket, and the states surrounding the area of eastern Massachusetts. A magnetized clairvoyant would demonstrate before a crowd how she could successfully diagnose the illness of a sick person brought before her by passing her hand over the body, describing the condition of each organ as she reached it. Curiously enough, this was just about the time the stethoscope was introduced into Europe. Its extrasensory powers were received with as much skepticism as magnetic healing.

Physical and social ills were then thought to be more closely tied together. Unjust laws—like a kind of bad air that surrounds us—were thought to lead to such maladies. Cures, therefore, would involve both taking a mineral bath and reading a book of philosophy. Mesmerism in America was more than *avant-garde* intellectual entertainment. It became part of a social movement when perfectionist political thinkers began to connect the idea of a decaying society with a lifeless medium, unaffected by contact with the universal fluid which flowed through it. One prominent lecturer blamed the corrupt institution of government for this condition and saw Mesmerism as a way to a free and purer world. The bond between radical politics and occult behavior is still intact today.

Many American secret societies worked actively for social reform—establishing social philosophies in direct opposition to the state. They all claimed to stand for the mom-and-apple pie tenets of the day: political progress, true democracy, and the defense of ideas. Spiritualism neatly fit into the picture because it advocated the rejection of the authority of the Bible. Sin was the action of a person whose character was not fully developed. There *was* no fall from grace and we shouldn't spend our time seeking atonement. Instead we all ought to work optimistically to improve ourselves and our status in life. If the dead can reach out to help us in our efforts, by all means let's grab on. We need all the help we can get.

You make your own bed—in the hereafter as well in your own here-and-now. Nobody had expressed this philosophy better in a context that combined science with religion than the Swedish scholar turned spirit communicator, Emmanuel Swedenborg (1688–1772). His ideas, like those of Mesmer, also were brought out and widely read during the spiritualist movement. Swedenborg, well-grounded in science (having studied metallurgy, math, geology, and anatomy) also spoke several languages. He was fifty-six years old, single (though seeing a number of women), held down a prestigious job as assessor of the Royal College of Mines under appointment by Charles XII King of Sweden, publishing important works on mining engineering, and worked on scientific inventions like an air-powered gun and a submarine craft. Then it happened. Into his placid life a series of vivid dreams suddenly intruded. In them, Swedenborg visited heaven and hell, spoke with God, Jesus, Plato, and Aristotle. They all convinced him to be the hereafter's ambassador to the human race and to report his findings about the world above to the people of the world here below. These apocalyptic visions caused him to jump the track of rational scientific skepticism rather abruptly and to latch onto the world of the occult.

Thanks to his methodical training, Swedenborg gave many future spiritualists just what they were looking for—a manifesto. He wrote out a detailed description of precisely what the afterlife was like—ideas the American spiritualists (and even today's New Agers) still borrow. Swedenborg took his dictation from angels and busied himself with hour after hour of trance-channeling with a variety of famous dead spirits. He even claims to have left his body for the Moon where he discovered a race of people, who for want of air, could speak only by belching through their stomachs. He learned to induce dream states by concentration and disciplined breathing exercises. Excited and busy with this work, he cut his government job to half-time, meanwhile becoming a vegetarian (to aid his concentration).

The main theoretical thrust of emissary Swedenborg's message was that all human life possesses two simultaneous existences: one in the natural, tangible outer world, the other in the inner spiritual one. Over time we lose intimate contact with this inner existence. What modern cryogenics tries to do with the body, Swedenborgianism did with the mind. The inner existence keeps its own memory bank after we die—a memory bank that preserves a record of everything that ever has transpired in our lifetime.[13]

We can think of Swedenborg as the father of the concept of a self-generated heaven or hell. Real hell, wrote Swedenborg, isn't really so bad. It is populated by dead spirits who get on with their lives much as they did here on earth. There is neither a Devil in hell, nor any angels in heaven. Like hell, heaven has its own form of government and social structure. When we die we pass through a process of self-evaluation assisted by those we once knew on earth. In effect, we choose our own heaven and hell. If you were a materialist you might choose the latter, because you could be as dishonest and underhanded in hell as you needed to be on earth to acquire your wealth—so long as you didn't exceed the magnitude of your earthly sins. Then your fellow souls would beat you up to keep you in line. The same for heaven. If you chose to belong there, then you opted for the communal way of life. This consisted of a permanent state of dedication to progress toward perfection in your own life as well as the lives of your neighbors.

Translations of Swedenborg's books were a huge hit in turn-of-the-century America, and it is not difficult to see why. His version of the afterlife was decidedly liberal and rife with individualism. He beat a true path between fundamentalism as taught by the church and the questioning agnosticism of the Enlightenment. Swedenborg's far-out anti-establishment spin on the spirit world had great appeal for the inhabitants of the American colonies. The hardworking Yankee fringe—those independent and rugged individualists who headed out of New England for distant but promising empty pastures—were adventurously forging new explorations. With ideas like Swedenborg's to back them up, they became cosmic pilgrims reaching for the infinite. In Oneida, New Lebanon, and the other utopian communities of the Burned-Over District they were ready for the challenge—to reconstruct Swedenborg's heaven here on earth.

During George Washington's presidency, a branch of the Church of New Jerusalem was established in the States, only fourteen years after the English sect dedicated to Swedenborg was set up.[14] Writers of the Romantic period, such as Blake, Henry James, and Coleridge were very much affected by the sort of delegation of the hereafter to human will proposed by Swedenborg. Emerson, the great New England transcendentalist, seemed caught on the stressful tightwire between scientism and spiritualism. Religious liberals were getting away from the Scriptures, searching for a scientific way of acquiring true knowledge and happiness. Serious romantics, they believed in recapturing a world in which ideas and ideals were more important than physical and material things and forces. As in the old Neoplatonic tradition, spirit came first.

Even though there were basic philosophical disagreements between the two, Mesmer and Swedenborg—designing architects of the early American occult movement—both were ostensibly scientists, at least as far as lay people were concerned. What they did, the public believed, was to tap into laws of the universe that hitherto had escaped human attention. Clairvoyance and mediumship offered a new form of science, an antidote to the dull scriptural rules about how to behave in the present world in order to earn a passage to the one above. Both of them helped bring together a new social, religious, and scientific philosophy. As the intellectual historian Whitney Cross described spiritualism:

> This philosophy, whose sire was American Universalism, and dame European mysticism, was a true cousin of transcendentalism, bred from the brother Unitarianism and the sister European idealism.[15]

Incidentally, today Boston is the hub of Swedenborgianism, with three chapels and a bookstore in the area along with a family-operated school where you can still be ordained as a minister—the only one in North America (sixteen are currently enrolled, up from two earlier in the century). Students read interpretations of Swedenborgian dreams. One of their teachers argues their hero would be a lot more famous today if he had had the foresight to leave out all the detailed spirit encounters—those angelic and demonic visions—and just stick to the philosophy (just as Mesmer should have wised up once he pulled those magnets from his pockets). Alas, he only described what he had experienced.[16]

And so, the rule-breaking spiritualistic fad of the first half of the nineteenth century emerged as an entanglement of strands from the braids of both science and religion. Very strong in both rural and urban America, it had its deep roots in unsettled Europe between the time of the French Revolution and the establishment of the industrially based nation states whose ethnic boundaries we still glimpse on today's European maps. As one aspect of occult thinking, the spiritualist movement would subside but then it would periodically rise again, for post–Civil War America was no better a place for a homogeneous Christian religion, given its class structure and racial mix.[17] Divided ideologies would give rise to alternative spiritual schools, like the Christian Science movement of Mary Baker Eddy and the Theosophical ideology of Helena Petrovna Blavatsky, not to mention later movements in the unsettled social world of the century we are about to conclude.

CHAPTER 18

"MR. SLUDGE"

Now, don't sir! Don't expose me! Just this once!
This was the first and only time, I'll swear—
Look at me,—see, I kneel,—the only time,
I swear, I ever cheated,—yes, by the soul
Of Her who hears—(your sainted mother, sir!)
All, except this last accident, was truth—
This little kind of slip!—and even this,
It was your own wine, sir, the good champagne,
(I took it for Catawba, you're so kind)
Which put the folly in my head! . . .

Why, now your face clears! I was sure it would!
Then, this one time . . . don't take your hand away,
Through yours I surely kiss your mother's hand . . .
You'll promise to forgive me?—or, at least,
Tell nobody of this? Consider, sir!
What harm can mercy do? Would but the shade
Of the venerable dead-one just vouchsafe

A rap or tip! What bit of paper's here?
Suppose we take a pencil, let her write,
Make the least sign, she urges on her child
Forgiveness? There now! Eh? Oh! 'Twas your foot,
And not a natural creak, sir?

Robert Browning, "Sludge the Medium"

W̶hile the Fox sisters were clearly two of a kind, the American
spiritualist stage was plenty large enough to accommodate
other actors and their acts—some of them very curious characters. The Foxes were controversial enough, but, as the poetic lines above
demonstrate, no occult figure of the age drew more venom than Daniel
Dunglas Home (sounds like "room") (1833–1886). The poet Robert

Browning (his sworn enemy) characterized him as "Mister Sludge"—the result of an odd set of circumstances involving the poet's own dear wife.

Home did all the things today's stage magicians do. He was an expert at elongating his body and floating through the air (Fig. 13); he "washed" his face with red-hot coals and moved furniture from a distance while tambourines shook in midair, bells tinkled, and white-gloved hands floated about waving handkerchiefs. As a medium he spoke to the departed in strange tongues and—as Browning's poem would indicate, through spirit writings. He did all of these things in a time when most people did not see magic as trickery—and, despite Browning's wishful verse, he never really got caught faking it.

Unlike most spiritualists, Home, who was born in Scotland but emigrated to the U.S. at the age of nine to live with his aunt, began to experience his visions relatively early in life. By the time he was four he claimed he could see things happening in other places. At thirteen he had a dream in which he saw a young friend circling over his bed. He thought the image to be an omen that his friend had died. He reported it to his aunt and the sign proved to be correct. By the time he was seventeen, house rapping began to accompany his prognostications. When the breakfast table began to lift, tilt, and rattle, his aunt, convinced he had delivered the Devil himself to their peaceful Connecticut doorstep, invited the boy to leave; the year was 1851 and DDH (as he is affectionately known to occult *literati*) had plenty of places to emigrate to, for the rapping fad already was in full swing.

Home's feats quickly captured the attention of the New England rationalist fringe, and, like most mediums, he was finally put to the test. When he ran a séance before a Harvard committee, William Cullen Bryant, the poet, swears he saw the table tilt and float off the floor in broad daylight despite the group's attempts to hold it down. The gentlemen crawled around under the table and took the room apart but failed to find any sign of deception. His self-elongations were equally inexplicable. One skeptic present at one of his feats says that he measured Home and found he had increased his height eleven inches.[1] The same applied for his self-levitations:

> On one occasion, while holding hands with a circle of spectators and in a trance, he floated upward until his head touched a high ceiling; they naturally had to let go. All the

TABLE TIPPING.

Fig. 13: The "Stammering" century's table tipping and levitation. Left: *Table tipping. (Anonymous, [A Searcher After the Truth],* The Rappers: or, the Mysteries Fallacies and Absurdities of Spirit Rapping, Table Tipping and Entrancement.) Right: *DDH in self-levitation. (L. Figuier,* Physical Science.)

while Home said he felt as if someone were drawing him upward as if by a belt or rope tied under his arms.

Though he was fast becoming famous at twenty-two, young Home coolly took it all in stride. He developed a flamboyant demeanor, wore lots of jewelry, and seemed to enjoy the trappings of his rich clients. He never asked directly for compensation, yet Home rarely declined to stay in their houses and savor their fine wines. And he never claimed to know the source of his magical powers. Things just happened when he was present; it was as simple as that, he said.

Home was ready to take on Europe, and he did it with a firestorm of magical prowess that attracted major attention. At Cox's Hotel in London, he lifted a table with people sitting on it, hanging off the edge himself as it tilted. Then he raised himself several feet off the ground to within a few inches of the high ceiling. He impressed Alfred Russell Wallace, cocreator with Darwin of the theory of biological evolution and a devout spiritualist, who noted that Home's feats took place in dozens of different private houses of people, all of whom could hardly be suspected of conspiring with him. Trickery, therefore, seemed out of the question, the respected scientist concluded. On the contrary, Charles Dickens, perhaps too proper a Victorian to subject himself to any of DDH's séances, called him a scoundrel.

The Browning episode began when Elizabeth Barrett Browning took a shine to DDH after he had selected her as one of the young ladies 'round the séance table to speak tender words to a spirit; the grateful ghost then crowned her head with a wreath, though her husband's jealous opposition prevented her from getting further involved with the magician.

Browning later recorded in careful detail what he experienced at this dramatic séance:

> At about 9 we were placed round a large table, as Mr. Home directed—and the results were some noises, a vibration of the table, then an up-tilting of it in various ways, and then more noises, or raps, which were distinguished as the utterance of the family's usual visitor, the spirit of their child 'Wat' who died three years ago, aged twelve. . . . Mrs. and Mr. Rymer were touched by what they recognized as the spirit of their child, and next my wife: whose dress, near the waist, I saw slightly but distinctly uplifted in a manner I cannot account for—as if by some object inside—which could hardly have been introduced there without her becoming aware of it—. The spirit then announced (by raps in answer to questions) that it would play on the accordion and show *myself* its hand. The lamp was then extinguished, and all the light permitted came from the two windows thro' their muslin curtains. A hand appeared from the edge of the table, opposite to my wife and myself; it was withdrawn, reappeared and moved about, rose and sank—it was clothed in white loose folds, like muslin, down the table's edge—from

which it never was separated—then another hand, larger, appeared, pushed a wreath, or pulled it, off the table, picked it from the ground, brought it to my wife—who had left my side for the purpose of receiving it, at Mr. Home's desire, and had taken the chair by him—and put it on her head—thence, at her request, it was carried, under the table, and given to me. I was touched several times under the table on one knee and the other—and on my hands alternately (a kind of soft and fleshy pat) but not so as that I could myself touch the object. . . . Then Mr. Home took an accordion in one hand, held it below the table, and sounds were produced and several tunes played—on it, I suppose,—but how, it is difficult to imagine—(there was light in the room for this experiment) . . . The lights being away, the first hand pulled a small bell off the table, picked it from the floor and rang it. Another hand was held up, which opened and shut the fingers, turning itself as if to be seen. I desired leave to touch it, but was refused (by the spirit). It was clothed to the *base* (for one can't say *elbow,* where form was not distinguishable beneath the muslin-like drapery) and, like the other, kept close to the table. . . . Mr. Home observed that he supposed the hand with the wreath was that of a particular relation of my wife's—raps confirmed this opinion, the alphabet was put in requisition to discover the *name*— . . . Hereupon Mr. Home went into a trance and began to address Mr. Rymer, in the character of his dead child—in a sort of whisper, at first, to represent a child's voice, but with Mr. Home's own inflexions, peculiarities, and characteristic expressions—beginning 'Dear Papa,—is not God *good,* isn't he *lovely?*' &c[sic]. As this continued, by degrees Mr. Home's natural tones were resumed, the talk affected the parents, as you might suppose.[2]

Compare this account with that of Elizabeth, who records things in a seemingly more subjective way.

We did not see quite as much as Mr. Lytton did, but we were touched by the invisible hands, heard the music and raps, saw the table moved and had sight of the hands. At the request of the medium, the spirit hands took from the table a garland which lay there and placed it upon my head. The particular hand which did this was of the largest human size, as white as snow and very beautiful. It was as near to me as this hand I write with and I saw it distinctly . . . The hands that appeared at a distance from me I put up my glass to look at—proving that it was not a mere mental impression and that they are subject to the usual laws of mental vision. These hands seemed to Robert and me to come from under the table, but Mr. Lytton saw them rise out of the *wood* of the table.[3]

Though she never touched the hands, "Mr. Lytton and Sir Edward both did. The feel was warm and human—rather warmer, in fact, than is common in a man's hand."[4]

"Everybody would be delighted to disbelieve in Home—but they can't. They hate him and believe the facts," wrote Elizabeth to her sister.[5] While she was convinced the apparitions were real, Elizabeth says she felt no real connection with the spirits; they behaved as if they belonged neither to her nor to anyone else around the table, which makes the motive for such spirit contact disinteresting if not suspicious in the eyes of critics.

Frank Podmore (1856–1910), a British natural scientist who dedicated two volumes[6] to exposing mediumistic fraud, notes that the longer the time between a happening and an account of it, the less reliable the account. Robert Browning's first description (the one quoted here), in which he seems to have professed a degree of belief, was composed forty-eight hours after the event. However, in a later testimony he reverses his opinion. The performance was clumsy, observed the poet. There must have been contrivances—flexible tubes—under Home's clothing, which, like the Fox sisters, he wore loosely. The man was a mere prestidigitator, opined the poet. To the contrary, though she disliked him as a character, Elizabeth was convinced of the efficacy of DDH's powers. And every time Browning's attractive young wife would utter Home's name, the poet would fly into a rage, swearing up and down at him, calling him a dungball. Browning's poem, published after the untimely death of Elizabeth, follows the meanderings of a fake medium who preys on the wealthy class and becomes rich and famous. It begins with the exposure of the magician by a one-time dupe, an obvious longing for the day when the imposter who had won over his wife would be exposed.

But beneath it all the poet seems to be saying there's a deep desire in all of us to be taken in, to be deceived:

> I'll go beyond: there's a real love of a lie,
> Liars find ready-made for lies they make,
> As hand for glove, or tongue for sugar-plum.[7]

"Sludge the Medium"—all 1,525 lines of it—is full of the venom of a crusading nonbeliever exploring one deceitful perpetration after another of a fictitious DDH-type character.

When DDH came to Browning's home after the death of the poet's wife looking to bury the hatchet with the man who had hounded and taunted him, the poet threatened to throw him bodily down the stairs and out of the house. Home fled to Italy where in Florence he made one Countess Orsini's piano rise in the air even as she played it. This feat had resulted from invitations issued by a number of Italian ladies of wealth to come stay with them in their villas for a while. Despite the ensuing scandal, Home still managed to acquire an audience with the Pope, at which time he converted to Catholicism. As a consequence, he says, he suffered in the loss of his magical powers for a whole year. Catholic opposition to Home's magic led to threats and one night he was attacked and beaten on the way back to his hotel. Soon he was on his way to France, where his powers miraculously returned at a séance attended by no less a dignitary than an emissary of Napoleon III. At the Tuileries he raised spirit hands that stroked the Empress Eugenie. She swore they were those of her dead father for she could feel specific arthritic defects in them. The emperor, himself an amateur occultist, listened to sonorous American tunes like "Home, Sweet Home" (a clever pun?) squeezed out on an ambient concertina,[8] as Napoleon spoke to him. DDH also gave séances for the Queen of Holland and he met the Czar of Russia, Alexander II, as he lectured and performed all across the continent—usually staying in homes of ladies of high society.

Of all Home's magical feats, probably none is more famous than the nocturnal performance he gave at Adare Manor back in London in the winter of 1868. In the presence of two witnesses and with a brandy glass in his hand, Home levitated himself, assumed a horizontal position, floated out a third story window opened twelve inches wide, then back into an adjacent room feet first via another window about seven feet away where the gentlemen stood watching. He then repeated the act, allowing the lord of the manor to follow him. One of the witnesses, Lindsay Earl of Crawford, describes the event:

> I was sitting with Mr. Home and Lord Adare and a cousin of his. During the sitting Mr. Home went into a trance, and in that state was carried out of the window in the room next to where we were, and was brought in at our window. The distance between the windows was about seven feet six inches, and there was not the slightest foothold between them, nor was there more than a twelve-inch projection to each window, which served as a ledge to put flowers on. We heard the window in the next room lifted up, and almost immediately after we saw Home floating in the air outside our window. The moon was shining full into the room; my back was to the light, and I saw the shadow on the wall of the windowsill, and Home's feet about six inches above it. He remained in this position for a few seconds, then raised the window and glided into the room feet foremost and sat down.[9]

Over the years this celebrated defenestration of December 16, 1868, has provoked endless discussion by a variety of believers and critics, from author Sir Arthur Conan Doyle and Sir William Crookes, the physicist (both were very pro-Home), to the indefatigable ghost-buster Frank Podmore and Sir William Brewster, also a physicist (they were the anti-Home contingent). Podmore found himself at a loss to explain the feat, finally retreating to a position that would become standard in the twentieth century: The witnesses had hallucinated and Home had mesmerized them. That evening both the gentlemen witnesses already had experienced a dazzling array of Homean legerdemain to soften them up: fireballs flying through the air, tongues of flame coming out of the magician's head, chirping birds, strange words babbled in foreign languages, flowers falling from the ceiling and so on. Writer Ruth Brandon suggests the magician had worked them up to a state where they would have believed just about anything.[10] Like Podmore, she thinks that fallacy of memory is a better explanation than fallacy of the senses.

A number of reputable scientists were taken with mediumistic capers like DDH's to the degree that they would at least comment upon them. Faraday himself was a critic. He believed rappings were due to an unconscious muscular movement, or so he wrote in a letter to the London Times in June 1853.[11] Some, like Sir David Brewster, the Scottish natural scientist, even studied the phenomena. Discoverer of one of the laws governing the refraction of polarized light (he also invented the kaleidoscope), Brewster certainly knew enough about optical illusions. He had written a book on natural magic in which he had reduced a number of extraordinary phenomena to the mundane via the basic laws of physics. After attending a séance, Sir David concurred with the Buffalo doctors' opinion of the Fox duo that the raps were generated in Home's anatomy. On the other hand, the equally famous Sir William Crookes was so convinced of the importance of studying the kind of prestidigitation DDH and others performed that he ruined his career.

How difficult it is for us in hindsight to penetrate the Victorian mind of a brilliant experimental scientist like Crookes—a mind in which both religion and metaphysics could not be denied a creative role. Crookes had created a device in his laboratory capable of producing a vacuum one millionth the density of Earth's atmosphere. His experiments with lightning and phosphorescent gases in his "Crooke's Tube" would ultimately make possible the discovery of X rays. It was his quest for understanding and exploring other states of matter that drew him toward the realm of the psychic.

Ever the empiricist, Crookes had started out a skeptic. He described, like a true rationalist, the tenets necessary to adopt if some of these feats were valid:

> The spiritualist tells of manifestations of power, which would be the equivalent of many thousands of 'foot-pounds' [a unit of force], taking place without known agency. The man of science, believing firmly in the conservation of force and that it is never produced without a corresponding exhaustion of something to replace it, asks for some such exhibitions of power to be manifested in his laboratory, where he can weigh, measure, and submit it to proper tests.[12]

Crookes published a long list of phenomena he had encountered. He concluded with what has been interpreted historically as a resounding endorsement of psychic phenomena when he suggested that the "experiments show the importance of further investigations."[13] Between 1870 and 1871 he wrote four articles on spiritualism in the prestigious *Quar-*

•

terly Journal of Science. But as much as Crookes held onto, looked under, and tested Home's turning tables with complex force-measuring apparati, he never could offer a natural explanation of how all of it was managed.

What seemed at odds to his colleagues was that during all of this fooling around with occult forces, Crookes was making great scientific breakthroughs in the field of thermodynamics. Did this great scientist simply possess a predilection to believe in magic and spirits, they wondered? Interestingly, like other eager believers, he had lost a twenty-one-year-old brother only two years before he took up his study of mediumistic techniques and he already had participated in spiritual séances as a means of contacting him. His peers never forgave Crookes for devoting so much of his creativity to such a worthless cause. Wrote a perplexed Charles Darwin: "I cannot dis-believe Mr. Crookes' statements, nor can I believe his results."[14]

Of all the scientific anti-magic pundits, there was no bulldog more ferocious than Frank Podmore—the Oxford-educated Perry Mason of Spiritualism. Like James "the Amazing" Randi today, Podmore was the bane of the spiritualists' existence, the scientific arch-debunker of the century. He descended upon séance after séance and by the late 1870s, helped by a number of committees, he had investigated everything from slate writing to haunted houses. Podmore's 1902 two-volume work entitled *Modern Spiritualism* gives the modern reader a sense of just how far spiritualism had spread by the end of the century and the kinds of questions and problems that surrounded it. It became the most thorough history and analysis of paranormal phenomena alleged to have been produced by the agency of both living people with extraordinary powers and by the dead—supposedly acting from another place of existence through these specially endowed mediums. Can spiritualism be justified both scientifically and religiously?, Podmore asked; and if not, how are we to explain the apparent capabilities of Home, the Foxes, and a host of others? This was Podmore's central question and he attacked it with gusto in one case study after another—from the Drummer of Tedworth to the Castle of Slawensik to Bealing's Bells and the Epworth knockings. For him the Foxes amounted to little more than "a couple of tricky little girls who had thrown about crockery and upset kitchen furniture . . . while onlookers accepted the portents as manifestation of super natural powers."[15]

Concerning the art of rap, Podmore concluded that there were dozens of methods for producing the different kinds of sounds described by reliable witnesses. For each type that he took the trouble to describe he also gave a precise analogy (i.e., a heavy stick falling, a rap with knuckles on a cloth-covered partition, a spark of transmitted electricity, or— my favorite for exactitude—"like the sound of a pheasant imprisoned in a wooden box and pecking vehemently to release itself").[16] Though it might appear that there were too many correct answers rapped out to complete strangers by any given medium to be explained by simple fraud, Podmore asked his early turn-of-the-century readers to consider the clever method of those who offered a series of possible answers until a rap gives the correct one. This gave the medium a chance to study the tone of voice movements and facial expressions of the inquisitor, thus:

> Is this person I inquire about a relative? *Yes* was at once indicated by the knocks. 'A near relative?' *Yes.* 'A man?' *No answer.* 'A woman?' *Yes.* 'A daughter? a mother? a wife?' *No answer.* 'A sister?' *Yes.* . . . 'Did she die of consumption?' naming several diseases, to which no answer was given. 'Did she die by accident?' *Yes.* 'Was she killed by lightning? Was she shot? Was she lost at sea? Did she fall from a carriage? Was she thrown from a horse?' *Yes* and so on.[17]

In seeming unbiased fashion, Podmore dismissed one incorrect scientific explanation after another—such as the idea that all mediums conduct their séances near electrical lines or that they fill their table legs with electricity from which they control explosive raps. Telepathy? It's all in the operator and trance intelligence is all in the mind. Nothing else is indicated from other living minds; the whole business is either outright fraud or fraudulently suggested hallucination.

So, where does this outburst of spiritualism that happened between Morse's telegraph and Edison's phonograph and Marconi's crystal radio fit within the shadow of history? Early twentieth-century critics such as Podmore traced it to pre-existing beliefs and viewed it as the logical successor to the alchemy and astrology of the Medieval and Renaissance Ages. They, too, advocated sympathetic relationships between mind and matter. The healing power of Paracelsus and his contemporaries was the psychological predecessor to the kind of self-help offered by contemporary clairvoyant and seer, Podmore argued. The major difference is that what once had been possessed by demons now evolved into a secular dialogue with overt occult forces. What the semi-learned believed in the

scientific behavior of their universal fluids acting through magnetic clair-
voyants, the vulgar sought in their poltergeists. All was according to fashion, he concluded.

Re-sounding Robert Browning's theme, so much about spiritualism
can be attributed to the power of suggestion in an age too filled with the
desire to be taken in. As Podmore concluded:

When the hand acts without the knowledge of the owner,
when the mouth speaks words foreign to the thoughts and character of the speaker, the inference, in an age of faith, is inevitable
that the utterance and the action are to be attributed to alien spiritual powers.[18]

CHAPTER 19

DDH TO HPB:
PIPELINES TO THE PAST

⌒

The ancients knew more concerning certain sciences than our
modern savants have yet discovered.

Helena Petrovna Blavatsky,

Isis Unveiled

Esotericism is the stuff of the so-called mystery schools, from the
Eleusinian of ancient Greece[1] to the theosophical movement of the
nineteenth century. That means the knowledge it professes is designed for and can be understood only by the adept, one who is initiated
into the domain of secret knowledge via special spiritual qualifications.

Recovering lost knowledge is really what lay behind the esoteric
movement that swept Europe and the Americas in the early nineteenth
century. What religious, philosophical, and scientific basis underlay the
occult practices of DDH, the Foxes, and others? Is there an ideology that
accords reason a valid place alongside traditional religious beliefs? Where
do new scientific discoveries such as evolution fit into religious dogma?
Among the most influential shapers of one such philosophy that attempted to deal with these questions was a colorful, charismatic Russian
immigrant woman born of radical parents—Helena Petrovna Blavatsky
(1831–1891). She founded the Theosophical Society, the branches and
publications of which played a profound role in introducing Eastern elements into the philosophy of the New Age.[2] Her efforts were part of a
major move to institutionalize occult beliefs in the name of progress.

The ancients knew more than we, Blavatsky boldly announced in
italics in the densest among a host of publications, *Isis Unveiled*—a title
appropriate to such a dictum—published in 1877. Attempting to redeem
magic from its disfavored position in the previous century, she built
theosophy (from theos = god and sophia = wisdom) on the theory that
all religion emanates from the identical roots of lost wisdom. It is based
on the practice of studying ancient secrets, now preserved in the minds

of the great Buddhist masters who reside in the remote regions of Tibet and India, in order to discover truth and spiritual identity.

Long ago and far away—why would a radical liberal in the great century of progress look outward and backward for answers to inward-directed questions? To entertain that question we need to know who Helena Blavatsky (known as HPB to aficionados of magic) was and how this enigmatic, mysterious woman acquired a way of looking at the world that seemed incongruent with the times, yet constituted a serious attempt at a spiritual synthesis that crossed many cultural lines.

Described as fiery, temperamental, and stubborn, Helena claimed psychic powers early on—voices emanating from organic and inorganic objects, including all the stuffed animals in her grandfather's private museum. She married out of spite against her guardian, she says, and separated in three months of her seventeenth year (all that seems to have survived the much older Mr. Blavatsky is the name he gave her) and spent the rest of that year and the next traveling around the world. Among her prolific activities during this period were stints as a concert pianist, a bareback rider in a Turkish circus, a businesswoman in Odessa, and—what was to play a profound role in her ultimate mission in life once she hit the Port of New York in 1873—initiation into the occult aspects of the spiritual lore of Tibet. From that time on the so-called Masters became the invisible mentors who willingly communicated to her the secrets of ancient esoteric knowledge at a distance (all this while she levitated her way across East Coast society, demonstrating her abilities at clairvoyance, clairsentience, and clairaudience to any audience she could muster).

HPB's cosmic convergence came in rural Vermont when, while observing the spiritualistic feats of the best of the local levitators, the Brothers Eddy, she ran into the lawyer-journalist Henry Steel Olcott (1832–1907). This rather proper, bushy-bearded middle class gent was intrigued by the exotic foreign pilgrim. Of her he wrote with fascination:

> H.P.B. had one trait of character that has made her memory so precious to most of her former colleagues—winsomeness. She might drive you almost mad with her sayings and doings, might make you feel ready to run as far away from her as possible, yet when she changed from one extreme to the other in her treatment of you, as she would in a flash, and looked and spoke to you with a sort of childlike

blandness, your anger would vanish and you would love her in spite of herself. . . .

One never knew at what moment she might do some wonderful feat of magic. . . . Association with her was a continual excitement, and the most sluggish temperament was roused into some show of activity. She was truly a great woman—to confound, if we may, the carcass with its indwelling entity, which seemed to me as far removed as possible from the ideal of the gentler sex.[3]

In the flesh the two did make quite a pair (Fig. 14), she short and squat, the penetrating gaze of her Slavic countenance protruding from a babushka, he tall and lanky with thick-lensed wire-rims balanced on an aquiline nose at the upper end of a monstrous square beard wider than her entire face. Their life together became an intellectual—he says never romantic—odyssey dedicated to disseminating through writings, colloquia, lectures, and parties at their 47th Street New York apartment attended by every category of imaginable Bohemian, their knowledge of the invisible forces that really made the world go around.

By 1875 the two would formalize the whole business into the Theosophical Society, a philosophic-religious organization dedicated to form-

Fig. 14: "The Odd Couple": H. P. Blavatsky and H. S. Olcott, the founders of the Theosophical Society. Lately she has been heralded as the "Mother of the New Age" (H. Olcott, Old Diary Leaves, The History of the Theosophical Society.)

•

ing a universal brotherhood of men, studying ancient religions, philosophies, and sciences and to investigating the unexplained laws of nature
and human psychic powers hidden within us.[4] They equipped themselves with the full weight of an administration, as was the Victorian custom. HPB, as the Recording Secretary of the Society, says she was
instructed to make the move at the suggestion of one of her Masters'
voices. The liberal social objective of the Theosophical Society was to
promote universal brotherhood without regard to race, creed, sex, or na-
tionality. But its charter also announced that it was an organization dedicated to the study of science, religion, and Eastern philosophical wisdom
all for the purpose of disclosing that set of laws that governed both nature and humanity and—the most controversial goal—the exploration of
the psychical powers latent in man.[5]

The two-volume *Isis Unveiled* was the great manifesto of the organization. It was said to have been written under the influence of spirits
who held Kabbalistic and Gnostic teachings in ancient books before her
very eyes while Helena smoked hashish and wrote them down. Full of
invective against straitlaced science's refusal to pay attention to spiritualist phenomena, anecdotal attempts to expose phony magic (HPB de-
spised the mediums),[6] and harsh criticism of the Christian faith, the book
became an instant bestseller, attracting a wide variety of dissidents from
the conventional approaches to the meaning of the real world. As one
commentator pointed out, the underlying theme of the book (and the
society) is the great nineteenth-century monomyth: that individual consciousness and matter in the universe are conjoined by an invisible ener-
gizing spirit in an all encompassing evolutionary scheme.[7] Generically
speaking, the impact of this alternative view of reality is now firmly implanted in the Western outlook, but vital subtleties of detail differ from
those professed by the scientific establishment.

That the concept of evolution might be incorporated in HPB's secret
doctrine should come as no surprise. Darwin's *On the Origin of Species by
Means of Natural Selection* was published in 1859 when HPB was only in
her late twenties. Unlike Darwin, HPB believed in evolution with a purpose. For her it was a designed growth process, not a fortuitous selection
process. Consciousness, she believed, grew as life passed upward through
progressive levels of existence from mineral to plant to animal to superhuman. A purposive cosmology can be very appealing, for it instills hope
in humanity through human participation in universal change. In *Isis* she
explains the progression of races: First came an invisible race made of fire

and mist that inhabited the polar region. Second were a red people who lived in northern Asia; they invented sexual intercourse. Then came the unreasoning ape people of the appropriately named lost continent of Lemuria. Next were the Atlanteans, who were done in by black magic. We are the fifth race—also doomed to destruction—but we will be followed by a sixth, even a seventh race on Earth, before our progenitors depart to the planet Mercury where we will take up yet another life cycle in the great hierarchy of being. With each evolutionary step we become increasingly spiritual—pulled forward in time toward the infinite, eternal deity. In effect, Blavatsky replaced the out-of-step transcendent God of the Old Testament with an immanent one who was in step with creation and evolution by natural means. Hers was a god in tune with science.

Other cultures from around the world share with the esoteric doctrine of theosophy a likeness in progress through human participation (see sidebar). HPB's basic argument is that while things may look rough, we can extricate ourselves from this deterministic evolutionary mess. We can become godlike—even change the course of events—by seeking true wisdom. She was impressed by a common thread in all myths of this sort. But what most historians view as parallels in the past she saw as designs for the future.

Today, anthropologists are inclined to explain parallels among world creation myths as part of the way most people think about renewable cycles of time—the same properties we observe in all biorythmic cycles. Day and night, the seasons, the phases of the Moon all work that way. They provide us with a story line and a temporal beat for expressing things past. We keep the heroic past of our gods alive by sharing and retelling these myths. In HPB's eyes the pipeline that channels present to past was direct and tangible; it was made of the concrete imagery of revealed truth. We must work at rediscovering lost meaning from the past through gifted seers like herself, for revelation is the only true way to knowledge. HPB argued that bits and pieces of the truth are all there to be rediscovered in ancient belief systems, but the connections are subtler than we have made them out to be. For example, Jesus knew about Buddhism, and the Chaldeans, Egyptians, and ancient Norsemen all conceived of the identical primal substance out of which the universe was made. We are not talking about abstract cosmic archetypes or human traits common to all, but the same universal truths down to the last detail passed on from seer to seer across the ages.

There is a ring of familiarity in this age-old cyclic myth of origin. We find the same storyline in creation mythologies as disparate as those of the Aztecs' *Legend of the Suns* (fifteenth century A.D.), the *Theogony* (eighth-century B.C. Greek), and the Babylonian *Enuma Elish* from 2000 B.C., to name just a few of the classics.★ The Aztec creation story carved in the great Sun Stone, one of ancient Mexico's most famous artifacts, pictures this repetitive dynamic story line: In the first creation, people were giants who dwelt in caves. But because they did not till the soil as expected, the gods destroyed them by sending jaguars to eat them. In the second creation, another imperfect race was blown away by the wind. Then the gods created apes that they might cling better to this world with their gripping appendages, but not well enough, and so they were destroyed by a rain of fire. Some of the survivors were changed into birds to enable them to escape the encroaching, death-dealing lava from erupting volcanoes. A flood did away with the fourth era; but the Aztecs, the myth goes on, live in the fifth age and it is up to them to keep the world going by spreading the word about the importance of making blood sacrifice to the sun god in order to keep him on his course, to keep the world in motion.

The Inca creation story is not so different. There were three previous creation cycles, each following a catastrophe in which "people" were successively turned to stone, inundated by water, and burned by fire, each creation having been connected with a protagonist god in a cosmic struggle. In the fourth age, the Inca are responsible for the destiny of the world and it is only through proper human action—through the sacrifices they make to their ancestors who still live, though in altered form in the body of mountain-mother earth—that the human race can remain in existence.

★ See, e.g. my *Empires of Time* for details on these and other stories.

Blavatsky's "monomyth" on the cyclic course of evolution of all the civilizations of the world had its parallel in science with the "monosubstance." This "astral substance," as it is termed (like the *alkahest* of alchemy), is a kind of stuff more ethereal than matter and energy that *invites* all things, she explains. It lies within every atom and it is the key to the gates of the biological unknown we today call embryology.[8]

HPB was quite in tune with her times. Indeed, eighteenth- and nineteenth-century physics was consumed with the search for ultimate hidden substances. The "luminiferous ether" was once thought to pervade the universe, thus making possible the transmission of electromagnetic energy across vast distances. Phlogiston—an inflammable substance—was conjured up in the minds of late-seventeenth-century physicists to account for the way things burn. It escaped to the domain of fire, thus causing all combustible reactions.[9] In the twentieth century, the search for the monosubstance has been replaced largely by the search for process. The ether has given way to the theory of transmission of energy across vacuous space and the combustion process witnessed in the lab is now explained by the chemical union of hydrogen and oxygen.[10]

HPB's account was one of many indictments of Darwin's theory of evolution by natural selection and we can understand the moral and social stresses that led to it. Imagine how frightening the implication of Darwin's determinism must have sounded to the progressive optimists who first heard about it. We are all but bystanders in a history of the universe that dictates that the survival of only *species*—not individuals—is governed by natural law. And even then the adaptive advantage that must be acquired to ensure survival comes about only by accident. HPB simply opted for a series of evolutionary rebirths that could be experienced at the individual level—births the Masters of the mystery schools knew about and from whom we must learn it all to save the world.

These unknown theosophical laws are not supernatural. They are as natural as gravity and magnetism and can be theorized like a scientific hypothesis. For example, on thought transference, Olcott speculated:

> . . . as the evolution of a thought is accompanied by a sort of galvanic discharge from the grey matter of the brain, and as this vibration passed beyond the periphery of the brain into the ether, and no one can say how far it may extend, it is conceivable that the evolution of thought in a human brain may affect a distant planet.[11]

I find it curious that despite the relentless diatribes against science in *Isis Unveiled* and other books, HPB curiously endows the heroes of mythology with scientific knowledge essentially in the same form as we know it through contemporary scientific experimentation. Why did

Thor need to put on his iron gauntlets when he grasped the handle of his thunderbolt hammer and why did he wear an iron belt (a closed electrical circuit?) and drive a chariot with a long iron pole (a lightning rod?) in it? ". . . how can this myth be interpreted but as showing that the Norse legend-makers were thoroughly acquainted with electricity?"[12] she asks. And on death, there is this scientific and materialist–sounding opinion, its syntax borrowed from physics:

> If death is but the stoppage of a digesting, locomotive and thought grinding machine, how can death be actual and not relative, before that machine is thoroughly broken up and its particles dispersed? So long as any of them cling together, the centripetal vital force may overmatch the dispersive centrifugal action.[13]

By 1884, HPB's individual fame was reaching a crescendo, thanks to the immensely popular *Isis*. Followers would range from Gandhi to Tennyson to Edison. (One purpose of the early phonograph was to speak to the spirit world.) But like every occult figure whose life I have traced, HPB rode the rapid roller coaster to a sudden downfall. The woman who would undo her was a Mrs. Coulomb. She and her one-eyed husband, a French missionary, had heard of HPB's exploits and the Theosophical Society and they had traveled all the way to Bombay, where Blavatsky was demonstrating her occult powers, to become her friends and ultimately her housekeepers. After a few years, admiration turned to hatred, especially after the diviner discovered the couple had been stealing from her. Divisive and jealous by nature, Mrs. C. decided, in retaliation, to expose Blavatsky as a fraud to a missionary magazine editor. The evidence included a disclosure of letters and eyewitness reports of fakery and madness. For example, once she allegedly made a papier-mâché dummy of her Master and paraded around in the garden with it perched on her shoulders on moonlit nights. The story made the London *Times,* whereupon the Society for Psychical Research duly dispatched an investigator, a Mr. Hodgson, to Madras to check it all out. He claimed to have discovered secret panels in HPB's boudoir and his detailed report concluded that the Madam was indeed a fraud. Her supporters countered that the Coulombs had planted the incriminatory evidence. Among Blavatsk-o-philes the piece is still regarded as controversial, even as recently as 1993.[14]

These misfortunes struck at an inopportune time. Already in her mid-fifties, Helena had begun to acquire a number of maladies (heart disease, gout, and rheumatism among them) exacerbated by her now obese condition. Carrying on the inevitable court proceedings that emanated from the accusations proved difficult. Still, another massive tome, *The Secret Doctrine* would follow in 1888 and two more in 1889. In these last books she struggled in vain to reunite the Gnostic ideas she felt Renaissance thinking regrettably had taken apart. She explored in further detail a nebulous scheme of evolution of humanity (anthropogenesis), which she suggested was related to cosmogenesis (the evolution of the universe). The same law of cycles that explains what happens in the universe governs what happens to us as well. All our souls—under the guidance of the Universal Oversoul—pass up a ladder of progress through degrees of intelligence via reincarnation.

Exhausted and weary, HPB died at age sixty in 1891. But other liberal intellectuals carry on the work of theosophy even to this day, when it seems to have undergone a rebirth. The Society now boasts thirty-five thousand members in thirty-seven countries.[15] *Sunrise,* a magazine on theosophic perspectives issued bimonthly, is currently in its forty-second volume. The Theosophical Press, based in Pasadena, carries a long list of titles including reprinted editions of eight of HPB's own works. In a recent issue appears a lengthy review of yet another biography[16] (there are eighteen others!) on this energetic rogue of a woman. Perhaps somewhat blinded by HPB's enduring charisma, it suggests that her influence on a new generation of New Age admirers is equal in intensity to that of her followers long ago when she was still alive.

In the shadow of nineteenth-century intellectual history, Helena Petrovna Blavatsky emerges as one of many spirit seekers who followed in the footsteps of Neoplatonists like Plotinus and Proclus and of Kabbalists and alchemists like Paracelsus and Agrippa. All have persisted in being reborn in the Middle Ages, the Renaissance, and every time the philosophy of looking backward toward what was perceived as better times intellectually and spiritually comes *en vogue.* They achieved popularity in the Victorian Age because they circumvented Christianity's bureaucratic layer of mediators from pastor to pope and the taboo official religion laid upon direct mystical experience. Their brand of spiritualism was simple and open to all. As members of a late twentieth-century existential society, it is difficult for us to imagine how pervasive this idealism had become a hundred or more years ago and to sense how ready were these idealists of the human spirit to lump mechanistic science, new technology, and crass materialism into a single conceptual basket and fight a war against it. They pictured themselves as social reformers.

Only in the last generation have scholars begun to realize that the study of the occult is a valid inquiry in the field of United States history.[17] Realizing its impact, a modern critic speaks of "the spiritualism" craze, from which we are not yet recovered.[18] Ideas about spiritualism and evolution were destined to fuse together in occult doctrines like theosophy in the hands of feisty extremists like HPB. She and others paved the interstate highway of the occult. They crafted spiritualism in more dilute form to respectable romantic intellects of the day like Coleridge and Hegel. These deep thinkers truly imagined themselves to be waging a war against diabolical social forces that sought to destroy what was left of the human spirit. Like today's *Chariots of the Gods* and Shirley MacLaine's stories of reincarnation, these optimistic crusaders against the Darth Vaders of the deterministic establishment made a far heavier impact on the public than they did in elite academic circles. Having taught science for thirty-three years, I too come to the conclusion that most ordinary people possess a deep desire for old traditions to win out. Except for today's extreme rationalist, we seem to accept that everything need not require a factual explanation.

CHAPTER 20

AFTER THE FOXES:
FROM PARLOR TO STAGE

On my expressing a wish, the medium parted her thighs, and I
saw that the material assumed a curious shape, resembling an
orchid, decreased slowly and entered the vagina. During the
whole process I held her hands. Eva then said, 'Wait, we will try
to facilitate the passage.' She rose, mounted on the chair, and sat
down on one of the arm-rests, her feet touching the seat. Before my eyes, and with the curtain open, a large spherical mass,
about 8 inches in diameter, emerged from the vagina and
quickly placed itself on her left thigh while she crossed her
legs. I distinctly recognized in the mass a still unfinished face,
whose eyes looked at me. As I bent forward in order to see better, the head-like structure rose before my eyes, and suddenly
vanished into the dark of the cabinet away from the medium,
disappearing from my view.

Slater Brown, *The Heyday of Spiritualism*

So many curious characters rode the rapids in the stream of occult
revival during the great century of the adept. In this section I have
chosen to focus on the lives of only a few—those who were the
most influential and who best exemplify the continuity and change in
beliefs and practices derived from their predecessors and modified to best
fit contemporary thought. Before passing on to the world of magic we
know today, let me touch briefly on the few extremists who were not
taken seriously even in their day. Why do so? Because, unlike the middle,
the late nineteenth century experienced a glut of phony mediums followed by fraudulent experimenters, all of which culminated during
those first few decades of the twentieth century in a great debate about
the physical reality of occult phenomena. Now the religious side of the
issue, along with an interest in talking to the dead, began to fade away. I
think we can better understand the separation between pretense and true
belief imparted on the one hand by stage magicians and conjurors like
David Copperfield, the Amazing Randi, and Houdini, and on the other

hand by crystallists, numerologists, and channelers, whose influence on a wide section of the public is well-established and growing even as we creep up on the millennium (I will deal with the latter characters in the next section).

After the Foxes, spirit rooms became Coney Island–style attractions starring apparitions from a real world beyond the here and now. For example, the Koonses' Spirit Room, located in a remote section of Eastern Ohio, featured luminous armless hands—cold to the touch—that wrote out messages from the beyond on glow-in-the-dark paper. At the other end of the same town, Tippie's Spirit Room specialized in musical performances by spirits.

The Davenport brothers of Buffalo, New York, were the first successful stage mediums. Their feats were so celebrated that they rented a hall and charged admission. Though they were Houdini's forerunners, their intent was still more or less to affect and influence a somewhat believing public.

The Davenports' *piéce de resistance* was the cabinet séance. According to a witness at one of their New York performances, the boys' wrists and legs were tied tightly. They were trussed, bound to a bench, and placed in a cabinet. As the lights dimmed, the hall fell into silence. Within a minute the door popped open and out walked one brother completely free, ropes in hand, every knot untied. The second brother's ropes remained intact, the door again was closed, and a minute later he had duplicated his brother's feat. But there was more to come. Both siblings reentered the cabinet and sat on their benches, the unknotted ropes lying between them. The doors were shut, the lights dimmed again—then silence for one or two minutes. An assistant opened the cabinet door and *voilá!,* they had run the gamut in reverse: There sat the Davenport duo tied just as tightly as they had been at the start of the act. Next, musical instruments, including a guitar and tambourine, were placed in the cabinet and the doors once again shut. Seconds later music was heard. Suddenly the cabinet doors were kicked open from the inside, the instruments tumbled out onto the stage, and there sat the brothers, still tied up. They even went so far as to put a witness into the box while the act was taking place. He reported feeling fingers passing all over his body, untying his cravat, and tapping him on the cheek with the tambourine subject to the boys' commands: "Will the spirit strike the stranger with the instrument gently on the head"?, "Will the violin play?", etc.[1] Combining magical entertainment with spiritualist philosophy, a lecturer later joined the fraternal act. He would expound on the vicissitudes of supramundane phenomena, explaining that what the audience saw was proof that there truly is life beyond death.

Harry Houdini, the most famous escape artist of the twentieth century, would learn this act very well. Escaping from a container while bound in ropes and chains, submerged in water, or hanging from a crane, would make him a very rich and famous man. Houdini knew the Davenports and even credited them with the idea for this particular trick. But the great prestidigitator, a decided nonbeliever in spiritualism who made a side career out of debunking magicians for their flummery, also stated that in old age one of the brothers had confessed to him that the whole act was indeed a hoax and he even told Houdini how the secret rope tie was managed so that the brothers could free themselves to play the violin in the darkened cabinet. Harry never revealed the secret.

As spirit demonstrators marched across the land (there were even séances in the Lincoln White House) with an increasing retinue of ever-larger committees of doctors, scientists, and psychologists, something very odd happened: The spirits began to communicate with the real world via unexpectedly sophisticated techniques. Kate and Maggie's rapping and tapping first gave way to more complex audio phenomena—those bells, tambourines, and guitars, and to such visual imagery as luminous hands, top hats, and floating umbrellas. By the 1870s phantoms endowed with extra arms and legs began to appear at séances along with yet another universal spirit substance—ectoplasm. Just as the Devil is the embodiment of evil in human form, ectoplasm is the tangible emanation come to us from the spirit world. Much to the horror of the true Victorian mind, this gooey stuff, described at the head of this chapter, began to emanate from every conceivable mediumistic orifice.

Eusapia Palladino, first to gush forth the weird substance, was a Neapolitan who "apported" (materialized out of thin air) everything from furniture to dead rats, all over the world. She dominated the spiritualist scene from 1870 to 1890 just as DDH had done the generation before—all this despite the fact that she was caught cheating on several occasions. Eusapia's appeal was overtly sexual. She seems to have been the first to produce a third arm from beneath her dress. One investigative committee explained that her menstrual secretions increased when she went into a trance and that she possessed a zone of hyperaesthesia about the ovaries. As a result she experienced erotic sensations—even orgasm as the phenomena she called up began to materialize. Like DDH, whose materializations we recall interested no less a distinguished scientist than Sir William Crookes, Eusapia attracted orthodox scientists including Cesare Lombroso (the Italian founder of criminology), British engineer William Crawford, and the French Nobel Laureate physiologist Charles-Robert Richet (who established an Institute for Metaphysics in Paris). All of them carried out investigations in search of scientific explanations of Eusapia's phenomena.

Richet is responsible for having named ectoplasm as that substance out of which mediums construct materializations from the spirit world.[2] The spiritual "helping hand" made its first appearance in 1894 during an investigative session at Richet's country cottage on the island of Hyères off the south coast of France. Among those present, British physicist Oliver Lodge wrote that there were definite protuberances, "pseudopods," that issued from various parts of Eusapia's clothing. These artifices performed the same function as hands—pushing, pulling, squeezing—but they looked very unreal. As far as the physics of their movement was concerned, Lodge said, everything was in accord with the laws that govern matter. The abnormality of this substance, he declared (perhaps with a sigh of relief), clearly belonged in the realm of physiology and human anatomy, not physics. Richet, who says he was disinclined to believe in forms that circulate blood, have warmth, speak, think, and can issue from a person's body, nonetheless wrote that "C'est absolument absurde, mais c'est vrai"—"strange but true"![3] The pair didn't just *want* to believe. They were true converts.

Even more tabloid-oriented were the ectoplasmic excreta of the mysterious Eva Carrière, a.k.a. Eva C., who titillated thousands just after the turn of the century. Her forte consisted of materializing phantoms, faces, and figures out of thin air in a darkened room; she later specialized in excrescences of the type mentioned above. Clad in a tight leotard beneath overalls, she would sit in a black, felt-lined partitioned section of a séance room. Could she have hidden rolled gauze and string cords in her private parts beneath her leotard that she could pull, expand, and manipulate?, skeptics inquired. To counteract such legerdemain her entire body would need to be fingered through the clothing by the examiners. Surprisingly, neither she nor Eusapia offered the slightest objection to being examined by the male investigators—all in the interest of science.

Lights dimmed, curtains closed, Eva C. would then go into a trance. With the onlookers singing mystical music and crying out to cheer on the medium, the excitement would build for an hour or more. When the curtains finally opened an incredible sight would reveal itself to the gasping throng. Gobs of gooey plasma variously described as luminous smoke, veiled substance, and a "flocculent mass"[4] were seen emerging from her nostrils, mouth, and leaking out her shoetops—a telltale clue for emission from her private parts. Totally uninhibited Eva would gasp, groan, and writhe, suggesting a combination of birth pain and sexual delight as she produced the visible "spirit stuff" itself. Eva's ectoplasm would take on various recognizable shapes, then it would seem either to withdraw mysteriously back into her body or float some distance away before it vanished into thin air. Because light damaged this delicate substance her séance room always was dimly lit, but at the end of a performance Eva would boldly turn on the lights and throw off her tights, demanding a physical examination for proof of her supernatural skills.

Harry Houdini and associates weren't sure of what they witnessed at an Eva C. séance:

> I saw distinctly that it was a heavy froth [coming from her nose] and was adhering to her veil on the inside. Dingwall, who sat next to the medium, agreed with me it had emanated from her mouth, but when she leaned forward it looked as though it was coming from her nose. She produced a white plaster and eventually managed to juggle it over her eye. There was a face in it which looked to me like a colored cartoon and seemed to have been unrolled.[5]

Attempts to employ the nascent science of photography to record this bizarre imagery (Fig. 15) today seem comical, yet the relatively new craft was regarded by many as having produced serious evidence at the time. Conjectured one believer in ectoplasm (in quasi-scientific terms):

> Could this mediumistic energy be one of the many new forces in the ever-widening boundaries of modern physics? It appears to have a polarity, for there are persons whose actions neutralize each other. . . .[6]

This was indeed a part of science.

As the career of Eva and her colleagues developed, the ectoplasmic forms began to assume ever more definable and detailed facial characteristics. One whole phantom named "Dorsmica" was described as hav-

Fig. 15: Spaghetti-faced spiritualist. This medium may have lost control over the great beyond when she emitted excess ectoplasm in a séance. For nearly thirty years the whitish manifestation of the spirit world oozed its way out of every mediumistic orifice. (Baron von Schrenck-Notzing, Phenomena of Materialisation.)

ing "an elegant moustache and beard, wearing what looked like a white lab coat over a shirt and tie."[7] Photos reveal a decidedly two-dimensional figure. With such concrete images some thought Eva had gone too far. She was accused of fraud by a woman who discovered pictures in a popular newspaper that bore a distinct resemblance to Eva C.'s phantom. Clearly the medium had doctored the pictures by adding beards, curls, and enhancing a forehead here or there, wrote her accuser in a popular magazine article. (Among the ectoplasmic subjects to issue from her spiritual conduit were President Woodrow Wilson and the King of Bulgaria!)

Fakery? Not possible, retorted believers such as engineer Crawford. The phenomena were real. Bestowing the language of science upon Eva's phantom spirits, he called them "ideoplasts": "ephemeral, externalized, precipitates of the medium's psychic impressions and reminiscences."[8] And so the accusations and rationalizations continued. Houdini was certain that Eva C. regurgitated the ectoplasm—chiffon gauze on which images were painted, carefully folded and then swallowed. She also may have hidden materials in the hollowed out part of her hair-comb, or for that matter in any other part of the cabinet that could cleverly escape detection. In any case:". . . There is no way the Great Almighty will allow emanations from a human body of such horrible revolting viscous sub-stances . . ." opined the great illusionist.[9]

Ectoplasm was still around in the 1920s, by which time it had reached the category of the absurd and became more a thing of showplace than serious séance parlor. But while extroverts like Eva and Eusapia stretched the limits of public imagination and the credibility of romantic spiritu-alism, another occult extremist was seeking to refashion the lost art of conjuring up the Devil. He was the Beast Himself, the Master Therion—called the "wickedest man in the world" by the attentive media; he spelled magic with a "ck" to distinguish it from the show business arti-cle. The British magus, Aleister Crowley (1875–1947),[10] is the last of the Romantic period characters I want to profile—and a late one at that—as a way of exploring the odd twists and turns the world of the occult took late in the voice-filled "Stammering Century."[11]

A brief review of Crowley's life will clearly establish the origin of those Dracula-like characters who have adorned Hollywood films since the turn of the century. Son of a wealthy British brewer (of Crowley's Ales) turned preacher, the young Edward Alexander Crowley was an attention-getting rebel and an exhibitionist who says he made his first sexual seduction at fourteen and nearly killed himself when exploding his own homemade ten-pound bomb at fifteen. (It left him unconscious for four days.) "My limbs possess a consciousness of their own which is infallible" and "My sexual life was very intense . . . a challenge to Chris-tianity"[12] he would proclaim as he immersed himself, while still a teenager, in translations of the *Zohar* and other books on ceremonial magic published by the Hermetic Order of the Golden Dawn, a society which he would later join and fight to control.

It took very special creative powers to apply the formulae that acti-vated communication between mind and matter, Crowley contended—powers he was absolutely sure he possessed. And he would apply them the way an artist creates a painting, both spontaneously and subcon-sciously. Wealthy sportsman and vain playboy, as he traveled around the world he would develop his power of concentration by sitting in front of a mirror trying to make his image disappear. Or he would go out, pick up a local prostitute, and employ his sadistic sexual powers of magic on her. He even filed his teeth so as to draw blood from the lips and throat of victims with each "serpent's kiss."

The occult fraternity Crowley had presided over was founded in the 1880s. Unlike HPB's Theosophical Society, the source of Golden Dawn's wisdom was the ancient Middle East—Egypt rather than Tibet. It was said to be based on an alleged ancient document on the Kabbalah and the Tarot. Whoever deciphers it shall be in care of its knowledge, the legend went. The members of a Rosicrucian[13] order, who claimed to have accomplished the feat, thus founded a sub-branch of that secret society. Like the larger parent organization, which had been around since the Protestant Reformation, it was dedicated to the ideal that a select brotherhood of adepts would reform the entire world by perfecting both self and nature as illuminated through secret doctrines passed down through the ages. Like Rosicrucians and later Masonic orders, the Golden Dawners had their own temple, a complex set of rites, and an initiation. Members could elevate themselves hierarchically up a kind of *sephirot* tree of life toward self-perfection as they penetrated ever more deeply into the repository of secret works possessed by the temple. (The great poet William Butler Yeats was a member.) Fraternal orders such as the Elks, the Odd Fellows, and the Greek letter fraternities (and now sororities) in our universities are the last remaining vestiges of such social bonding organizations, though their goals and membership qualifications—often still held secret—have been modified considerably to suit the times.

In Crowley's day, Golden Dawn as a Rosicrucian outgrowth had about one hundred members spread over several lodges bound by the celebration of secret rites. Members of the club would practice the Kabbalah, learn how to set up magic circles, and make use of magical technology like talismans and amulets. Their autocratic leader was the charismatic Samuel Liddell (MacGregor) Mathers. He claimed to be in touch with secret chiefs who communed with him on the astral plane, clairaudiently divulging piecemeal all the secrets of ancient magic in the Western tradition.

An early confidant of Mathers, Crowley was sent by him to head the London lodge. But the eccentric was too much for Yeats, who recorded what happened upon Crowley's arrival:

> This person 'seized' the rooms and on being ejected attempted to take possession wearing [a] black mask and in full Highland costume and with a gilt dagger at his side. Having failed in this he has taken out a summons on the ground that he is Mathers' 'envoy', and that there is nothing in the constitution of the Society enabling us to depose Mathers.[14]

While all this brotherly philosophy about making the world a better place sounds very humanitarian, Crowley seemed more interested in the discipline's potential to turn man into a godlike creature. He would swish around in black robes often hooded and penetrated only by eye slits as he developed his powerful formulae to invoke the Devil.[15] He would practice drawing the protective circle about himself, scenting it with cinnamon, myrrh, aromatic roots, and oils. Sacrificing and drawing blood from three pigeons at the apices of a triangle drawn within the circle, he would utter a conjuration from the *grimoires*.[16]

One of Crowley's disciples describes what happened when he and the Master uttered such a chant in the middle of the Moroccan desert as they attempted to exhort a mighty demon named Choronzon. He (Crowley) looked into a crystal of topaz to perceive the embedded image of the demon which would talk back to him: "I have made every living thing my concubine. . . . From me come leprosy and pox and plagues. . . ." Then, to open the gates of hell, Crowley babbled the words: "Zazas, Zazas, Nosatanada, Zazas."

> . . . Suddenly there was a loud, wild laugh and Choronzon appeared visibly in the triangle [in place of Crowley]. He heaped flattery on [me] and asked permission to come and put his head under [my] feet to adore and serve me. [I] recognized this as another ruse, an attempt to get into the circle, and refused. Choronzon [who was now in the shape of Crowley but naked] begged for water to quench his thirst. [I] again refused, commanding the demon to obey him by the Names of God and by the Pentagram. Choronzon was not in the least subdued by this and . . . becoming increasingly frightened, I threatened him with anger and pain and the torments of hell. But Choronzon answered magnificently, in the manner of Marlowe's Mephistopheles. 'Thinkest thou, O fool, that there is any anger and any pain that I am not, or any hell but this my spirit?'
>
> The demon broke into a torrent of furious and obscene blasphemies. [I] was frantically trying to write down all Choronzon's words and while his attention was distracted Choronzon craftily threw sand from the triangle on to the line of the circle, broke it and sprang into the circle.[17]

A battle between assistant and demon then ensued in which the sharp-fanged one attempted to tear at the disciple's throat; but the young mortal managed to subdue the Evil One with a magic knife. Suddenly Choronzon retreated into the circle and metamorphosed into a beautiful woman who tried to seduce the assistant—all in vain. By this time the pigeon's blood had dried up in the hot desert sand and the diabolical imagery consequently faded away. During the whole proceeding Crowley indicated that he did not participate. He claims only to have witnessed the Devil in the face of a woman, a snake, a wise man, and so on.

Today—to some degree even then—we might attribute such madness to "impression management" (hallucinations self-induced in the extreme emotional state in which the magician finds himself after employing stimulants, sleep deprivation, hypnotism, and other tactics to get high). We know Crowley was hooked on mescaline. But as in the case of miracles, for those who experience one, the phenomenon is real and it exists independent of a magician, at least in most cases. Proponents of magical conjuration argue that the state of extreme intoxication does not *cause* what takes place. It is necessary to *allow* it to take place even if it comes from within the magician—for the spirit, not being part of the ordinary world, cannot be experienced through the state of mind through which we sense everyday things. Does reality consist only of what we perceive in normal conditions of life? And is what we see, feel, and hear in any other conceivable state of mind unreal? As we have discovered, wise people like Plato who have thought a lot about it would offer a very different answer than the modern world to this vexing question.

So what happened to "the Devil Himself"? Like Mathers, Crowley predictably got kicked out of the Golden Dawn for being too eccentric, ambitious, and power-hungry. He experimented further with drugs—heroin, opium, hashish, cocaine—as a way of inducing religious ecstasy. Once he rented a hall and charged admission to those who might care to witness him in a series of seven successive weekly rituals in which he got higher and higher. The more extreme his actions became the more he opened himself to attack; for example, he was accused by the Golden Dawners of divulging one of their top secrets, namely that sex could be used for magical purposes[18] and of practicing sex magic with a companion of Isadora Duncan at a secret location in Italy along with onstage sodomy.

When he came briefly to America, the Devil Himself conjured up a little cult of his own in lower Manhattan. He roused attention when he spent forty days and nights painting his "Do What Thou Wilt . . ." motto in immense red letters on the high cliffs up the Hudson River. But his life became pathetic, like that of so many fallen masters of the occult.[19] Restless and in a weakened condition from the excessive consumption of drugs and alcohol, Crowley acquired a series of respiratory ailments which his return to the damp climate of England did little to improve. From there he darted about—to Tunis, Paris, and Italy—rebounding each time back to London worn out. Consuming a bottle of gin a day, that he even lasted until 1947 is magic in itself, a testimony to his strength and willpower. Aleister Crowley was surely an adept who symbolized perhaps the most bizarre, socially unwelcome aspect of the occult, a forerunner to the handful of serious cults of the Devil today.

CHAPTER 21

MY BODY, MY MAP:
"BUMPOLOGY"

Phrenology . . . reduces the mind to the mere accidental shape
of the head. All the phrenologists ought to be avoided as a mortal pestilence. Their secret purpose is to subvert all mortals—all
free agency and volition. They reduce man to a mere machine—and woman to a silly toy. . . .

Anonymous source quoted in John D. Davies,
Phrenology: Fad and Science;
A Nineteenth-Century American Crusade

It may seem a long way from Crowley to craniometry, but the range
of extremes plumbed in nineteenth-century occult beliefs cannot
be fully spanned without charting the other end of the spectrum of
beliefs, which is positioned about as far from Devil conjuration as you
can get, and close enough to science to have attained quasi-respectability
for a time.

"Body type and physical characteristics may offer clues about the origins and progression of disease," proclaims a recent article in a popular
magazine.[1] The best predictor of heart disease after forty is a crease in the
earlobe. Short thumbs and fewer ridges in your fingerprints may be pre-
cursors of schizophrenia. People shaped more like apples than pears exhibit a higher risk for diabetes and heart disease. Men with long, skinny
torsos have a two-out-of-three lifetime chance of getting prostate cancer. The science of anthropometry—determining what the mind and
health of a person are like on the basis of physical measurements and observable characteristics of the body—is lately being retrieved from the
trash heap of science. It had been discarded there long ago because of the
false conclusions it produced about brain capacity, intelligence, and racial
type based on measurements of the human skull.

But what could creases in your earlobes possibly have to do with the
way your heart functions? And how can your fingertips be connected
with your state of mind? Biotypologists explain that miniature blood ves-

sels behave like big ones, so any narrowing in the tiny arterioles of the ear would produce those visible creases. The same effect would be duplicated in the major veins and arteries that traffic blood in and out of the heart. What about thumbs and schizophrenia? One theory has it that the disorder develops from some sort of disruption during the fourth to sixth month of pregnancy—precisely when both finger and cerebral cortical development proceed at a rapid pace. While many of these ideas are controversial, this much is clear: The body *is* a map, and if carefully read, it can tell you who you will become both mentally and physiologically, at least to a degree. This idea, termed *metoposcopy,* is older than Hippocrates and scientists are now beginning to reexamine its deepest hidden secrets by reading the body's contours and studying its subtle topology.

The notion that the body is like a map harboring information about the highway of your personality seems at first sight too deterministic, too materialistic. Ideologically, it ought to lie at the opposite pole of thought from the spiritualist practices that captured the imagination of idealist Europe and innocent America in the century of the occult. Yet body topology as a route to knowledge somehow does spark a gap with animal magnetism in that its practice also consists of manipulating your outside to discover what's happening on your inside.

The idea of divining by consulting parts of the body is as old as the Babylonian hepatoscopist, who saw the future in perforations in a sheep's liver. If sheep, why not people? If holes, why not moles? Ancient diviners often would carefully examine moles on the skin, noting the position of such bodily markings on one's anatomy. A mole on a man's forehead indicates happiness and wealth, wrote the fifth-century B.C. Greek diviner Melampus. On a woman it means she will be powerful, maybe a ruler. On the bridge of your nose, lust; on your lips, you'll be a glutton; on the neck and ear, lucky; on the loins, unlucky.[2] Anthropologist William Lessa shows how these forms of body divination enjoyed their first great resurgence in popularity during the Renaissance. Insecure about how to deal with the newfound individualism and freedoms of that age, many chose to believe that the unknown is already written in the cards—or in the face—rather than imagining we can influence it.[3]

In a book published in 1658, the ambitious, energetic Italian mathematician/physician Cardano (Jerome Cardan, or Cardanus, 1501–76) coupled skin divination with astrology and generated a scheme wherein the situation of moles on your face and body were alleged to be an indication of which sign of the zodiac governed a particular behavior.

Thus, a mole on the nape of the neck, which predicts decapitation, is also assigned to the ill-fortuned planet Saturn. As in acupuncture, the body is not just the sum of its parts; thus, moles on the face are related to those on other parts of the body. One seventeenth-century text consisted of no less than 150 numbered moles mapped out on a female figure accompanied by an extensive description of each one and its relation to the others. Cardan, as ambitious a taxonomist as Roman Pliny, also published a scheme with 800 illustrations (four of which are shown in Fig. 16a) delineating lines on the forehead (metoposcopy) to tease out character traits. Why the forehead? Because it's the part of your body closest to heaven. He claims to have based his conclusions on observations of several hundred foreheads. When studying his subjects, Cardan would use a sort of magic marker to sketch out horizontal bands on their heads. These he said correlated in descending zones, from the top, with the

Fig. 16a: A catalog of foreheads. Metoposcopy. One of countless forms of body divination, it says that you can tell what a person is all about by studying the lines on his/her forehead. From left to right and top to bottom: a blasphemer, a vagabond, a perjurer, and a homicidal maniac. (La Metoposcopié de H. Cardanus.)

order of the planetary influences from highest to lowest according to the Babylonian-derived index of the speed with which they appear to move: Saturn, Jupiter, Mars, Sun, Venus, Mercury, Moon.[4]

You can see it in her face: Figure 16b demonstrates that the circular strokes used to create the face of the woman (is she Mother Nature?) represent the very circular orbits of the stars and planets that make up the

Fig. 16b: Looking like a computer-generated diagram consisting of closely ruled circles centered on the nose, this seventeenth-century facial map shows how to determine character traits by the location of moles and beauty spots on the face. The level zones on the forehead represent the heavens of the several planets, the Moon being the lowest and Saturn the highest. (Richard Saunders, Physiognomie.)

heavens. A short diagonal that touches the left eyebrow foretells death by violence. Curvy lines, like the waves of the sea, portend drowning. Three parallel lines on the uppermost part of the forehead connote a quiet and successful person. The catalogue of associative possibilities is endless: musical, immoderate, adventurous, vicious, unhappy, loving, infirm, successful in war, imbecilic, and so on.

Natural physiognomy was another system of association that made use of body and facial types as an index of character. There are in all of us signs of sympathy with other animals, wrote the Italian sixteenth-century physiognomist/alchemist Giambattista della Porta. He attempted to reduce every variation he observed in human facial features to recognizable differences found among animals. In other words, if you had a head shaped like that of an ostrich, you'd be inclined to behave like that nervous, untrusting bird; but if your cranium is elongated like a donkey's, you were asinine; a leonine countenance deemed you courageous, and so on. In eighteenth-century Austria, these ideas were cleverly transformed to connote racial types. A famous painting from Steiermark depicts a row of ten archetypical citizens of neighboring nation-states ranging from Spanish to Turkish, below which is given a list of their characteristics regarding manners, personality, physical features, likes, and dislikes. At the bottom of the painting there is an animal comparison. The French (lynx-like) are frivolous, garrulous, and deceitful; the Poles, timid, disdainful peasants—very bearlike. Catlike Turks are superficially clever as well as fickle, lazy, and self-loving. Close to the middle of the chart are positioned the open hearted, witty, physically superior—if slightly extravagant—and (you guessed it) leonine Germans and Austrians. This intriguing map of the theory of racial types was a portent of racist opinions that would be converted to practice with devastating political consequences just a handful of generations later.[5]

When I was a kid phrenology was regarded as harmless boardwalk quackery. This was not the case a century earlier when it was the most popular and popularized science in the early nineteenth century—a new way to study the connection between mind and the human character that was at last *objective*.[6]

The phrenomaniacal wave that swept over the United States traces its roots to the last years of the eighteenth century and specifically to the German doctor-philosopher Franz Joseph Gall. His basic thesis went like this: First: The mind consists of thirty-seven independent faculties that can be mapped out on different regions of the brain: veneration at the top, self-esteem at the back, individuality at the front (just above the bridge of the nose), destructiveness over the ear top, amativeness behind it, and so on. Second: Every point within the landscape of your skull is a direct indicator of what's happening in the brain directly below it. So stated, Gall's theory became an experimental, inductive science. What also helped phrenology acquire its scientific veneer was the dehumanized, abstract-looking map of the head; with its faculties mapped out in orderly array, it offered as controlled a scientific formula as one of Newton's Laws of Motion (Fig. 17a.)

Gall would compare the bumps on the head of a mathematical whiz against the cranial contour of a person who couldn't add two and two. Then he would use his data to analyze the bulges on an unknown subject's head to see if he could predict various character traits. Gall's disciples and collaborators included brilliant lecturers, among them one Johann Gaspar Spurzheim, who was responsible for bringing the latest findings to America via lectures at Harvard, that great American fountainhead of learning. From there evangelical preachers carried the message across the Berkshires, through the Burned-Over District, and out onto the Great Plains. Character readings at "two cents per caput" by expert cranioscopists fit right in with séances, spirit rappings, and other parlor entertainments among the spirit seekers on the fringe of America. Phrenology made human behavior all so clear, so explicable in layman's terms—so unbiased. Getting your head examined became a fad on college campuses. Wrote a Union College (Schenectady, New York) student in his diary in 1835:

> Last night attended a lecture on phrenology and today have had my cranium partially examined. Phrenology is fast rising to be a science and will no doubt ere long be studied as such. . . . The faculties the phrenologist made mention that I possessed were in almost all cases very true so far as I can judge of my own mind. I am rather inclined to think he neglects to tell the evil passion as in my case and many others none were noticed which I am confident we possessed. Perhaps interest promp[t]s him.[7]

Like Weight Watchers and exercise clubs, phrenological popular societies quickly sprang up in New York, Baltimore, and Boston, some of them verging on cults. Members shared information on the latest lotions

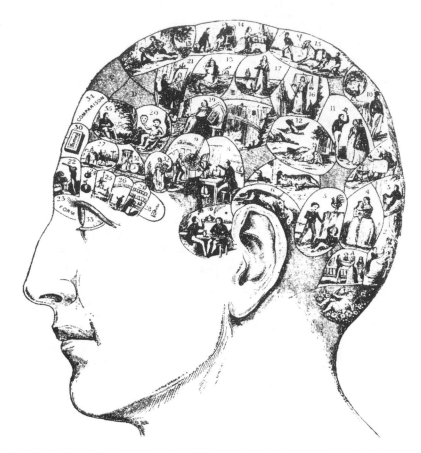

Fig. 17a: "It's all in your head." Phrenological diagram of the head picturing *character traits and mental abilities in their appropriate cerebral compartments. (The Mary Evans Picture Gallery.)*

to be rubbed on the body or the special hats to be worn on the head to develop various regions of the brain. Fortune-tellers flourished. You could get a reading by mail for four bucks—just send a three-quarter pose of your daguerreotype. Serious academics eventually disavowed such nonsense with the same vehemence HPB decried the mediums. They created their own journal which carried articles debunking char-latan fringe phrenology and otherwise crass commercialization of what they regarded as *their* serious practice. But like today's astrology, despite round condemnation by the scientific *literati,* the movement continued to rise from the ashes of the grave to flourish again and again.

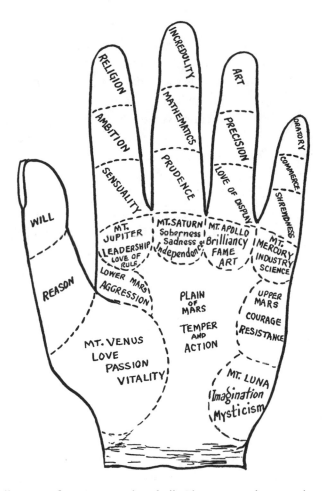

Fig. 17b: "Your Life is in your hands." Chiromantic diagram showing similar qualities mapped out on the sections of the fingers and mounts of the palm. (James Sandstrom, Palmystery.)

Exactly where does this seemingly materialistic, deterministic science (or pseudoscience) of phrenology link up with the occult world of nineteenth-century spiritualism? The key to its appeal lay in combining phrenology and animal magnetism to create a new power—phrenomagnetism. It was claimed that when a subject was magnetized, an operator, via the fluid imparted by his or her fingers, could touch one of the cranial bumps, thereby agitating certain parts of the skull and thus observe the resulting reflexes. For example, magnetically agitate the destructiveness sec-

•

tor and you can induce the subject to act out his or her own version of that particular faculty. Equipped with Swedenborgian philosophy, some phrenomagnetizers turned their craft toward the art of communicating with spirits. Phrenomagnetism also served as a healing technique. By deducing the cause of one's ailment as writ on the cranium you could cure a person. Some magneto-extremists went so far as to deny the reality of all physical diseases; it was all in the mind. The Christian Science doctrine advocated by Mary Baker Eddy was one outcome of this basically spiritualistic belief that started out in the wake of Mesmer's use of magnets.[8]

Though not as popular in nineteenth-century America, palmistry (or chiromancy) is distinctly related to phrenology as one of the techniques of body divining (Fig. 17b). Oddly enough, having peaked in popularity in the sixteenth and seventeenth centuries, it lay submerged for nearly two hundred years before inexplicably resurfacing in the New Age. Today it has become as strongly allied with fortune-telling as crystal ball gazing.

"The hand is the organ of organs, the active agent of the passive powers of the entire human system," said Aristotle.[9] How long will I live? When will I marry? Will I have money? In adept hands this form of body divination is said to be capable of reading potentialities and insights into the most perplexing problems of life. Those who object say: "Don't those telltale lines in your palm just come from opening and closing your hands?" Ah, but if so, retort the believers, how come the markings and signs are just as numerous on the palms of idle people as they are in working people, in the hands of infants as well as old people?

How does palmistry work? Basically your life is in your own hands. Even the Bible says so—Long life is in her right hand; in her left hand are riches and honor (Prov. 3:16). In the highly dualistic system of association found in traditional palm reading, the left hand shows the inherited qualities you are born with (natural tendencies), while the right is all about what you make of yourself (development through experience). In other words, the hands complement one another. You need to read them both. Vertical lines in the hands are the most favorable—they indicate advancement; the horizontal are contradictory—they involve opposing forces. Mired among them are the life, heart, head, and Sun (creative power) lines.

Like the hepatoscopist of old, the palmist looks at structural details: Do the lines cross, break, or become disoriented? Something could be awry. In the lifeline, for example, cross lines might denote sadness, worry, or family friction. Then there are the mountains and valleys that comprise your manual topography: reason, will, shrewdness, oratory, religious views, ambition. Pronounced elevations indicate a superabundance of each quality which has its own position on the hand. There also are different *kinds* of hands: elementary ones (thick short fingers and thumb), artistic ones (conically shaped), psychic and philosophic ones, and so on. Serious chiromancers pay attention to color: pale lines, red lines, yellow lines; and to marks: triangles, grilles, dots, crosses, squares. Some strive for metric accuracy: To estimate the timing of life's many expectations, they measure the distance from the center of the Mount of Venus (the roundish area at the base of the palm on the same side as and just below the trunk of the thumb) to the crotches below each of the fingers. Thus, born thieves have an exaggerated Mercury mount (the bulge on the palm located at the base of the index finger).

All these forms of body divination are not so remote from the theory of criminal types once elaborated by criminal anthropologists and today enjoying something of a rejuvenation. Some biologists (or should I call them genetic diviners?) believe there may be genes that play a role in some of us who commit violent crime.[10] Does your physique really provide the framework for your psyche? Are fat people lazy? Short people feisty? Red-faced people apoplectic? Are thin people beautiful by standards of that norm? If divining means predicting, then in a sense aren't we all self-diviners when we inspect our own constitutions in a mirror in the same way if not in the same detail as phrenologist or palmist?

Or maybe good divining is just good psychology? "You will suffer a violent death," a chiromancer uttered as he read the hand of one of the Medicis. That it actually came to pass was entirely predictable given the intrigue in the Medicean court at the time. Historian of magic Kurt Seligmann has pointed out how ready were the palmists of old to indicate bad omens, in contrast to the rather positive dispositions of the palm readers we find at the State Fair. Either way, the predictions, like those of newspaper astrology, are amply endowed with the power of suggestion.

Orthodox medical doctors of the nineteenth century attacked various forms of body divining; they were especially critical of phrenology. The shape of your skull has nothing to do with the shape of your brain, they blustered, and the dissected human brain fails to reveal any such division into compartments. And even if it did, the protective cranial bones are far too thick for any phrenologist to read through. Furthermore, when an area of the brain is damaged there is no demonstrable corresponding impairment of the faculty that is supposed to reside there. Brain functions are interdependent, not isolated—period.

Orthodox religion joined in the fray. If phrenology were correct, then we would all be little more than intellectual machines, irresponsible for any action to God (the clear implication of the diatribe uttered by the anonymous clergyman quoted in my epigraph). Others saw phrenology as not at all inimical to revelation and spiritualism. "The Bible addresses man, as Phrenology sketches him," wrote Calvinist barrister George Combe.[11] In his view, there was a harmonious connection between the Christianity of the scriptures and the science of your head bone. Phrenology only classifies your propensities and singles out the moral and intellectual nature of man from his animal nature, as laid out in the Ten Commandments. It serves as a vehicle, a motivation for us to explore the sentiments and morally based characteristics listed among the thirty-seven faculties.

In Combe's influential hands, phrenology became a kind of religion itself—"optimistic and sentimental deism," historian John Davies calls it.[12] Allied lecturer-missionaries called to the faith conducted revivals and set out the dragnet of conversion. In tune with many New Age teachings of the present era, phrenological promoters argued that to improve ourselves we needed to be in touch with a whole new philosophy of human nature. If you could use the indications of head bump analysis to improve the mind, you could do the same for your body—"to attain success in this object, all moral, religious, and intellectual teaching must be conducted in harmony with the laws of physiology,"[13] wrote the enthusiastic Combe.

How to bring our bodies into oneness with nature, to acquire the knowledge nature offers us free of charge? For one thing, we should all open our windows to let in fresh air at night. Women in particular should emancipate their constitutions—get rid of those tight corsets that constrict their natural development. Instead, get into the newly designed liberating fashion items, such as the long, loose, Turkish-looking undergarments recently designed by Amelia Bloomer. We should all eat healthier, too: lay off those sinful comestibles like coffee, tea, and cucumbers—and definitely no alcohol. "Total abstinence or no husbands," said the reformist wife. "Natural waists or no wives," retorted her spouse.[14]

In the end, phrenology did not add much to the debate about whether and how to contact spirits and today it is regarded as a dead end on the occult road that wound through the nineteenth century. Washed away by the shift of public interest to the tide of abolitionism before the Civil War, it nevertheless deserves a firm place in the ornamentation of fascinating somatomatic techniques that flourished in one form or another since civilization began in the ancient Middle East. At least for a short while in the nineteenth century, it was an important part of the way people struggled with the mind-body question.

We can easily look back at the whole phrenological movement as totally valueless on the grounds that the phenomena it took to represent the truth were totally irrelevant. But why bash phrenology along with all the other "ologies" we no longer hold sacred at the altar of contemporary science, as if to imagine our own enterprises are not only true but also free of value? Like so many pseudosciences of the past, it disappeared, not because it was scientifically proven false but because it simply was no longer socially useful in the ways it had been in the past.

CHAPTER 22

SUMMARY:
A LIGHT THAT FAILED?

In the case of primitive men and savages it is possible that little thought accompanies their actions.

Lynn Thorndike,
A History of Magic and Experimental Science

The exotic substances, visions, and summonings of turn-of-the-
century spiritualism-turned-stage magic coincided with a time
of dizzying scientific progress—the discovery of radium and
other radioactive elements, of X-rays and other mysterious emissions
possessing great and inexplicable power. Could such powers also penetrate the psychic domain?

Although it raised the question, the study of paranormal phenomena
never seemed to ripen or progress; it died on the vine. Even the most
qualified experimenters, like Crookes and Richet, never got beyond the
stage of concluding, to the objection of many, that the phenomena celebrated by spiritualism were real. Ruth Brandon thinks that what held
parascience back at the turn of the century—and still does so today—
was the absence of an overarching theory to tie together all its peculiar,
diverse phenomena. "They are merely repetitions: of ghost stories supposed to have been experienced, of attempts at guessing numbers, of the
different kinds of ectoplasm materialized by Eva C."[1]

Scholars who wrote about magic early in the twentieth century labeled it pseudo-science—science that didn't work out, science gone
awry. Magic is a pernicious delusion based on incorrect associations,
claimed the influential nineteenth-century anthropologist Edward Tylor.
The way it works is this: A rooster crows with the rising sun. Make a
rooster crow and you can make the sun rise. A blood sacrifice is connected to the movement of the sun across the sky; therefore, to make the
sun traverse the heavens, offer blood to it. Now, everybody knows neither the call of a rooster nor a rooster's blood can cause the sun to rise

and move; therefore, these associations are false stupidities. Sounds reasonable, doesn't it?—except that such logic makes the mistake of applying *our* system of understanding how the world works to *somebody else's* interaction with it.

Tylor and his nineteenth-century contemporaries also were very much influenced by Darwin's recent discoveries. They saw the animism in magic (the doctrine that living phenomena are actuated by a vital principle distinct from the substance of the body) as a form of primitive thought. Civilized man had yet to rise above the belief that the spiritual world is a part of the material one. People once believed that animals, plants, and even rocks had souls. All that survives this belief is that humans have souls, Tylor argued as he misapplied the theory of evolution by natural selection, endowing it with the forward-pulling force of human destiny.

If magic is erroneous—a vestigial appendix in the body of human knowledge—then why has it persisted through the fifty-odd centuries through which I have thus far charted it? Because it seemed to work. Natural events, like the rainmaking that magic is supposed to bring about, usually occur anyway. And if the events foretold do not occur, a magician can blame improperly conducted rites and spells or perhaps some form of superpowerful counter-magic. Some percentage of success would be enough to reinforce a belief in it—a self-fulfilling prophecy. Savages and civilized people don't think alike, argued the turn-of-the-century British rationalist James G. Frazer (1854–1941). His *The Golden Bough,* one of the most influential books of its day, acquainted millions of lay readers with the habits and customs of exotic people around the world via an extraordinary collection of myths (most of them taken out of context). More or less following Tylor's line, he believed that savages are reasonable people who have failed in their attempts to reach the Truth. The superstitions they harbor are the beliefs of immature minds. They are errors committed on the upward winding pathway of logical thinking.

Frazer proposed an extraordinary course of evolution from science to magic. Yes, magic was recognized as a failure by the higher intellects in primitive cultures; only those with weaker minds clung to it, he said. The cerebral cortex of such people simply was not well developed enough for them to know about causation, echoed psychologist Carveth Read in 1920.[2] But the brighter half were smart enough to realize that the gods can't be coerced; they can, however, be entreated, offered an exchange, maybe a sacrifice of a first-born child or a pulsating human heart. Where one idea failed, a better one was ushered in to take its place. Thus did the age of religion succeed the age of magic, reasoned Frazer. Only the demonstrably effective processes from the old age of magic survived and these served as the foundation for the age of science in which we now live. Only in the last four hundred years has this higher form of common sense that leads to rational truth taken root and become a social reality. How had Tylor and Frazer acquired this special window into the minds of these exotic people? Asked if he'd ever seen a single one of the primitive folk from the faraway colonies on whose customs he had written so many volumes, Victorian gentleman Frazer replied in horror, "God forbid!"[3] Such was the progressive evolutionary reasoning of anthropologists a hundred years ago.

By century's turn, personal magnetism, clairvoyance, crystal gazing, astrology, phrenology, and palmistry were all big-time. In that Gilded Age, society rode a wave of moonstruck optimism—a New Thought movement. Despite how predetermined the state of the world might be owing to circumstances beyond our control, we can nevertheless do something about ourselves via the power of the mind—and a little help from technology. Cure baldness by rubbing your head and thinking good thoughts; chew your food with the right mental attitude and you'll digest better; smoke nicotineless cigars and use an "air burning" machine to help you induce silence and contemplation so that you can put your mind into harmony with the universe before going into the office. Gilbert Seldes, a 1920s historian, who saw it as the peak of radicalism that had marked American ideology since its inception, wrote of the all-inclusive New Thought movement:

> It loved Jesus and Buddha, Tolstoi, and Nietzsche, liberalism and socialism and anarchism, Unitarianism and Ethical Culture and the wisdom of the East, free love and monogamy, wealth and ascetic virtue. It was scientific and poetic and adored Nature and exalted man. It was pacifist and admired successful brutality. It was precious and went in for simplicity. It was soft.[4]

A popular magazine of the time declared that this new liberal philosophy was sweeping away everything from materialism and bigotry, to poverty and disease—maybe even death, bringing with it human ad-vancement, development of latent powers, good health, and success.[5]

Unlike the "Burned-Overs," New Thinkers were influenced by sci-ence's proof of waves and rays in the air. If *things* could radiate and broad-cast, why not *people?* A redoubled faith in divine goodness led to the notion that we all can perfect ourselves gradually as we climb that old Kabbalah tree of life toward an ultimate "at-oneness" with the universe. As one follower put it:

> In just the degree in which you realize your oneness with the Infinite Spirit, you will exchange dis-ease for ease, in-harmony for harmony, suffering and pain for abounding health and strength. To recognize our own divinity, and our intimate relation to the Universal, is to attach the belts of our machinery to the power house of the Universe. One need remain in hell no longer than one chooses to; we can rise to any heaven we ourselves choose; and when we choose so to rise, all the higher powers of the Universe combine to help us heavenward.[6]

As Romanticism declined, a less tolerant, impatient new century wit-nessed the publication of many establishment treatises, some with purpo-sive sounding titles,[7] debunking practically all aspects of spiritualism and the occult: There is nothing to animal magnetism except what has be-come scientific under the name of hypnotism. Table turning really hap-pens, but when it isn't a fraud (Fig. 18), unconscious muscular reactions are responsible. As to the raising of spirits, it is fully hallucinatory. Spiritu-alism had yet to yield up its proofs; therefore everything that happens takes place in the mind of the medium. Mused one skeptic: In Germany, all spirits are mystical and transcendental; in France, liberal and frivolous; in England, skeptics who talk incessantly; and in the United States, dog-matic and matter-of-fact; but evermore, they are atheistic or pantheistic materialists.[8]

If the occult is the promised land, then science is its constant invader. And those occult phenomena that do not yet belong to science someday will be conquered.[9] When this happens, they will cease to be occult—and they also will cease to be wonderful.

Remember William Crawford? After concluding his study of Eusapia Palladino and Eva C., he suffered a nervous collapse. During his recov-

Fig. 18: Debunking "pseudopods." Joseph Dunninger, the early twentieth-century magician, like many of his colleagues, was dedicated to exposing mediumistic fraud. Here he illustrates how a medium can reach out and touch someone during a seance. (*J. Dunninger,* Inside the Medium's Cabinet.)

ery period he wrote that his psychic research had been his greatest achievement and that he was convinced that everything he did to demonstrate the validity of psychic phenomena would truly withstand the test of time. Shortly thereafter, in 1920, he committed suicide—a fitting symbol of the unripe fruits that grew on the transplanted tree of spiritualism in the nineteenth century.

PART IV

A MODERN KALEIDOSCOPE OF MAGIC

CHAPTER 23

WHO'S A MAGICIAN?: THE HOUDINI LEGEND

I don't even know how he does these things.
Playwright/director David Mamet,
referring to his friend, magician Ricky Jay

Staging and showmanship were Harry Houdini's middle names; his real name was Ehrich Weiss (1874–1926). When he executed one of his celebrated escapes—usually on a dare or a challenge— from a locked box tossed into chilled waters beneath a Detroit bridge, or out of a straitjacket while dangling from a crane before a wildly enthusiastic throng in front of the Washington Monument, he always led his audience to believe he had struggled mightily.

Harry's feats always induced nail-biting anticipation. The handcuff king would try the attention span of his anxious onlookers with waits of twenty, thirty, often forty minutes. Then he would spring from his self-imposed prison, his clothing rumpled, dripping perspiration, displaying the marks upon his wrists and ankles where ropes and chains had chafed his skin raw. Houdini had learned by experience how to make his act exciting:

> If I got out too quickly the audience would reason that escape was easy. Every second that ticks by during my struggle builds up the climax. When they are sure I am licked, that the box will have to be smashed open to give me air, then— and only then—do I appear.[1]

Houdini stories give you a real sense of what a super-magician can do. Harry Houdini's disappearing elephant trick is exemplary—a trick, deception pure and simple. A trainer would bring ten-thousand-pound Jane on stage, while fifteen attendants turned the huge rectangular cabinet around to show that nothing else was there—nothing but a box with open front placed flush up against a brick wall. After marching the pachyderm around the box the trainer would walk her inside. A 1918 witness writing for *Variety* magazine describes what happened next:

> Curtains closed, curtains opened. No elephant. No trap. No *papier mâché* animal. It had gone. . . . Mr. Houdini has provided a headache for every child in New York. The matinee crowds will worry themselves into sleep nightly wondering what Houdini did with his elephant.[2]

What the audience didn't realize was that the rear wall of the box had been cleverly made up to look just like the backdrop. Actually the box stood a full fifteen feet from the wall. So, once the elephant was locked in via the front door, she could simply be led, unbeknownst to anyone, out the back. Credit Houdini with performing a miracle. He had conquered the spectator's eye.

Houdini's legendary lock picking and feats of memory were less illusionary—more a matter of extraordinary skills he had somehow acquired through constant practice. In 1903 he extricated himself from a *carette,* one of the secret portable jails of the Russian police—an allegedly escape-proof horse-drawn contraption used to transport condemned exiles to Siberia (Fig. 19). It consisted of six metal plates, one of them an entrance door padlocked from the outside and fitted with a tiny barred window. Harry did it in twenty-eight minutes. (Furthermore, he already had been shackled when they put him in.) A biographer theorizes:

> . . . [he] pierced the "zinc" floor of the transport cell with a "cutter," folded back the metal, removed the wooden planking beneath it, and slipped out.[3]

Believe what you like. When you possess extraordinary powers your admirers never will fail to multiply them. That's how you become a legend. More likely, Houdini had managed somehow to slide his practiced, nimble fingers through the bars and pick the lock from the outside. Precisely how he did it still remains a mystery. Witnesses testify that he had been doubly strip-searched before entering the cell, so there is no way he could have possessed any implements or keys. Isn't it interesting how the power of suggestion can lead to conclusions that may be far from the truth?

In one famous incident on transatlantic shipboard, Houdini mystified then-President Teddy Roosevelt. The magician had been invited to put

Chief of the Secret Russian Police LEBEDOEFF has HARRY HOUDINI stripped stark naked and searched then locked up in the Siberian Transport Cell or Carette, May 10/1903 in Moscow and in 28 minutes HOUDINI had made his escape to the unspeakable astonishment of the Russian Police.

Fig. 19: Conjurer Harry Houdini, synonymous with the word magician, about to be incarcerated in the Siberian Transport Cell—the world's most escape-proof device, bar none. From a 1903 poster. (W. Gibson, The Original Houdini Scrapbook.*)*

on a Grand Magical Review, one act of which consisted of members of the audience writing questions on slips of paper and Houdini answering them "with the aid of a spirit." Even after the President was warned by composer Victor Herbert, who sat next to him, to cover his hand as he wrote so that the magician could not decipher the writing by following the movement of the top of the pencil, Houdini was undeterred. His correct answer to the President's question: "Near the Andes," along with a map of South America, appeared sketched out on a pair of slates bound together facing one another. Between these lay the folded tab Roosevelt had earlier submitted and on which he had written the question: "Where was I last Christmas?"

What no one on board the ship knew was that a few days before the voyage from London to New York, when Houdini had picked up his tickets, he learned in confidence that Roosevelt would be on board. At the *London Telegraph* newspaper office, which he also had visited, the trickster had heard of a series of stories the paper was planning on the publicity-seeking President's expedition to South America. A reporter friend gave Houdini access to much of the unpublished information, including a map of the itinerary.

Doing your homework, having access to knowledge before the fact, clever guesswork—and supposing that a self-aware man like Roosevelt might ask such a question about himself—are the sorts of skills honed by the genius-magician that permitted the feats of the legendary Houdini to outstrip all the efforts of his competitors.

Who hasn't heard about the Chinese Water Torture Cell (Houdini's concoction right down to the exotic, captivating label)?[4] It was a major contribution to the staying power of the Houdini myth. In it he performed his final act. Houdini often had emerged from behind a black curtain that enveloped the oversized water-filled milk can after being immersed in it upside down garbed in a straitjacket. When he insisted on attempting the feat with a broken ankle and a ruptured appendix that had already spread poison throughout his system, he emerged as never before. No sooner had Houdini extricated himself than he staggered and fainted—in full view of a piqued audience. A few days later, only in his mid-fifties, the great deceiver was dead.

Paradoxically, though he always was a trickster, Houdini expended considerable effort, especially late in life, exposing trickery—what he called fraud. He targeted spiritualism in particular. In the 1920s, séances conducted by professional mediums were still fashionable, so popular in fact that the editorial board of *Scientific American* magazine formed a Spirit Truths Committee to investigate the phenomenon. They offered a prize to any *serious* medium (some were obvious frauds, declared the group) who could demonstrate he or she could bring back the dead and talk to them. Now, Houdini had done just such an act, though it was devoid of the elevating table, rapping noises, and luminous images still associated with séances of that day. After being sealed in a cabinet—the whole audience experiencing bell-ringing sounds and jangling tambourines as they watched the swaying box that contained him—Houdini would talk about the spirit world he had just encountered. He would name names, dates and blurt out old family secrets that could be known only to select members of the audience. How could Houdini know about local resident Efrem Alexander, who had died years before the magician performed his spiritualistic feats in Galena, Kansas? By spending a quiet Saturday afternoon the day before the show memorizing facts carved in stone on monuments in the Galena cemetery. Thus did the great deceiver deceive Efrem's descendants—folks he anticipated just might turn up at the only show in town that Sunday. He took in the Alexanders the same way he conned Teddy Roosevelt.

As advisor to the *Scientific American* committee, Houdini specialized in exposing details of fraudulent procedure in séances. How did spirits make rapping noises? Even when both her hands were held, the celebrated Maggie Fox had managed to slide her foot out of her right shoe and place it on a stool just under the table. Contact between the stool and the first joint of her big toe produced all that knocking, according to Houdini.[5] How did DDH manage to sail out the window at Ashley House? It was all a ruse, said the skeptical Harry; here's how *he'd* do it:

> First actually get out the window, or pretend to; then, go back and noiselessly crawl on all fours through the door into the next room and shake the window; and lastly, boldly return to the first room, closing the door with a bang.

or

> There is a possibility that a man of Home's audacity with levitation feats might have resorted to swinging from one window to another, which means nothing to any acrobat with a wire properly placed in readiness.[6]

What about Eva C.'s ectoplasm? I've done it, claimed Houdini, by swallowing and regurgitating various materials. Spirit messages on blank cards? Give the medium a set of cards that can be identified by pricking each of them with a pin. If the spirit writing appears on any cards without pinpricks, then you know the medium has switched cards. How to elevate a table? The *Scientific American* committee had come close to awarding its prize for doing just that to "Margery the Medium" (aka Mina Crandon, wife of a prominent Boston surgeon, who claimed she'd been told by a psychic that she possessed remarkable latent clairvoyant powers). But Houdini was able to convince the committee it was all done with a stealthful movement of the legs. Even while her arms were held down, so agile were Margery's free limbs that in the darkened environment of the séance room she could remove a shoe and stocking, manipulate luminous forms in the dark, and ring a bell by gripping its handle between her big and first toe. In order to detect Margery's leg motion, for a whole day until the time of the test-séance Houdini had worn a surgical bandage between the knee and ankle of the leg nearest Margery, next to whom he sat. Every time Margery tightened the muscle of her leg to make a move, Houdini could feel her actions against the sensitive skin of his leg, which he had exposed just before the performance by rolling up his trouser leg.

At considerable expense, Houdini constructed demonstration schemes: trick tables, cabinets, bell boxes. He sold kits that told how to perfect illusions—even wrote a book exposing Margery the Medium. But what moves an exconfederate, master conjurer like Harry Houdini to go through so much effort to expose fellow pretenders? Their tricks were fraudulent, he argued, simpleminded deceptions when compared to the contortions he needed to learn to escape from a milk can, hand-cuffs, or a straitjacket—or the subtle finger manipulations he had tire-lessly perfected for his card tricks. *He* used skill; *they* used trickery. Houdini seemed to be saying: "What *I* do is the real thing; what *they* do is phony."

In the eyes of Harry Houdini, genius was a matter of degree. What made him a genius in his own eyes, and in the eyes of his followers, was that he could make possible what to all others had seemed impossible. Houdini was simply so much better at his craft than all his competi-tors, so superior in confidence, so much more willing to expand his ef-forts to break new horizons—to substitute eagles for doves, elephants for rabbits.

Where Houdini left off, Dunninger and others picked up the slack.[7] Magician Joseph Dunninger wrote in 1935 that the Great War was re-sponsible for all the misguided spiritualism that materialized in the séance parlor. Gullible moms and wives who lost the men in their lives succumbed to spiritualist hocus-pocus that promised them a dialogue with the departed. A great technologist of magic, Dunninger boastfully exposed fraudulent mediums by showing how to make spirit hands by dipping your own in water, then in melted wax—and offering instruc-tions on how to make a telescoping "reaching rod" out of a strip of thin fiber with a wax or rubber glove on the end of it that could make body contact with a client several feet away (see Fig. 18). He showed how to levitate tables with hidden bars strapped up his sleeve that plugged into rods bolted beneath the table and how to use trick slates to write out the answer to a spectator's concealed questions. Dunninger also fought back a whole gang of mediums who claimed to have materialized messages from the dead Harry himself.

Today, stage magicians perform before record crowds. Thanks to high-tech devices, they can easily one-up old Harry. For example, David Copperfield saws *himself* in half and substitutes airplanes and the Orient Express for Harry's elephants. And "Ricky Jay and his fifty-two assistants," after fifteen years of languishing, turned into an off-Broadway hit—an eight-week run sold out on opening day. Jay babbles fifteenth-century poetry while manipulating cards—pitching them cross stage with enough force to penetrate a watermelon and decapitate a toy duck. His written works on the subject of magic sell very well.[8]

Magical conjuring has a long and impressive history, but there is one major difference between nineteenth-century magic, like the Davenport Bros.' cabinet act, and Tricky Ricky's or Dazzling David's performances of the twentieth: There is no doubt in *anybody's* contemporary mind that their kind of conjuring is 100 percent smoke and mirrors. Or is it?

CHAPTER 24

WHO'S A MAGICIAN?: TRICKSTER FROM FAR ROCKAWAY

I'd be in there alone and I'd open the safe in a few minutes . . . then sit around, reading a magazine or something, for fifteen or twenty minutes. There was no use trying to make it look too easy; somebody would figure out there was a trick to it. After a while I'd open the door and say, "It's open".

Richard Feynman,
Surely You're Joking, Mr. Feynman!

Genius. A great mathematician once defined it as the ability to perform magic—to do things nobody else can do. In the eyes of his fellow scientists, Richard Feynman (1918–1988) was a magician. His colleagues knew him as an intellectually adventurous, highly unconventional academic who shattered all the professional archetypes. You and I might recognize him as the Nobel laureate in physics who solved the mystery of the 1986 *Challenger* space shuttle disaster. The problem, you may remember, lay in the quarter-inch-thick O-rings that sealed the joints of the rocket booster together. Gas pressure from inside was supposed to push outward on the O-rings, thus automatically making the seal. But that isn't what happened on the frigid January morning of liftoff at Cape Kennedy. As Feynman, a member of the investigative committee, explained to the press in plain English:

> I took this stuff that I got out of your seal and put it in ice water, and I discovered that when you put some pressure on it for a while and then undo it it doesn't stretch back. It stays the same dimension. In other words, for a few seconds at least and more seconds than that, there is no resilience in this particular material when it is at a temperature of 32 degrees. I believe that has some significance for our problem.[1]

Reporters were stunned by the simplicity of Feynman's answer and the practical way he seems to have arrived at it. But even as a child, Dick was fascinated by gadgets. Colleagues say he had an uncanny way of perceiving problems from an independent perspective, one that bypassed and usually ignored conventional approaches. Captivated by formulas and diagrams, Feynman, who was always quick to bolster his own ego, believed the reason he was so good at repairing radios as a kid growing up in Far Rockaway was because he could see the gadget as a map of itself, each part expressing its own function. But unlike a mechanical clock, the magic of the radio lay in its abstract ability to change invisible waves into live sound, all without employing any moving, interconnected parts.[2] Waves would come to dominate Feynman's attention for the rest of his life—hydrodynamic waves of fluids, plasma waves, and the probability waves of quantum physics.

But Feynman the genius was also Feynman the deceiver. He could be brilliant at concealing the way he solved a problem and equally brilliant at showboating his arrival at the answer. As one biographer relates: He was able to master "mental tricks covering the deeper landscape of algebraic analysis."[3] Feynman tells how he learned such tricks from another genius and Nobel winner, Hans Bethe of Cornell University:

> One time we were putting some numbers into a formula, and got to 48 squared. I reached for the Marchant calculator, and he said, "That's 2300." I began to push the buttons, and he says, "If you want it exactly, it's 2304." The machine says 2304. "Gee! That's pretty remarkable!," I say. "Don't you know how to square numbers near 50?," he says. "You square 50—that's 2500—and subtract 100 times the difference of your number from 50, (in this case it's 2), so you have 2300. If you want the correction, square the difference and add it on. That makes 2304."[4]

Feynman would amaze his friends with numerological sleight-of-hand of this sort at every turn. If you asked him what time it was, he'd be likely to quickly respond, "Six hours and seven minutes ago it was half past eleven," or "In two hours and fifty-three minutes it will be three thirteen." How did he do it? By setting his watch every day to a different offset from real time. Remembering one fixed number in his head, he would need only read the other from his watch. What it took to accomplish such feats was a lot of memorization and mental exercise with arithmetic—more of both than most ordinary mortals might entertain. But if you want the performance to be effective, Feynman seemed to be saying: You need to know how to do it *and* you've got to make it look amazing.

Feynman once bragged that he could crack any safe at Los Alamos National Labs, the secret government research facility where he worked during the war period. "I opened the safes which contained behind them the entire secret of the atomic bomb: the schedule of production, how the bomb worked—the whole schmeer," he boasted.[5] His coworkers were impressed. Most of them believed he had mastered the difficult art of listening to clicks. Feynman cleverly nurtured the legend, evoking nervous anticipation by taking longer than he needed to penetrate the inner sanctum of government secrecy. He even brought along unnecessary tools as foils. In reality, Feynman knew by tinkering with them in his spare time that most safes of that day could be opened even when each setting lay within two or three digits of the correct combination. Second, most people chose birthday numbers as combinations. So, as a first approximation, the less experienced safe cracker can try months 0, 5, and 10, each of which covers the margin of error. Half a dozen trials at 0, 5, 10, 15, 20, and 25 will cover the days of the month and several more trials the range of years in which users of the safe might have been born. If you knew whose safe it was, you conceivably could narrow the year range. Feynman could perform the eighty or so combination trials in a matter of minutes. And if that didn't work, being an experienced safe cracker, Feynman knew a few other rules from an allied discipline—spying. Most people usually don't lock their safes; they leave their combinations at factory settings and they often write down the combinations on the edges of their desk drawers.

There is every indication that Feynman did physics the same way he cracked safes. In addition to possessing a vast storehouse of knowledge, he had a way of seeing the entire landscape of a problem—how it related to other areas of thought not conventionally attached to it. To give an example: At an astrophysical meeting in the early sixties concerning where the quasars—high energy sources that lie at the edge of the universe—came from, one physicist who had worked on the problem for a long time offered the proposition that these denizens of deep space were supermassive stars. Almost immediately Feynman popped out of his chair and confidently announced to the group that such objects could not exist in the real world because they would not be stable. Lengthy calculations by his colleagues later proved him correct—calculations one hundred pages long that Feynman had performed years before but never bothered to publish.

Feynman acquired his unconventional boldness—this rebelliousness against authority—early on. He enjoyed playing the role of nonconformist, the anti-intellectual in a cerebral environment. He suggests maybe it was because in the working-class environment where he grew up, being a practical man mattered more than being either cultured or intelligent. Also, he was secure enough not to be offset by any adverse reaction he got when he behaved in an unorthodox manner. Like the time in his student days when, given the choice, he asked for both milk *and* lemon in his tea at a Princeton social. He reveled in being the iconoclast. Recounting a talk he gave on ancient Maya hieroglyphic writing at a Cal Tech colloquium, he comments, almost irreverently, "There I was, being something I'm not, again."[6] In his amusing book of reminiscences, entitled *Surely You're Joking, Mr. Feynman!* (the response of the Ivy League hostess who had served him his tea), Feynman testifies to his own cleverness with story after story detailing the way he would always manage to think up questions that were very interesting yet no one knew the answer to—questions that would rattle philosopher and biologist, as well as fellow physicist, because they came from a totally foreign perspective. "Is a brick an essential object?" he asked one professor in an informal philosophy seminar. This in response to a similar question about electrons that had been put to him. Said Feynman to himself, "I was only trying to establish whether these people were willing to admit that theoretical constructs were essential."[7]

As much as we might view Richard Feynman's behavior as that of a wizard and a master of deception (a person who knew the invisible secrets that lay hidden just beneath the skin of the real world), scientist Dick, like magician Harry, was strangely emphatic in the way he spoke out against deception. In science we must never deceive, he preached. If you are a scientist, you must provide all the information to help others to judge your theory. You need to give even the details that might end up proving you wrong. And you must make sure the things your theory fits are not just those that gave rise to the ideas that ultimately led to the theory, but that the theory also makes something else, even something that might seem remote, come out right, too. He once characterized doing physics as something that looks like magic to the outsider but is really more like imagination confined to a straitjacket. For Feynman, like all practicing scientists, the major difference between science and the occult lies in self-initiated skepticism. In science you bend over backward to prove yourself wrong. You report *all* the data in your experiment—not just the data that makes sense from the point of view of your theory. Then you go out of your way to try to punch holes in your own theory.

The difference between a scientist and a witch doctor is that what witch doctors propose usually doesn't work, says Feynman:

> In the South Seas there is a cargo cult of people. During the war they saw airplanes land with lots of good materials, and they want the same thing to happen now. So they've arranged to make things like runways, to put fires along sides of the runways, to make a wooden hut for a man to sit in, with two wooden pieces on his head like headphones and bars of bamboo sticking out like antennas—he's the controller—and then wait for the airplanes to land. They're doing everything right. The form is perfect. It looks exactly the way it looked before. But it doesn't work. No airplanes land.[8]

The South Sea islanders are missing a key element—probing and questioning where they might be wrong; that's why their method gets no results, argued Feynman. They are deceiving themselves.

But did the golden boy of twentieth-century science really practice what he preached? Colleagues who watched Richard Feynman at work admit they never knew where his thoughts were going from moment to moment. He seemed to exhibit mental flights that lay outside of their grasp. Then he would suddenly arrive at an answer. It was almost as if the truth came from divine revelation, as one close observer characterized it. Was this witness just using a metaphorical term, I wonder—or was he serious?

Generations of psychologists, neurologists, and biologists have tried to master the material basis of what makes a genius a genius. When Einstein died, pathologists removed his (under average size) two and two-thirds-pound brain for study. It took twenty-five years of countless anatomical tests on microscopic sections to reduce his gray matter to a mass of shreds. What's left sits in a jar on a shelf in a dusty medical office in the middle of Kansas. The question still goes unanswered. . . .

•

Feynman would have agreed: Genius or magician—neither possesses more brain cells or neuron branches than you or I. It's all a matter of degree. Just as some people are faster and stronger, some are naturally smarter than others. And some develop the capacity to think in bold and original ways. When these qualities are coupled with a photographic mind that can perform rapid-fire calculations encased in a brain prepossessed with a monomaniacal attraction to an area of study, then whether it be violin playing, chess, or physics, you get a Feynman—someone who could, as one admirer put it, "get away with being unconventional because he was so goddamn smart."[9]

Were the acts of the twentieth century's greatest magician, Harry Houdini, and perhaps its greatest scientist, Richard Feynman really all that different? Houdini the magician seemed to know more than all the others about what the eye and mind could apprehend and what contortions his body was capable of performing. Feynman the scientist understood the imaginary mathematical terrain and the interrelated underlying structure of the world of physical experience. Both were obsessive in their zeal to master the skills of their craft. Possessed with the same showboat quality, each thrilled to the roar of the crowd upon giving a masterful performance. And both Dick and Harry had the savvy to string out the act—to play to the audience. One was as unconventional as the other.

Had we made such a comparison around the last turn of century, say between Alexander Graham Bell and Scottish prestidigitator John Henry Anderson (the "Wizard of the North"), or between Madame Curie and Jean-Eugène Robert-Houdin (the French illusionist from whom Houdini derived his stage name), we might have discovered fewer parallels. James Gleick, who has written a whole book on the subject of genius, argues that's only because science by then had completely demystified its geniuses.

They understood the entire universe in a more deterministic way in those days. Before quantum theory and relativity, physics was not so full of the abstraction and indeterminacy that gave rise to the Einsteins and submerged the Edisons in the public image that surrounds science. Sure, Edison could make the voices of the dead be heard again. He could even raise ghosts of their images and parade them around in front of flickering lights, but he did it all by logical experimentation with circuits and wires. That wasn't magic. By his own admission, his experiments were subjected to thousands of trials and rejections before he arrived at something that worked. What Einstein and Feynman did was not so easy to explain. These guys were the real Houdinis.

These brief vignettes from the lives of a pair of very curious characters help outline one of the main signposts on this segment of our journey through the occult forest: that during most of Western history and especially since the Renaissance, the thoughtways of magic and science, though in historical retreat *from* one another, now begin to bend ever so slightly back *toward* one another. The heavy thicket that forms the contemporary boundary between them is well worth hacking through and exploring. Both science and magic have a complex technology, a body of organized knowledge, their own logic, and a set of methods. Moreover, each has its own efficacy. Each addresses needs, solves problems, and serves a purpose. The differences lie in who possesses the requisite knowledge to practice the craft and exactly what constitutes its effectiveness. And this, in turn, is tied to the attitude both practitioner and audience display toward the real world.

CHAPTER 25

MAGIC IN THE
TWENTIETH CENTURY:
WHAT THE POLLSTERS SAY

Psychoanalysis is no longer chic. Encounter therapies and group grope have gone with the New Age winds. *Est* can rest in peace. The dead are alive and talking to us. The Occult Revolution shows no signs of abating.

Martin Gardner,
The New Age: Notes of a Fringe Watcher

L et's graph the progress of science and magic over the ages. To judge from our exploration of the profiles I've been sketching from then to now, it would appear that while the magic curve has steadily declined, the curve of science has risen at the expense of its rival. Cliffs of ascendancy on the science curve would include the Greek invention of the rational approach to the world through the logic of geometry, the formulation of the theory of the open-ended, Sun-centered solar system by Copernicus two thousand years later, the Renaissance idea of developing controlled experimentation as a way of testing scientific ideas, and the rationalist attitude of Descartes that pried the corporeal world away from the age-old idea that mind and body were one—and the rise of the mechanical philosophy that followed: All the real world's just a machine governed by a collection of mathematically determinable statements.

There have been valleys on the science curve, too. One was the chasm caused by the recognition of the Uncertainty Principle, which boldly demonstrated that there are *unseeable* crags and crannies in the microscopic unknown. In other words, there's at least some knowledge about nature you can't mathematize exactly because the deck of physical measurement is stacked against you. Another dip on the learning curve of science came with the recent revelation that coalescing all the laws of the forces of nature under a single mathematical umbrella has proven far more difficult than we had previously thought. The audience is beginning to be turned off by too many "-ons" (leptons, muons, anti-protons—top quark or no top quark) in a universe that appears too complex for its own invention. It reminds me of the sad, sorry state of affairs five hundred years after Ptolemy laid out his epicyclic model of the solar system. As they were barraged with new data on the motions of the planets acquired with ever greater precision, those who followed him could do little more to improve upon his scheme than to simply add circle upon circle to an already geometrically overburdened convocation of tangled orbs. No God would create a universe as complex as this one and tell us about it!

What about the curve of magic? Its downward-spiraling time line also has its upturns. Recall the effects of the age of anxiety and the religiously myopic Middle Ages—both major peaks on the magic curve. And during the "stammering century" there was that unpredictable spiritualistic burst that started in the young heartland of America.

My imaginary curves travel along together, the gap between them widening as they go forward in time. I think they were about as far apart as they ever had been when we reached the threshold of the last century of the second millennium—all that remains of the thicket between two worlds of thought we've been exploring. What constitutes belief in magical phenomena today? Who believes in it and why? Suppose we were to walk through an occult bookstore at ten-year intervals in the late twentieth century, asking who's reading what? Homeopathy—big in the nineties as are channeling, crystals, and geomancy (I call it environmental magic). Psychokinesis—huge in the seventies, but pretty quiescent today. UFOs—making a definite comeback but well below the peak of activity attained in the fifties. Demons are down, but as I write this chapter, angels are experiencing a definite upswing. As time moves forward, the kaleidoscope rotates. But what do magic's ever-changing shiny facets have in common? Can we predict what we'll see at the next turn of the tube?

As far as I know, nobody conducted polls back in the Middle Ages. The earliest survey data I could turn up on magical beliefs in the United States comes from a questionnaire on superstitious beliefs given to Columbia University students in 1920. Mind you, we can't expect pollsters to have asked the same questions at the beginning of our century as at its end. And surveys don't always sample the same segment of the population. Nonetheless, only 4 percent of those surveyed in 1920 believed a planet's position in the sky could influence their character; 2 percent agreed that lines on their hands could foretell their future; but 10 percent thought that bumps on your head did (I was surprised to find phrenology so alive and well in the 20s!). About the same percentage said they also consciously avoided the number thirteen because it was bad luck and that you can make a person turn around and look at you if you stare at his or her back long enough.[1]

By the 1950s the responses to similar questions showed few significant changes among Americans.[2] On the contrary, surveys conducted at the same time in Europe revealed that fully one in five English believed in horoscopic astrology; 17 percent of the English[3] believed in ghosts (42 percent of them actually claimed to have seen one); and about one out of six believed in lucky and unlucky days, numbers, and mascots. In Germany the latter numbers were up around 50 percent, and nearly one in three Germans professed a connection between human fate and the stars. By the middle of the 1970s, polls placed American belief in astrology in the 15 to 18 percent range. In a more penetrating Roper survey conducted in 1977, these numbers leaped up to 25 percent, with 14 percent professing to a belief in reincarnation, 53 percent in ESP, and 74 percent in heaven and hell. Twenty-nine percent of all Americans believed in UFOs as evidence of extraterrestrial intelligence.[4]

Time magazine declared the mid-1970s "boom times on the psychic frontier."[5] Explained the social pundits, it was all part of the revolt against the materialist/rationalist explanation of how the world works. Proponents of rejuvenated Jungian psychology spread the notion of synchronized events that lay outside the realm of probability. The parasciences gained new respect; the number of offerings on parapsychology at college campuses around the nation increased to more than one hundred.[6] Meanwhile, Israeli psychic Uri Geller gave demonstrations of spoon and key bending by the force of his own thoughts, psychic surgeons were healing tennis elbow by touch, and a best seller entitled *The Secret Life of Plants* suggested that frustrated gardeners should employ brain rather than thumb and carry on a meaningful dialogue with their own greenery.[7]

By 1978, a new survey indicated that ghosts and witches stood at about 10 percent on the I-believe meter, the Devil was positioned at 37 percent, angels at 54 percent, and UFOs led the effigy pack at 57 percent. More than one in three Americans believed in precognition.[8] Nearly half of those polled said that they regarded astrologers as scholars; one in three labeled them charlatans, one in six as magicians. Concerning reincarnation, in 1969 20 percent of Americans believed, but by 1981 this number rose by 3 percent (to thirty-eight million people). Whether you attended high school or college seemed not to matter significantly, though the numbers were slightly higher among women as opposed to men, among Blacks than Whites, among lower rather than higher income classes, and in the younger as opposed to the older set.

As the 1990s approached, even though slightly different questions were being asked, popular trends in magical beliefs still prominently revealed themselves. Can crystals be used to heal people? Four percent say yes (20 percent uncertain). Can pyramids? Seven percent (26 percent). Can channeling? Eleven percent (22 percent). Ever been touched by the deceased? (17 percent yes); been in a haunted house (9 percent); consulted a psychic (14 percent).[9] "A strange mix of spirituality and superstition is sweeping across the country" heralded *Time* magazine once again in a 1987 cover story,[10] as the percentage of believers in psi-phenomena rose from one-out-of-two to two-out-of-three in the period 1974–1987. (During this period Bantam Books recorded New Age titles up a factor of ten with the number of New Age bookstores doubling.) Believe in the Devil? Sixty-two percent said yes and 54 percent believed in devil possession. Witches? Fourteen percent. Have you ever seen a UFO? Fifteen percent. Do you believe in astrology? *Still* 25 percent. By 1993, 69 percent had said yes to angels (up 15 percent in fifteen years), 49 percent to devil(s) (up 12 percent).[11] ESP? (46 percent); *déja vu?* (51 percent); clairvoyance (22 percent); communication with dead? (14 percent).[12]

What surprised me after digesting all these numbers was, first of all, how high most of the positive responses were and second, despite the public's fancy for fads, the age dominated by middle-aged baby boomers remains as steadfastly entrenched in belief in occult phenomena as their predecessors were two generations ago—people who were raised in the pre-World War II depression years and ultimately became the pillars of society in the postwar economic boom. Occult beliefs have transcended gaps throughout the century that boasted the space age and the age of the miracle drug. Despite the superficial appearance that our society operates in the realm of reason, a significant percentage of Americans remain fascinated with the possibility that there may be something "out there" beyond the objective world—some form of experience that operates beyond the five senses and some phenomena that penetrate the barrier of physical law in which science has taught us to have faith.

The pattern changes but it remains a pattern. The Top Ten list is altered but there's always a list. I will not argue that a New New Age Cult is about to form, only that old wine—carefully filtered to weed out the dregs—continually reappears in new bottles. It is a spirit of the same sort of vintage that always has been flavored with a desire for the mysterious and irrational. There is a recycling—a recovering and reconfiguring of a general belief that trades in the uneasy certainty and security generally offered by establishment common sense.

To arrive at this prognosis I must first walk you over the old and proven turf on which the New Age has been built—the landfill of nine-teenth-century spiritualistic beliefs that has been combed over more than once this century by new and revised sets of social needs. For a good part of the twentieth century, magic (other than stage magic) and occult phenomena have been lumped together in a loosely defined, very wide-spread philosophy known as the New Age—a reenvisioning of the New Thought of the turn of the century. In 1989, CSICOP (the Committee for the Scientific Investigation of Claims of the Paranormal) devoted an entire conference to the New Age. These are just a few of the responses offered by conference leaders to the question, What is the New Age?:

> . . . A religious/social movement, *religious* because it uses religion's languages, *social* because it's inclusive, not exclusive.

> . . . An example of confusion between inner and outer truth, subjective and objective reality.

> . . . A strange and blurred category that includes a lot of things you might not have thought to find there.

> . . . An extremely confused area where useful books spill over into muddy religious areas.[13]

(The meeting was so popular, reported one member, that participants at other conferences sneaked out to kibitz with the skeptics!) Though use of the term New Age has now begun to decline (it has largely been re-placed by terms like alternative religious movements, planetary con-sciousness, and so on), its immediate past is worth probing.

As far as I know, the term New Age was first used in 1914 when a Freemasonry journal and a London newspaper of the same title both ap-peared, offering articles on social, psychological, and spiritual issues of the day. The concept was revived in America in the calm aftermath of the turbulent social revolution of the sixties. The notion of the anticipated "Age of Aquarius" made popular in a rock musical of the sixties contributed to the diffusion of this term.[14] Such a major change in the cosmos—a spiritual knocking of the earth off its pivot—was a sign that something big was about to happen to its inhabitants. And those who had been socially active and involved in protest movements and who had turned to spiritual contemplation via networking, writing periodicals, and establishing clubs were ready for it.

While nineteenth-century spiritual efforts were directed toward communicating with the dead in order to learn the secrets of what awaits us in the afterworld, today the quest after the meaning of death has been traded in for a yearning that addresses the meaning of life itself. The contemporary occult fringe seems more interested in the philosophy of spiritualism than in acquiring proofs of survival of the soul later on. If any single goal has unified all the efforts of this loosely gathered eclectic movement, it is the professed desire for wholeness. Mixing Christianity, animate nature, and active humanity, one New Age author calls it a metaphor for being in the world in a manner that opens us to the presence of God—the presence of love and possibility—in the midst of our ordinariness.[15] It is a response to the idea that our planet is sacred and the desire "to create a world in which humanity, nature and the domain of spirit work together in ways that are mutually empowering and cocreative,"[16] declares one New Age philosopher. But New Age also has a more secular, individualistic ring to it. That same author calls it a condition that emerges when I live life "in a creative, empowering, compassionate manner," one that recognizes and honors both the inherent wholeness in the world and the value and importance of each of its component parts.

Time magazine gave us the late eighties' pop view when it called the New Age "a combination of spirituality and superstition—fad and farce . . . not new":

> The underlying faith is a lack of faith in the orthodoxies of rationalism, high technology, routine living, spiritual law-and-order. Somehow, the New Agers believe, there must be some secret and mysterious shortcut or alternative path to happiness and health. And nobody ever really dies.[17]

Qualities correctly or incorrectly attributed to New Age folks include the tendency to experiment with Eastern religions on the one hand and psychedelic drugs on the other—both with the goal of attaining a higher state of consciousness; but, paradoxically, those who profess nineties-style New Age beliefs (as opposed to, say the seventies) are squeaky-clean-livers, more inclined to beat the path toward the health food store than the drug commune. Environmental consciousness and activism are another growing part of the movement.

The New Age has its detractors. Some intolerant traditionalists on the theological side call it too easy and undemanding a faith because it rejects confronting the problem of good and evil—a mainstream Christian idea; or because most of its so-called practitioners are superficial and narcissistic and a few (like Paracelsus of old) pose serious dangers to society because they are mere mountebanks who exploit decent people. Finally, there is, as perhaps there deserves to be in our age, a conspiracy theory: Some fundamentalists say organized New Age cults are deliberately out to destroy all order with an intent to dominate the world—Satan leading his army of demons against Christianity and Western civilization.

But these critiques are all generic. To understand the course of magic and the occult in the development of the New Age, we need to look at its many components. Precisely where has New Age thought emerged? What theaters of human consciousness has it penetrated and what jagged crystals of thought have tumbled around to color the patterns we view through the New Age kaleidoscope? And, most importantly, how are these ideas connected with the roots of magic in the past that we have already explored?

CHAPTER 26

DIFFERENT TIME, SAME CHANNEL

When you turn on your television set and watch the evening news, you don't for a moment suspect that the anchor person is sitting inside that little box. The system of vibration [energy from another physical plane] enters your reality . . . much as a television signal to the antenna—and then is amplified and comes out of the vocal chords, the mouth and the speaking structure of that which is the Channel.

Lazaris, High Spirit of channeler Jack Pursel
Quoted in Rosemary E. Guiley's
Harper's Encyclopedia of Mystical and Paranormal Experience

L et's call it the communication of information not known consciously to the one who communicates it. Channeling is the 1990s' number-one form of mediumship, holding out at the top of the charts since the late 1980s. It is to contemporary occult culture what spiritualistic séances were to the 1920s, except it has a much wider repertoire. Sources are said to be not only the dead, but also angels, spirits of nature, extraterrestrials, and the "Higher Self"—a universal form of Soul that finds its roots back in the Middle Ages.

All channeling proceeds through an individual perceived to be someone other than his or her conscious self. Pay $150 and you can join the crowd at the local Holiday Inn to experience J. Z. Knight, an attractive blonde charismatic adept, being taken over in voice and in spirit by a 35,000-year-old Hindu warrior god named Ramtha, her father in a previous life. As she ties back her hair and the lights go down, J.Z. begins to enter her self-imposed trance: "Come forward into truth and knowingness and wisdom"—her voice descends into lower, more guttural tones and her body writhes.[1] She stamps her feet on the ground, imitating a sumo wrestler as her fans chant and cheer her on. After making a few predictions about the forthcoming state of the world (earthquakes, volcanic eruptions, the stock market and the like) she (he) dives down into the audience, portable mike in hand, and begins to answer questions and offer individual advice to inquiring believer and nonbeliever alike: "Why do I get an upset stomach when I take vitamins?" "What can I do to get out of debt?" "To get my autistic child to talk to me?" The answers are rather basic: "Learn to love your fat," "The Ram" tells a corpulent complainer; "I will send a runner (a person of experience) to help solve your problem"; "Just let it be and don't worry so much about it." These are the answers to just about anything. Many have acted on J.Z./Ramtha's advice—even uprooting their homes and businesses or ditching their spouses and moving to another place in order to save themselves from impending physical or economic disaster.

Ex-insurance man Jack Pursel, another premier channeler, squints his eyes and clenches his fists as he calls up Lazaris, a High Spirit like J.Z.'s Ramtha except he's much warmer and wittier than his rather violent Indian counterpart. Also like J.Z., after spending a few private years with the spirit in which he honed his skills and began to learn about the evolutionary development of his several past lifetimes, Pursel quit his job and began to share Lazaris' wisdom with the public. He did it via a series of books, seminars, and workshops ("energy blendings" he calls them), thereby also acquiring an alternate source of income. Jack Pursel's upscale clients include a number of Hollywood stars, Shirley MacLaine once among them.[2] MacLaine's intrinsic fame, her popular books, and the media coverage have all played a role in catapulting channeling to the head of the occult charts in the eighties and nineties.[3]

Love and learning is the message beamed to your inner self if your antennae are up. Lying outside our space-time continuum, Lazaris' mission is to educate, Pursel tells his audience. He's around to make people aware of the fact that they are multiple selves. He's not out to dominate anybody—doesn't want to be a master or a guru—just a friend who's here to help you get to your own self-designed higher place of reality. To get there, you need to endure pain, but you grow through joy and love, for the "God and Goddess—All" loves you.

Despite channeling's obvious media-derived name, this calling up of supernaturals via trance goes all the way back to the Oracle at Delphi. Swedenborg channeled and so did Nostradamus. And recall those late-nineteenth-century séances of DDH and HPB. The contemporary wave (skeptic Martin Gardner calls it a flood) of spirit conjuring was revived in the late 1960s when seer Jane Roberts,[4] like Mesmer, laid aside her technological aid (a ouija board) and via deep trance alone took on the

vocal features of Seth, a kind of higher entity of the spirit world. Roberts
described him as an energy-personality essence in non-physical form
reincarnated from previous lives in the lost continent of Atlantis. Prior to
that he had been a Roman contemporary of Christ, a Renaissance mer-
chant, a pope, a monk, and several different Turks and Ethiopians. Seth's
optimistic message sounds a lot like Lazaris'; at least it has a decided Swedenborgian origin. One difference is that Swedenborg claims to have
talked directly to the great figures from the golden ages of history while
Roberts' channel source only represents the great luminaries as a contemporary—TV has made its impact!

In the West, the idea of the reincarnated soul has always been less popular than in the rest of the world (two-thirds of the world's population
believes in one or another form of it) but with the slow warming to alternative philosophies like Hinduism, Islam, and even Native American
beliefs, the popularity of the concept has been steadily on the rise in the
United States. Reincarnation fits very well with cyclic notions of time,
and phenomena like channeling readily lend themselves to it. Your past
lives, thoughts, actions, and beliefs create all that there is to reality; this is
an idea that has always been closely tuned in to channeling. Picking up
on the idea of evolution according to Madame Blavatsky, Roberts advocated that the growth and development of the self is a limitless possibility. But successive reincarnations don't derive from the karma—the deeds
both mental and physical that make up your life; rather it is your Soul
that progresses. And it advances only in proportion to the effort you put
into psychic and spiritual matters. Other Sethian historical tidbits of
truth focus on Christian beliefs: Christ was really three different blended
lives and his disciples merely fragments of this personality. The crucifix-
ion was a psychic event. The Second Coming (it will happen before
2075) will be a similar event but you'll need to be tuned in to experience
it, for like the first time it won't happen physically.

What's going on in channeling, say some psychologists, is "mass hypnosis—a process of collective suggestion and the transfer of conscious
content"[5] from channeler to client, usually lost souls and seekers looking
for new ways of life. Social commentators at the soft end of the spectrum
think of channeling as a simple form of divination and many skeptics say
that's all there is to it—minus the charlatanry. In other words, the
medium simply uses his or her own imagination, intuition, and inspiration to give basic advice to those in need (what I claim to do when I advise my students). If the message is positive, simple, and uplifting (as often

mine must be to my young anxiety-prone charges: Don't worry, forget about it, get a good night's sleep, and things will look better in the morning) then it is not surprising to see how channelers like J.Z. and Jack, both described as charismatic individuals who *look* like they know what they're talking about, have developed such a vast following.

This annoys the rationalists who hate to see the public being duped by a bunch of ego-enhanced materialists who spread about low-level intelligence for profit. Systematized delusions, they call it,[6] if not out-and-out fakery. But they are bothered by the security blanket channelers throw about themselves by blaming everything they babble on somebody elses' voices from the past and consequently they find it difficult to devise tests to evaluate their authenticity.[7]

Middle-of-the-road channelers admit the mental forms associated with their craft derive from dreams and deep meditation; but hardline physical channelers claim to produce direct material results: apports, levitation, spoon bending, and that old universal spirit substance, ectoplasm. Psychokinesis, or PK as it is now called,[8] is the stuff of this far-out realm. It's what provokes most of the scientific spleen, those who feel their territorial toes being stepped on. Damn it!—Anything that operates in the material realm, the empirical rationalists argue, ought to be subjectable to physical tests before being declared true and real. Adepts, who tend to be less blissed-out than their purely meditative counterparts, clash head-on with the scientific debunkers; they are aided, oddly enough, by a new cadre of Houdinis, who seek to explore ways alleged phenomena of unknown origin can be reduced to known explanations such as the rational laws of physics—or to out-and-out deception.

CHAPTER 27

PK WARS:
PSYCHICS VS. PHYSICS

. . . no science modeled after physics or chemistry can offer much of interest to parapsychology.
> Stephen Braude, *The Limits of Influence*

Paramedic, paralegal, parapsychology. The prefix is Greek and it means "beyond" (translate, "at the edge of")—medicine, law, or in the present instance, the boundary of the relationship between our consciousness and the things in the physical, material world of which we are aware. The phenomena with which parapsychology deals were categorized with the spirit visions, angels, and demons once relegated to the domain of religion; that is until about 1900, when Sigmund Freud (1856–1939) proposed his revolutionary theory that much of what we say we experience is locked away in our "unconscious"—a state of mind so powerful and far-reaching that it directly influences many aspects of our behavior.

If Copernicus exteriorized the universe, Freud interiorized human consciousness. He plunged us into the vast abyss of the human mind. Behind and below our intelligence in the shadows of our existence other mental forces operate, no less a part of our being than the conscious actions of which we are all aware. And they can be explored, Freud said. Though he resisted the possibility of supernatural phenomena, in his work on psychoanalysis Freud did have occasion to mine telepathy and clairvoyance; but he was inclined to attribute a physiological rather than a psychic explanation to "uncanny" phenomena, something on the order of the physical transfer of thought waves.

He may be getting rapped by contemporary science for blaming too much on sexual repression; nevertheless, Freud tore down the limits of our cognitive experience and extended the potential to receive, store, and disseminate information about the world outside.[1] People with a sixth sense, a kind of extrasensory perception (ESP), for example, believe they can acquire information about the past, present, and future. At the hard edge of psi phenomena lies psychokinesis. When it reached the occult hit parade in Cold War America, its crescendo produced a war of its own.

Can the simple roll of dice be influenced by mental concentration and can they be made to fall as someone wills it, with a specific combination of faces straight up? One logical-minded researcher defines psychokinesis (PK) as "the causal influence of an organism on a region [r] of the physical world, without any known sort of physical interaction between the organism's body and [r]."[2] In lay terms, that means mind over matter and it includes metal bending, levitation, healing by touch, and mental picture taking (thoughtography). (DDH's body stretching probably belongs here. So does the evil eye.) The response of the scientist–stage magician axis to such feats has been particularly harsh. Maybe this is because the claims of PK are extra-extraordinary, and there have been many demonstrated instances of fraud.

On the rise since the 1930s, when psychologist J. B. Rhine lent scientific legitimacy to PK by establishing a lab at Duke University to investigate it,[3] mental spoon bending seems to have peaked in the 1970s after the media latched onto the antics of high-profile characters like Ted Serios and Uri Geller and their antagonist and combatant, magician James (the Amazing) Randi.

Spoon-bending Geller says he acquired his abilities as a child when one day out of curiosity he reached out and touched a spark that emanated from his mother's sewing machine. Immediately, he says, he could read his mother's mind, make his father's watch speed up, see through metal containers, and—what would ultimately develop into his stage specialty—bend pieces of metal by concentrating on them.

Frequent TV appearances gave Geller more exposure than any occult figure of his time. Thanks to TV personality Johnny Carson's passing interest in skepticizing psychic phenomena, Geller made an appearance on the nationally televised "Tonight" show; but he was duped by his host, who cleverly refused to employ any of Geller's devices and insisted instead on supplying his own. Surprisingly, the Israeli psychic's inability to perform—he said it was because the atmosphere was too hostile—did little to defuse his audience appeal. A few years later magician Randi demonstrated that he could produce the phenomenon of spoon bending and breaking through simple illusion and concealment—by using a spoon that already had a hairline fracture in it and stealthily holding thumb and index finger over the crack while thinking on it.

Following in Houdini's footsteps, in the late 1960s James Randi joined the war being waged by the ubiquitous vigilante scientific committees against parapsychologists under the caveat that no experiment on the paranormal can be considered worthy unless an expert illusionist is present while it is being conducted. This was supposed to counter the possibility of using techniques of trickery with which illusionists are familiar but scientists—who seem always to believe Mother Nature would never trick them—are not. This relationship was consummated when Randi became a member of CSICOP,[4] an offshoot of the American Humanist Association. This organization had achieved some notoriety when it issued a famous manifesto: "Objections Against Astrology," signed by 182 prominent scientists. Incidentally, Randi was aided considerably in his task when, in 1986, the MacArthur Foundation awarded him a $272,000 "genius grant" to continue with his debunking efforts.

Oddly enough, while Geller couldn't bend entertainer Johnny Carson's will, he had sufficiently impressed Stanford Physicist Russell Targ and his colleagues for them to offer to test him. He passed! Geller was officially pronounced effective at guessing the roll of dice imprisoned in a metal box. Targ and an associate describe one experiment they conducted with the Israeli in the prestigious scientific journal *Nature:*

> A double-blind experiment was performed in which a single ¾-inch die was placed in a 3″ × 4″ × 5″ steel box. The box was then vigorously shaken by one of the experimenters and placed on the table, a technique found in control runs to produce a distribution of die faces differing nonsignificantly from chance. The orientation of the die within the box was unknown to the experimenters at that time. Geller would then write down which face was uppermost. The target pool was known, but the targets were individually prepared in a manner blind to all persons involved in the experiment. This experiment was performed ten times, with Geller passing twice and giving a response eight times. In the eight times in which he gave a response, he was correct each time. The distribution of responses consisted of three 2s, one 4, two 5s, and two 6s. The probability of this occurring by chance is approximately one in 10^6.[5]

One in a million sounds impressive. That the test was double-blind, the die being hidden in the box from both Geller and the scientists, is impressive, too. Could Geller have cheated? Did he have a way of peeking inside the box? Yes, suggested Randi, and he even offered a means by which he might have done so. Was the evidence presented by the Stanford group bogus? A videotape that revealed the omission of some unsuccessful trials cast some doubt on their findings. In sum, critics concluded that what seemed to be a carefully controlled die test could be reduced to a collection of mere anecdotes.[6]

Countless lab tests have been conducted to determine whether PK is valid. As in the Geller case, psi hits and misses are recorded against the statistics of pure chance. Do the lab conditions affect performance? Do hostile onlookers cause sensitives to lose their paranormal abilities? Does boredom and distraction produce more misses? Are the conditions too artificial and restricted to activate any psychic manifestations? What about the comfort level in the lab? (Medical doctors routinely report inconsistencies in blood pressure readings taken in the office when compared with those obtained via a monitoring machine in the home environment.) The problems are myriad and to date few scientists will admit that such tests have produced any remarkable results. George Price, a research associate of the University of Minnesota's Department of Medicine, launched an exemplary attack: There's too much noise in the data, he said, and too many instances of unreported failed tests. The data are simply not trustworthy.[7] Even those who admit there may be something to it unanimously declare that no physical variable can affect what happens in the lab—no nuclear forces, not gravity nor any known force produced by wave, particle, or field. Nothing that is measurable seems to have any connection with whatever takes place. As long as empirical science is society's preferred form of explanation, dissatisfaction and disbelief will remain the standard response.

Ted Serios was a 1950s Chicago bellhop who claimed to have deduced the location of buried treasure in Florida while conversing in a telepathic trance with the departed spirit of pirate Jean Lafitte. (Maybe he was just a bit further out there than Geller.) No doubloons ever were found, Serios explained, because the information was leaked to another source who had beat him to pay dirt. When Serios met Jule Eisenbud (a psychiatrist and professor of the University of Colorado Medical School) both their lives changed. The two experimented together and Serios developed into a master "thoughtographer," claiming the uncanny ability to produce images in Polaroid simply by looking into the lens of a camera.[8] Together, adept and scientific professional claimed to have catalogued hundreds of images obtained when Serios held a small tube (a "gismo" that aided in his concentration), before his eyes and stared into the camera lens. They published some of them in a book controversial enough to get the attention of Randi and the reductionists.

In 1967 a skeptical pair of reporters published an article in the magazine *Popular Photography* claiming to show how Serios used optical gimmickry and sleight of hand to dupe everybody, including scientist Eisenbud. The trick, they demonstrated, was to hold a negative over the lens of the camera, the whole of the apparatus being hidden away in the "gismo." Just because James Randi can create the illusion of bending a spoon and a couple of photographs obtained with a "gismo" can fake a thoughtograph—does this prove that Geller and Serios are fakes? In other words does the *possibility* of fraud mean that it actually had occurred?, retorted PK buff Curtis Fuller, cofounder of pro-PK *Fate Magazine.*[9]

The plot thickened. Like Sir William Crookes one hundred years before, Eisenbud was so convinced of the psychic's ability to produce thought images that he took a public pledge stating that if any jury could duplicate under similar conditions the range of phenomena he had experienced with Ted Serios, he would personally buy back at list price and burn all copies of his book on Serios[10] and spend the rest of his life selling door-to-door copies of *Popular Photography*—in a future issue of which he promised to appear wearing a dunce cap!

Not surprisingly, Randi headed the queue of takers. His technique, announced in a meeting with Eisenbud and Randi on the NBC "Today Show," would duplicate what Serios had done, namely palm a small lens and a picture, then transfer the picture through the lens and onto the film of the camera. The dare never came off. Instead, the whole affair turned into a war of words and in a series of published letters and exchanges—again with the full attention of the media—the two sides quibbled lengthily over the term "similar conditions." One demand was that Randi have his body orifices inspected before being sewn into a monkey suit; another that his blood alcohol level be sufficiently high (Serios usually performed his miracles while intoxicated!). Within a year the media fanfare attracted the wider scientific community. The journals *Science* and *The Journal of the American Psychoanalytic Association* each published articles proclaiming the *Popular Photography* exposé devastating and condemning the PK duo for refusing to submit to controlled experimentation. Theirs, wrote one author, were "decaying minds" with "thinking defects and disturbed relations to reality."[11]

Sure, cheating and fraud are common occurrences that contribute to scientific disbelief in PK. But, some ask, what about those instances that *are* believable? How *could* the mind triumph over matter? Physicists say there is only one course to take. But, as philosopher of science Stephen Braude has pointed out, the vigilantes may be seeking the wrong indictment. In many instances they assume that psi phenomena do have unobservable underlying structures that are analyzable by the methods of the physical and biological sciences; for example, the way heat is reducible to molecular motion, the inheritance of disease to DNA, and time to a chain of events that follow causally one after the other, with an arrow of progress pointing only in one direction.[12] Who is to say this is the only way to explain what happens in the world around us?

Whatever encompasses the physical world also unifies human intellectual behavior. Right? Maybe not. Maybe we're too hung up on reducing everything mental to something physical. We tend to think on faith that there is nothing that is not unanalyzable—reducible to subsidiary laws that we are capable of articulating, and that such laws rest on tacit unquestioned assumptions about the universe; for example, that there is a continuity to its happenings and that all its parts always add up to the same total. While Braude and other critics are a long way from framing that much scientifically maligned, nonexistent theory of PK, they do offer a few novel propositions that might take us out of the realm of PK warfare and toward such a theory. Maybe PK processes just don't reduce to underlying phenomena, Braude concludes.

Instead, what if actions between organisms and observable states are direct? What if a bending spoon doesn't result from some microscopic molecular action that then causes a large-scale change? What if, in defiance of the reductionist way of viewing the world, changes on the quantum level happen as a result of action that takes place on the large-scale level?[13] Maybe thought processes have a way of collapsing the "state vector" that we cannot further break down, theorizes Braude. The question of how to bridge the gap between mental intention and resulting physical effect may have no definitive answer after all.

To put it another way, can simple laws of nature, by being repeatedly applied and interacting with one another, automatically lead to complex, seemingly chaotic phenomena like aggression or compassion—phenomena that might not be predictable in a straightforward manner by those laws? Advocates of the new science of complexity theory think so.[14] As we have seen time and time again, parascience has a habit of borrowing implements from the scientific tool shed. Quantum mechanics, with all of its implied improbabilities and uncertainties, needless to say, has provided a haven for explanations of occult phenomena, for any world devoid of certainties is also free of impossibilities. Physicist David Bohm tested scientific orthodoxy when his work on causality culminated in a book on the "Implicate Order."[15] It would profoundly influence occult readers and thinkers like Braude. Bohm suggested that beyond the tangible or "explicate" world there exists a deeper, imperceptible reality of undivided wholeness. Entities in the explicate world are all "implicated" as subtotalities of that other imperceptible order. A stream has waves, splashes, and vortices, each arising from the flow of water, but each transitory aberration can be abstracted temporarily and experienced separately from the flowing motion of the stream even though it depends on it. This is the "hidden variable" theory physicists often speak about.

Sounds like the doorway into complexity theory, doesn't it? Physicist Murray Gell-Mann also believes an interplay between nature's laws and chance exists on the frontier between order and disorder. As we directly perceive only the coarse-grained phenomena of the macroscopic world, we are only beginning to be aware of the existence of such a frontier. But Gell-Mann is careful to point out that he believes *this* universe is knowable and that the laws governing it will be understood to be simple at their basic level once we discover them. And—the key point for us—the description of everything that happens in the universe via these laws will indeed be complete and just as strict as classical physics in disallowing paranormal phenomena.[16] Confidence of this order is a rare and precious possession. Critics of the quantum mechanics theory of PK argue that all consciousness is non-physical and that if the mental-physical link is still causal then it resists further analysis by the laws of physics; therefore, how it is that human consciousness causes the "state of affairs" to change has no real answer—either from classical or quantum physics.

Granted, all of this is far more complex than I've made it out to be, but it should illuminate the context of the epigraph I chose to open this chapter. Maybe we've reached the time when we need to prepare to think of the possibility that some phenomena at the macroscopic level of human behavior may be unexplainable, just as some scientists (not Gell-Mann and a sizeable majority) already believe is the case at the quantum level. In the final analysis, the turf over which PK war combatants have been feuding may be confined to the domain of human will.

CHAPTER 28

THE PERSONALIZED MAGIC OF HEALING: MENDING THE CARTESIAN SPLIT

~~~

Moyers: You know I think millions of Americans are ahead of your profession in the practice of mind/body medicine. They often go off into the superficial aspects of it, pop psych and all of that. But they're searching for something and they seem to know that the mind has something to do with health.

Dr.: Yes—Science often lags behind popular experience.

William Moyers, *Healing and the Mind*

Exploring the mind-body connection has become a major move-ment in behavioral medicine today; over one third of all Ameri-cans have tried alternative therapies in the nineties. Believing what you think influences how you feel, so surgeons and anesthetists hold hands with patients—tell them to relax and imagine themselves in a favorite place. Relaxation therapy, meditation, and hypnosis are actively being used to deal with serious, even terminal diseases. Group therapy is employed in the healing process. There seem to be three legs to the med-ical support structure: pills, surgery, and the paranormal leg inherent in the "relaxation response."[1]

Few medical researchers today doubt that our immune and nervous systems are linked. Indeed, we *are* wired together. Nerve fibers connect all the way down to the cellular level of the immune system. First dis-cussed in laypersons' terms in the 1970s by a Harvard medical professor, this link has led to wide adoption of the idea that the physical effects of stress can be alleviated by a variety of thought and exercise techniques.

Demonstrating that the placebo effect (the response of the body to a neutral substance like plain water or a sugar pill) is often indistinguish-able from a standard drug therapy had a profound effect on building up the third leg of contemporary medicine's accepted support stool, for it proved that healing can be a process that involves learning. If it's not all in the mind, at least Dr. Herbert Benson's relaxation response theory began with the well-known idea that all animals react to chronic stressful situations by the "fight or flight response." So, when we need to adjust our behavior (i.e., what to do when we're suddenly attacked by a wild boar), an involuntary response automatically triggers our rate of blood pressure, heartbeat, blood flow, and metabolism as we prepare either to stand and fight or flee. But in twentieth-century sedentary people, Benson reasoned, the fight or flight response could be instead a shock to the system leading to heart attack and stroke. This is where relaxation therapy comes in: By concentrating on your breathing, heartbeat, and other life-sustaining processes you can control your own flow of juices. Through meditation you become something above the animal that instinctively reacts to threats via signals in the environment.

If this sounds a long way from PK and channeling, it isn't really, for at the heart of relaxation therapy lies human will. You can take the same role as the magician; you are the active agent in the mind-body encounter. Mental control—mind over body—was the main thrust of Benson's bestseller and it all was nurtured by the process of biofeedback. As he explained:

> We have long been aware that man's skeletal muscles are commanded by his voluntary nerves acting through the brain. However, Western man has only recently recognized that he can control his involuntary responses. The regulator of these involuntary processes such as blood pressure, heart beat, and amount of blood flow to various parts of the body is called the autonomic nervous system. Visceral learning, or biofeedback, as it is popularly called, established that man could control his involuntary or autonomic nervous system.[2]

Benson contended that by learning biofeedback techniques you could lower your blood pressure and heart rate, and even change the electrical activity in your brain—all by thinking relaxing thoughts. One way to do this, claimed the doctor, was to learn the Eastern meditational techniques of yoga and Zen Buddhism. To prove his claim he tested ten practicing pros in his Harvard medical lab. The subjects included TM's most celebrated habitué, the Guru Maharishi Mahesh Yogi, who knocked out all the time-consuming, boring aspects of Yogic practice that might otherwise be unappealing to the attention-impaired. In other words, the grinning guru made it easy. Benson describes the Maharishi's influence on him:

> Transcendental Meditation involves a surprisingly simple technique. A trained instructor gives you a secret word or sound or phrase, a mantra, which you promise not to divulge. This sound is allegedly chosen to suit the individual and is to be silently "perceived". The meditator receives the mantra from his teacher and then repeats it mentally over and over again while sitting in a comfortable position. The purpose of this repetition is to prevent distracting thoughts. Meditators are told to assume a passive attitude and if other thoughts come into mind to disregard them, going back to the mantra. Practitioners are advised to meditate twenty minutes in the morning, usually before breakfast, and twenty minutes in the evening, usually before dinner.[3]

Follow your will; make your work in keeping with your purpose; find your own individual place in the world. These are the slogans that hang in the offices of the new Zen masters of business and industry a generation later—leaders who provide regular workshops in stress management for their employees. Meditating is now taught via computers and clubs and it is deemed as sound in marketing as in medicine for producing results, if not miracles. Taking on many of the trappings of high-tech science, the mind-over-body concept implicit in the relaxation response has adjusted itself to the self-help industry, proliferating as a result. A woman with severe cramps, another with persistent headaches, a third with a right arm so stiff she cannot bear the pain of lifting it flock to a local Healing Arts Center for an encounter with a Kenkocreator, a rubber-handled metal rod that passes through a pair of magnetic spheres. The massage therapist, a latter-day young Mesmer, gently rolls the metallic balls over the affected area. "My left arm felt like it was freer; like it wasn't so stuck anymore,"[4] claimed one patient. Taping magnetic pads to her arm and shoulders prolongs relief, she says. For asthmatics there are magnetic jackets. Others squat on magnets to mesmerize their lower back pain and some put them in shoes that house their arthritic feet. Still others stuff them in their pillow to stop snoring or sleep on them to awake refreshed.

Tools of an expanding trade: A middle-aged executive suffers from chronic back pain and headaches. He enrolls in a six-week course consisting of biofeedback training sessions at a local Psychological Health Service Center. While a mechanic down the street tunes up his Chrysler, our patient lies in a relaxed posture as he is hooked up to an Electromyographic (EMG) biofeedback machine. He sticks his finger into a sleeve attached to a wire that goes to a beeping black box that measures his muscular tension. A relaxation tape consisting of soothing sounds is turned on and over several sessions he learns to practice controlling the beeps by tensing and relaxing various muscles. As he slowly elevates his skin temperature, both frequency and tone register the changes on the machine. Other sensors are connected to the sites of his aches and pains—still others monitor heartbeat and brainwave activity. He is in charge, but the machine monitors all his standard bodily rhythms. The original theory behind the black box was that if you are continuously fed data on your brain wave patterns you can learn to regulate them. The idea is to keep the brain's alpha waves, which correspond to being in a completely relaxed state, turned on.

Just as Mesmer tried to do it without magnets, some proponents of the new "therapeutic touch" (TT) therapy, a no-touch form of the laying on of hands, move only their hands over the body of their patients from head to toe, thereby claiming not only to soothe them but also to produce chemical changes in the blood that relieve pain. They say they operate by smoothing out kinks in the human energy field, specifically by assessing which areas of it feel out of balance; their movements clear, mobilize, and then redirect the field to facilitate healing. Practitioners— most of them nurses— draw as much fire from the medical establishment as Mesmer did when he abandoned the technology that gave some semblance of legitimacy to a would-be science and decided to go it alone. *What* human energy field?, they gripe.

Magic always tries to be in tune with the technology of the age in which it develops. That's what makes it thrive. Remember Mary the Jewess' *bain marie* and Mesmer's *baquet?* Today's magneto-revival indeed would have pleased Franz Mesmer, who might be surprised to learn that it emanates not from Europe but from Japan. Dr. Kyoichi Nakagawa holds that the earth's magnetic field has a lot to do with ailments like insomnia and backache. Did you know that when a magnet is passed across a blood vessel it deflects ions in opposite directions?, claims one distributor of magnetic apparatus. Though this hasn't exactly been borne out in tests, an MIT group did discover a marginal increase in the flow of saline solution through capillaries. The FDA has not approved of such devices in the fight against pain control and while physicists and medical researchers decry the efficacy of static magnetic pads, some claim to have successfully treated osteoarthritis with pulsed electromagnetic fields (PEMF)[5] and various pulse frequencies have been shown to aid in the healing of damaged and broken bones.

Comments one skeptical researcher on do-it-yourself healing technology:

> If you believe in it and it feels good, that's half the benefit you're getting. . . . The first rule of medicine is do no harm. That's probably why the people selling these aren't getting their wrists slapped.[6]

Like their reaction to astrology, this is an attitude that some scientists lately have taken toward harmless forms of experimental medicine.

Remember deep-muscle body massages a decade ago?—close to a Medieval form of torture, rife with crunching bodily abuse usually administered by a heavy-handed bruiser. So maybe you were rewarded either before or after with a turkish bath or a trip to the sauna. You were supposed to get that feel-good attitude engendered by restoring your muscular structure to normalcy through forcible manipulation. The net effect is no different today but the process is decidedly a kinder and gentler one. Visit a high-tech massage therapist today and you might begin by entering into a computer the history of your body and all its ailments—the questionnaire replete with a release stating that (a) if you experience the slightest discomfort you will immediately inform the practitioner so that she or he may adjust the pressure to suit your comfort level, and (b) if you make any sexual advances toward the therapist you will immediately be "terminated." Such are the potentially ruinous risks of today's resort to the relaxation response. When you finally enter the theater of therapeutical arts—a quiet, often dimly lit and tastefully decorated room enhanced by New Age background music—the person you confront is no sadistic Brunhilde. A nicely dressed youthful massage therapist gives you a hot pack on the back and a hot oil rubdown on your feet, being careful to expose only the part of your body being worked—it's the law. Fingers then work their magic on the affected problem area, usually gleaned from the questionnaire. Maybe it's a knot in the neck or tension in the upper back. The most violent part of the whole treatment is the final gentle karate chop that travels up and down each side of the spine (it still gives me goosebumps). Time flies when you're having fun as $50 buys an hour that seems only ten minutes long—an aftershock of the treatment.

Given this description, I was surprised that a few of the painful, vehement forms of bodywork—such as Rolfing, which was common in the 1960s—have undergone a recent resurgence (a 10 percent increase in the number of practitioners per annum since 1990).[7] When you get Rolfed you literally get realigned—at least that was Ida Rolf's theory about how to deal with really bad posture. She was the Swiss chemist who developed the theory that unless your deep muscular connective tissue is straightened out, you can't really move or breathe properly. Consequently, you get all slumped over with back pain and you walk crooked. In the nineties form of the art, the Rolfer stands on the table you're seated upon and jerkily pushes down on your back. In this condition a Rolfee is enabled to vividly reclaim true epiphanies of his or her past life—perhaps even a forgotten episode of sexual abuse. Recalled one client:

> When (Amodeo) [the therapist] was working on some of the muscles on my right side, I got some really strong images of my father, who has been dead since 1972. . . . These were good memories of childhood events with my father that I hadn't thought about for a long time.

With those memories came vast physical improvement. One practitioner stated:

> I really see it as a very natural process and a process we don't understand. . . . The mind isn't only in the brain; the mind is throughout the body. I think the connection between the mind and the body is something we really don't understand.

According to one scientific disclaimer, Dr. John Renner of the National Council Against Health Fraud (a newly created arm of the National Institutes of Health), the benefits of the process remain questionable:

> Rolfing probably makes some people feel better, but you
> have to be extremely cautious. . . . It has tended to become
> a cult, and I'm not sure Rolfing is a necessity of life.

All of the therapies I have described fall under the New Age generic heading of bodywork. The theory behind acupuncture—at least in our culture—is similar. The idea that there's a connection between your organs and your skin goes back five thousand years to ancient China. When you're ill, your inner energies are out of balance. Taking herbs is a way of unsticking your *chi*—the universal life force that flows in all of us along energy pathways or meridians. Having needles stuck in your skin is a way of intervening in the energy system and attempting to control the flow (in effect doing what Galen sought to do with the bodily humors). An expert spins a needle with the emission of his own *chi* before inserting it into a specified location in order to gain access to a particular meridian.

Chiropractic is another popular form of natural bodywork that dispenses with drugs and surgery, those two other conventional support stilts upon which the stool of medical practice rests. The Foundation for Chiropractic Education and Research says that since 1980 the number of people visiting chiropractors has doubled. Chiropractic basically involves manipulation of the spine to repair neurological asymmetries attributable to a variety of causes ranging from accidents to stress to poor posture. To the chiropractor the spine is all. When you get on the table in his office, he doesn't hook you up to anything; instead he lays you on your stomach and works on your back the way Rodin might have labored over a mass of clay about to become a statue. He flips you onto your side as he twists, pulls, and wrestles with your body, which responds with snaps, crackles, and pops in sometimes painful resonance with his digital kinetics. Remove the impedance and let the body heal itself, seem to be chiropractic bywords. Having had a minor back problem recently, I am well aware via first-hand testimony of the public's attitude toward this profession. Of all the alternative medical curers, I think the chiropractors elicit the greatest extremes on the continuum of response. For every friend or relative I'd heard offer up the "I swear by him" testimony, there was another who charged: "He ruined me and my back for good!" (Incidentally, my problem went away before I could decide what to do about it—or maybe I *did* do something about it subconsciously?)

Tai Chi is yet another contemporary popular form of self-manipulation. It means "great ultimate feat" and it derives from Chinese boxing. While we think of *Tai Chi* as being tied to the martial arts, the slow, fluid movements and controlled breathing associated with it can be used as a treatment for balancing, loosening up, and coordinating the body—a way to keep you limber as you grow older and your joints and muscles begin to dry out, stiffen, and atrophy. Done slowly, the moves are often related to forms of dance or meditation. When you engage in them you are literally going with the natural flow of energy in the universe; but each move speeded up does have a martial arts application. According to the Taoist philosophy behind *Tai Chi,* as you move you become aware of energy waves or breaths of vitality (*Qi*) that interact within the body. As you breathe you pull up yin (or female) energy from the earth below you and *yang* (or male) energy down from the heavens above to comprise this *Qi,* which flows through eight psychic channels and a dozen meridional lines in the body. Getting the two commingled kinds of energy together and in balance is the secret of keeping you healthy and happy.

Dating from the first century A.D. *kundalini* is another yogic philosophy that is user friendly to the evolutionary theory of advancing the human race toward higher consciousness. A bit farther out on the spectrum, it evokes a non-physical sort of energy called the *prana,* which can activate psychic power centers in the body called *chakras* (wheels)—invisible ganglia that radiate throughout the body. The practitioner visualizes the *kundalini* as a "fiery serpent" coiled at the base of the spine (Fig. 20). Normally dormant, when activated through stepwise meditation this creature within us all, though rarely harnessed, releases his awesome powers as his force passes upward along an invisible channel, the *sushumna,* or Rod of Brahma, that parallels the spinal column. Getting all that *prana* to flow all the way up your spine to the top of your head isn't easy. You experience weird sounds, shrills that descend into cricket chirps, then like the buzzing of a bee, a flute, a bell, and finally, a boom and a roar of a distant ocean. Novices report being dizzy and nauseated—even foaming at the mouth.[8] The goal of the whole process is to attain the Resplendent Void. In this highest state of bliss acquired through the activation of the fire serpent, all your normal processes of thought are suspended, your ego vanishes and all things become one. This is the ultimate union—the absorption of the self into the infinite, the ultimate transcendent, blissful state of being.

In all of these Eastern meditative philosophies that have become so popular in the New Age, one is not just body or mind but something

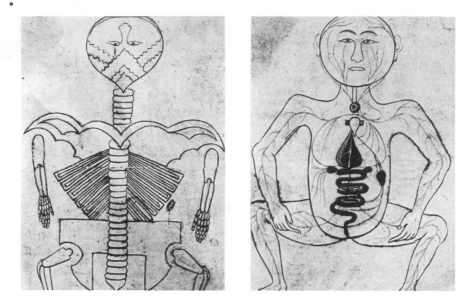

Fig. 20: Kundalini—the body serpent which, when awakened through yogic discipline, rises along the spinal shaft. As you condition it to pierce ever higher openings you experience more powerful sensations of higher reality. These culminate in the "supreme radiance," a shining whiteness where all things become one. (From a first-century A.D. anatomical drawing.)

quite separate, something greater—a part of the universal consciousness, devout practitioners say. The ultimate goal of yoga is to liberate your spirit from all material existence and join it with the absolute. *Hatha yoga,* one of many forms the discipline takes, consists of purifying the body through exercise along with the development of various postures. It has become the most popular of the yogic techniques for resolving the mind-body gap in contemporary American society—though most lay practioners, as might be expected, tend to concentrate primarily on the physical benefits it offers.

Rosemary Guiley's Encyclopedia catalogues fourteen major types of bodywork including the Alexander technique, a manipulation technique combined with verbal utterances, and *Shiatsu,* a Japanese finger therapy resembling acupuncture.[9] At the extreme outer limits of bodywork manipulation itself lies the simple therapeutic touch, perhaps another relic of the Mesmerian age. "I place my hands to connect them to their healing source. My hands are able to feel hot spots, cold spots, pain and symptoms of problems in the body—the radiant inner light," says one of the modern touch healers.[10] I wonder: Are they closer to adepts than chiropractors because of the way they practice their art?

Regardless of the current flap over the efficacy of TT, medicine has now begun to acknowledge that the self really does play a definite role in the treatment of disease—and meditation alongside medication has its proven beneficial effects, as countless self-help books written by a cadre of medical doctors on alternative therapies have proffered. But as the spiritualistic and scientific threads intertwine to weave a new health care fabric, those who study meditation and try to deliver its physical benefits seem disinterested in carrying over the full Buddhist framework. Deep down there is still a tendency at the explanatory level to think of neuropeptides and their receptors as the correlates of our emotions.

CHAPTER 29

YOU ARE WHAT YOU EAT

⌒

. . . the yellow corn, white corn [which] came from there. . . .
There were four animals who brought the news of the ears
of yellow corn and white corn. They were coming from
over there at Broken Place, they showed the way to the
break.

And this was when they found the staple foods.

And these were the ingredients for the flesh of the human
work, the human design, and the water was the blood. It became human blood. . . .

Verse from *Popol Vuh: The Definitive Edition*
of the Mayan Book of the Dawn of Life
and the Glories of Gods and Kings
Dennis Tedlock, translator

A Maya Indian creation story still told today tells how the human
race was formed. As the first dawn approached, the four cre-
ators—they call them maker-modelers—gathered together to
search out the appropriate ingredients to make up the human body. Suddenly they were hit with the flash of a great idea for what to use. And so
they all departed for Bitter Water Place to acquire . . . corn.

Then the grandmother of all creation, Xmucane they called her, im-
itated the God of Genesis—only she used corn instead of earth,[1] and the
creation process was far more complicated. The story continues:

. . . the water she rinsed her hands with, for the creation
of grease; it became human fat when it was worked by the
Bearer, Begetter, Sovereign Plumed Serpent, as they are
called.

After that, they put it into words:

the making, the modeling of our first mother-father,
with yellow corn, white corn alone for the flesh,
food alone for the human legs and arms,
for our first fathers, the four human works.

It was staples alone that made up their flesh.[2]

When we say "you are what you eat," maybe we don't take it quite so literally as the contemporary Maya. You don't have to dine on fajitas in
Cancún to realize nothing could be more natural for a Maya person than
to think he or she is made of the most nurturing substance in existence—the Maya manna. It's good stuff![3]

But suppose it's bad. Tommasso Campanella, the Renaissance philoso-
pher-scientist, once said that if it stinks, it's bad—even right down to the
root. So lay off the fruit of any tree grown in dung and don't consume
animals that eat dead bodies for

. . . whatever is not suited to live long, when changed and
transmuted into us, still retains atoms and particles that produce the same tendency when taken internally, stir up the
same feeling and perishable conditions and dispose us to
their native condition.[4]

Spoken like a true Renaissance budding scientist. In line with this philosophy of "association equals participation," dry flesh having something
of aging animals on it is supposed to incline us to senescence. What to
eat then? Dine on fruits and light vegetables—particularly the tasty fra-
grant ones, wrote Campanella. Eat red meat to benefit your blood, not
white food that burdens your bones.

"The cult of the diet is the greatest of all American fads," wrote historian Gilbert Seldes in the 1920s.[5] Never have Americans *not* held some
special attitude toward food. And whatever that attitude, it is rarely based
on taste. Ben Franklin gave up meat to save money and to keep himself
thinking clearly. By the end of the spiritualistic nineteenth century, fad
diets were the ultimate expression of revivalism. Eat nuts and grains to be
in tune with nature. Slaughter not thy fellow creatures for consumption.

The modern approach to taking in the right stuff was popularized in the 1950s by Gaylord Hauser and by Euell Gibbons[6] in the sixties and seventies. And the eat-lots-of-vitamins approach has been revivified over and over again. So none of the modern diet regimens is terribly new.

The homeopathic route to healing is based on the Law of Similars—the idea that you have the healing force within you and that it must be stimulated by consuming products that produce the same symptoms as the disease, but in tiny doses was first charted out in late eighteenth-century Germany by physician Samuel Hahnemann. Despairing of the inability of the standard medical techniques (especially purging and blood-letting) to cure disease, he experimented on himself. When he took quinine he discovered that it produced mild forms of the same symptoms (chills and fever) that it was supposed to cure. This led him to the Law of Similars.

Flying in the face of scientific common sense, homeopathy also relies on the principle that the weaker the solution of an effective substance, the stronger the effect (the so-called Law of Infinitesimals). Hahnemann argued that vigorous shaking of the solution activated the medicine that kick-started your vital spirit.

Homeopathy (from homios = like and pathos = suffering) took a huge step in the 1970s when magazine editor Norman Cousins wrote a bestseller telling how he cured himself of a degenerative disease of the spinal connective tissue.[7] Given less than a 1 percent chance of survival, Cousins did two things. He abandoned the drug therapy his doctors had recommended and got into ingesting massive doses of vitamin C. He also sought numerous ways of modifying his emotional attitude through good humor, thus bringing mind back to the problem of healing.

Is Cousins' Vitamin C, which can be found in any health food store, the elixir of the turn of the millennium? There have been other panaceas in the past. The erudite and wealthy French Count of St. Germain thought he had it nailed in 1759 with his secret "water of rejuvenation," which he proudly presented to Madame Pompadour. He claims to have lived more than five hundred years on this wonderful stuff—coupled with a dish of oatmeal, white chicken meat, and a good French wine. The book of Kings (1 Kings 1) advocates inhaling the breath of young girls; to do it effectively you would need to sleep with them. Alcohol as an elixir has a long history.[8] As I noted earlier, elixir means "water of life." Our modern translation of the word "whiskey" comes from shortening the Irish word for same (uisgebeatha); it is also aqua ardens (Latin), aguardi-

ente (Spanish) for "water that burns"; *aqua vital* (also Latin); *eau-de-vie* (French); *lebenswasser* (German); and *aquavit* (Nordic).

Great taste and strong passion go together. Traditionally, good sex and good food have always been linked, simply because indulging fervently in either can be a sensual pleasure. (But some will argue that food induces more fear than fun in the hearts of today's diet-conscious American.) If the way to a man's heart once was through his stomach, maybe it's because the woman of the house, via kitchen alchemy, could gain control of him who brought home the bacon.

Carrots, eggplants, and bananas on the one hand, figs and oysters on the other, were among the early American foods thought to be powerful aphrodisiacs. (Question: What do their shapes have in common with the male and female generative organs?) When we give the gift of chocolates on St. Valentine's Day, we continue to pay Cupid's homage to chocolate power. First brought over to Europe from America after the conquest, chocolate was treated as an exotic substance. Highest of all on the list of seductive consumables in pre-Columbian Mexico, it had long been used in the Maya and Aztec religions as an offering to the gods. The Inquisition tried a number of women for drinking hot chocolate and using its latent powers to conjure up the Devil to aid them in casting love spells. (Chocolate, by the way, contains phenylethylamine, which is a stimulant similar to those the human body releases during intercourse.)

Food power is still very important in southeast Asia, so important that some of the rarer aphrodisiacs are dealt on the black market amid concerns about the extinction of rare species. The tiger is the animal of choice. They say that to sharpen your vision, you should eat the eyes of a tiger; to hone sexual acuity, men should eat the penis of a tiger (those of a deer or seal are lesser substitutes). Tigers from colder climates, like those from China's northern provinces, are best. At least they produce the most potent tiger penis soup. At a posh Taiwanese restaurant you can get soup for eight out of one Amur tiger member (there are only some three hundred left in the wild at this writing!) for about $2,500. Ground-up tiger bone is one of the great panaceas for pain, functioning a bit like our aspirin and then some. It is good for specific ailments such as rheumatism, ulcers, malaria, typhoid, animal bites, and boils, as well as more general maladies—even getting rid of the Devil or of your fear of water.

In our world, science and technology dictate the written agenda concerning what ought to belong on the shelves of the health food store by offering precise measurements of every element and compound printed out on every bag and carton. They chart the recommended route, if not toward eternal life, at least in the direction of prolonging our earthly existence by avoiding those disease-inducing evil missiles hurled at our digestive systems in the form of fat and protein. Still, in 1995 Americans spent more than $165 million for homeopathic preparations, with a rise in sales of 25 percent. Taking one part per trillion of cuttlefish ink to cure hemorrhoids (a standard homeopathic remedy of the 1990s) may seem a long way from swallowing raw oysters to conjure up a Medieval love spell, but I see this as a vestige of the occult connection between today and yesteryear. Homeopathy is a reaction to the inability of standard medicine to cure all our ills. Today's road to good health seems to consist of a holistic synthesis of science and self—of medication and meditation. Genes are only a part of the story.

CHAPTER 30

COME FLY WITH ME:
UFO ABDUCTIONS

. . . angels of a blueish colour and about the bigness of a capon,
having faces . . . like owls.

From *UFO's, A Scientific Debate*
Carl Sagan and Thornton Page, editors

Apr il 16, 1651, sunset. Two English country women claim to have
witnessed a battle in the sky followed by just such an apparition. Others tell of birds fluttering over death beds, celestial apparitions wrecking ships at sea, galloping horses, fiery chariots, and other
contemporary conveyances taking flight. Usually, great moral significance was attached to these stories—divine warnings of God's plan and
purpose. Like this story from the Old Testament Book of Ezekiel, which
opens with a fantastic and surprisingly detailed description of a vision:

> In the thirteenth year, in the fourth month, on the fifth
> day of the month, as I was among the exiles by the river
> Chebar, the heavens were opened, and I saw visions of God.
> On the fifth day of the month . . . As I looked, behold, a
> stormy wind came out of the north, and a great cloud, with
> brightness round about it, and fire flashing forth continually,
> and in the midst of the fire, as it were gleaming bronze. And
> from the midst of it came the likeness of four living crea-
> tures. And this was their appearance: they had the form of
> men, but each had four faces, and each of them had four
> wings. Their legs were straight, and the soles of their feet
> were like the sole of a calf's foot; and they sparkled like bur-
> nished bronze. Under their wings on their four sides they
> had human hands. And the four had their faces and their
> wings thus: their wings touched one another; they went
> every one straight forward, without turning as they
> went. . . . Now as I looked at the living creatures, I saw a

wheel upon the earth beside the living creatures, one for each of the four of them. As for the appearance of the wheels and their construction: their appearance was like the gleaming of a chrysolite; and the four had the same likeness, their construction being as it were a wheel within a wheel. When they went, they went in any of their four directions without turning as they went. The four wheels had rims and they had spokes; and their rims were full of eyes round about. And when the living creatures went, the wheels went beside them; and when the living creatures rose from the earth, the wheels rose. Wherever the spirit would go, they went, and the wheels rose along.[1]

What was this alien-bearing, wheeled chariot that lifted off before the eyes of the prophet and his exiled people? It has been regarded by some as a vision of the glory of the Lord, for the "aliens" go on to give God's message to the prophet, telling him to embrace the god of Israel; but, ask religious skeptics, could it have been real?[2]

Atmospheric scientists say that you get a luminous phenomenon not so different from the description in Ezekiel when sunlight passes through clouds of ice crystals. Sometimes you can observe a double circular rain-bow with "mock suns" twenty-three degrees to the left and right of the solar image when it is low in the sky. The Bible may be describing this very phenomenon in symbolic and picturesque language. Donald Men-zel, the astronomer who offered that explanation, had a reputation for being one of the premier UFO debunkers of the last generation. (Inci-dentally, he took the trouble to clear his detailed explanation with the expert on Ezekiel in the Vatican, who said this account was all right with him provided the astronomer did not suggest Ezekiel's vision was *not* di-vinely inspired.) Other scriptural examples of visions in the natural en-vironment occur in Isaiah 66:15, Jeremiah 4:13, Genesis 9:13 (probably a rainbow), and the much analyzed burning bush witnessed by Moses and his followers in Exodus 3:2; the phenomenon of St. Elmo's fire[3] accord-ing to Menzel.

Even if the first extraterrestrial contact episode happened 2,500 years ago in the Holy Land, it was not until our century came along that vi-sions started to produce visitations of a more secular nature. By 1892 large telescopes had begun to reveal the enigmatic Martian canals and

Camille Flammarion's popular astronomy books picked up on Sweden-borg's notions of habitable worlds, spreading the word to an intrigued and receptive public. The more techno-oriented among them specu-lated: Could we some day use the telephone to communicate with the peace-loving inhabitants of a red desert-covered planet imperiled by a drastic water shortage?

Helen Smith, the renowned turn-of-the-century medium of Geneva, and French author Victor Hugo wrote novels on séances she had con-ducted while out of body on the landscape of Mars. She describes Mar-tian people, places, and things (note how their primary mode of transportation bears an uncanny resemblance to the *avant-garde* electric trolley of the day):

> . . . carriages without horses and wheels and which by gliding throw out sparks; houses with jets of water playing on their roofs; a cradle whose curtains are an angel made of iron, with wings unfolded. The people are quite similar to us except that both men and women are attired in long blouses with the waist brightened and trimmed with orna-ments . . . different from earthly multitudes solely as to the ample robes worn by both sexes, the flat hats and fencing shoes fastened with straps. The people have at their disposal instruments . . . making yellow and red flames. They use them to fly with through the air.[4]

Like Donald Menzel, who came fifty years after him, the French psy-chiatrist and skeptic Joseph Grasset hurled arrows of hallucination at the ignorant woman as he scientifically picked her argument apart. Much has been overlooked by Helen Smith in the realm of scientific questions, he points out:

> The famous canals in which astronomers have taken such interest are never mentioned. Nothing is said with regard to biology and sociology on Mars. Up there life is identical with life on earth, and the manners follow ours. There is less difference between Martian habits and our European habits than between ours and the Mussulman's [Turkish] civiliza-tion, or the habits of the savage.[5]

One of my most vivid childhood memories (I was about seven) was my first sighting of a jet plane crossing the sky. I remember the portentous way sound preceded sight with a thunderous crack that rattled the kitchen windows of our upstairs urban flat and fairly knocked me off my feet. Too late to get a closeup view, I craned my neck out the window wondering where to spot the fleeting black arrow that seemed to run ahead of time.

Aircraft and spaceships do not enter the lexicon of mysterious objects sighted in the sky until after World War II, when jet planes fell into the mainstream of aviation and America's thoughts turned to the exploration of space. This period also ushered in a rush of popular excitement. It began on the 26th of June in 1947 when the *Eastern Oregonian* carried a piece from a reliable witness—a respectable businessman and pilot— who had seen nine little round aircraft whizzing by Mt. Rainier at approximately 1,600 miles per hour. Their shape and movement, he says, reminded him of the erratic motions of saucers skimmed over water— hence the term "flying saucers" was born.

Conditioned by all those World War II blackouts, then living in the Cold War era, the public constantly cast wary eyes skyward in anticipation of an attack from their now hostile Soviet allies. Whatever the underlying cause, between 1947 and 1951 the government filed close to two hundred reports of unidentified flying objects.[6] As postwar America built fallout shelters and turned on its early warning radar nets, excitement pertaining to things in the sky reached a crescendo. By 1952, hysteria reigned, as 1,500 sightings of objects, ranging in form from disks to cigars to eggs, spheres, and pencils, followed a major spread on UFOs in *Life* magazine. Many observers reported having been personally contacted. The ten major contact books published between 1953 and 1954 were widely read, but mostly for entertainment. Then Hollywood took hold. As an impressionable teenager, I can remember seeing just about every one of the spate of low-budget science fiction films that followed. On "buck night" at the local drive-in theater we'd load up the car with friends and plenty of refreshments and watch the same set of grade B actors cycle through sci-fi flick after flick. (*War of the Worlds, When Worlds Collide,* and the classic *Forbidden Planet* were favorites worthy of multiple viewings.) Plot? Saucerians usually were portrayed as coming here either for a fast-food drop by—consisting of us (less often), or to colonize us (relatively often), or maybe just to warn us (very often), just as God's chariot-born angels had come to admonish Ezekiel. "If you earthlings don't mend your ways, you're going to mess up the universe for us" (its wiser galactic denizens). Wisdom that comes from beyond—a common theme of the occult seekers of the saucerian cults of the fifties.

Under public pressure in 1953, the Air Force organized Project Blue Book, an official scientific investigative committee to look into UFO reports systematically and with a skeptical eye. This commission was charged with determining, once and for all, whether the explanation of each set of individual phenomena could be reduced to known physical processes. By the mid-sixties, feeling some measure of public distrust, the Air Force chose the University of Colorado and respected physicist Edward Condon to conduct an independent investigation outside its jurisdiction. Members of his team traveled to sites, conducted interviews, and read reports of several dozen select cases. Two years and half a million dollars later, the commission released its controversial "Condon Report."[7] What are UFOs? Hot air balloons, bright meteors, debris from space, high altitude aircraft, firefly clusters, bright planets, and stars seen through fast moving clouds and hoaxes, hoaxes, hoaxes. . . .

> . . . nothing has come from the study of UFO's in the past 21 years that has added to scientific knowledge . . . and further extensive studies of UFO's probably cannot be justified in the expectation that science will be advanced thereby.[8]

In other words, there's nothing in it for us. The report, however, did have a deleterious effect on the public awareness of UFOs. The number of sightings fell from 1,100, the year in which the Colorado project was initiated, to 150 after the report came out three years later. Meanwhile cries of cover-up filled the air. Today, in the wake of a major UFO comeback and in an era of distrust of institutions in general, it is not surprising to see the government concealment hypothesis being resurrected.[9]

Meanwhile, the mid-fifties witnessed a resurgence of sightings along with the formation of a number of cultlike "contact clubs" in the U.S. Who belonged to these clubs? Mostly middle-aged middle-income people, women (widowed) with limited education, a significant number of them in poor mental and physical health. Members would travel from club to club sharing their stories with fellow believers, crying cover-up on the part of the government and championing the daring members of the scientific community who dared speak against the Condon Report—like committee member James McDonald. This renowned senior scientist from the University of Arizona's Institute for Atmospheric Sciences charged that the investigations were inadequate—a foul-up rather than a cover-up. Members of the committee often did not fully investigate, rather preferring to offer the same broad explanation for a variety of sightings he regarded as quite diverse. On the contrary, he contended, UFOs are "the greatest scientific problem of our times; there should be more studies, not fewer."[10]

I find it curious that the theme of alien saviors finds current support in the scientific search for extraterrestrial intelligence. Optimistic astronomer Frank Drake of the now independently financed project SETI (Search for Extraterrestrial Intelligence) was among the first to realize that, even if they're out there, direct visitation by aliens is unlikely simply because it would be too costly. The extraterrestrials, he figured, would probably rather communicate by radio signals. In the sixties the veteran seeker of intelligent life in the universe launched Project Ozma (after the princess of the mythical land of the Wizard), an attempt to tune in to potential alien signals. It involved setting up a receiver using the (now-collapsed) big "dish" at the National Radio Astronomical Observatory in Green Bank, West Virginia, to pick up transmissions that might come from planets orbiting a pair of nearby stars similar to the sun.

Nothing came of it, but Drake's enthusiasm somehow survived the seventies and even the early eighties, when his mathematical attempt to estimate the extent of habitable worlds in the universe (there *should* be hundreds of millions of them) began to fall under attack by an ever-growing number of skeptical naysayers. These detractors argued that no civilization could survive long enough to deliver interplanetary missives, and that even if any supposed aliens could manage to do so, the fact that none had yet arrived at our terrestrial doorstep was sufficient to prove that either they had no technology or they didn't exist. Drake's response to his critics was characteristically hopeful: The fact that we have not yet received word from the aliens, he said, may simply be because it takes a long time to gear up and transmit messages, and because we haven't been listening for very long.

Drake's pro-life argument goes like this: A little logical extrapolation naturally leads to the idea that extraterrestrial intelligence in some form ought to exist. Astronomers have calculated that there is plenty of liveable stellar acreage for folks like us to populate. Chemists have demonstrated that life can be created out of a few basic elements. Biologists have shown that intelligence has evolved in more than one species on earth. And many scientists share the belief that any intelligent being anywhere would arrive at the same truths about nature as we have, and that such a being would thus decide to send messages through radio waves.

The immanence of the end of the millennium gives many people the feeling that something really big is about to happen. That's probably why the federal government had given (and later withdrew because of budgetary cutbacks) $100 million to the National Aeronautics and Space Administration's Search for Extraterrestrial Intelligence project, thus elevating it to mission status. What was all that money for? While scientists interested in attracting alien attention had once suggested drawing huge geometrical figures in the Sahara or reflecting sunlight toward Mars by using gigantic mirrors, now they proposed, with the help of the Arecibo Ionospheric Observatory's thousand-foot radio dish in Puerto Rico, to conduct a twenty-eight-million-channel search of radio noise, to tune in to messages penetrating the earth's atmosphere from deep space.

What can we expect to hear from a real extraterrestrial? Drake's buoyant prediction is that we can look forward to an era of universal harmony.[11] This message is not so radically different from that of the UFO cults that sprang up all over America beginning in the fifties. Indeed, the need to conduct a search for extraterrestrial intelligence today seems more driven by a religious than a scientific compulsion. Drake expects the interstellar message to be broadcast by the benign members of an intergalactic club. Its content could well amount to a grand instruction book on how to acquire immortality.

In the 1970s UFO cults took on a form of historical backshifting when they garbed themselves in the ancient astronaut hypothesis. Promulgated principally by popular writer Erich von Däniken,[12] the idea was that extraterrestrial intelligence *has* visited the Earth in the past. Specifically, ancient astronauts came here to Earth in space ships between 10,000 and 40,000 B.C. and mated with Earth women. The aliens were responsible for a number of ancient works of architecture, documents, and legends that survive today. How else would there be so many unexplained mysteries—like the Terraces of Baalbek built out of huge stone blocks sixty feet long weighing two thousand tons apiece that even modern technology would have difficulty setting in place; or the quadrangular wall at Tiahuanaco (Tiwanaku), Bolivia, consisting of sculptured not-of-this-earth faces, or the mysterious lines of Nazca that run dead straight for miles and miles on the floor of Peru's coastal desert? Lost know-how, that's how.[13]

In von Däniken's interpretation, Nazca's straight tracks become runways upon which astronauts, visiting us from another world, once landed their spacecraft. In another case, he describes certain odd face masks worn by Maya gods on carved stelae as space helmets of cosmic drop-bys (whose visits evidently were rather widespread). As he examines the past, von Däniken, like Helen Smith, molds the specters of the alien world into images that look more and more like reflections of ourselves in a mirror. In effect, we demystify our forebears by making them more like us—by "discovering" that they shared our own contemporary ideas, motives, and concerns.[14]

The contact message of the 1990s has changed somewhat: Grossly disturbed by our fiddling with atomic energy and the environment, intelligent beings have come here to renew us spiritually. In fact, selected members of our species already have been contacted, swooped up to the overhead lab, thoroughly felt and fingered by alien internists, had their semen or ovarian contents sampled, (maybe even indulged in a little extraterrestrial breeding), and—before being patted on the head and returned safely to home—initiated into an indoctrination process that will culminate in the aliens lending us a helping appendage.[15]

Recently, Pulitzer Prize-winning Harvard psychiatrist John Mack created a major stir in the halls of science when he seemingly validated the experiences of a number of men and women who claim to have been abducted by space ships.[16] The cases Mack culled out are related neither to psychotic, delusional people nor to hoaxers and self-promoters. Instead, their experiences were real, reasons the doctor, and the contact phenomenon has as deep a spiritual and social significance for us now as the anticipated blip on one of SETI's computer terminals.

When he placed them under hypnosis, Mack's patients revealed a variety of stories. One says he was forced to drop his shorts for a brief checkup in front of a gang of short gray guys. Another claims to have been surgically adjusted so as to be less hostile and more open to change. The alien goal is to sensitize us to the eco-disaster we're all headed for. That's why they are hybridizing survivors for the impending environmental holocaust—or so the dozens of abductees tell the good doctor.

There is a new myth unfolding in contemporary culture's brand-new set of UFO stories: openness to a universe that is not alien but familiar, not hostile but enabling. The basic theme behind both scientific SETI and occult UFO abductions is, as I suggested earlier, an inspirational one. There's a bigger reality out there for us to connect with. Whatever it may be, it is forthcoming, generous, and helping—a positive force that wafts between that of great wisdom in carnate form and pure spirit. And it's out there to reunite us with the forces from which we've cut ourselves off—to see us through the complex web of individual and social problems we are responsible for having gotten ourselves into. Like so many other instances of extraterrestrial encounters, the tales change with the times. In the late 1940s one merely saw lights in the sky; today's victims have evolved to be part-ET themselves.

Contemporary Americans have taken to UFOs the way their forebears flocked to table-tipping a century ago. Interestingly, the European community has leaned more in the direction of UFOs being a parapsychological phenomenon—projections from the collective unconscious that have always been part of the human need to ascend out of the ordinary—than a concrete reality. UFOs are like the fairies of old portrayed in Medieval romances, diminutive humans, guardians of souls of the dead, or nature spirits who came out of the woods to assist us with their magical powers. Oddly enough, fairies and aliens share another characteristic. They, too, used to be fond of kidnapping women and taking them for wives.

Sociologist H. T. Buckner makes the interesting suggestion that belief in one kind of magic often promotes another. He uses the term "open door" to imply that UFO audiences thus established now become open to other occult ideas such as mind-to-mind communications (ESP) and mind-to-matter (PK). They are all seeking connective explanations. Like many of the latter-day New Age cults, they are *for* a better world; they want to hear something new, and they want to be helped.[17]

Closely related to the suppressed form of the UFO experience are the recall of past lives and near-death experiences that have been widely reported in the pop literature of the 90s. (Two books on these topics head the bestseller charts as I write these words.[18])

CHAPTER 31

LIFE AFTER LIFE

My heart had stopped . . . Everything was just completely
black . . . this void became the shape of a tunnel, and then before me was the most magnificent light; it's The Light in capital letters, and it's—very bluntly—the essence of God.

Carol Zaleski,
*Otherworld Journeys: Accounts of Near-death
Experience in Medieval and Modern Times*

As far as we know, we are the only species ever to exist that is
conscious of its own individual mortality. I remember twenty-
five years ago entering a dear young artist friend's hospital
room at the instant that he died. The experience of seeing life replaced
by death is an unforgettable one. I recall a wave of whiteness gradually
descend over him as the natural color of his flesh withdrew like a diminishing gas flame from the tips of his fingers and toes toward the center of his body. I remember seeing individual capillaries on the surface
of his rosy cheeks wither away, no longer pulsed with life as they were
drained of his once red and shining consciousness; the hand that I held
turned colder and colder, stiffer and stiffer. For a fleeting moment I understood the logic of quack experimenters who seek to weigh the Soul
physically by noting whether a dying body tips the scales any differently
before and after the big event. The transformation that affected the en-
casement of the Soul was more drastic than I ever could have imagined.
I had witnessed human remains in a state of death before, but never had
I been on the scene at the actual moment of departure. It was—in a
word—horrifying. What might have transpired on the other side of that
metamorphosed countenance during my friend's descent into darkness,
I wondered?

And what of those who claim to have returned from the precipice on
which my friend stood for an instant before slipping over to the other
side? A 1982 Gallup Poll revealed that eight million Americans have had

a Near-Death Experience, as American doctor Raymond Moody[1] once dubbed that mystical, blissed-out, out-of-body experience. An NDE is usually described as a feeling of looking down on yourself or through a dark tunnel toward a source of light; sometimes you even can see non-physical beings. NDEs, like UFO contacts, are almost always positive, frequently joyful, and ecstatic—a reaching out into the great beyond to another time rather than another space dimension.

The message contemporary returning NDEs have to offer bears a likeness to that of UFO abductees. After confronting their visions while clinically dead, interviewees often become evangelistic; they want to spread the word that we have nothing to fear—that what happened to them was enlightening and if other people on the planet could only share it with them maybe all of humanity would be transformed:

> My consciousness was going out and getting larger and taking in more; I expanded and more and more came in. It was such rapture, such bliss. And then, and then, a piece of knowledge came in: it was that I was immortal, indestructible. I cannot be hurt, cannot be lost. We don't have any thing to worry about. And that the world is perfect; everything that happens is part of a perfect plan.[2]

Such messages for all humanity from the world beyond have been the stuff of myths and stories from Sumeria to Swedenborg. Seeing angels, channeling, out-of-body experiences—from NDEs to UFOs—involve the same feelings of love, wonder, and awe; all are described as encounters with alternative realities of one sort or another that accord the same revered messenger status to those involved. But are they real or are they, as religionist Carol Zaleski suggests in an excellent historical overview of the problem, a modern counterpart of universal cosmic outreach—the religious imagination in search of ultimate truth?

In all cultures, in all of history, Zaleski recounts, people have told of traveling to underworld and afterworld, passing the gates of death only to return with a message for the living. The frequency of such stories follows the hypothetical magic curve I talked about earlier in this section. It peaked in Christian antiquity and the Middle Ages, fell during the Reformation, and peaked again in nineteenth-century spiritualism. Such stories have been with us full force since the 1970s, when Moody's popular *Life After Life* first hit the bookstores.

There is no question that culture has had its effect on producing variations on the theme of concurrence. There is an uncanny resemblance between the encounter passage from Old Testament Ezekiel and the NDE testimonies I just quoted. But there is wide disagreement about whether these phenomena are cosmological or physiological, whether they are best explained by religion or science. Physiologists attribute the tunnel effect to a lack of oxygen (hypoxia), the photoreceptor associated with peripheral vision being highly sensitive to the amount of oxygen received. But unconscious projections probably play a role, too. Psychiatrist Carl Jung believed UFOs—like mass religious conversions that happen under the tent of the evangelist—are a deep-seated archetypal expression of a collective desire to change the world.

Medical explanations for NDE phenomena range from psychological to psychopharmacological. They include drug-induced altered states of experience, either by drugs ingested near the time of death or by morphinelike chemicals known as endorphins secreted by the brain cells during times of stress; the effects of hypoxia; seizure of that section of the brain which controls memory and emotion; and simple hallucination engendered by sense deprivation—like a lonely hiker on the Sahara Desert who compensates for his or her own loneliness by conjuring up mirages.

Psi-cop authorities on the world of experience offer the typical "nothing but" reductionist explanation for NDE, as Zaleski characterizes it. If they ever succeed, all we'll need to tell anybody who's had an NDE, or any other vision for that matter, is that we have a very complex mechanism you'll never understand to explain it, but you can be sure whatever you experienced has nothing to do with revelation. But we will never come to a decision; the battle between relativist and skeptic will forever be a draw. The action of the debunker does little more than polarize the opposition:

> . . . fringe causes tend to cluster together, and their champions begin to speak a common language even when they have little in common beyond the fact of being labeled fringe.[3]

However, something beneficial does wash out of all of NDE, contends Zaleski. It is the religious imagery and imagination of human culture—the wonderful stories of the supernatural that we tell, the myths we create. Perhaps we should pay more attention to *them*.

CHAPTER 32

CRYSTALS:
WHO'S SCRYING NOW?

She sat directly under the apex, pausing to face each cardinal direction for several minutes. Looking east, and with little effort
her perception became acutely visual. Meanwhile, lying down
nearby, I felt my entire body vibrating. Directed south, she described a feeling of quietude and relaxation. To the west, the
subject became extremely clairaudient, sensing the sounds of
the woods. Turning to the north, she once again felt strong, high
vibrations and saw a bright, white light. Of all directions, she
favored northeast, surprised at the effortless flow of energy
through her sensing vehicles while inside the pyramid chamber.

Letter to the editor, *The Pyramid Guide*

T he ancient Egyptians did it with pools of ink or blood. Siberian
tribes used a puddle of water; the Olmecs shiny obsidian, the
Greeks brass, the Arabs a polished fingernail; our own Medieval
ancestors employed a perfectly spherical polished ball made out of crystal. Through the ages gazing into a clear translucent object to descry (literally to make out dimly) what awaits us in the future and beyond
ordinary experience has been one of the most persistent of all human pastimes. But today's scryers profess to be better healers than prognosticators.

If you bought a crystal mine five years ago, writes a contemporary
physicist, you'd be rich today. Some specimens go for up to two hundred
grand![1] Modest believers (such as my arthritic aunt) wear crystals about
the neck because they say it makes them feel good—and besides, pills
don't seem to have much of an effect on her pain anymore. Some go further—like the eccentric Pittsburgh optician who suspends a huge quartz
crystal from the ceiling of his workroom. He says it filters out negative
vibrations emanated by those whose ailments he treats. The negative energy gets rerouted to earth via a grounding rod in the room below while
an array of various crystals strategically planted about the property keep
out additional energetic pollutants, he explains.[2] Amethyst, rose quartz,

blue quartz, and black onyx are the lithic choices of a Stone Mountain, Georgia, crystal therapist who says she uses them because she believes her patients' physical problems emanate from a negative attitude toward God—a negativity that can be electrically zapped, quietly and painlessly out of your body with the aid of crystal technology. "Hate your body and you've got lung trouble—hate God and it's a gall bladder problem."[3]

No question there is power locked in crystals. Old radio buffs still can remember the crystal radio sets of years gone by. They operated on the principle of piezoelectricity (pressure electricity[4]). When a quartz crystal is subjected to pressure, say by sending voltage through it, charges appear on its surface, positive on some faces and negative on others, thus generating an electrical current. This curious effect has found a number of practical applications, particularly as a means of converting mechanical vibrations into electrical ones and the converse. The current flow from a deformed crystal, amplified to huge proportions, is what first allowed Enrico Caruso's booming tenor voice to come to life to everyone's amazement in my Grandma's living room. Another attraction crystals exert on the mind is that people seem to be aware of their near-perfect technical qualities and so they willingly borrow for psychic application the scientific set of terms associated with crystallography: energy, resonance, bonding, field, and so on.

Channelers and crystal healers share the belief that different stones affect psychic channels of communication (see table). Green fluorite grounds your excess energies, rose quartz heals the heart, and blue celestite is for the highest truth. Wearing the right combo—like consuming the proper dosage of an array of drugs or vitamins—gets you back into equilibrium; it keeps your energies centered. When you're talking energy we can *measure* that means we're talking science. If there's a healing force locked within crystals we ought to be able to measure its effect. But, retorts one CSICOP investigator:

> Crystal power lies not in understanding the physical or electrical properties of the crystals themselves but rather in understanding the terminology and thought processes of people who practice crystal healing. The energies and powers they claim to use and capture in crystals have nothing to do with the everyday electromagnetic, chemical or other energies we ordinary humans are familiar with.[5]

THE SYMPATHIES OF
METALS, PLANETS, STONES, AND DAYS OF THE WEEK

METAL	PLANET	STONE	DAY OF THE WEEK
Silver	Moon	Quartz	Monday
Mercury	Mercury	Lodestone	Wednesday
Copper	Venus	Amethyst, Pearl, Sapphire	Friday
Gold	Sun	Diamond	Sunday
Iron	Mars	Emerald, Jasper	Tuesday
Tin	Jupiter	Carnelian	Thursday
Lead	Saturn	Turquoise	Saturday

Adapted from S. T. Ali Shah, Occultism, Its Theory and Practice, *New York: Dorset, 1969, p. 143.*

And so the war goes on.

The shining epiphany of crystal power is the nineties version of pyramid power and the geodesic dome of a generation ago. After all, what is a perfect polygon but a huge geometrical structure you climb inside for a personal energy tune-up? The bigger the crystal, the quicker the enlightenment. The leap between crystals and pyramids is not a huge one and it does have a definite history. The pyramid theory goes all the way back to that glorious heyday of the occult—the mid-nineteenth century. It maintained that the Egyptian Great Pyramid's proportions were intended to reflect geometrical and geodesical truths such as the value of pi.[6] This whole idea got stretched further into the belief that ancient biblical prophesies and God's divine plan for the ages—the religious antidote to evolution and scientific determinism—were also encoded Kabbalistically into the pyramid's structure. By the Victorian age, the pyramid was thought to have predated the Egyptians and the whole project conceived and carried out by divine inspiration for the express purpose of passing secret wisdom across the ages from the pre-Egyptian Ten Lost Tribes of Israel to the enlightened believers in fundamentalist truth of the Scriptures, namely their Anglo-Saxon descendants.

The undiscovered chamber in the Great Pyramid has long been the mega-crystal *par excellence.* Its location has been sought by geomancer and astrologer, by Rosicrucian and spiritualist alike. Stonehenge, the Tower of Babel, and more recently the pyramids of Mexico (the great Pyramid of the Sun at Teotihúacan especially) have received the same power-pack interpretation. They are high-precision cosmic markers—archaic centers of power that locate all of humanity in the great space-time manifold.[7]

Believers began climbing into homemade versions of these cosmic focusing devices in great numbers in the late 1970s. What do you do when you get there? You get rejuvenated. No need to travel to Egypt. Like easy-on, easy-off meditators, pyramid advocates of the late hippie generation were content with buying kits and self-assembling personal polygons. One package consisted of four 12-foot cherry wood poles for the base and four more to make the sides; it included mosquito netting in case you didn't have the 144 square feet of interior floor space needed to house it. You'd sit in a lotus position inside your energy balancing transparent tetrahedron with your eyes shut. Or if you felt like it you could read, talk, or just plain relax to pass the time, the way you do when you get an indoor tan or a hairdo. The clairvoyant responsible for the testimony quoted in this chapter's epigraph reported an array of vibes she experienced when she turned herself like a rotor antenna around the cardinal directions to which she had carefully aligned her client's pyramid.

Aside from a few extreme applications, there's a lesson in the tale of crystals. It's a message to be learned from our contact with all forms of otherness—one we've heard before. While ancient cultures were able to create crystals and pyramids because they possessed a high-tech science beyond our own in scope, they also were capable of destroying themselves. Whatever good came of their knowledge went into the crystals which constitute a record from which we can now recover the potential to teach and heal ourselves.

CHAPTER 33

GEOMANCY:
FROM SAWS TO SAUSAGES

The Powers of the earth are still strong and we are beginning
to recognize that they exist.

> Derek and Julia Parker,
> *The Power of Magic*

W hat takes a homing pigeon home? What natural instinct enabled ancient people to live so fruitfully off the environment? They knew about the Earth's numinous qualities, the sacred places from which her helping powers emanated. Because they were unencumbered by the settled life, undulled by technological aids, their environmental sensory skills were honed into a kind of natural religion.

What nineteenth-century theists saw as spiritism, moderns see as superstition, but it's really natural religion and the goal of geomancy—the process of divining via signs in the earth environment—to recover our lost power from the earth and put the human habitat back into harmony with the world. Using that power to transform the Earth back to what it was before we changed it overlaps with the ends of the less mystical but equally spiritual planetary consciousness movement.

As with the Tarot, there's a principle of orientation to geomancy that can instill the right state of harmony. Chhiu Yen Han, the eighth-century Chinese geomancer who used the first magnetic compass to lay out a north-south meridian, knew that. And so the Chinese employed the compass in the art of *feng-shui* (Winds and Waters), a divinatory art that seeks to balance the controlling forces of nature so that society can find its correct place and orientation in relation to these forces. Then, when imbalance does occur, it can be skillfully righted.

Finding a sacred water source is a good example—sacred because once found it would need to be guarded against pollution and access by others, for it was a guarantee against drought.[1] Being in touch with the water's spirit and making offerings to it at the wellhead would be the only way to gain assurance of continuity of the lifeline it offered. That's why water diviners have always occupied positions of importance in the religious hierarchy. Moses may have been the first water diviner when he struck a rock with his wand and water gushed out of it. But how can a nonscientific belief like water witching persevere within our culture today?

I can still remember my geologist colleagues back in the late 60s and early 70s responding to student queries about water witching. It was just about the same time I was confronting demands to include a segment on astrology in my beginner's astronomy course. (Having done so, never before or since have I been more successful at getting my students motivated to learn to identify the constellations!) A survey reported in the first issue of *Psychology Today* revealed that divining for water was most popular in regions of the United States where water might be thought to come close to a sacred commodity, namely in the arid regions of the southwest, like southern Arizona and the deserts of Nevada and coastal California, where there were an estimated 25,000 water witches.

What do you witch with? Anthropologists R. Hyman and E. Vogt[2] offer a veritable catalog of water witching technology (a uniquely American term because of the colonial practice of using witch hazel twigs). Usually a divining rod (often called a dowsing rod in the northeast after the old British term[3]) is a few feet long and it's forked. But it needn't be made of wood. My friend Sig Lonegren, past president of the American Society of Dowsers, based in Danville, Vermont, is a sensitive who employs a pair of shiny stainless steel rods that screw into a ball joint that connects to a pointing shaft. His device looks like a Radio Shack TV booster antenna I recently purchased for our cabin in the Adirondacks. Sig claims crystal-clear aqueous reception with it. When he enlisted in my Earthwatch field expedition to Peru several years ago, I watched him parade around on the Nazca lines, holding one tine of the forked device in each hand while extending its prong upward and outward. Later he entertained our research group by walking in front of some slides of maps he had projected on a screen. Damned if his bifurcate gizmo didn't deviate ever so slightly in the direction of certain points on the screen where water was pictured!

Water witching devices from the old days included a crossed knife and fork and open scissors. A seventeenth-century painting shows a dowser operating a hand-held sausage (yes, the painting is from Germany).[4] Still other tools of this versatile trade listed by Hyman and Vogt include saws, baling wire, coat hangers, bucket handles, welding rods, pliers, crowbars, files, stalks of grass, walking sticks, open books, horse whips, shovels, and pendula.

How does dowsing work? Sensitives' answers range from "I don't know; I just think it and it happens" to "supernatural power" (the dowsing rod being only a kind of mental pointer), to what psychologists call the *adaptive response:* "my muscles are affected by electromagnetic disturbances that emanate from underground." One New Hampshire diviner, when asked why he always took one long additional step after finding the spot where the rod pointed earthward and before ordering his clients to "Dig here," replied "Oh, I was just correctin' for the hypotenuse."[5] Physiologists offer an alternative explanation. They say the whole performance has to do with how you grip and release the rod, which in some instances can result in an involuntary movement to it that in some hands appears convincingly paranormal. Researchers explain that if you hold each fork of the twig with your palms up, pointed forward at an angle of forty-five degrees, and compress your hands toward each other then you can make the rod move by any of four very slight changes of grip. First a slight easing of the grip can make the rod rotate. Second, a slight twist of the wrists toward one another might cause the rod to dip (rotate them outward and the rod moves upward). Pulling your hands slightly apart or pushing them slightly together are the third and fourth ways to make it move. By upsetting its balance with the slightest of these moves, experts tell us the rod can straighten out with such a force that the bark (assuming it is made out of wood) literally can come off in your hands. (Don't try this at home, kids!) In simple terms, the rod magnifies small automatic movements made independent of the operator's consciousness. Everything else having to do with it is the product of the superstition of a bygone age.

Of course, all this explanatory psychophysical ideo-motor action doesn't preclude the possibility that it all works. But as the reader—now immersed in the midst of my exhaustive survey of the Old and New Age theaters of sensate phenomena from ouija boards and table tipping to UFOs, crystals, and spoon bending—might be able to predict, this sector of the occult battleground, too, has been overcrowded with committed soldiers and a lot of blood has been drawn.

On the front line of combat, the water witching war pretty much boils down to the geologists versus the diviners. The geologists believe they have the upper hand. In one test at sixteen preselected sites that were later test dug, they claim they scored higher than the water witches.

Divining is motor automatism, pure and simple, they conclude, and furthermore it doesn't even work. The diviners counter with the same parry the astrologers make on their astronomer critics: We've been doing it for seven thousand years and you geologists have been around only for a few centuries, so we've better met the true test of time. We *must* be doing something right if we've persisted this long. Besides, even if water witching can't be demonstrated scientifically, that doesn't mean it can't happen. Furthermore, diviners (like many other sensitives we've met) just don't perform well under scrutiny, because lab conditions are inimical to their art. And lastly, there are plenty of testimonials and plenty of believers willing to pay us $100 instead of $20,000 for a bunch of academic water witches.

Like UFO enthusiasts, today's dowsers[6] often go further than their predecessors. Not content simply to find veins of water, some of them claim to transmit as well as receive. One diviner claims to be able to move the supply to a desired location by generating resonant waves that jibe with the water waves. Others say you can use the art to recover lost objects, and—not surprisingly in an age that reaches out for alternative techniques of healing—even find bodily tumors and track down the roots of emotional conflict.[7]

Geomancy encompasses the power of land as well as water:

> . . . the laying out of the land by these invisible lines predates the foundation of cities, as it is these which eventually led to another reordering of the areas which became dependent upon them—the countryside.[8]

The Old Straight Track Club was a British fraternity founded in the 1920s by Alfred Watkins, a businessman, inventor, and photographic technologist. He was dedicated to bringing forth evidence to support the hypothesis that sacred sites—camps, tumuli, churches—are laid out all over the British landscape in straight lines (*leys* he called them). These power centers are geometrically related to one another, the distances between them often expressing universal geometrical truths—such as the spacings of the planets and the structure of the atom. Their careful and deliberate placement, like the deity's arrangement of the planetary wanderers on the celestial orb, indicates that our ancient predecessors not only understood the harmonious balance of elements but also exhibited mastery of a degree of order and control of the landscape far beyond our own capacity.

Watkins originally started out as an active member of a typical Victorian era naturalist antiquarian club that traveled about picnicking, lecturing, and documenting and excavating ancient sites. With his engineering background it didn't take long for him to discover that three British sites—all of them ancient Roman ruins—lay in a straight line that ran undeviated over the top of a hill. What originally started out in Watkins' mind as straight tracks, practical shortest-distance routes taken by merchants and traders, would later develop into deliberately arranged sacred alignments. Why, after all, would such lineations pass unswervingly over bogs and surmount inaccessible hilltops?

Terrestrial geometry got linked up to UFOlogy in the 1960s. This happened in an odd way, when it became evident that all flying saucers traveled in straight lines. Some wondered: Could they be parallel to the paths of energy of the alignments on the surface of the earth from which they drew sustenance?[9] Thus the notion that alignments all over the world might have something in common, whether they were grooves marked out on the ground such as we find on Peru's coastal desert at Nazca; connections among an array of objects in the landscape (as in Watkins' ley lines); or geoglyphs (giant earth drawings) in general (like the Serpent Mound in Ohio, the great spider on the Nazca desert, or the Uffington White Horse carved on the chalk downs of south England). Even the axes of ceremonial structures like the megalithic horseshoe of Stonehenge and other arrangements of Bronze Age standing stones were fair game. All of these could be interpreted not as simple "earth art" or sites along practical pathways, but the result of a force or power beyond our comprehension, if well within the grasp of ancient sensitives.

Researchers who have put the alignment hypothesis to quantitative statistical tests often find it wanting.[10] In my own experience, straight tracks or alignments may be concerned not so much with harboring secret forces or powers that sound a lot like what we'd invent if we lived in the past, but rather with expressing indigenous peoples' concepts of the sacred landscape. Take those straight Nazca lines, for example, which date from the first few centuries A.D., I doubt they are the artifacts of von Däniken's interplanetary "Air Nazca." Having spent a fair amount of time on the Nazca desert studying the lines, I am more convinced that water rather than air was probably the foremost element in the mind's eye of the designers. When you stand on one of the natural hillocks out in the middle of the desert (locals call it the pampa), which is about as lifeless as the surface of the Moon, and you see dead-straight pathways radiating like rays of colored light passing out of a prism in every conceivable compass direction, each one connecting to a distinct and distant land form, the last thing you think about is ancient astronauts.

At least water emerged as a central explanation of their origin when our research group studied and measured the straight lines on the pampa in the early 1980s. We correlated line orientations with natural geographic benchmarks and discovered that most of the line network centers were crowded toward the edges of the pampa; they lay either at the ends of the rows of hills that extend like fingers out onto the flat pampa from the mountains on the east or along the elevated rim that separates it from the river valleys on the north and south. Lines radiating from the ends of the fingers, we noticed, tended to continue in roughly the same direction as the rows of hills. These hilly promontories, like the ridges on a drainboard, define the direction in which water flows as it cascades down the mountains onto the pampa during the exceedingly rare rainstorms that occur in this very arid part of the world. This led us to suspect that the lines had been laid out to mimic the direction of water flow. Perhaps they were part of an indigenous water-divining scheme. Then we discovered another correlation that seemed to bear out the importance of water flow. Many of the large geometric figures (trapezoids, triangles, and zig-zags) that also accompany the lines are themselves elongated, and seem to define the favored direction. In addition to surveying the figures from the ground, we studied aerial photographs, measuring the difference between the orientation of each figure and that of the nearest dry gully. The match was impressive. That's why we figured it was not so much an obsession with what's *up* as an inescapable concern about what's *down* that drove the Nazca line makers.[11]

Alignments of other ancient sites around the world are also explainable in terms of solar and lunar orientations. These may have been employed as a way of preserving an "unwritten" orientation calendar—a way of keeping track of the flow of environmental time by incorporating the pulse of the seasons into both sacred architecture and the landscape—where people go to worship their gods of time.[12] As late as the 1940s in highland Guatemala, a Maya shaman still laid out orientations to the sun at the equinox, which, an anthropologist was told, occurred around twenty days before the time of planting.

Despite many documented, rational explanations for earthly geometry and alignments in individual cultures, many persist in believing what we're really looking at are remains of a mega-land survey undertaken by a vanished civilization of Atlanteans. I think what's really at stake here is the attempt to reestablish in our own minds the preeminence of the pastoral way of life over the evils the urban condition has laid upon us. Another hidden agenda seems to be that scientific rationalism has alienated us from what we perceive to be a better world—the ancient, primitive world of which geomancy was a part. We can't reconcile advanced ideas and methods we discover in the past with our own preconceived bias that civilization advances and progresses with time, suggests author Nigel Pennick. While our nineteenth-century predecessors stirred their imaginations with tales of Atlantis, we space-agers rationalize what we (believe we) find by positing ancient astronauts.

Archaeologists are to weird alignments what geologists are to dowsing and what astronomers are to UFOs. Why do they ignore geomancy? Because it is pernicious, anti-science's "findings" are not covered by the pathways of reason; therefore, it must be viewed as it is—a fraud, a plot to undermine the scientific way of thinking, a body of pseudo-knowledge to be debunked with all the fervor they can muster!

Closer to the ecology movement and religion than it is to the astronaut hypothesis or science, planetary consciousness is a dilute form of 1990s geomancy. This is particularly true in the United States, where it takes the form that regardless of what happened in antiquity, we sentient beings need to be aware of how delicately balanced the earth energies really are and how fragile is their connection to our own existence.

When I wrote in my book, *Conversing With the Planets,* about the influence of Gaia theory on scientific rationalism as well as its role in millennialism, I argued that the demonstrable sensitivity of the environment to humanity—the awareness of how special and precious life on Earth has become—has produced new tensions. These tensions have prompted many earth scientists to think about the biosphere not as a bunch of

> . . . coevolving organic and inorganic parts but rather as a single entity made up of living organisms: an atmosphere, an ocean, and a planetary surface all interacting with one another through a series of complex feedback processes.[13]

I was referring to the Gaia hypothesis, named after the old Greek goddess, an idea which tries to restore planet Earth to capital-letter status.[14]

Is the world more than the sum of its parts? Does it possess a purposive element? Is it conscious? The theory of Gaia seems to be part of the drive to rehitch culture to nature. Milder in form and positioned as it is in the penumbra of the many millennial offspring of its occult sisterhood of astrology, it nonetheless invites open conflict with scientific catechism.

What better time to look forward to the future than the year 2000? But as we already have learned, every new idea always seems to have an underlying predecessor seeking the same kind of universal consciousness. What forward-looking Gaians strive for was foreseen in the 1920s by French Christian philosopher and theologian Pierre Teilhard de Chardin (1881–1955), one of the great proponents of the concept of *directed* evolution—a desperate antidote to the cold, random cruelty of Darwinism. It was he who coined the oft-used New Age term "noosphere" (meaning "mind sphere") to characterize a state of universal human consciousness—a kind of "supermind" we will all attain once cosmic evolution acquires its most advanced culminating state. It's all a part of Madame Helena Blavatsky's anthroposophic notion of evolution taking place in cosmic phases: galactic, Earth, life, and human. As matter becomes more advanced, so too does our consciousness. Physically and psychically we progress on the road toward being ultra humans, argued Teilhard. When we reach our "Omega Point" we all converge in Christ, who is the ultimate unity. In this planetization of the mind advocated by many modern New Age Earth worshippers lies the notion of fulfillment of the custodianship of spaceship earth bestowed upon us long ago by Old Testament Genesis.

The planetary consciousness movement has become both passionate and action oriented. Advocates stress that as cocreators in the evolutionary production we are in a take-charge position—far from simple losers in the big crapshoot in the cosmic casino envisioned by the Darwinian naysayers. When we exploit Earth's resources we undercut the evolutionary base that got us to where we are. So, we'd better start worshipping Earth if we want to get to our Omega point. Then we will all make the great leap to "Gaiafield," the form that universal planetary consciousness will take. According to Peter Russell, a British physicist, we will all attain "self-reflective consciousness that emerges from the interaction of all the minds within the social super organism."[15] The outcome can be hastened by universal meditation, rebonding ourselves with Mother Earth, and realigning ourselves with her psychic centers—a collective goal worthy of achievement.

CHAPTER 34

SUMMARY:
ON SHIFTING GROUND

⟿

We learned in this section that today's occult movement is very personal, highly noninstitutional, and democratic in the extreme. Just walk through the occult section of any bookstore, pick up some of the books on the subjects I've referred to, and ask yourself: Is it pop-science, pop-religion, pop-what? Can it be the new truth? It is hardly "fringe literature," for those occult shelves command a fair share of bookstore space—almost as much as the science and natural history section usually positioned opposite them.

Some of the subjects on the shape and content of contemporary magic we have touched upon, like self-healing and homeopathy, defy classification. Sometimes we find these subjects treated as hard science; elsewhere they acquire the softer label "nature"—usually considered to be somewhere between science and occult. While I have looked at what's on those shelves and who reads it, I haven't fully answered why. This is the goal of the final section. How do the different titles and themes answer the question for the reader: Wherein lies the truth? The titles and subjects were a little different a few generations ago. That observation tells us something about the way popular culture confronts traditional thoughtways like religion and science and how the confrontation has shifted ground. Phrenology and palmistry then, though a bit more deterministic, still evoked what the homeopath and self-healer believe today: The answer lies within ourselves. You can read truth in the map of the human body—the head, the hand, the working of the internal organs—for the design of humanity and nature is exactly the same.

Books on magical remedies seem to focus on how people and nature are connected. Folk medicine, magic, and homeopathic medicine still offer up a host of examples of the same *similia similibus curantur* (like-cures-like) philosophy we read about in ancient world magic. As above, so below. As in the macrocosm, so in the microcosm. On a roll from the sixties' Age of Aquarius, astrology books, we have learned, still attract the attention of occult enthusiasts. The birth and development of everything that lives is ruled by celestial Virtue and the qualified astrologer is the one to interpret how we fit the cosmic design—what we bring into life and how we can maximize our astrally derived potentials.[1] Alchemy books still direct their inquirers to look to matter in general if you seek the ultimate bond with the human spirit.[2] For the alchemist, primal matter does not reside in the hundred-odd elements of the chemists' modern periodic table, with its taxonomy of electronic charge and the basic affinity the elements possess to combine with one another to produce hydrocarbons and DNA. The *materia prima*—the basic substances that remain irreducible—derive from the ancient world: earth and water, air and fire. Sulphur still marries quicksilver just as sun conjugates moon and man communes with woman. In all the New Age disciplines, the structure of the universe is based on a different set of principles from that of science—a system of correspondences that tells what is active and what is passive in a kind of human chemistry that articulates the interaction of matter with *us* rather than with *itself.*

PART V

GOD, DICK, AND HARRY:

MAGIC AT THE MILLENNIUM

CHAPTER 35

IS MAGIC A RELIGION?

The Indian not only knows his nature but he knows also how much he himself is nature. The European, on the other hand, has a science of nature and knows astonishingly little of his own nature, the nature within him.

Gerhard Wehr,
"C. G. Jung in the Context of Christian
Esotericism and Cultural History"

"Are you practicing medicine or religion?", Bill Moyers questions one of his interviewees who deals in holistic medicine: "It depends on what you mean by religion" comes the answer.[1] Traditionally religion binds the soul, the mind, emotions, and human consciousness to an organized institution. But a lot of what's going on here has more to do with the integration of mind and matter, not with institutions. The integration is a very personal one and the personal dimension is why I think magic, if it hasn't been totally successful all these years, is nonetheless still alive and well.

Magic succeeds at the popular level not because it passes the empirical tests of science, which few laypeople really understand or pay attention to, but simply because it satisfies. Magic is a feeling—an attitude. It is emotional and tactile and whether it consists of gazing into a crystal ball or making an incantation, it is a one-on-one operation. Like religion, magic possesses an active principle because it is all about responding to our own self-centered psychic needs.

If homeopathy, phrenology, and palmistry argue that secret knowledge lies hidden somewhere within our very bodies, then astrology, alchemy, witchcraft, and sorcery seem to contend that the answers come from the way we commune with the world around us. Crystal gazers say that humanity has yet to reach the purity, the clarity of quartz crystals, the major source of light and energy on this planet. Geomancers ask us to get in touch with ancient architecture and earthworks, which give the true expression of the lost and living cosmos. Astrology, alchemy, geomancy, and UFOlogy seek a solidarity with nature by contemplating the stars, ponderable matter, earth signs, and extraterrestrial space. Spiritualism, Kabbalism, clairvoyance, faith-healing, and the cult of witchcraft—we have trotted all of them out and followed their rides up and down the Top Ten occult lists of our century. What they have in common that is so appealing to so many is that they evoke a special relationship between the receiver of knowledge and the transcendent world. Like cable TV, you can pick your station from among a multitude of offerings. Each purports to make the unknown knowable, to channel knowledge of the divine, the beyond, what is secret, what is hidden, via a direct and personal pipeline—often through a special individual who is naturally endowed to receive and transmit such knowledge.

All the vehicles of present-day esoteric beliefs from computerized astrology, whose software has replaced the old style hand-drawn chart and visitation procedure, to reincarnation, to Native American philosophy (based on the assumption that our concept of nature is exploitative and theirs isn't), to the others I have included in my own current Top Ten—channeling, PK, NDE, and so on—all have a decided religious ring. But today's secular brand of religious self-centeredness is a part of the God-is-in-You movement, in which we each try to create our own personal reality.

Oddly enough, even though the anti-establishment occult rebellion is also directed against science (we will tour that battlefield later in this section), we have become so ingrained in the ways of rational thinking that our science education, though underfinanced, has taken root in the religious domain. Firmly implanted, its tentacles have strangled traditional religious beliefs. Modern biologists may stand horror-stricken at the very existence of anti-evolutionist teachings in some religious schools, but let's face it: Darwin's theory has made considerable headway and it has caused the church's Genesis cosmology to back off. You can't stitch up the immense tear in the fabric that connects God and the theory of evolution with a simple needle-and-thread motto like "God moves in mysterious ways."[2] Forget it, say the unbelievers, God doesn't move in mysterious ways. If He really put together a theory like Darwin's, He is either incompetent or he didn't have creating the world in our image in mind.[3]

Even if both God and evolution are real, why did God initially choose to allow us to turn back to our past, to Biblical scripture's Paradise Lost in search of truth, only to have us look the other way a century ago? If Darwin really speaks the truth, why is he a mere mortal rather than a savior like Moses or Jesus Christ? And if God is really out there, why would he conspire to lead us to doubt our faith in Him? These are the kinds of questions on the minds of ordinary people trying to reconcile belief in the extraordinary with their own religious doctrines.

The sweeping dissatisfaction with traditional religion exhibited in those who turn to neo-pagan cults also stems from a disappointment that all the church seems to offer is social ethics. The message on spiritual instruction doesn't constitute the *renovation* they are looking for, as Mircea Eliade puts it.[4] What they want is a private initiation into old and venerable secrets. Esoteric gnosis has just that personal element they find so appealing. Being selected from the anonymous masses gives you a very special feeling. It soothes the ego. In the fully secularized "cosmos 2000," the traditional way of the Western church takes the role of second fiddle. So if you want to get to God in today's busy world, take the express route because it avoids the liturgy and rite-cluttered ecclesiastical subway station. You go direct to Him for God-is-in-You.

Here is where the appeal of Eastern religion meets the psychic test. What in the world, you may wonder, is responsible for attracting a nation of 250 million pragmatic, logical, high-tech, progress-oriented individuals living in technocratic, capitalistic American society to the thoughtways of a remote, isolated Himalayan country of four million inhabitants about twice the size of Florida and under siege by its gargantuan Asiatic neighbors?

As the frontiers of faith recede in the inundating impersonal wave of rational scientific knowledge and religious litany that together daze us into robotic dullness,[5] many feel the need to retreat to a more personal set of beliefs. The love of anything alien is common at times when traditional values lose their force. Zen Buddhism, Hinduism, Sufism, and all the other winds from the East that have blown over American society with increasing force since late in the nineteenth century breathe an air of discipline. The idea of passing through gradations of religious life turns on individuals who are inbred in a society that sees itself as progressive in every way—from the way we diet to how we power walk, from minimalist TM to yoga exercise and the attainment of the highest forms of the religious life. The inward-directed, self-improvement quality of these fringe religions suits contemporary American sensibilities a lot better than the Old Testament Thou shalt not this and Thou shalt not that.

Psychologist Carl Jung, one of the great applicators of Eastern philosophy to Western thought, wrote the epigraph that begins this section. I think it aptly expresses what kind of cosmos twenty-first-century humanity desires to create. From von Däniken to MacLaine, this nostalgia for reconnecting with a long-lost solidarity with nature is the cardinal religious quality of the occult explosion in the second half of the twentieth century—the wished-for "charismatic cosmos," Eliade calls it. The tight bureaucratic society we live in has numbed us almost to the point where we cannot experience the intriguing, the inspiring, and the awesome dimensions of our imaginations. There's no room for magic in a production- and efficiency-oriented society, religionist Edward Heenan writes.[6] (Maybe that's why there's such an anti-institutional corporate mistrust inherent in the millennial occult.) The new love of matter is a response to dissatisfaction with what history has done to it, how science has explained it, and technology transformed it. We are just not happy with the existential condition of the world bequeathed us by the modern philosophers and nothing short of the recovery of that primeval situation in which (we suppose) man and environment lived in harmony will satisfy our wishes.

I have argued elsewhere that we create the cosmos we desire and we end up with the cosmos we deserve. In effect, we continually reinvent our own universe for different sets of reasons. What we conceive as the real world in the end is what matters most to us—whether it be our own backyard neighborhood or a once-fiery firmament filled with protogalaxies retreating from one another at screaming speeds. The contemporary occult focus on the glorification of nature seems more centered on satisfying our own particular *physical* desires. Environmentally conscious New Agers want to breathe the unpolluted air and live in the nontoxic environment once shared by their seemingly wiser ancestors. The wisdom they seek to channel up from the past is concerned with ways of both attaining emotional gratification in the present form of life as well as extending that life and all of its pleasures to the next dimension. (No wonder Swedenborg's philosophy had such appeal!)

Remember Jack Pursel's Lazaris? He instructs us to go through a four-stage, twenty-eight-day meditative process to help heal the angry hurt and lonely child within us.[7] Ruth Rydon,[8] an ex-legal secretary, offers a Book of Lessons that teaches how to explore out-of-body states. "The soul is the ignition key to Christed Consciousness" but to get to the ultimate realization that you are "a light being," "you need to experience and coalesce a number of perspectives," says Vywamus, Janet McClure's primary contact in the spirit world.[9] Through meditation he (she) can successfully align you with the galactic perspective. Swami Anandakapila (John Mumford) offers a series of lecture tapes on Tantric Occultism. The fourth installment, "Sexual Magick and Tantric Psychosexual Kriya, Part I," gets you to the level of better sex—a level "in which sex is as 'organic' to the view of the Universe as it is to the life of Man."

Are we shallow, superficial, and naive enough to think we can embrace the traditions of an alien, remote culture with so little effort while most of our attention is focused on the necessary business of making a living and getting on with life? Do we really think we can turn back the clock to ancient religious structures and live the perceived simple lives we imagine once were lived in this world?

To judge by the way we behave as a society the answer for many of us seems to be: Yes. And so in our spare time we try to satisfy our inner appetite for truth by mixing mantra and massage. Not only do we subscribe to these more facile courses to the truth but also, to help us along on our journey of mind and body, there is a host of technological aids. The subject matter in today's shopping malls of the mind includes good sex, loving your body, food and fitness, healing, nontoxic substances, dream analysis, natural products, anti-smoking, anti-polluting devices, herbal medicine, and homeopathy. The *Inner Harmony* catalogue, for example, offers:

> . . . mind machines. Also, smart pills and brain foods, cyberactive software and mind-expanding videos, brainwave entrainment and Ericksonian hypnosis cassette tapes, professional and salon equipment, subtle energy and health products.[10]

If occultism has a beneficial liberating aspect to it one of its dangers today may be that it's too fattening—for the ego. Hierarchies get set up and spiritual authority is assumed. Self-appointed gurus who were never pupils become avatars of the age. They decree what tests need to be passed to attain higher levels. There is, as philosopher Jacob Needleman puts it, "a certain smell" to it all, characterized by the institutionalized absence of questioning along with the idea that knowledge is an easy commodity to come by. As one novice guru told him:

> It's as if you had no knowledge of chemistry and asked me how to make a cup. There would be no sense in my

telling you all about the chemical composition of this cup. I would just say, well, I have the knowledge of how to give mantras. Knowledge is not difficult to obtain. Knowledge is very simple, the simplicity of life. Mistakes are impossible.[11]

And so, we find ourselves in a private "spiritual explosion" in the closing decades of the second millennium. The flight-to-alternate-reality bestseller list changes because our needs, our desires, and our tastes change. When we confront the medium and the message of modern occultism, we aren't so much seeing through a looking glass to an absolute reality as we are viewing our own cultural image. After reviewing otherworldly visions of NDE from the Old Testament to the New Age, author Carol Zaleski concludes:

> To put it bluntly, I do not believe that any of our notions of God, the soul, or the other world are likely to be true in the ordinary sense of the word. . . . our concepts are too abstract and one-dimensional, while our images and symbols are too concrete; we sense that both modes of understanding are necessary, yet they seem incompatible. . . . We can intuit and be forever changed by a higher reality, but we cannot apprehend or describe it in the direct and unequivocal manner with which we seem to know the objects of ordinary experience. Such understanding as we do receive of the transcendent comes to us through symbols, and it is through symbols that we communicate this understanding to one another.[12]

Let me loudly echo her view: I think that as we perceive the reflection of our own cultural image in this symbol-faceted mirror, maybe we should pay less attention to trying to objectively verify or deny every reported paranormal experience and pay more attention to how our imaginations and perception work together. What we see or what we say we see in those lights in the sky, at the end of the tunnel, or through the channel, *is* important because it shows us that every religion we devise will always harbor a message that is mysterious, fantastic, at odds with what is rational—and above all special to the believer. Religion *is* by definition the realm of the uncommon, the extraordinary. That is where magic really belongs.

CHAPTER 36

MAGIC AND SCIENCE: J.Z. AND THE RAMSTERS MEET ARCH DEBUNKER

Knowledge and the search for it are not so transient as the cities
of river and plain. Venus remains neither demon nor maiden
but a rocky globe, whatever the metaphor her scattered rays
adorn.

Philip Morrison, "What We Seek in the Sky"

When we compare magic's by-laws to those of science, it becomes very clear why the two constitute ways of knowing that are totally at odds with one another concerning both what knowledge is valid and how that knowledge gets passed on. First of all, as MIT physicist Philip Morrison suggests in the epigraph above, science has faith that the universe *is* what it *is*—an objective collection of interacting things no matter what we have to say about it. In other words, Morrison seems to be saying, "After all is said and done, the planet Venus is *physically* a round globe, even if we choose to call it a love goddess." Question the premise that you cannot make up your own world out there and scientists display all the symptoms of "Cartesian anxiety syndrome."[1]

Science advertises itself as a self-questioning enterprise. The knowledge it prizes is deemed valid or invalid by virtue of experiments—observational tests performed on that tangible collection of things that makes up the natural world. If you have an idea about how that stuff out there interacts, it must pass the test. If a test that can be designed out of your idea is repeated over and over and over again and gives identical positive results, then your idea is worthy; but if it fails the test, then either that idea is false or it has been incorrectly stated—maybe something is left out. In any case, it needs to be modified and it must retest positive before it is admitted to the armada of information that forms the stock of accepted scientific truths about the world.

Here's how it works in principle: Suppose an astronomer determines the speed of a distant quasar by measuring the red shift in its spectrum. The result will either help validate the Big Bang theory of the origin of the universe or it will provide evidence against it. One of many empirical tests of falsifiability deliberately thrown up by cosmologists against their own theories, the procedure involves manipulating special instruments and grinding together numbers that emerge from the data in formulaic machinations (an oft-abstract process that can cause disagreement even among consenting partners—there may be physical mechanisms other than the expansion of the universe that account for the red shift). To no surprise, such complexity commonly evades all understanding by laypeople whose mental skills are insufficiently attuned to what is really going on (what lay reader really understands how the theory of general relativity affects the red shift?). Nonetheless, the final performance comes with the orderly presentation of the results in a professional journal or on the stage of a national scientific meeting for all the indoctrinated world to see, and then in magazines like *Scientific American, Science News,* and *Omni,* which are attuned to the palates of the progressively less indoctrinated but ever-growing population as one descends the pyramid of specialization. These activities are all part of the scientific ritual of model making.

In the rites of magic, you reciprocate and exchange with superhuman forces you know are already there. You take it on faith and you are as sure of it as the scientist is certain that the universe is impersonal. In science you deliberately distance yourself from the thing you want to know. You set out all the objects for your rite. Then you flick the switch, withdraw, and dispassionately watch truth unfold. You hope—even pray—that the controls you need to impose on the whole process to keep it going will not affect the outcome of what it will reveal. I find it curious that in both endeavors—science and magic—you transform yourself into a being who consciously manifests power. When a scientist increases control over nature, he or she can do things that seem magical.

Even though we all covet power, and science is today's gateway to acquiring and using it in the physical sense, paradoxically most people don't feel at home in its milieu. I think it's because science paints too logical and inflexible a picture of the world. Everything happens chronologically, one event after another, each connected to its predecessor via cause and effect. For everything we see happening, there is a specific previous cause and that cause is discoverable. What gives outsiders another kind of queasiness about science (and I find this doubly paradoxical) is that by its own definition it is incomplete—and, moreover, self-satisfied with its deliberately designed state of eternal incompleteness. In science, any hypothesis worth its salt is supposed to remain forever open to being retested. In other words, it must be capable of yielding to the possibility of being falsified. At the same time, its results—even if they appear to be more outlandish and more anti-common sense than those of magic—must be admitted to the halls of scientific truth if they pass the test of controlled experimentation. That's the bottom line.

When physicist Max Planck thought up the concept of the quantum of energy around the turn of the century he (somewhat modestly) recognized the unlikely nature of his very own claim; yet he believed it to be the best approximation to the truth for one reason:

> It is true that we shall not thereby prove that this hypothesis represents the only possible or even the most adequate expression of the elementary dynamical law of the vibration of oscillators. On the contrary I think it very probable that it may be greatly improved as regards form and contents. There is, however, no method of testing its admissibility except by the investigation of its consequences, and as long as no contradiction in itself or with experiment is discovered in it, and as long as no more adequate hypothesis can be advanced to replace it, it may justly claim a certain importance.[2]

His idea had passed the test!

No wonder science is at loggerheads with magic. To be effective, its practitioners must act ceaselessly upon the world and manipulate its parts. In turn, the world is required to respond to their inquiries and incantations in a way that is consistent with their own idea of reason and order. In honest science, what the cosmologist wishes for is not a part of the act. On the other hand, for effective magic the outcome of the performance intentionally affects the participant. Magic is personal and social while science is apersonal and physical. I think Renaissance magician Marsilio Ficino said it best: "When I sing a song to the sun it is not because I expect the sun to change its course but (because) I expect to put myself into a different state of mind in relation to the sun."[3]

After Planck, we can echo the same sentiment he expressed about the half dozen particles on the subnuclear scene, including the bizarre top quark which simply has no business being what it is. As physicist Paul Davies characterizes the situation:

> I am often asked why I find it comparatively easy to believe in evaporating black holes and invisible cosmic matter, but not in straightforward things like ghosts and flying saucers that ordinary people apparently see all the time. The reason is not easy to explain to someone unfamiliar with the scientific process because the nature of scientific evidence and the relationship between theory and experiment can be very subtle.[4]

Good science is crafted to be value free and totally objective—"a human adventure without parallel that permits us to glimpse nature's innermost secrets with reasonable confidence that we are not misleading ourselves," as one believer puts it.[5] Nobody in all of science is an expert and the only gurus are folks like Einstein and Feynman, the rare handful who possess that uncanny skill—call it intuition—for repeatedly coming up with bright ideas that somehow manage to pass all the tests. But as we have already discovered, even these master teachers and their followers cannot exactly say how they do it.

Science characterizes truth as something hidden beneath the veneer of a superficial face that nature puts on as a way of deceiving us. But it also has faith in progress. While primitive people could answer questions about nature only in terms of fiction, we, by virtue of having developed the means of extending our senses, are able to probe more deeply into the stuff that makes up the universe and consequently root out those underlying secret truths that await us. The ancients never had the slightest hint that the management of matter consists of the laws of physics, so no wonder they conjured up sun gods riding chariots across the noonday sky and dragons taking bites out of golden Apollo, say the scientists. But there's no need to fear the natural order any more. Thanks to our new procedure to satisfy our quest for knowledge, gradually cultivated, nurtured, and improved (and fully set in place about five hundred years ago), we now can acquire meaningful data about how the universe really is—not how anybody wishes it to be.

With its uncompromising, rule-bound rigor, and the difficulties involved in penetrating it implied in Paul Davies' earlier statement, no wonder impersonal science has a hard time attracting a lot of fans. But it gets even harder: To break into the game of science, you also need to cop the attitude that we have unlimited rights and powers over the Earth. The work of science neither recognizes any higher power (as organized religion does by being subservient to it), nor does it play "Let's Make a Deal" with it (as magic does). The universe of science is nonpurposive, its inquiry served only by human curiosity. Science can tell us how we're constituted but it can never tell us who we are. Mess with any of these laws of the scientific constitution and you arouse the guardians at the gate. Consider Philip Morrison's considerably toned down but fundamentally similar reaction to one who would challenge the notion that there is only one correct way to know the universe:

> . . . if science winds up teaching us that the universe is a clock [a mechanism] in which God [the creator] left us "home alone," then, so be it! It's time for us to grow up, anyway. And let's not "throw out the baby with the bathwater," but let's get on with real science.[6]

Whether the author is a member of CSICOP I know not, but it is noteworthy that the *Skeptical Inquirer,* which published his commentary, advertises itself as the most reliable source of scientific information on paranormal claims—from the Bermuda Triangle, crop circles, and UFO abductions to the Shroud of Turin. The Committee for the Scientific Investigation of Claims of the Paranormal first drew the Maginot line of organized occult skepticism twenty years ago when 186 fed-up scientists (including eighteen Nobel laureates) signed a manifesto entitled "Objections to Astrology."[7] In it they pronounced astrology a mistaken process without scientific formulation. Despite living in a rational age when the debunking of such beliefs might seem unnecessary, the signatories declared themselves disturbed enough to strike out stridently at all beliefs based on magic and superstition. CSICOP's editor supervised production and publication of the manifesto. Today, members of the organization include a curious concatenation of scientists, writers, journalists, and magicians.

Anthropologist David Hess sees the psi-cops as one of three, not two, opposing cultures—anti-antiscientists from the opposite pole to the New Age movement's shamanic voyagers, harmonic convergers, California channelers, and pagan ritualists. The parapsychologists, academics who study PK, ESP, and other psychic phenomena, form a kind of "demilitarized zone" between the two. What the parapsychologists (i.e., Rhine and Eisenbud) take more seriously (namely, the paranormal), both the skeptics and, oddly enough, the media in general label as occult.[8] This parochial attitude may come about because magic is still perceived as science's competitor. It crowds the stage. Its rites are wrongs as far as the debunkers are concerned.

Godfather of the psi-cops is Martin Gardner, mathematician and longtime popular science writer, whose debunking volumes, which undauntingly span this generation as well as the last, are legion. His brusque dialogue with the enemy extends no olive branches:

> . . . life is short, scientists are busy, and cranks have a habit
> of writing lots of books.[9]

Gardner's muckraking diatribe on J. Z. Knight is a good example of the entertaining way he expresses his skepticism: She stands in a doorway with a pyramid on her head to conjure up her image of the Ram, gets the word Ramtha copyrighted, and then tells fellow Ramsters the money they pay to be at the receiving end of the Ram channel is tax-deductible. No wonder ex-Ramsters are filing suit in droves. Look at the ridiculous predictions she makes:

> Ram's predictions for the close of 1985 were wild. A great
> pyramid would be found in Turkey, with a shaft leading to the
> earth's center. Sabotage of the World Bank, by a high official,
> would plunge the United States into a major war. MacLaine,
> by the way, isn't much better as a prophet. In a *Playboy* inter-
> view (September 1984) she predicted that George Bush
> would get the '84 Republican nomination for president.
> Maybe she got the year wrong and really meant 1988.[10]

Why does Gardner attack with such zeal? Because he believes passionately that this stuff is so obviously fraudulent and because it cons too many unwitting dupes. A barometer of the state of warfare between science and occult beliefs, his campaign against psi-research exceeds that of Houdini against the nineteenth-century and early twentieth-century spiritualists. David Hess argues that many New Age thought police see themselves as heroes, defenders of a way of life threatened by the New Age movement, which—if it catches on—could be as bad for the social system as AIDS is for the immune system.[11] Science for them is the only course to human salvation and misusing it could destroy us.

If Gardner is the godfather, CSICOP's chief hitman is the aforementioned magician James "the Amazing" Randi. What Ralph Nader is to consumerism, Randi is to the occult. Writes the illusionist turned activist:

> We critics of supernaturalism are accustomed to having words put into our mouths by the opposition and by the media, and it is about time that we struck back. In this book I will hit as hard as I can, as often as I can, and sometimes quite bluntly and even rudely. Good manners will be sacrificed to honesty, and the Marquis of Queensbury be damned.[12]

A recent *Time* magazine article begins: "Scientists, it seems, are becoming the new villains of western society."[13] We read about them in newspapers faking and stealing data and we see them in front of congressional committees defending billion-dollar research budgets. We hear them in sound bites trampling our sensibilities by comparing the Big Bang or some subatomic particle to God. It has become standard operating procedure to blame the environmental crisis on science because of its suspicious and aggressive goal of mastering nature through technology. Institution battles institution as government questions the value of science by canceling NASA's Search for Extra Terrestrial Intelligence and the Superconducting Supercollider. Mirroring a report of three government academies, an editorial in the prestigious journal *Science* admits that maybe scientists haven't been careful enough to be aware of when science is necessary but not sufficient. It can't be blamed for all the ills of society and maybe it ought to pay more attention to human needs.[14] I, too, have suggested that science *has* been getting a bum rap lately[15] but I don't think the turn to the occult, even in the benign form it has taken in America, is the *cause* of it. Instead, it may be one *effect* of the outcome.

Why this anti-science attitude now—at this particular point in time? Today we are very much conditioned by the notion that reality and the knowledge that constitutes it are in constant change and that no single thought system should decide what we ought to believe. Those who parade in intellectual circles call it postmodernism (the expression of a perceived breakdown of established certainties in general and of which science is very much a part).[16] If all truths are perceived to be relative in the extreme, then we who operate on and in the universe can never do so from an external vantage point. There is no division between mind and spirit—no Cartesian split. This attitude is very inimical to science, whose perspective no longer has the upper hand. There is no protocol. Whether argued against organized religion or institutionalized science, openness to alternative views seems to be the order of the day.

What is also so typically postmodernist about the New Age, says anthropologist Hess, is the way it mixes high and mass culture and the way it tries to incorporate into its discourse the findings of science and anthropology, just as it also fluidly juxtaposes philosophies spanning a range of time from ancient Egypt to the contemporary Native American.[17]

In sum, all the uncertainties twentieth-century science had promised to rescue us from—all the substantial reality bases of the universe—have begun to evaporate. Thanks to relativity, once-simple notions such as time and distance suddenly got too complicated, too warped, and intertwined; atoms once thought to be solid now dissolve beyond reach of our eyes into probabilistic uncertainties, a subnuclear zoo, each denizen with fractional electronic charge. And matter under chaos theory now is said to demonstrate the remarkable capacity to "self-organize" in non-Newtonian lumps. Gone is the secure optimism of nineteenth-century scientific humanism and here (perhaps to stay) is a cynical view of the world—a "cosmos of the absurd."[18]

Complained one physicist to his colleagues in a recent issue of *Physics Today:*

> . . . against all expectations, particle physics has turned into a nightmare, in spite of the many deep insights from which we have profited now for some time.[19]

Despite the upbeat face science has a habit of putting on, there is strife from within. This abyss of indeterminacy and fallibility in which science finds itself has helped to resurrect the notion that perhaps we alone can determine our own fate. Once the idea that a more secure knowledge of the future could be ascertained through science began to erode, it was gradually replaced by experiments with new ideas. Maybe we influence the universe and it influences us. And so we resurrect some of the old dictates of magic.

Still, there are optimists to respond to this tawdry state of physical affairs. For example, physicists Paul Davies and John Gribbin foresee a salvageable, more purposive science.[20] Their new paradigm is one among many purposive "theories of everything" (TOEs). They argue that physical processes have both a creative and a progressive nature, the origin of life being but one step along the pathway of the progressive complexification and organization of matter. Think of the possibilities—the universe should be teeming with ETs for Frank Drake to discover. Teilhard de Chardin, that apostle of purposeful progress, would have loved it! Only a couple of generations ago he was preaching the theory of guided evolution of the universe to ever higher stages of complex consciousness. Davies and Gribbin deliver the same goods minus the Cosmic Christ and love as a binding force.

Astrophysicist Frank Tipler goes further. His utopian view imagines a cosmos amalgamated into a single intelligent computing system. In *The Physics of Immortality,* he argues that attaining a knowledge of the hereafter is basically a battle between progress and technology on the one hand versus the collapse of the universe that will terminate all tangible human experience on the other. Tipler calls the end the Omega point (the last letter in the Greek alphabet) after a term coined by Teilhard de Chardin. Recall that as one of the early twentieth-century architects of directed evolution, Teilhard tried to soften Darwin's blows against purposiveness by ladling onto evolutionary theory a heavy dose of Judeo-Christian teleology. According to Teilhard, our hidden psychic energy grows as science and civilization develop and one day it will detach the collective human mind from the corporeal world and join God in the hereafter. Like Teilhard, Tipler sees the Omega point as a time of fulfillment of humankind's greatest ambitions. We will beat the big crunch and win the race to immortality. We will win it by building intelligent machines that will recreate themselves in an information-processing chain reaction that will spread the essence of the human mind throughout the universe, increasing knowledge limitlessly as it goes. Our manmade intergalactic robots will coalesce into a Teilhardian supersapient mind just in the nick of time before the ultimate black hole swallows what's left of the material world, Tipler predicts. This mind will be capable of resurrecting every conceivable human thought, concept, emotion, and desire and casting any combination of them in any conceivable bodily form. Detached from the universe's point singularity, ultimate reality will become virtual reality—a cyberspace in the memory of a supercomputer that processes information *ad infinitum.* If all of Tipler's visionary prognostications aren't audacious enough, he caps the test with a mathematical proof of the physical existence of God and the resurrection of the dead. In a lengthy "Appendix for Scientists," he tells us that ". . . intelligence will have hijacked the 'natural' information-processing system we call the Universe, and used it for its own ends."

Allen Dressler, in the last chapter of his *Voyage to the Great Attractor,* preaches essentially the same line as Tipler, with the imaginative twist that as cultural conquers biological evolution, human hosts will achieve actual union with the intelligence machines (I married a teenage computer?), thus carrying the DNA-encoded human message on humanity's greatest adventure. Writes Dressler, we have only lately become aware that the scientific process of discovery is the secret of life: "Only once in the evolution of sentient beings is this corner turned, and we who are now alive are that most fortunate generation, the people of the awakening."[21] From Disney World to virtual reality! The TOE of Davies and Gribbin also views the universe as an interlocking network of information exchange—a holistic, indeterministic, and open system.

Where does God fit into this scientific picture? A godlike intelligence could develop from our own descendants, or better, from that of computerized intelligence. He becomes the scientist par excellence who controls the natural world to such an extent that he becomes a part of it:

> One can envisage intelligent life or machine intelligence gradually becoming more advanced and spreading throughout the cosmos, gaining control over larger and larger portions until its manipulation of matter and energy is so refined that this intelligence would be indistinguishable from nature itself.[22]

Out of the mouths of scientists come new cosmologies. Their stories remind us of those told by nineteenth-century spiritualists like Madame Blavatsky. The new twist, however, is that we help create the divine spark through technology rather than pure spirit. Thus, we propel the universe on its evolutionary course to loftier orders of information processing, and when it finally all coalesces into the infinite and eternal world soul, man becomes Superman.

Who knows—maybe we're all just bugs in some giant computer or maybe my brain is a hologram. As one psychologist put it:

> In this post-Heisenberg, post-Freud, post-Marx, post-television, post-constructionist, post-modern world, we

have finally come to realize that there is no system of truth
with which to account for all aspects of being.[23]

We have discovered in this chapter that both science and magic, two ver-
tices of the triangle whose connecting axioms we have been trying to
comprehend, have definite tools and methods, separate technologies,
contrastable rational procedures, and systematic bodies of knowledge.
One difference is this: What the magician once stole from the gods, the
scientist now steals from an abstract objective entity that operates totally
outside the sphere of human concern. And a second important difference
is that each enterprise arrives at valid knowledge by different standards.
In magic, the truth of it all—the efficacy of the magical act—is judged
by the way you feel after you've gone through it, not by any objectively
based proof in a controlled environment designed to decide whether a
formula or a transfer works.

CHAPTER 37

ANTHROPOLOGISTS ENCOUNTER THE OCCULT

⌒

... the extraordinary similarity of savage and classical spiritualistic rites, with the corresponding similarity of alleged modern phenomena, raises problems which it is more easy to state
than to solve.

Andrew Lang, *Cock Lane and Common-Sense*

Here's the ultimate question about magic: Why is it that so many of the principles of magic we have discussed in our own past—nature as an animate force, the principle of correspondences through association, the notion that only the gifted adept can make the connection between the individual and the world beyond—seem to have patterns of behavior that occur in cultures all over the world, from Indonesia to Siberia to Africa to the Native American southwest? Every society in the world seems imbued with what we call magical ideas and despite the fact that established institutions teach us to shun such beliefs, even our own popular culture is not free of them. Why is medicine all over the world dominated by magic? Why do people persist in their attempts to control environmental forces through magical rites? How come everybody but us twentieth-century rational beings has developed that uncanny knack for talking to the dead? They live by magic and we resist it. Why? To find out, in this chapter I want to explore just a few examples to illustrate the cross-cultural common ground of magic.

Azande tribespeople of the Central African Republic prick the stalks of their banana trees with crocodile teeth: "May bananas be prolific like crocodile teeth," they say. They also place a stone in the fork of a tree to keep the sun in the sky: "May the sun not be quick to fall today. You stone, retard the sun so I can get home before sunset." These customs are part of organized Azande magic,[1] and the analogies these rites and customs depict in the minds of the people who practice them are strikingly similar to those in ancient Rome described in Pliny's *Natural History*.

An example worth mentioning brings out yet another universal principle of magic we've encountered before. To get rid of ringworm, one Azande cure says, rub the infected area with fowl excrement. Why? Because ringworm looks like fowl excrement, which is, therefore, associated with both the cause and cure of the malady. Symptoms are supposed to yield to treatment by the object that resembles and causes them. This is nothing more than the old like-cures-like principle. But be careful: What do I mean when I use the words "yield to treatment"? Do we know whether the connection is a causal one? The active principle seems to be that you try to control certain objects or aspects of one thing by manipulating other things that resemble them. You attack a disease by resorting to a natural object that resembles the disease. But again the rite expresses something more like a wish rather than a scientific prediction. You do it with the intention of evoking an attitude, a desire, a wish to cure the disease—magic—rather than to determine its outcome—science.[2]

Not to be lost in our comparison is that in both science and magic an analogy is being used as a model for the thing or phenomenon that requires exploration. If exploring and exploiting similarities between ringworm and chicken excrement seems absurd, consider some of the analogies made by rational scientists. For example, we've all heard it said that the brain is like a sponge. In what way? If we manipulate an ordinary kitchen sponge, we will discover that to a certain extent it isn't such a bad model for what scientists and philosophers think about thinking. If thoughts to be memorized are like water, some sponges, like people's brains, have a higher capacity to absorb knowledge than others and some retain it longer. Absorption and retention are suitable operative words to describe the way we think the brain works. At least at the macroscopic level, the porifera of the pantry is a vivid model to explain the process of the acquisition of knowledge and ideas. When we get to the microscopic level this won't do, so we substitute the computer model of the brain. We imagine electrical bits and bytes of information being downloaded and coursing through neural pathways like blood through our veins from one storage terminal to another. Indeed, early computers were termed "electronic brains." No self-respecting psychologist would argue that the brain really is a sponge any more than a biologist would propose that DNA is really a computer information network or, for that matter, a physicist that atomic nuclei in an accelerator actually are an array of colliding billiard balls.

All of these devices—the Azande's and ours—are metaphors, simple substitutions of familiar devices that are so deeply ingrained in our culture that they easily can stand in for things and processes about which we really don't know very much. We use this mental substitution—the familiar for the unfamiliar—as a way of making the mysterious universe a little less mysterious. While we use mechanical models as metaphors, the Azande liken the brain to a walnut because, in a nutshell, it *looks* like a brain in its cranial case.[3] Pull the top shell from the nut and you can trace the creases and folds in the nutmeat (it's an even more remarkable visual likeness to our grey matter than a sponge). For the Azande in this instance it is the physical resemblance that matters. To say that a walnut is a bad metaphor for the brain and its thought processes is to suggest that the Azande ought to think about brains and thinking the way we do. If they did that, they would realize that the sponge, not the walnut, is the better metaphor. Rather than miseducate them, I find it more interesting to try to understand what African people think about brains (and walnuts) and where both fit into their world view.

Remember the amulets—charms that protect against evil—described by Pliny and the Egyptians? Other cultures have them too. But oddly enough, anthropologists usually give them a different name. They call them fetishes—objects said to have mysterious powers that give a feeling of awe that comes from habitation by a deity. Actually, the root word is Roman—*facticius* (man made), as opposed to natural. In the hands of early Christian writers, this led to the term "factitious," meaning fraudulent. Pliny discusses them in his thirty-fourth volume where he says that they represent the worship of false images and idolatry—bad stuff. In the Biblical tradition anything altered by man was thought to countermand God's perfect work as decreed in Genesis. Tertullian, the Christian Roman philosopher (A.D. 150–230), once condemned bodybuilding on the grounds that it attempted "to create an artificial body as a way of surpassing god's work."[4] Reading Webster, you and I would assign a negative meaning to "fetishism," perhaps because there is an inherent falsity in attributing anything personal or spiritual to an object of nature. This is in part because our society, grounded in modern materialism, teaches us that the real worth of a stone is measured by its commercial value and technological usage. Any personification of the object is pure caprice.

The anthropologist J. R. Fox has described a modern Cochiti (New Mexico) rite that is notable for the host of fetishes it involves.[5] It starts with the creation of a huge sand painting. Then stone figures of lions, bears, badgers, and so forth, along with parts of the real animals (e.g., bear claws) are positioned around it. Each represents one of the participating spirit doctors, who alone possess curative power, though they can transfer it to the medicine men. Like a modern surgical team, four or five of them can be present at the ceremony, especially if the patient is gravely ill. They carry rock crystals to give themselves second sight and an ear of corn, the grain of life; these serve as badges of office. The doctors then sing songs and dance as they exhort all present to believe in them, for they are doing their best to make the patient well. They lay out lines of sand from the sick person's doorway to each of the animal fetishes to draw the animal spirits in from the outdoors. Water from the six directions of the universe[6] is poured into a bowl. Herbs are added. Then the doctors go to work massaging the patient with ashes. They detect foreign objects in the body with a rock crystal, objects that witches have shot into the body to make the patient sick. They draw them out one by one and spit them into the bowl as they use their bear claw necklace, flint knife, and bear bone whistle to combat the witches who are trying to steal the sick person's heart. Sometimes the doctors find it necessary to go outside the curing place where witches rap at the door and beckon to them. In confusion and cacophony, doctors and witches fly through the air; they make crashing noises and let loose blood curdling howls as they fight for the return of the victim's heart. In retaliation the witches try to blow their foul breath into the doctors' faces to overpower them. But the medicos stay their ground and if they are lucky enough to capture a witch (often portrayed by an animal in the ceremony), they bring it to the hearth and shoot it with a bow and arrow and smear themselves with its blood. Then they bring back the heart (in the ceremony it is described as a ball of rags wrapped around a bunch of corn kernels). Exhausted after four days of this frenetic activity, they finally collapse into unconsciousness on the ground.

Now, modern psychologists would describe the whole process of Puebloan curing as shock therapy. We might liken its drama and emotion to a faith healer's cure by touch. It certainly isn't medicine as we practice it. One anthropologist says the cure usually works because illness among these people is largely psychosomatic. You're sick because you're bewitched and when you believe you're bewitched the illness gets worse. Medicine men capitalize on the emotion of fear by creating a ceremony for good medicine that outdoes the fear of evil in the heart of the patient. They literally scare the hell out of him and drive out the disease!

By manipulating and talking to the fetishes, chanting more loudly and dancing ever more spastically night after night, they build up tension. The final battle comes on the last night, when the frenzied doctors fly out the doorway into the darkness to physically confront the evil spirits. The audience hangs in suspense. Will they return? Will they be harmed? What message will they bring? When they finally do come back, bloodied and disheveled, the tension is snapped in an instant; the patient is saved. One old man made well by this process was heard to remark that his relief was so profound that he could actually feel the disease go out of his body. When it comes to dramatic magical cures, the theatrical Cochiti ceremony has few parallels.

As far as we know, the practice of using fetishes often may have had little to do with invoking good or evil spirits, like Christian souls, argues anthropologist William Pietz. More in line with the wish theory, he sees the fetish as an artifact that bonds an oath enacted through a physical performance. In this sense tying an object to the body is little different from consuming an exotic substance. If we believe fetishes were intended to conjure up the Devil (the usual interpretation in grade B movies and novels) we may be falsely conferring upon native practices devoid of Christianity a belief inherent in Western religion—that demonic spirits can interact with people through idols. We have no right to inflict that belief on others.

Would I recommend that one of my academically-troubled students place books around his or her bedside when he or she goes to sleep the night before a final exam? I would if I believed that manipulating these objects of knowledge in some sort of ritual of performance was a concrete way of manifesting my wish that my student would do well on the test. I would if I believed it to be a persuasive device to exhort the student to study hard before retiring and to encourage him or her to remember to relax when taking the exam. Maybe verbal encouragement (i.e., advising my student to spread the books out and what to say to oneself while doing so) would psych him or her up for the big test. (Steven Hawking is fond of mentioning how many millions of those who purchased his bestselling, but tediously difficult *A Brief History of Time* scarcely were able to absorb its content. But then isn't there something to the theory that if you keep that text on the coffee table long enough you will somehow absorb the knowledge crammed between its covers?)

The idea of transferring knowledge from book to brain, I think, is not so remote from what happens in a magical rite. Assuming that there is an invisible attractive force in the form of an intangible field or stream of corpuscles that passes from words on a page to cells in the cerebral cortex, is just the way a scientifically acculturated person might insist upon interpreting this sort of magic in his or her mind's eye. Our perception of what's really happening could be as far off base as the Christian notion that the only way to perceive what idol worshippers are doing is through the (presumably) false agency of the interaction of the spirit with the material world. The problem is that modern culture is so deeply imbued in Judeo–Christian and scientific ways of thinking. How can we possibly be expected to perceive someone else's ideas and actions in any other framework than our own? The task is so very daunting.

Since communing with the dead has occupied a central position in the history of Western magic, let's turn for comparison to an example of necromancy in a non-Western culture. Sisala diviners of northern Ghana foretell the future through contact with their dead ancestors. In a typical case reported in the literature,[7] a Sisala man visits another lineage under the pretense of collecting bride wealth, but instead he keeps the money for himself. When the real collectors finally arrive to acquire the tribute, they are told that a young man already came to collect it three months ago. They return to their village to confront the embezzler. He denies the charge and because there is no real proof of his guilt he is released. Soon, the thief is taken seriously ill. Neither native nor institutional medicines seem to work on him. He dies in the government hospital and his body is taken back home and buried. This is where the diviner comes in. He is consulted and asked to determine the cause of death. Did the ancestors do him in for being dishonest? When it is finally determined that this is exactly what happened, the family must reciprocate by sacrificing a goat to the ancestors to keep their lineage from being punished for the bogus collector's crime.

Just how is this deadly divining accomplished? In cases of suspicious death, at the funeral of the deceased the body is used as a device similar to that employed in water witching to point to the person who caused the death. Because law now forbids keeping the body out of the grave too long, they carry a bundle of sticks tied with the coffin cover cloth instead. The Sisala diviner totes a bag out of which he pulls cowrie shells and casts them in order to answer questions that lead to information about a disease that afflicts his client. Specially endowed Sisala witches can call up fairies and spirits—God's messengers who live in the trees, bushes, and rivers. To divine you must (usually) be male, though old women are permitted to practice; since they no longer bear children they are said to be more like men. You must exhibit a knowledge of the past and you should live by the ways of your ancestors (i.e., be conservative). Above all, you must be disinclined to travel. Though there are parallels between African and western divining, all of the Sisala methods of tapping into the world beyond are directed toward a different end: to reveal the power of their ancestors, who are the preservers of the moral order and who alone have the power of affliction. Little concerned with clueing us in about the hereafter, it is they who direct those of us who live here in the present about how to behave in the immediate future. Their dead are simply more like social beings than ours. They are as concerned about the present as we are.

The same for witches. The Azande blame just about everything bad that we might attribute to luck or fate or coincidence on witchcraft, but they do not do so idly nor do they live in fear of witchery. Some events can result from idleness or lack of self-control. But unexplainable accidents, illnesses, and deaths get categorized under the heading of malicious activities of sorcerers and witches—a kind of philosophical catchall of the unknown. They can activate the inner malevolent powers that lie within their intestines and make their power strike out and eat away a person's strength and will. A wise Azande male will consult the oracle for witch-proofing before embarking on a hunting trip or getting married, often changing plans if the consultation proves inauspicious. He might consult the termites to inquire whether his wife-to-be had been unfaithful. To do so he would insert two branches into the termite mound and ask the termites to answer his question by either eating or not eating the offering. Then if the answer is affirmative he might go on to another oracle to acquire the name of his rival. To do this he could use an oracle board with the names of suspects placed upon it. It works just like a ouija board. He would squeeze juice on the board and slide a lid across it until it sticks at the name of the adulterer.[8]

To excise your evil spirits in West Malaysia you might go to one of the handful of specialists or *dukun* (healers). These are like our adepts, only they are said to possess *ilmu,* an esoteric knowledge of how the body is interrelated with the universe. Anthropologist Michael Peletz has observed and recorded the activities of various *dukun* in the West Malaysian village of Bogang, especially those who specialize in cases of poisoning and spirit possession. The *dukun* usually acquire their *ilmu* from their fathers and grandfathers after years of fasting, praying, battling spirits, and ingesting a wide variety of foods. To give an idea of how sorcery enters into the explanation of misfortune, Peletz recounts the case of his friend Rashid, a young man from a relatively prosperous household who was very sick:

> . . . I encountered him at the local provision shop (kedai) that his mother runs. I expected the worst from the stories I had heard but still was not prepared for what I saw. Rashid was lying on a chaise lounge that had been covered with a blanket and was propped up behind one of the tables in the kedai. His head appeared freakishly large as the rest of his body was emaciated and withered. He looked all skin and bones, and his feet were covered with flaking skin and a red substance that I initially mistook for blood (it turned out to be medicine). Rashid greeted me by explaining that I looked well and fat, and that he was sick and thin. He had been very ill, he added, and could not walk, which is why his legs had withered; this was his fate (nasib). He said that he is much better now and not nearly as thin as before; at least now he has an appetite and can sleep, and has feelings in his legs.[9]

Why was Rashid taken ill? Because he violated one of the territorial codes involving a rival group. According to his own account he got sick a month after his father died. He was working on the East Coast in the family lumber mill. Whoever made him ill—most likely somebody he worked with—did so deliberately and probably out of envy, he explained. But another interpretation, that of an elder, blames the illness on aborigines—non-Muslims who spat their poisonous saliva on the ground which then entered Rashid's body through his feet. (Walking in the forest and stepping on somebody's poisonous spit is an occupational hazard in Rashid's sort of work.)

According to the dukun informant, one technique for removing such poisons starts with a healthy dose of coconut juice, thanks to its cooling properties. First the sorcerer makes a barely audible (secret) incantation over a hole drilled in the coconut shell. This usually includes a passage from the Koran recited in Arabic, the most sacred of all languages. In many ritual-oriented societies this sort of spontaneous, irregular—even incoherent—speech is taken to come straight from the heart. Unre-

•

hearsed and unadulterated, it is a true expression of one's thoughts—a higher form of knowledge. (In a Pentecostal sermon the more unintelligible the words, the greater the belief of the congregation in the gift of the communicant's interaction with higher powers.)[10]

The patient drinks the juice. Then he removes his shirt and leans over a banana leaf that rests on a table. He places his head inches above the leaf's surface. The sorcerer pats his back in a circular motion and does a rhythmic chant—also scarcely audible. Diviner and assistant then examine the content of the leaf (spittle, breath, foreign particles) to make sure the bad substances have been expelled. Sometimes several sessions are necessary for the treatment to take effect. Meanwhile, the patient is instructed on what he should and especially should not eat—lay off "scratchy" foods like shrimp, snails, and certain types of fish (as opposed to cooling foods like papaya, sugar cane, bananas, and tea). By all means, don't attend any funerals. In other words, the cured patient must not distress either his emotional or digestive balance—an admonition that reminds us of the idea of maintaining humoral imbalances. (In fact, it may well be a western Medieval influence that intruded into southeast Asian culture.)

The treatment for possession by demons in Bogang is a little different. One particularly frightening demon, who takes the form of a razor-toothed bloody-mouthed grasshopper, gains control of the body when its master instructs it to attack. You know you've been possessed by the grasshopper demon if you experience cramps and body twitches accompanied by visible rashes. If you have fits of screaming and begin to utter abusive language and make nonsensical talk, that's another sign. The healer treats possession by a hands-on technique. He localizes the telltale bodily blemishes and pinches the area occupied by the spirit, a common locale being at the joints where the fingers join the hand. He employs incense, sacred water, and incantations to exorcise the spirit, inquiring of it who is its master. Then he calls the victim's spirit back into the body by blowing on the head of the afflicted one.

What's behind all this Malaysian magic? In a society preoccupied with greed and envy, with people putting on displays of status and prestige and trying to gain control over one anothers' resources, Peletz finds that *ilmu* and the institution of *dukun* give one Malay villager a kind of social one-upsmanship over another. Trafficking in evil spirits is still widely practiced, even though many of these communities have been thoroughly industrialized.

Anthropologists today are less inclined than their Gilded Age predecessors to trace the roots of magic in other cultures to gaps in universal knowledge—deficiencies or failures that automatically led other societies away from developing a scientific approach to dealing with the natural world, the way we did. Instead, they look for explanations such as belief in the Devil when they study the practices of witchcraft and voodoo that are rooted in social beliefs and customs. Take, for example, the magic of envy. It may be the result of a social ethic that seeks to delegitimize people of one group who have more money than another: No wonder he's rich and famous—they say he acquired his power through allegiance with the Devil. Likewise, I rationalize the extraordinary size of my neighbor's swimming pool compared to my own by jokingly suggesting to other admiring (and probably also envious) neighbors that he can afford it because he cheats on his income tax.[11]

Voodoo[12] (it means worshipping the gods who control the universe) is the last example of the "magic of the other" that I want to mention that bears the trappings of pagan Old World practice. Actually, voodoo finds its origin in spirit possession cults that came from West Africa to the New World via the slave trade. Casting spells (e.g., using magical powders and potions to attract a lover) are as common and familiar as Old World methods we explored earlier—so similar they could well have been scripted by Pliny himself. A girl serves the man she desires portions of food laced with a part of her body—like ground up fingernail clippings or menstrual blood. If she does not desire him, she blows a powder consisting of dried herbs and the flesh of a hummingbird at him. He uses a dead man's bones to blind or paralyze his enemy. Say the Pater Noster backwards seven times and you can use it to invoke a priest or priestess you can personally talk with to get advice about how to cure illness.

The idea is to influence the host of spirits, good and bad alike, who make up a very real part of the world, to be your friends and allies and to act in your behalf. Like the Cochiti curing ceremony, many of the voodoo cures and other rites are accompanied by wild gyrations, dancing, and trance states, so we have had a tendency to rationalize the whole business as hysterical mumbo jumbo—this just isn't the way we deal with our problems! Because the witches of our Renaissance past were thought to consort with the Devil, we project that image, too, on the contemporary Haitian witch doctor. Finally, our attitude toward voodoo is also very much conditioned by our categorization of all magic as trickery and delusion—Houdinism.

To really understand voodoo we must look again at the fabric of culture out of which it is patterned. Far from a secret society bent on malicious ways and the perpetration of Satan-worshipping superstition, voodoo is a social system with deep religious underpinnings that caters to the needs of people who truly require a happier existence after death. When your life is as miserable as that of ordinary Haitians, voodoo practice can give you a sense of power and help you make your way. It offers a path to your wishes—a means of putting a hex or an anticipation into action—a kind of terrorist act committed in a situation of tension or competition and designed to create anxiety, either good or bad, in the victim. But this sort of terrorism is effective only if both perpetrator and victim share in its belief.

Voodoo may have a lot more to do with a people's way of clinging to a style of life over which they are rapidly losing control; the Devil is responsible for what's happening here, not us, people say. Just as we might neglect the social value of the Greek oracle at Delphi and focus upon the imagined rantings of an incense-inhaling priestess who deals in exercises in nonsensical mumbo jumbo, so too might we expect to find that there is little to be learned in discussing a voodoo witch who sticks pins in a doll or for that matter a Malaysian adept who whispers sweet nothings into a coconut. Far from imprisoning the mind, Delphi's Oracle, the Sisala diviner's sacred bundle, the Malaysian wizard's bag of tricks, and the voodoo witches' magic powder—they all kick-start people along the road of decision making.

Us and them—what we called magician and adept in our own past we label shaman and medicine man in other societies. Altered states of consciousness, out-of-body experiences, impregnating objects with life via the power of the word, developing magical formulae to acquire potency, magic spells, chanting, potions, ecstatic trances, alternate realities, like-cures-like—the whole array of beliefs we explored from anonymous Babylonian exorcist to modern channeler—are all there in one form or another in descriptions and accounts of ritual behavior in non-Western societies. Makes you wonder, if it works the same the world over, are *we* the ones who make it work? And deep down, are we all really the same?

To seek answers to these rather basic human questions, let's backtrack a little and trace the threads of the relatively young discipline that is supposed to deal with questions like these—the study of the "other." Nineteenth-century anthropologists tried to rationalize magic as a way people fill in the uncertainty gap in life's big questions by expressing their optimism through ritual. (Given that they lived in an age in which the screws of scientific rationalism were being tightened on the explanations of all things, this is not so surprising.) Ask a magician why he chants as he plants and he will tell you it is the correct procedure to produce crops. If you ask him what would happen if he did not chant, he probably would tell you that then the seeds would not grow.

Scientists try to do something similar in our culture. They assume regularities in nature and try to manipulate matter in order to clarify what they believe. Language, performance, the intellectual approach—they're the same in both endeavors. Trouble is, a large number of these early anthropologists agreed, magic doesn't work. They saw it as failed science, science gone wrong. Crude in its operation, shallow in its belief—the whole of it carried out with a monotonous sameness—magic was declared no match for progressive science's logical and orderly way of dealing with the uncertainty gap. But, we must remember, the nineteenth century also was noted for its ethnocentric outlook on cultures the western world had scarcely begun to explore. For the first time, anthropologists were getting a close look at societies whose values they tended to regard as unworthy of serious exploration in and of themselves. Doing a magical act—chanting over newly planted seeds—has nothing to do with the outcome, the direction toward practical ends, they reasoned. After all, the ends are what concern us most. According to the anthropologists, magic also had negative connotations that separated it from religion as well as science; where religion unifies, magic divides; where religion is sacred, magic is profane; religion mollifies and supplicates, magic provokes and manipulates[13]—it is full of errors and stupidities—a monstrous farrago, as Edward Tylor, dean of early twentieth-century anthropologists, once characterized it.[14]

Instead of stressing the split between magic and science on the one hand and magic and religion on the other, the next generation of anthropologists, who began to study the lifeways of exotic cultures more deeply—and who practiced their discipline in an age far less inclined to the overt rationalism to which we've become accustomed—found themselves switching paradigms. They began to see all three (magic, science, and religion) as intertwined, part of a magical world view ordered by relationships totally different from our own. Not so much concerned with its efficacy, the mid-twentieth-century view of magic seemed more tolerant; it dwelled more on demonstrating how different it was from our own way of dealing with the world.[15] Different cards, different games. As

anthropologist John Beattie put it (when speaking about the West
African people he studied), their common sense is different from ours:

> ... the beliefs of this highly intelligent people ...
> are ... not ... a set of weird and irrational delusions about
> occult forces, but rather ... a mode of adjustment to the
> strains and frustrations of everyday life which, in the whole
> context of Zande culture, appears as eminently practical and
> sensible.[16]

In other words, those who practice magic, said the anthropologists,
simply do not deal with the same world as we. Their reality is a social
world of *mana* or power exchanged among beings both human and nonhuman via rites that constantly reestablish social equilibrium in a universe that *they* perceive. This makes magic a symbolic system, a way of
expressive rather than practical behavior, a vehicle for saying and doing
something you can't do directly.

Despite these differences, even when we view it cross-culturally,
magic really should be thought of as part of a people's religion, as one of
the many types of practices that make up religious ritual, rather than a
separate phenomenon. We focus too much on proving or disproving the
power of magic and not enough on what it means to those who practice it. If you look carefully at the handful of examples I discussed, you
will see in all of them a common element: They are used as techniques
and practices that reflect a belief in the effectiveness of human activities
that are no different from praying and sacrificing. Both prayer and sacrifice are accepted parts of religious ritual. The Sisala diviner, like any
modern religious counselor, guides moral action—he works in the field
of ethics. Whether they read tea leaves or decipher an inflated pair of
lungs of a sacrificed animal, what the diviners are trying to do is to mediate in some sort of apparent conflict between an individual or society
and the powers they believe reside in the mysterious world around them.
The course of action is decided not by reason or dialogue but by manipulating symbols and images that relate to a world view shared by all
believers—*their* common sense. In all instances, people seem to be acting
on the belief that superordinate agencies (rather than transcendent or
spiritual "beings") do not run the universe alone but that our power, our
will, our forces can influence the future course of events. We make a mistake, I think, when we insist (in the western tradition) that anybody who

views people as part of a ruling cosmic hierarchy either lives in a total fantasy world or deliberately lies as a way of palliating nature's circumstances to the ignorant masses. Magic isn't just a form of politics.

When we cast modern scientific spells upon the world in order to control it we too are engaging in a form of religious ritual, albeit one that depends more on the worship of the book and the computer than on eliciting the power of the spoken word. Incidentally, this religion too has its fanatics. Recently I participated in a solar eclipse expedition to the South Atlantic. One passenger, a computer hack and astro buff, tracked the diminishing solar disk on his desktop planetarium all the way to mid-totality even as the eclipse developed. Finally, concerned friends found it necessary to forcibly drag him from his cabin out onto the deck of the ship so that he could bask in the final few minutes of genuine coronal light.

What came to pass in the subatomic world at century's beginning now comes back to haunt the social anthropologist at its end. In contrast to the nineteenth-century hierarchical order (with Central European scientifically minded man positioned at the top of the heap), cultural pluralism today is accounted for not by absences or deficiencies that reside within the *other*, but instead by a Gouldian kind of punctuated equilibrium of social life (reflecting the idea that evolution proceeds as a result of sudden episodic change as well as continuous and steady change over a long period, or gradualism). In this new age of uncertainty and recognition of cultural diversity, we are forced to live with the possibility that in other times and places there were and are other ways of comprehending the external world that are impossible to translate, much less appreciate. Internal connections, logic, and coherence not only exist in such systems of thought, but also we have little hope of comprehending or explaining them—an uncertainty principle of the social sciences.

In the 1930s, French anthropologist Lucien Lévy-Bruhl proposed that our capacity to engage in magic is an evolutionary leftover from the primacy of our cultural youth. Magic is in all of us, he said—an undiscarded intellectual appendage of our thoughts. It is like the bump at the base of our spine that used to be our tailbone—a reminder that we once swung from trees. The typical evolutionist of his time, however, Lévy-Bruhl also suggested that there is a mystical and a rational side to all mentalities, the former having been more marked in primitive times, the latter in our own (i.e., we have evolved from pre-logical into logical thinkers). Like so many early twentieth-century views of human behavior, Lévy-Bruhl's idea was based upon a direct if misguided application of Darwin's theory of evolution.

Why have I plumbed the depths of magic from a multitude of perspectives? Because I believe too many of the academic disciplinary approaches to the subject unwittingly operate with blinders on. The subdiscipline of cognitive psychology has become a stock-in-trade of modern anthropology's exploration of the world of magic. Many psychologists think that when Lévy-Bruhl spoke about our magic versus our rational side, he tapped into a question Freud and others had long contemplated: Are there multiple realities, other subuniverses of the mind that lie beneath the concrete, sensible world in which we place all our faith? Is there a dream plane versus an action plane, a scientific way of thinking about the world versus a mythological one? Perhaps the thought planes that we perceive are all there at the same time and we spend our days and nights switching channels from one to the other. Some of us give better Nielsens to the magic channel than to the reason channel because we enjoy its programs more. Like biological organisms, societies develop in an open-ended way and there are myriad possibilities for an outcome. Our culture has experienced one of those ways and we cannot say whether it is the best because culture can't be reduced to a common measure. There is no room for value judgment here. Nor is there a measure of unity in this explanation of how people understand the world—no psychic unity for humankind. Still, as anthropologist Stanley Tambiah emphasizes, we need to strive for an integrative explanation, for there really are problems that envelop all cultures and times—like coping with the prospect of death, questions about the afterlife, the problems of origin, and of human suffering.[17]

CHAPTER 38

SUMMARY:
CROSSING CURVES IN AN AGE
OF INTERCONNECTEDNESS

~~~

... for the first time an American renaissance is taking place in
all the disciplines, breaking the boundaries between them,
transforming them at their farthest reaches—where they all
converge.

Max Lerner, in Marilyn Ferguson's
The Aquarian Conspiracy

L ike the Renaissance man who sings a song to the sun, not to physically change its course, but to put himself into a different state of
mind, the Azande traveler chucks a stone into the fork of a tree,
not to stop the sun in the sky, but to remind himself to hurry along to
beat the sun in his homeward race. Each magical act is really a wish—an
attempt to persuade a charismatic cosmos he is confident he can talk to.
Magic is an attitude that makes you aware that you must act accordingly.
It is a form of activism and participation as sensible and practical in many
cultures of the world as scientific trial-and-error testing is in our own.
Maybe one of Mesmer's examiners from the scientific establishment was
not too far off the mark when he explained that the hypnotist's acts
called into play the genial influences of hope.

Magic is the way to your wishes—from the Oracle at Delphi to the
masterminding of the god-supercomputer some contemporary scientists
say will extricate us from the messy death that awaits us at the Omega
point. Both oracle and computer put a share of the power of God in us.
If divining means giving a sign of future things to come, then magic's role
in society is to imbue the future's possible course with that wished-for
element. No wonder pre-Christian Gnosticism has always looked so
good to us. It offers us the opportunity to participate. Believing in a par-
ticipatory cosmology spurs us on to action. It leads to the notion that our

actions have a real stake in what will happen in the future. We really *can* affect what happens in the world.

Maybe we *all* do magic. Maybe there's even a piece of everybody's brain that buys into the magical world. Where does all this psychological and anthropological theorizing and the debate about cultural relativism leave us regarding the recent upswing in occult beliefs? Sociologists Edward Tiryakian and Marcello Truzzi are among the scholars who have taken a hard look at the sociology of the occult.[1] Though each wrote in the immediate aftermath of the sixties revolution, a time when occult bookstores sprang up in university neighborhoods like dandelions on a neglected lawn, what they had to say is still fresh and it makes pretty good sense even after thirty years of hindsight.

The hydraulics of the modern interlink between magic and science consists of a downward-angled pipe from the former to the latter, Truzzi seems to argue. You can't bend spoons without touching them and Darwin's theory leaves no room for an abominable snowman. Truzzi sees the occult as a kind of wastebasket chock full of claims to truths that don't fit established science or religion. Magic's zone of influence is a lot less limited today than it was a few centuries ago. Gone from its fold and over to the science camp are herbals and meteorites. As its once basic tenets get tested and approved by science they are co-opted and relabeled. What belongs and what doesn't belong to magic depends on who's doing the sorting and the labeling as well as when in history and in what social context it gets done. Whatever coincidences still defy a causal explanation get shelved in that in-between par-occult (my term, not Truzzi's) category. Jung's synchronicity, transcendental experiences of the mind—there may be something to it, there may not. Let's just wait and see whether we can scientize it.

"Far out!" was a familiar cry of the hippie age. It usually referred to beliefs positioned on the hard end of the occult continuum, such as those least likely to be integrated into the mainstream of common sense: Kabbalism and demonology very much so; UFOlogy and crystals less so; astrology even less; parapsychology and ESP, *déjà vu,* and hypnosis less still. Today's magic is far less elite and much more democratic than that of Paracelsus, even than DDH's or HPB's kind of magic. Remember, they were radical activists who worked their way into the upper echelon of the social and financial hall of fame, not benign mainstream middle-aged baby boomers. Today magic is for everybody.

The canons of occult thought are no longer mysterious. If you want to know the secret, just go into any New Age bookstore and you can buy all the special know-how you need—formulas and even the paraphernalia that goes with them. The more public magic becomes, the greater the need of the rational element in society to check people's indulgence in it (ergo the letter by 186 scientists condemning astrology) or at least to try to justify their belief in it through scientific validation (Bill Moyers' book).

Max Lerner's foreword to *The Aquarian Conspiracy* (the epigraph I chose for this section) reflects the optimism in Marilyn Ferguson's popular book on the personal and social transformation that enveloped New Age thinking a decade or more ago. *The Aquarian Conspiracy* isn't about an underground menace—it's about a movement consisting of activists asking questions about the establishment and challenging it from within, in areas as diverse as brain research, holistic medicine, biological evolution, and parapsychology. It all coalesces around a spiritualist tradition centered in the personal meditative disciplines like Zen Buddhism, yoga, Christian mysticism, Transcendental Meditation, Sufism, and Kabbalah.

Except for a small percentage at the hard end of the spectrum, most practitioners of the occult enter into it playfully, openly—as in a trip to Disneyland. What once was feared by society—what once was threatening—now becomes slowly demystified by the age of reason. Would any inquisitive teenager enter an old abandoned house on Friday the thirteenth if she really thought it was haunted? asks sociologist Marcello Truzzi.

> It is precisely because we no longer believe in fearsome aspects of the occult that we are willing to experiment with them. If we really believe in demons we wouldn't draw a pentagram on the floor and call them up. The more we eliminate the myths the more we develop a scientific naturalistic rationalism.[2]

In line with what Truzzi says about the occult, Tiryakian thinks much of what is modern has its source in what once was esoteric. In the face of social instability and uncertainty, mass shifts in social inertia turn us inside out, carrying us away from the exoteric to the esoteric. This happened early on in the Renaissance in Europe, on the American frontier in the 1850s, and on our campuses in the 1960s. He underlines the alienation of disillusioned youth—disillusioned with the ideology of progress, overt materialism, and bureaucracy. This was a major development that led to the escapist, otherworldly concerns of many hippies of the sixties, much of it manifested through the drug campaign, trends toward new religions, and the neo-evangelical movement.

Today the organization of New Age philosophy has become more formalized, more varied—embracing a broader span of ages of the people it influences. And yet, despite all the openness and optimism within the occult fringe, the world outside it remains suspicious and ever fear-wracked. Modern witchcraft poses a striking contrast with its historical counterpart. It is a good example of the political and religious mainstreaming effect of occult practice. Today they call it Wicca—feminine for the English word for witch, *wicce*. It is a largely urban feminist religious cult that draws in middle-class women in the thirty- to forty-something age category. The high priestess is said to be the mother goddess of a once violent and patriarchal—but now turned peaceful and matriarchal—society. Most neopagan cults believe in ecofeminism and they tend to lay the woes of the world on the male element of western society, which they consider to be alien to their causes.

In Britain, where Wicca is more highly organized than in America, it is largely a fertility cult. Like UFOs and Atlantis, it is believed to come from a place and time before the creation of the present form of the corrupt world. Rituals usually are conducted on dates geared to the changing seasons—the equinoxes and solstices. On these occasions the coven, a working unit averaging about a dozen persons, for example, might gather in a large circle to draw down power from the mother goddess with magical utterances and written words accompanied by nude frantic dancing. Binding parts of the body to control the blood and ritually whipping initiates (albeit with an embroidered piece of silk), as practiced by some covens, unfortunately adds to the charges leveled by critics that Wicca is just a titillating form of sado-masochism, not to mention an excuse for sexual orgies. Typically, a book of Wicca liturgy stands on an altar at the center, along with wand, pentacle, and chalice. And though it bears comparison to its archaic derivative, Wicca's magic circle is benign. While it once may have been employed to make pacts with evil forces that it sought to unleash upon its enemy, today it symbolizes feminine bonding and fertility.

The 1990s version of American Wicca is quite active. I know of at least five covens within an hour's drive of my house. They do not practice their rituals openly for fear of harrasment by a public that still associates the Devil with their craft. One practitioner, the proprietor of a respectable local business, said hers is a religion that believes that humans do not have dominion over nature; they are merely guardians of a living Earth, of which we are an appendage. "We don't perform evil spells and we don't worship the Devil, naked or otherwise." The witches had found the limelight in our Burned-Over District just a year ago, when concerned citizens claimed the absence of a baby Jesus from our local creche during Christmas week was a statement emanating from the occult segment of the community that Jesus never was born. Explained the pastor of the town church in a letter to the weekly newspaper, we never put the figure out until Christmas day because that is when Jesus was born. "As above so below; as within so without; as the universe, so the soul. . . ." So say the local witches on the winter solstice as they greet the sun with all-night vigils to celebrate the arrival of its new rays.

Back in Aleister Crowley's day and especially in the 1920s and 1930s, a hot debate raged about the authenticity of the roots of modern witchcraft. Margaret Murray's controversial book[3] claimed it was a survival of pre-Christian paganism—not an unusual claim for any category of magical practice as we have learned. Modern witch-hunts?—they exist too, as the writer M. G. Marwick reminds us:

> Though modern man may have given up the more specific beliefs in witchcraft, he has retained many of its associated tendencies. He has not yet completely escaped from the charmed circle of taboos and magical beings that confines primitive man, and moved into an open society in which he has no qualms about adjusting his social institutions in the light of rational analysis. Some twentieth-century movements have many of the characteristics of a sixteenth-century European or a contemporary primitive witch-scare. An accusation of political deviance may, like an accusation of witchcraft, prove an infallible means of destroying a reputation or a career.[4]

He cites Joseph McCarthy's anti-Communist witch-hunt, which was played out in nineteenth-century Salem in Arthur Miller's play, *The Crucible,* as a parallel.

In the spirit of tracing the history of magic through the habits and beliefs of some of its most notable practitioners of different times, people, and places, I began this section by making what might seem to have been an absurd contrast between Harry Houdini and Richard Feynman—magician and scientist; one pulls rabbits out of hats, the other formulas out of the air. Public conception could not place the two in more opposing camps: Magicians indulge in trickery while scientists seek a higher truth; a magician practices deception but a scientist reasons; magicians deal in the supernatural, scientists describe and explain what belongs to nature. Today's scientists remand the modern magic of astrology, crystals, telekinesis, and channeling to the trash heap of superstition and render them articles of an undeserved faith based on a lack of material evidence. Yet, in the eyes of a palmist, homeopath, or Tarot reader, science offers only an incomplete reading of the real world, for it unhooks the human spirit from the wheels that drive the material universe. In my profiles of these two curious characters, my goal was to demonstrate that deep down science and magic are perhaps more alike than we might care to admit.

I think there is a twinge more fear and pessimism in the nineties occult than in the Aquarian joy and optimism of the 1980s—and an increased interest in it as well. Sociologists tend to label most occult practices forms of cult—today a pejorative term—for two reasons: First, they lie outside the mainstream of normal common-sense thought; second, they try to solve your problems by resorting to the experience of a single individual purported to have some special knowledge or wisdom above that of all the other members who make up the group. There is bound to be fear and overreaction against new and different forms of cult, particularly those who are extreme or emphatic in their beliefs (i.e., the Shakers and Millerites of the last century or the Moonies and Branch Davidians of the present one). Anti-cult groups lash out against them because they see a threat to organized religion and they become especially bothered when they see cultic rites practiced so fervently.[5] Or there is the feeling that cult leaders use their deception as a form of "mind control" to hoodwink the naive and weak-minded into joining them only to convince them to part with their pocketbooks to advance their own personal cause—decidedly a negative one.

From computerized virtual reality to the movies we watch, the books we read[6] to the white and black magical powers of the foods we eat (oat bran vs. cholesterol), to the ads touting potions we are directed to rub on our bodies to attract the opposite sex, today we are without a doubt riding the wave of yet another magical tidal surge. Why the resurgence of an interest in magic in late 1990s America—magic of all kinds, from spiritualism to sleight of hand, from Madame Blavatsky to David Copperfield? James Randi's answer is that in times of social stress—like the present, thanks to the complicated world we all live in—people hunger for simple answers and magic gives them what they want[7]—old wine in new bottles, even if a highly watered-down version of the old elixir.

The *New* New Age isn't just about the harmonic convergence and *Out on a Limb*—that's media stuff. Today's is a much quieter revolution. A mainstreaming process has developed, a desire to synthesize because all the problems we face seem so complex that we no longer feel we can seek monolineal solutions to them.[8] The New Age theory of Gaia becomes a subset of science, ESP of psychology, homeopathy of medicine, and TM surely belongs to religion. Fitness embraces yoga as sweat and spandex yield to meditative exercise in Jane Fonda's new version of working out. We heal our own bodies by realigning them with the help of at-home institutional cassettes. Sports incorporates a New Age technique as Sugar Ray Leonard narrates a course in boxing for women—advertised as a form of stress release involving strenuous exercise. Ads in airline magazines reveal that even the corporate world has accommodated itself to the new spirituality. If you want to be more creative and more adaptable you've got to bring more of yourself into the company. How? With this simple six-part audiotape course on meditation that you can learn without even budging from your business-class seat. That's the easiest kind of magic.

We find ourselves in the throes of change—economic uncertainty, a shift in the ethnic makeup of our populace, and a growing perception that all life's problems, from health insurance to getting a job and owning a home to paying taxes, have become too hopelessly complex to cope with successfully. And so we fly to alternate realities.

Where is New Age magic going as the new century approaches? Is it disintegrating, melting in the tepid waters of scientific rationalism? As I look into my own crystal ball, I think that if there's a single cord that binds together the diversity of practices I've been talking about, it is a resurrection of the belief in the underlying connectedness of things—the quest for the tie that binds the individual to the global in an age that constantly craves alternatives. It is only the *way* of seeking alternatives that shifts as magic forever becomes absorbed and retransformed by culture. Wrote New Age publisher Ehud Sperling at the end of the 1980s:

> What you're seeing happening is almost a biological cor-
> rective. . . . In the 1960s you had this incredible surge of ac-
> tivity that wanted to explore the culture. That went back to
> itself and is now reemerging as the New Age. . . .
>
> If you really look at the New Age. . . . It's an attempt to
> create a synthesis of cultural movements. And America the
> melting pot is the place where the synthesis is being created.
> Right now you've got everything from Native American
> traditions to Zen Buddhism, all flowing into one pot.[9]

Even the scientists are diving into the holistic melting pot as their
curve now begins to merge with that of religion and spiritual belief. Recently the Templeton Prize for Progress in Religion, which carries the
largest monetary award ($1 million) for achievement in any field, was
awarded to physicist Paul Davies. Books by scientists entertaining religious questions flood today's trade book market: *The Mind of God, God
and the Astronomers, Does God Play Dice?*[10] Their content reflects the
changing nature of the dialog between science and religion; their message is decidedly conciliatory. Evidently science and religion do not operate independently, and if you want to engage the question of whether
we live in a universe of design and purpose, you'd better learn what science has to say about knowing the real world.

Our generation has a love-hate relationship with science. We have become so imbued in its ways and methods that we cannot seem to get
away from the notion that science offers the correct method for telling
it like it is. Yet we know all too well that science's tangible technological
outcomes have contributed to environmental destruction, population
problems, and a huge health crisis as well by prolonging life. If only we
could unleash the power of science on the great ethical questions—the
big ones that deal with design and meaning in the world and the existence of the hereafter—on which the humanists have delivered nothing
but senseless songs and sermons. This is our *zeitgeist;* the desire to search
out the design of a universe with purpose we somehow feel is out there
and to use science as a way of doing it.

As I witness this scientific heist of the engaging questions traditionally assigned to the domain of magic and religion, I wonder whether
Tipler, Davies, Dressler, and company, are the modern-day direct descendants of Agrippa and Paracelsus. The particle accelerator and space
telescope become the state-of-the-art instruments for penetrating the

divine plan of creation. The computer is their philosopher's stone and their goal the simulation of all possible future versions of ourselves. Artificial intelligence emerges as the contemporary key to transmutation—the gateway to eternal life, estrogen for the human race. And this magic, like that of old, is turf on which no one but the adept ought dare to tread, for it is as elitist as the Paracelsian version. At least more than a modicum of knowledge of math and physics is required to penetrate Tipler's "Appendix for Scientists," which is as complex and confusing to the layperson as Aleister Crowley's *Magick in Theory and Practice.*[11]

Like the spoken word of the alchemist and philosopher of old, the message of optimism conveyed by many of these works palliates the negative missives traditional science has offered ever since Descartes dished up his universe of colliding billiard balls and left life's outcome to the role of the cosmic dice.

Are the curves of science and magic destined to cross? This is not the first time we've seen science and spirituality converge. Medieval scholars once combined the ancient Greek wisdom of Plato and Aristotle with the teachings of theology. Thomas Aquinas offered five proofs of the existence of God, all of which required an intimate knowledge of the physics of the day. To be sure, there were discoverable laws that governed the behavior of matter; yet nature operated toward an inherent kind of perfection; there was movement toward an end—a purpose to it all. Today's bold scientific assertions about omniscience and immortality test the limits of the scientific method. Just how far will they take us?

OF BACON AND BLACK HOLES

ornamental flourish

When I was a kid I remember being terrifically impressed by Edwin Abbot's book, *Flatland*.[1] It's a takeoff on Plato's "allegory of the cave," in which a group of people are imprisoned practically all of their lives in a cave. Their heads are chained so that they are restricted to facing a blank wall. Behind them is a huge fire. Other people walk back and forth in front of it, posing and holding various objects so that their shadows are cast on the cave wall. The prisoners, having no recollection of life before the cave, think that what they see is the real thing and not just a set of incomplete and imperfect representations of actuality. In Abbot's Flatland, a race of people inhabit a two-dimensional world as flat as my kitchen table. Their physical existence is made up only of length and width. They know no "up." If I lay my coffee mug on top of their space they can only sense its cross-section—the part that touches the world of their senses. What is a hollow cylinder (with a handle on it) to me comes across to them as a filled circle.

I used to imagine what I'd tell Flatlanders about the universe I perceive if I could communicate with them. First, I'd make it clear that they could never see, never experience the reality I'm talking about. They just aren't wired for it. Look, I'd have to say, what I have to tell you is only an idea. Yet we believe our world is real because the projection of that idea—that all things that occupy space have three dimensions—onto our senses shows it for what it is. But what you Flatlanders see, I'd go on, projects onto your senses as stationary circles. The reality of what you're seeing is a far cry from the deceptive imagery you detect. A brazen Flatlander might respond by saying that reality is *only* what you see—observation and knowledge of the truth go together; the former defines the latter (Plato would have disagreed). Likewise, a three-D'er might argue that the four-dimensional world of space-time is just an idea, too. In fact, an informed citizen of the universe might go so far as to say that everything we see, feel, and touch is just a manifestation of an idea. Which is primary—what you observe or what you think? That's the issue with magic. I have portrayed magic as the world view that will not die. Opponents think it's the cosmology from Hell. The more tolerant among us view it as another religion. Agree or disagree, there is an enduring body of knowledge that encases our rotating kaleidoscope of experience. Having looked at magic as a *social* phenomenon, we have seen where today's scientists, theologians, social psychologists, and anthropologists place it in human history.

We have discovered that magic has always had that sense of appeal to what lies beyond the tangible—that faith that you *can* fathom things that are not accessible to reason. In magic you look beyond the outward appearances of things by using your insight, your intuition, your inspiration, and your imagination. To gain access to the higher world of reality, you break the chains that bind you, you distrust your senses rather than follow them. You fly above the kitchen table, out of the cave, for this is the only way to get to reality's higher plane—the transcendent turf on which both spirits *and* people are real.

Though this regimen for entering reality's wider circle has gotten out of tune with the times, paradoxically it never dies. Most of us have become so accustomed to dissociating the tangible from the ideal that we find practically all transcendental explanations unreal. That's why we discard as a silly superstition Mike Griffin's habit of eating bacon the day before he pitches for the Texas Rangers. We take Paul Davies' faith in the reality of black holes a lot more seriously, even though we and he know we can never get close enough to set foot into a black hole to look around for ourselves—not in a billion billion lifetimes—and even if we could, word would never leak out about what we experienced. The difference between Mike and Paul is that we can connect what Paul believes to an imagery we think represents a projection of the idea of a black hole—thanks to the convictions of prestigious science, which we adopt as setting the standards of a sort of "truth that works." But we cannot for the life of us tie eating bacon to throwing baseballs. That transcends the rational approach to acquiring true knowledge established by society's norms. It defies common sense.

Tell that to Mike. He needs to win baseball games and all he knows is that his actions, whether they work or not, make him feel right; they give him the impression that he is in control. But Mike is only taking back a role that, for better or for worse, has been denied him by events that took place long before the game of baseball was invented—the notion that human consciousness really can influence the course of the cosmos. Mike is a magician!

NOTES

PREFACE

1. H. P. Blavatsky, quoted in S. Cranston, *HPB, The Extraordinary Life and Influence of Helena Blavatsky, Founder of the Modern Theosophical Movement,* p. 132.

INTRODUCTION   ABOVE THE ORDINARY

1. For a delightful excursion through some of the rites of baseball magic by a player-anthropologist, see G. Gmelch's "Baseball Magic." I have sampled but a few items in his rich collection. Gmelch points out that most of the magical rites he observes in baseball pertain to hitting and pitching rather than fielding because these are the parts of the game where each act, throwing or swinging, is more risky and has a lower success ratio than catching.

2. A. A. Milne, *When We Were Very Young.* The English origins of so many American pop-superstitions betray our colonial past. For a complete collection of children's superstitions in England, see I. and P. Opie, *The Lore and Language of Children,* and *A Treasury of American Superstition* by Claudia deLys.

3. On trees and tree worship: In Mesoamerica, see D. Heyden, "El Arbol en el Mito y el Simbolo." Anthropologist/art historian Heyden demonstrates that all over ancient Mexico trees are associated with creation. For example the Seven Heavens of the ancient Maya were created one above the other each with a hole in the middle. A giant ceiba tree passes through the holes and connects to the highest heaven where the great god lives. Spirits of the dead ascend to heaven via the tree. In the Maya world the tree of life's branches continue beyond the sky in the form of the summer Milky Way. See, for example, D. Freidel and L. Schele, *Maya Cosmos,* especially Ch. II. For other tree stories, see R. Brasch, *How Did It Begin?: Customs and Superstitions and Their Romantic Origins* and G. Jahoda, *The Psychology of Superstition.*

4. G. Gmelch, *op. cit.,* p. 299.

5. See, e.g., R. Guiley, *Harper's Encyclopedia of Mystical and Paranormal Experience,* p. xi. Among the other encyclopedic references on magic that I consulted in writing this work are the following: A. Crabtree, *Animal Magnetism, Early Hypnotism and Psychical Research 1760–1925: An Annotated Bibliography;* J. G. Melton, *Magic, Witchcraft and Paganism in America: A Bibliography,* 2nd ed.; I. Opie and M. Tatem (ed.), *Dictionary of Superstitions;* S. Kaplan, *The Encyclopedia of Tarot*

•

(2 vols.); and R. Cavendish (ed.), *Man, Myth and Magic: The Illustrated Encyclopedia of Mythology, Religion and the Unknown*.

CHAPTER 1   MIDDLE EAST EXOTICA

1. On amulets, see C. Andrews, *Amulets of Ancient Egypt*.
2. A. Heidel, *The Babylonian Genesis, Enuma Elish,* Tab 4, line 19, p. 37.
3. T. Jacobsen, "Enuma Elish—The Babylonian Genesis," p. 16.
4. R. Thompson, *Reports of Magicians and Astrologers of Nineveh and Babylon in the British Museum,* 2: ciii, no. 98 (obv. 1–8).

CHAPTER 2   THE ANCIENT ART OF HEPATOSCOPY

1. The instructions for reading "the View" and the holes in the liver are from U. Jeyes, *Old Babylonian Extispicy.*
2. Weighing about ½ kg, it can be held comfortably in the hand. Its top side is divided into forty-one compartments, sixteen of which ring the outer rim. These are labeled with the names of the Gods who inhabited the various directions of space. Etruscan painted vases found in tombs often depict the haruspex, liver in hand, scoping out the future.
3. Readers interested in the divining practices of the Incas, Aztecs, and Kodi can refer to, respectively: Garcilaso de la Vega, El Inca, *Royal Commentaries of the Incas and a General History of Peru* (2 vols.); B. de Sahagun, *Florentine Codex, General History of the Things of New Spain,* ed. C. Dibble and A. J. O. Anderson; and J. Hoskins, *The Play of Time: Kodi Perspectives on Calendars, History, and Exchange.*

CHAPTER 3   THE GREEK PARADOX: MAGIC CONFRONTS SCIENCE

1. Plato, *Phaedo,* quoted in Seligmann, *op. cit.,* p. 46.
2. In ancient Babylonia, Aries the Ram was the first 30° longitude segment of the ecliptic. (The measurement begins at the vernal equinox, one of the points of intersection of the ecliptic—the median strip of the zodiac—and the celestial equator, or the extension onto the sky of the geographic equator of the earth.) Taurus occupies the 30° to 60° zone, Gemini 60° to 90°, Cancer 90° to 120°, Leo 120° to 150°, Virgo 150° to 180°, Libra 180° to 210°, Scorpio 210° to 240°, Sagittarius 240° to 270°, Capricorn 270° to 300°, Aquarius 300° to 330°, and finally Pisces 330° to 360°.
3. What characteristics were assigned to the segmented stellar path? Whether a constellation is masculine or feminine seems to have mattered. This was based

on the Pythagorean notion that odd numbers were male, even female. Whether they are human (like Virgo), bestial (like Leo), or a combination of the two (like Sagittarius) was another. Do they rise right side up (like Virgo) or upside down (like Taurus)? Are they day signs (in which the sun resides when the day becomes longer) or night signs (when the day's length decreases)? Are they aquatic (Cancer and Pisces) or terrene (Gemini or Sagittarius)? Fertile (Cancer, Scorpio, and Pisces—animals that proliferate in great numbers) or unfruitful (Leo's mate bears cubs infrequently and then only in small numbers, while Virgo is barren)? And do they run (Leo and Sagittarius), stand (Gemini and Aquarius), or sit (Taurus and Libra) in the sky?

4. To visualize this local system, imagine slicing the sky into twelve 30° segments, like the sections of an orange. Make the cuts along lines symmetric about your local meridian, which passes overhead and through the north and south points of the local horizon. This divides the sky into twelve zones, called *houses,* each of which includes a 30° strip of the ecliptic. The intersection points of house boundaries and ecliptic are the familiar *cusps* of astrological lingo. These divisions do not necessarily coincide with the division of the zodiac into signs, which are based on a different beginning point.

5. Why divide the ecliptic into segments marked off relative to the local horizon and why assign prominence to the first segment below the eastern horizon? We do not really know, but the idea likely had a practical basis; for example, early agricultural people were well aware that the sun's rays had different effects on their crops at different times of the day. How many gardeners still insist that their plants must bask in the morning sun? And recall that worshipers in many lands were required to face the sun's first rays, which appear at dawn in the east.

6. For a fuller discussion of how the system works, with charts and examples, see my *Conversing with the Planets,* Ch. 5.

7. We will encounter this principle again in a discussion of Galen's theory of healing (p. 49).

8. Our list of birthstones by zodiacal sign is a remnant of the principle of associating terrestrial and celestial properties and entities (mine is amethyst, once supposed to prevent drunkenness—a natural malady associated with watery signs such as Pisces).

9. L. Thorndike, *A History of Magic and Experimental Science,* vol. I, p. 598.

10. R. Lattimore (tr.), *The Odyssey of Homer,* p. 160.

11. R. R. Marett (ed.), *Anthropology and the Classics,* p. 108.

12. S. Price, "Delphi and Divination."

13. G.M.A. Grube (tr.), *Plato's Republic,* (527 e), p. 17.

14. G.M.A. Grube (tr.), *Plato: Five Dialogs, Phaedo,* 102b, (p. 140).

15. The full argument is given in *Phaedo,* G.M.A. Grube, *ibid.,* pp. 138–47.

CHAPTER 4   MAGIC IN THE ROMAN EMPIRE

1. Called Pliny, The Elder. There were two Plinys. The younger, his adopted nephew, wrote on Roman military history and other subjects.

2. J. Carcopino, *Daily Life in Ancient Rome,* p. 205.

3. W. H. S. Jones (tr.), *Pliny, Natural History,* XXIX, 25.

4. See L. Thorndike, *op. cit.,* Ch. IV, for a compendium of Galenic treatises.

5. Though I have focused, for want of space, mostly on medicinal cures, other magical practices were relatively widespread in the Roman Empire. These included divining by the flights of birds (from whence our word *augury*), divining by observing strokes of lightning (the work of a *fulguriator*) and, of course, astrology, the deathless half-sister of astronomy.

CHAPTER 5   THE NEW OUTCASTS: THE RISE OF
SECRET DOCTRINES

1. K. Seligmann, *The History of Magic and the Occult,* pp. 73–4.

2. R. M. Grant (ed.), *Gnosticism,* p. 18.

3. Moon, Sun, Mercury, Venus, Mars, Jupiter, and Saturn, in order from lowest to highest in heaven. The other planets were not known to the ancients; Earth, conceived to be the center of the universe, was not thought to be a planet of coordinate rank until Copernicus and the Renaissance; therefore it was not a part of the count.

4. His skills actually combined those of Thoth, God of Wisdom, healing, magic, and writing, and Hermes, the swift-footed messenger, both of whom were associated with necromancy (communicating with the dead). Thoth weighed souls and Hermes escorted them to Hades. The principles of astrology, alchemy, crystal power, numerology, herbals, etc., espoused by various early Christian writers all ultimately trace back to Hermes Trismegistus or to some other god-priest of equivalent power and Middle Eastern antiquity; e.g., Manetho, Nechepso, Zoroaster. For details see Thorndike, *op. cit.,* pp. 292–7.

5. An early Christian contemporary claims Hermes Trismegistus actually wrote 36,525 books—one for each hundredth decimal fraction of the length of the year! A more modest historian puts the number at a mere 20,000.

6. The earliest copy of this document, dated to 1828, was found in the tomb of an anonymous magician in Thebes. (Seligmann, *op. cit.,* p. 87.)

7. Seligmann, *ibid.,* p. 85.

CHAPTER 6   KNOWLEDGE THROUGH NUMBER AND THE WORD

1. H. Weiner, *9½ Mystics,* explains the relationship between the wisdom of the Kabbalah and contemporary searches for relevance.

2. In the strictest definition of anagram (= back write) you read the letters in backward order to get the other word; for example, live = evil.

3. "Duodecim Scripta" according to O. A. W. Dilke, *Mathematics and Measurement,* p. 55, Fig. 52.

4. Actually the modern crossword didn't appear until 1913 (Dec. 21 to be exact) in the *New York World.* It developed out of the old word-square which comprised a set of words made up of the same number of letters that one was required to arrange in a square so that they read the same horizontally, as well as vertically.

5. Because all Hebrew letters are consonants, vowels must be indicated by a special notation—placing dots above or below the letters to denote elisions from one hard sound to another. Since YHVH was never to be spoken, the word for lord, "adonai," was used in its place. Often its vowel markings were added to YHVH, but a sixteenth-century scribe who erroneously applied these vowel sounds to YHVH ended up with a new word: Jehovah (see R. F. Smith, *Prelude to Science,* p. 87).

6. There is good neither in this number that marks the beast nor where it comes from—at the tail end of unlucky Chapter 13 of Revelation. Today we think of a "baker's dozen" as generosity but some of the early mystic religions conceived of thirteen as being excessive in that it counted one more than a dozen, the perfect measure of things, e.g., the twelve tribes of Israel. In Christ's time thirteen also was tied in a negative way to the Last Supper.

7. R. Cavendish, *The Black Arts,* p. 128. During World War II modern Kabbalists were consulted to fabricate and decode secret messages. In one elaborate calculation they managed to rearrange the letters of Syria to make Russia.

8. S. Ikbal Ali Shah, *Occultism: Its Theory and Practice,* p. 140. R. Brasch, *How Did It Begin? Customs and Superstitions and Their Romantic Origins,* p. 163, gives several explanations for this magic formula, which he regards as Hebrew or Aramaic. According to one tradition, it is a combination of the initials of the Hebrew words for FATHER, SON, and HOLY GHOST. Another solution has it as a corruption of the Hebrew words for "blessing"—*bracha*—and "word"—*dabar.* Finally, it may be the name of an ancient demon whose identity is no longer known.

9. Technically a charm brings good luck, an amulet keeps away bad luck and acts as a disease prevention. A talisman can do both and conjure up demons as well.

10. See esp. J. Gager, *Curse Tablets and Binding Spells from the Ancient World,* pp. 25–30.

11. The Pythagorean school was so powerfully tied to the significance of number that one of its branches hypothesized the existence of an invisible counter-Earth interposed between Earth and the central fire around which it orbits in order to bring to a perfect ten the total number of world bodies in the universe.

12.   A. Beer, "Kepler's Astrology and Mysticism."

13.   H. Weiner, *op. cit.,* p. 116.

14.   R. Cavendish (ed.), *op. cit.,* p. 2208.

15.   This is E. R. Dodds' term, after W. H. Auden; see E. R. Dodds, *Pagan and Christian in an Age of Anxiety,* p. 18.

CHAPTER 7   PATHWAYS TO KNOWLEDGE

1.   Gibbon, the great Roman historian recorded major episodes of plague in Rome in 531 and 590 and Bede, the philosopher, in England in 664, 672, 678, and 683.

CHAPTER 8   RESURRECTION OF THE KABBALAH

1.   According to one Renaissance Kabbalist, the number of heavenly hosts can be calculated to be 301,655,172! (Seligmann, *op. cit.,* p. 236).

2.   See F. Yates, *Giordano Bruno and the Hermetic Tradition,* Ch. VII, for a brief survey of the content of these books.

3.   In Hebrew tradition air was not an element; rather it was the binding spirit that mediates among the other three.

4.   The world catalog of "mancys" is enormous. Richard Cavendish (*op. cit.,* p. 658) lists a page full, including some rather humorous ones, such as: *axinomancy*—divining by a balanced axe; *bibliomancy*—by random passages in books; *capnomancy*—by smoke; *chiromancy*—palm reading; *cledonomancy*—by chance remarks; *coscinomancy*—by shears; *gyromancy*—by whirling around until you get dizzy and fall down; *ichthyomancy*—by fishes; *leconomancy*—from the shape oil takes when you pour it on the ground; *margaritomancy*—by pears; *myomancy*—by watching mice move; *onychomancy*—by studying fingernails; *pegomancy*—by fountains; *scapulomancy*—by reading an animal's shoulder blades; *spudomancy*—from ashes; and *uromancy*—by gazing into streams or puddles of urine.

5.   W. Shumaker, *The Occult Sciences in the Renaissance,* p. 138. This along with other descriptions of Agrippa's text, are taken from this source.

6.   M. Edwardes, *The Dark Side of History,* p. 51.

7.   J. Goody, *The Domestication of the Savage Mind,* pp. 40 and 68, derives this idea from Chinese historian Joseph Needham, who originally interpreted it (mistakenly, I believe) as a form of thinking linked with primitive societies. Needham tied it principally to oral as opposed to literate societies and applied it to ancient Chinese societies in particular. Unlike causal thought, associative or coordinative thought sought to systematize all events and things into a structural pattern that conditioned the mutual influences of all of its parts.

8.   R. Cavendish, *op. cit.,* p. 109.

CHAPTER 9   MUSIC OF THE SPHERES

1. Born in Elizabethan England into a military family, Fludd became a student of music and Hebrew studies when he attended college in Oxford. He was the author of *History of Macrocosm and Microcosm* (see J. Godwin, *Robert Fludd, Hermetic Philosopher and Surveyor of Two Worlds*).

2. Both the Kepler quote and the following commentary are from A. Koestler, *The Watershed: A Biography of Johannes Kepler*, p. 17.

3. The first law describes the shapes of planetary orbits. These turned out to be ellipses rather than the divine Pythagorean circle Kepler and other astronomers had steadfastly clung to for two thousand years; the second law relates the variable speed of a planet on its orbit to how far away it is from the sun—an obvious harbinger of the law of gravity.

4. The connotation "spyglass" employed at the time of the invention of the telescope came very early on when its military advantage was realized.

5. S. Drake (ed.), *Galileo, Dialogue Concerning the Two Chief World Systems*, p. 11.

CHAPTER 10   TWO SIDES OF THE COIN OF ALCHEMY

1. Significant because of Einstein's equation, $E = mc^2$; for the amount of energy, E, equivalent to a mass, m, of transmuted nuclear material carries a very big number (c-*squared*) as a multiplicative factor. By the way, the sun converts 600 million tons of energy from hydrogen to helium every second and has been doing so for the past 4½ billion years. Even at that phenomenal rate it will survive for another 10 billion years!

2. Actually, it isn't quite as simple as I make it out to be. There are various intermediary processes involving the formation of isotopes of helium and the decay of short-lived nuclear species; still the net effect is that hydrogen is transformed into helium.

3. The first transmutation in a terrestrial lab actually took place in 1919 when Lord Ernest Rutherford succeeded in bombarding nitrogen nuclei with helium atoms (called alpha particles) to produce oxygen.

4. See the derivation of this word discussed earlier (p. 38). Also see H. Salzberg (1991), *From Caveman to Chemist*, for a thorough early history of the subject as approached from the viewpoint of the history of chemistry.

5. W. Shumaker, *op. cit.*, p. 167.

6. Among Mary's other inventions is a low temperature dung-fed furnace made out of metal that produces a constant temperature.

7. Other elixirs included Paracelsus' white powder (of unknown composition), usually dissolved in warm beer, or his secret stone dipped in milk or oil to make a "tincture." One seventeenth-century French remedy even Julia Child would have difficulty reproducing. It was made out of Aristotle's ele-

ments: Take 3 parts earth, 1½ parts each water and air; grind this into a paste adding 1½ parts fire. When the mass congeals, after heating, put it in a pot into a red stove and reduce it back to a liquid. Cf. Cavendish, *Man, Myth and Magic,* pp. 809–812.

8. K. von Helmont in Seligmann, *op. cit.,* pp. 112.

9. R. Cavendish, *The Black Arts,* p. 168.

10. K. Seligmann, *op. cit.,* pp. 123, 170.

11. M. Eliade, *The Forge and the Crucible, The Origins and Structures of Alchemy,* p. 169.

12. E. Ashmole, *Theatrum Chemicum Brittanicum.* Quoted in Shumaker, *op. cit.,* p. 172.

13. M. Edwardes, *op. cit.,* p. 43.

14. M. Eliade, *op. cit.,* p. 116.

15. Both Majer quotes are taken from K. Seligmann, *op. cit.,* pp. 107–8.

16. Edwardes, *op. cit.,* p. 48.

17. Edwardes, *ibid.,* p. 50.

18. R. Guiley, *op. cit.,* p. 426.

CHAPTER 11   RISE OF THE CLEAR SEER

1. R. Guiley, *op. cit.,* pp. 408–9.

2. G. Kunz, *The Curious Lore of Precious Stones,* p. 176.

3. The Nostradamus quatrains are from C. Wilson's *Prophecy of Nostradamus,* pp. 264–5.

CHAPTER 12   MEDIEVAL ASTROLOGY

1. M. Graubard, *Astrology and Alchemy, Two Fossil Sciences,* p. 253.

2. Virtue was that substance or quality possessed by all bodies and by which they affect all other bodies. Remember this was before Newton invented gravity!

3. S. J. Tester, *History of Western Astrology,* p. 194.

4. In *Conversing, op. cit.,* Ch. 5, I discuss astrological allegory in greater detail. For a discussion on Venus and love reflected in Renaissance painting, see pp. 163–6.

CHAPTER 13   THE DEVIL AND THE PROLIFERATION OF GOOD AND EVIL

1. In Leviticus 16:10 the high priest on judgment day symbolically transfers all human sin to a goat which he allows to escape into the desert—whence our term "scapegoat." Thus the bearer of all sins is depicted with horns.

2. F. Horcasitas and D. Heyden (tr. and ed.), *Fray Diego Duran, Book of the Gods and Rites and Ancient Calendars,* pp. 127 and 247.

3. "Diabolos," from whence "diabolical," means "accuser" in Greek, translated from the Old Testament. And Satan is literally "the adversary" (of man).

4. As Lucifer, the morning star, he still proudly defies the sun who is about to rise. The morning star in Greece was Phosphoros (or Eosphoros, after the Greek goddess of dawn, Eos), the Greek equivalent of Ishtar (Aphrodite or Venus). From this name we derive terms such as *phosphorescent* and *phosphoric* to connote a sudden shining as well as the name of the wax-colored element that ignites at low temperature. Lucifer (Luciferos), the later Latin equivalent, likewise means "bearer of light." (The ancestors of today's nearly extinct safety matches once were called "Lucifers.")

5. According to a recent survey, nearly half of all Americans believe in the Devil (see p. 248, for details).

6. R. M. Frazer (tr., ed.), *The Poems of Hesiod,* pp. 74–6.

7. M. Musa (ed.), *Dante's Inferno,* p. 206.

8. J. Crehan, "Exorcism."

9. K. Thomas, *Religion and the Decline of Magic,* p. 488.

10. A.P., Syracuse *Herald Journal,* July 20, 1993.

11. On cursing, see esp. K. Thomas, *op. cit.,* pp. 506–512.

12. M. Mauss, *A General Theory of Magic,* p. 29.

13. S. Ikbal Ali Shah, *op. cit.,* p. 117.

CHAPTER 14   IT'S WITCHCRAFT

1. W. Shumaker, *op. cit.,* pp. 86–7.

2. M. Buonanno, "Becoming White: Notes on an Italian–American Explanation of Evil Eye," offers an interesting series of case studies on the evil eye in a contemporary Buffalo, New York, community of Italian immigrants. He relates the extension of this old world custom as a reminder of obstacles to acculturation in the American environment.

3. C. Maloney (ed.), *The Evil Eye.*

4. J. Teitelbaum, "The Leer and the Loom—Social Controls in Handloom Weavers," in C. Maloney (ed.), *ibid.,* pp. 63–75.

5. J. B. Russell, "Witchcraft."

6. Cf. R. Cavendish, *Man, Myth and Magic,* pp. 7–8, 1657–61.

7. K. Thomas, *op. cit.,* see esp. Ch. I.

8. K. Thomas, *ibid.,* pp. 7–8.

9. M. Douglas, *Natural Symbols.*

10. K. Thomas, *op. cit.,* p. 558.

CHAPTER 15   WHO TURNED ON THE LIGHTS?

1.   See, e.g., F. Yates, *Giordano Bruno and the Hermetic Tradition*, pp. 153–6.
2.   R. Nisbet, *History of the Idea of Progress*, p. 253.

CHAPTER 16   ROCHESTER RAP: THE FIRST HAUNTED HOUSE

1.   S. Brown's *The Heyday of Spiritualism* is the best account of the Fox sisters' story in my opinion. (See esp. Ch. 8.)

2.   E. Lewis, (1848), "A Report of the Mysterious Noises Heard in the House of Mr. John D. Fox" (Canandaigua: Privately Published). The pamphlet contains twenty-two signatures of witnesses to the phenomena.

3.   Actually, communication by rapping has an early precedent. In 1534 French monks conversed with a recently deceased person who rapped once when his name was mentioned, twice to signal yes, thrice no. The rapper later proved to be a conjurer. See R. Brandon, *The Spiritualists*, p. 4.

4.   J. Feola, "Parapsychology Today." This is Lewis' testimony.

5.   A. Gauld, *The Founders of Psychical Research*, pp. 4–5.

6.   The "peddler's bones" were on display in the house until 1927, when the place burned down. It had been moved to Canandaigua by a wealthy spiritualist where it was set up as a sort of shrine for believers in spiritualism.

7.   E. Capron, *Modern Spiritualism, Its Facts and Fanaticisms, Its Consistencies and Contradictions*, p. 72.

8.   Séance, from the French word for session, as of some public body, came to be applied specifically to a meeting of spiritualists.

9.   S. Brown, *op. cit.*, p. 113, both quotes.

10.   S. Brown, *ibid.*, p. 117.

11.   S. Brown, *ibid.*, p. 119.

12.   Quoted in F. Podmore, *Mediums of the 19th Century* (Originally *Modern Spiritualism: A History and a Criticism* (2 vols.), Vol. I, p. 184.

13.   S. Brown, *op. cit.*, pp. 120–1, note 1.

14.   S. Brown, *ibid.*, p. 121.

15.   *New York World*, 21–2 Oct. 1888.

16.   Quoted in Podmore, *op. cit.*, Vol. I, p. 186.

17.   F. Goodman, *How About Demons? Possession and Exorcism in the Modern World*, p. 125.

18.   E. Isaacs, "The Fox Sisters and American Spiritualism," pp. 79–110 (pp. 105–6).

19.   The debate about who controls the pointer (the ouija board effect) recently resurfaced in the controversy over facilitated learning—whether a special word processor used for communicating with autistic children is actually being guided unconsciously by the therapist. For a critique, see J. Mulick, J. Jacobson, and

F. Kobe, "Anguished Silence and Helping Hands: Autism and Facilitated Communication" and K. Dillon, "Facilitated Communication, Autism and Ouija."

20.   F. Podmore, *op. cit.,* Vol. I, p. 306.

21.   Controlled by a natural force called "od," named in 1845 by one Karl Ludwig (Baron) Reichenbach to explain luminous phenomena, raps, and other psychic phenomena. Present on all bodies, this force was thought to be especially concentrated in magnets and crystals.

CHAPTER 17   BEFORE HYDESVILLE: FROM REASON TO ROMANCE

1.   *Society for Psychic Research, Proceedings,* 1882, Vol. I, pp. 4, 9.

2.   H. A. Bruce, *Historic Ghosts and Ghost Hunters,* pp. 17–35, argues that the Tedworth case was a combination of witchcraft perpetrated by the disgruntled drummer, a crude practical joke, *and* a hoax.

3.   (1782–1849) Influential New England preacher who predicted a pre-twentieth-century millennial Second Coming due around 1843. After the date passed, he and his followers founded the Millerite branch of the Adventist church dedicated to preparing for it.

4.   For a full account of the lives and times of the Burned-Over District, see W. R. Cross, *The Burned-Over District, the Social and Intellectual History of Enthusiastic Religion in Western New York 1800–1850.*

5.   Anonymous, *The Rappers or the Mysteries, Fallacies and Absurdities of Spirit Rapping, Table Tipping and Entrancement,* pp. 266–7.

6.   Quoted in R. Brandon, *op. cit.,* p. 40 (orig. *The New York Times,* 6 Dec. 1858).

7.   F. Podmore, *op. cit.,* Vol. I, p. 290.

8.   The holding of hands at a séance, kissing spirit materializations, engaging in affairs under the direction of spirits, women being ordered by a mad man to leave their husbands—all would later develop as manifestations of sexual liberalism in the spiritist movement. Indeed, most mediums were and still are women.

9.   Comte de Montbrison (ed.), 1854, *Memoires de la baronne d'Oberkirch sur la cour de Louis XVI et la société Francaise avant 1789* Brussels (quoted in Edwardes, *op. cit.,* p. 89).

10.   Recalcitrant patients were removed to side rooms where they were further massaged and manipulated, especially about the soft mid-body parts, for the poles of the body—the head and feet—were thought to be too heavily influenced by terrestrial and celestial magnetism, respectively.

11.   M. Edwardes, *op. cit.,* p. 100. "Rapport des Commissaires Changes par le Roi de L'examen de Magnetisme Animal."

12.   R. Weyant, "Metaphors and Animal Magnetism" in M. Hanen et al., *Science, Pseudoscience and Society,* pp. 100 and 104.

●

13. A modern resurrection of this memory bank idea lies at the basis of scientology.

14. For the connection between radical religion in the colonies and Swedenborg's writings see M. Block, *The New Church in the New World.*

15. W. R. Cross, *op. cit.,* p. 343.

16. "Swedenborgians in Newton," *Bostonia* Summer (2), 1994, pp. 12–13.

17. On the relation of the occult movement to issues of American race and social class structure, see J. Butler, "The Dark Ages of American Occultism, 1760–1848."

CHAPTER 18 "MR. SLUDGE"

1. On self-elongation, see also: Brandon, *op. cit.,* Ch. II (this quote is from p. 68).

2. Brandon, *ibid,* pp. 59–60.

3. There are at least three other accounts of this séance. Cf. E. Jenkins, *The Shadow and the Light, A Defense of Daniel Dunglas Home, the Medium,* pp. 41–42.

4. Brandon, *ibid.*

5. EBB to Henrietta, 18 Nov 1856. Quoted in Brandon, *op. cit.,* p. 63.

6. F. Podmore, *op. cit.,* p. 4. We will sketch out his contributions to the study of occult phenomena later in this section.

7. J. Pettigrew (ed.), *Robert Browning: The Poems,* Vol. 1, p. 839. Sir Arthur Conan Doyle was so convinced of the authenticity of Houdini's magic that he refused to believe even Houdini's own direct denial of mediumistic powers. He wrote to his good friend in 1920: "Yes, you have driven me to the occult! My reason tells me that you have this wonderful power, for there is no alternative, tho' I have no doubt that, up to a point, your strength and skill avail you." W. Gresham, *Houdini, the Man Who Walked Through Walls,* p. 193.

8. M. Edwardes, *op. cit.,* p. 148.

9. Lindsay, Earl of Crawford, 1871, "Psychic Power—Spirit Power and Experimental Investigation" (London: Privately Printed). Quoted in Podmore, *op. cit.,* v. 2, p. 255. As to what the whole experience felt like to him, Home nonchalantly wrote: "During these elevations, or levitations, I usually experience in my body no particular sensations than what I can only describe as an electrical fullness about the feet. I feel no hands supporting me, and . . . I have never felt fear, though should I have fallen from the ceiling of some rooms in which I have been raised, I could not have escaped serious injury. I am generally lifted up perpendicularly; my arms frequently become rigid and drawn above my head, as if I were grasping the unseen power which slowly raises me from the floor." D. D. Home, *Incidents in My Life,* p. 66.

10. R. Brandon, *op. cit.,* p. 71.

11. M. Edwardes, *op. cit.,* p. 146.

12. R. Brandon, *op. cit.*, p. 78.

13. R. Brandon, *ibid.*, p. 82.

14. R. Cavendish, *Man, Myth and Magic*, p. 548. For a thorough discussion of all the weights and measures involved in Crookes' experiments on Home, see S. Braude, *The Limits of Influence, Psychokinesis and the Philosophy of Science*, pp. 85–101.

15. F. Podmore, *op. cit.*, Vol. II, p. 40.

16. *Ibid.*, Vol. I, p. 189.

17. *Ibid.*, Vol. I, p. 191.

18. *Ibid.*, Vol. II, p. 354.

CHAPTER 19   DDH TO HPB: PIPELINES TO THE PAST

1. Dating from the sixth century B.C., this cult, organized by the city of Athens and supervised by its king, was devoted to Demeter, goddess of grain and her daughter, Persephone, who brought grain, the staff of civilized life, to Eleusis. See W. Burkert, *Ancient Mystery Cults*.

2. See J. P. Laurant, "The Primitive Characteristics of 19th-century Esotericism," for a brief review of this movement.

3. H. S. Olcott, *Old Diary Leaves, The History of the Theosophical Society*, pp. 148 and 326.

4. Among the early members: Thomas A. Edison and Abner Doubleday, military man and reputed baseball inventor.

5. S. Cranston, *HPB: The Extraordinary Life and Influence of Helena Blavatsky, Founder of the Modern Theosophical Movement*.

6. They were experimenters with the shadows of terrestrial bodies whose souls and spirits had long ago departed; most mediums, she contends, are only playing with the material dregs of personages that any average medium and even the public can see. S. Cranston, *ibid.*, pp. 128–9.

7. R. Ellwood Jr., "The American Theosophical Synthesis."

8. H. P. Blavatsky, *op. cit.*, I, p. 219.

9. In the science of astronomy, coronium and nebulium were said to be the mystery elements responsible for bright lines in the spectra of the eclipsed sun and the Great Orion Nebula, respectively.

10. And those bright lines in astronomical spectra are attributed to the same elements we are familiar with in the laboratory, except that they are emitted via processes taking place at extraordinary conditions of pressure and/or temperature.

11. H. S. Olcott, *op. cit.*, pp. 146–7.

12. H. P. Blavatsky, *op. cit.*, I, p. 480.

13. *Ibid.*

14. Cf. *Sunrise, Theosophic Perspectives* 42 (3): 65–77, 1993. S. Cranston, *op. cit.*, pp. 265–277, gives a full account of the case offering documentation that dis-

credits the report and suggests the whole Coulomb–Hodgson affair was a frame-up.

15. See, e.g., E. Sellon and R. Weber, "Theosophy and the Theosophical Society." This is an excellent brief review of the impact of theosophy on Western religion, science, art, and ethics.

16. S. Cranston, *op. cit.*

17. Cf. Kerr and Crow, *The Occult in America, New Historical Perspectives,* p. 2.

18. J. Randi, *Conjuring,* p. 53.

CHAPTER 20   AFTER THE FOXES: FROM PARLOR TO STAGE

1. Baron von Schrenck-Notzing, *Phenomena of Materialisation,* p. 116.

2. As Ruth Brandon, *op. cit.,* pp. 130–1, points out, these investigators, who laid the foundation of modern "parascience" (which still floats about on the fringes of orthodox science), sought to explain the powers inherent in psychic phenomena in terms of concepts and ideas with which they were familiar in their own disciplines. Thus Crookes the physicist spoke of psychic forces and fields paralleling electricity and magnetism and engineer Crawford of psychic structures and force lines, etc.

3. Sir O. Lodge, 1931; Quoted in R. Brandon, *ibid.,* p. 134.

4. Encyclopedist Rosemary Ellen Guiley, *op. cit.,* pp. 178–9, gives two recipes for making ectoplasm. One consists of a mixture of soap, gelatin, and egg white, the other of toothpaste and peroxide.

5. H. Houdini, *A Magician Among the Spirits,* pp. 169–70.

6. Schrenck-Notzing, *op. cit.,* p. 31.

7. R. Brandon, *op. cit.,* p. 156.

8. R. Brandon, *ibid.,* p. 157. In an odd twist, Houdini the magician later would declare Crawford the scientist to be a madman.

9. R. Brandon, *ibid.,* p. 127.

10. See C. Wilson, *op. cit.,* pp. 351–78, for a compact biography.

11. Horace Greeley's term; cf. G. Seldes, *The Stammering Century,* p. 3.

12. C. Wilson, *op. cit.,* pp. 352 and 350.

13. After Brother CRC (Christian Rosen Creutz = Christ of the Rosy Cross), the legendary fifteenth-century ancestor—founder of the society. He was said to have acquired all his knowledge from ancient Egyptian seers. The Rosicrucian Order still operates today (headquartered in San Jose, California) as a worldwide educational and philosophical organization promoting exercises on enhancing one's physical, mental, and spiritual wellbeing based on the theory of reincarnation (or so reads an ad appearing in the July 1994 issue of *Omni* magazine, p. 95).

14. R. Cavendish, *Man, Myth and Magic,* p. 1133.

15. His book, *Magick in Theory and Practice,* is the Devil conjurer's Bible, considered by the few remaining serious practitioners to be the most superb work

on how to make black magic. A jumble of demonic hymns and conjuration formulae, its frontispiece/parable reads: "Do what thou wilt shall be the whole of the law."

16. These textbooks, most of them dating from the sixteenth to the eighteenth centuries, on the European tradition of magic give instructions for summoning up spirits and demons and for making talismans, etc. The word *grimoire* is a corruption of "gram arye," whence our word grammar, an old term for magic.

17. R. Cavendish, *The Black Arts,* p. 281; my brackets.

18. C. Wilson, *op. cit.,* p. 364. This notion of sexual magic was revivified in the 1970s. For example, cover articles of the popular New Age magazine *Gnostica* are titled "Sexual Rites and Nature Worship" and "Modern Couples Rediscovering Tantric Sex Magic" (No. 46, 1978), "Occult Sex—Union of God and Goddess within the Whole Person," and "Multiple Male Orgasm" (No. 51, 1979), and "Tantra—The *One* Yoga for Today and the Answer to Sexual Discontent" (No. 48, 1978).

19. C. Wilson, *ibid.,* p. 395.

CHAPTER 21 MY BODY, MY MAP: "BUMPOLOGY"

1. March 1993 *Good Housekeeping,* "Living Well" section.

2. K. Seligmann, *op. cit.,* p. 55. Like hepatoscopy, the art of divination by moles is much more complicated than I've made it out to be. For example left side vs. right side and the size and color of the spot also matter—not to mention its relationship to other spots.

3. W. Lessa, "Somatomancy: Precursor of the Science of Human Constitution." Other somatomatic (Lessa's term for using any part of the human body to divine) divination devices of the past are listed in this section, Ch. 8, note 4 (p. 356).

4. H. Cardanus, *La Metoposcopié.*

5. The picture and the list are reproduced in full in a number of places, e.g., J. Goody, *op. cit.,* pp. 154–5.

6. R. Cooter, "Deploying Pseudoscience."

7. J. Davies, *Phrenology: Fad and Science; A 19th-Century American Crusade,* p. 35.

8. S. Zweig, *Mental Healers,* pp. 103–250, gives an excellent biography that follows the mesmeric line on Eddy.

9. J. Sandstrom, *Palmystery,* p. vii. See also the classic L. Hamon, *Cheiro's Language of the Hand.*

10. See, e.g., T. Duster, "Genetics, Race and Crime: Recurring Seduction to a False Precision."

11. G. Combe, *The Constitution of Man Considered in Relation to External Objects,* p. 351.

12. J. Davies, *op. cit.,* p. 157.

13. G. Combe, quoted in Davies, *ibid.*, p. 107.

14. Both were popular mottoes of the evangelical reformist Orson Fowler. J. Davies, *ibid.*, p. 111.

CHAPTER 22   SUMMARY: A LIGHT THAT FAILED?

1. R. Brandon, *op. cit.*, p. 163.

2. C. Read, *The Origin of Man and His Superstitions,* p. 85.

3. G. Jahoda, *op. cit.*, p. 99.

4. G. Seldes, *op. cit.*, p. 349.

5. *Ibid.*, p. 356.

6. *Ibid.*, p. 355.

7. Cf. J. Grasset, *The Marvels Beyond Science, Being a Record of Progress Made in the Reduction of Occult Phenomena to a Scientific Basis.* A similar reductionism is expressed half a century later in C. D. Broad's *Lectures on Psychical Research.*

8. J. Grasset, *ibid.*, p. 193.

9. J. Grasset, *ibid.*, p. 376.

CHAPTER 23   WHO'S A MAGICIAN?: THE HOUDINI LEGEND

1. M. Christopher, *Houdini: The Untold Story,* p. 5. Among his more recent biographies is R. Brandon's, *The Life and Many Deaths of Harry Houdini.*

2. M. Christopher, *ibid.*, p. 46.

3. *Ibid.*, p. 71. W. Gresham, *Houdini, the Man Who Walked Through Walls,* pp. 90–1, writes that the magician's wife smuggled him (via a lingering kiss) a pair of tools she had hidden in her mouth.

4. W. Gibson, *The Original Houdini Scrapbook,* p. 71.

5. Some mediums, said Houdini, used mechanical devices, like a rapping mechanism hidden in the heel of a shoe that could be activated by pulling a string, which would cause a lead-tipped cord to make contact with the blunt end of a heavy metal pin. H. Houdini, *op. cit.*, pp. 110–11.

6. H. Houdini, *ibid.*, p. 48.

7. J. Dunninger, *Inside the Medium's Cabinet.*

8. See his *The Magic, Magic Book.*

CHAPTER 24   WHO'S A MAGICIAN?: TRICKSTER FROM FAR ROCKAWAY

1. J. Gleick, *Genius: The Life and Science of Richard Feynman,* p. 423.

2. R. Feynman, *Surely You're Joking, Mr. Feynman! Adventures of a Curious Character,* pp. 3–12.

3. J. Gleick, *op. cit.*, p. 177.

4. R. Feynman, *op. cit.*, p. 197.
5. J. Gleick, *op. cit.*, p. 189.
6. R. Feynman *op. cit.*, p. 290.
7. *Ibid.*, p. 57.
8. *Ibid.*, pp. 310–11.
9. J. Gleick, *op. cit.*, p. 324.

CHAPTER 25   MAGIC IN THE TWENTIETH CENTURY: WHAT THE POLLSTERS SAY

1. G. Jahoda, *op. cit.*, pp. 31–2. The sample consisted of adult students, half of them women, enrolled in an elementary psychology class.

2. Also Columbia students, but no women. See E. Levitt, "Superstitions: Twenty Five Years Ago and Today." (G. Jahoda, *ibid.*, pp. 31–2.)

3. But only 7 percent of the Scottish people! (The English always have loved their poltergeist.)

4. Adults, 2,006 in number, contributed to this survey. See Roper, in F. Fullam, "Contemporary Belief in Astrology."

5. "Boom Times on the Psychic Frontier," *Time*, Mar. 4, 1974, pp. 65–72.

6. *Ibid.*, p. 65.

7. This idea is still alive, if somewhat scientifically sanitized. The USDA concluded in 1988 that in times of drought certain plants (corn being one of them) emit high pitched sounds as their cellular structure breaks down. Electronic detection of the noisy emissions can be used to tell farmers when to irrigate. Can you tune in to a transmitting corncob directly? Probably not—the sounds are in the 100 kilohertz range and our ears are good only to 20. Cf. "Scientists Listen to Noises of Plants in Drought" in *The New York Times*, 4 Sept., 1988, p. 29.

8. There were 1,553 adults interviewed in the 1980 Gallup poll (Gallup Polls, Wilmington, Del., Scholarly Resources, Inc.). The closest European comparison I could find came from a 1980 Gallup poll conducted in England: 27 percent said yes to flying saucers; 20 percent to ghosts (twice as many as in America), 20 percent to astrology, 48 percent to precognition, 27 percent to faith healing. One person out of ten believed in black magic of some sort and in the possibility of exchanging messages with dead people. In Sweden, one in seven believed in good and bad luck signs such as days, numbers, four-leaf clovers, black cats, walking under a ladder, etc.; 39 percent believed in clairvoyance and 19 percent in communication with the dead.

9. Gallup Poll (Gallup Org.), 5 Aug. 1990.

10. *Time*, 7 Dec. 1987.

11. *Time*, 27 Dec. 1993.

12. *American Public Opinion Index*, 1991, Vol. 1.

13. L. Shore, "New Light on the New Age."

14. Recall that the end of the twentieth century also was one of those times said to have been prophesied by Nostradamus for the onset of cataclysmic disturbances ranging from the start of a world war to the shifting of Earth on its axis.

15. R. Guiley *op. cit.,* p. 403, from D. Spangler, (1976), *Revelation: The Birth of a New Age.*

16. D. Spangler and W. Thompson, (1991), *Reimagination of the World: A Critique of the New Age, Science, and Popular Culture,* p. 57.

17. O. Friedrich, "New Age Harmonies."

CHAPTER 26   DIFFERENT TIME, SAME CHANNEL

1. From K. Lowry, "Channelers."

2. Among the channel-surfing celebs: Barry Manilow, Sharon Gless, Richard Gere, Lesley Ann Warren, Michael York, Ted Danson, and Linda Evans.

3. Curiously enough, we rarely see the term "channeling" to characterize MacLaine's work. Her own passages to a higher plane of reality happen via out-of-body experiences that she claims are not induced by any channeling technique, but instead through a form of self-hypnosis and meditation.

4. J. Roberts, *The Coming of Seth.*

5. Lowry, *op. cit.,* p. 48.

6. G. Reed, "The Psychology of Channeling."

7. But recently Sarah Grey Thompson, a linguistics professor at the University of Pittsburgh, has analyzed the accent and word usage of a number of channelers and pronounced them fake—a real Scots English speaker of the tenth century, for example, never would have slurred those r's! See S. G. Thompson, " 'Entities' in the Linguistic Minefield."

8. I.e., mind-to-matter as opposed to ESP, which connotes mind-to-mind communication.

CHAPTER 27   PK WARS: PSYCHICS VS. PHYSICS

1. One of the best biographies, in my opinion, is P. Gay's *Freud.*

2. S. Braude, *The Limits of Influence, Psychokinesis and the Philosophy of Science,* p. 220. Again, not to be confused with precognition or ESP; e.g., Can I guess the card you're holding in your hand? Today ESP and PK are loosely categorized together as "psi" abilities.

3. Rhine conducted controlled experiments consisting, for example, of subject concentration to see whether coin flips and dice rolls could be affected by pure thought. According to some critics, the controls weren't strict enough and that explained his (false) conclusions that PK is subject neither to the laws of physics nor to any known process working in the human brain.

4. I am not the first to recognize the clever pun in this acronym. The outfit is indeed conceived as the "COPS" by many moderate PK researchers. The organization's journal, *Skeptical Inquirer,* which claims to be unbiased, takes a fairly hard line toward paranormal phenomena and regards most of them as dangers to society.

5. H. Puthoff and R. Targ, "Information Transmission Under Conditions of Sensory Shielding."

6. M. Gardner, *The New Age: Notes of a Fringe Watcher,* p. 142. Recently, Geller was ordered by the U.S. Court of Appeals to pay CSICOP $149,000 in expenses resulting from a defamation suit he had filed against Randi and CSICOP. *Washington Post,* Dec. 10, 1994.

7. G. Price, "Science and the Supernatural."

8. Serios says he acquired the technique quite by accident when a scoffer mockingly handed him a camera and said: "Here, take a picture of your mind" (to record the precise location of the buried treasure). The result was Serios' first "thoughtograph"—a recognizable landscape. Guiley, *op. cit.,* p. 618.

9. C. Fuller, "Dr. Jule Eisenbud and the Amazing Randi."

10. J. Eisenbud, *The World of Ted Serios.*

11. C. Fuller, *op. cit.,* p. 72, and B. Löfgren (1968), "Psychoanalytic Theory of Affects."

12. A counterexample I am fond of using in the last instance concerns the avid gardeners of the Trobriand Islands of southeast Asia. They despise directive behavior; they perceive reality atemporally, in terms of fixed-patterned wholes. For example, a tree is supported by its trunk, a house by posts, an incantation by its opening lines, a hunting expedition by its leader. In each case the latter term has the same meaning and is identified by the same word: *u'ula.* Pattern is the source of truth in this culture, not demonstrable cause and effect. Linear connections, causality, and sequentiality are no concerns of theirs. They place no value on the future as we do when we use the word progress to describe which way we shall go to get to it. For them, the present is not the road to the future, and the future is neither good nor bad, better nor worse than the past. We are forced to admit that there are alternative approaches to reality that admit the possibility of phenomena and behavior that do not fit scientific classification and explanation.

13. The quantum mechanical analysis of PK has become a legitimate topic of research among parapsychologists, if not physicists and psychologists. See, e.g., E. H. Walker, "A Review of Criticisms of the Quantum Mechanical theory of Psi Phenomena."

14. This is the thesis of Nobel laureate physicist Murray Gell-Mann's 1994 book, *The Quark and the Jaguar.*

15. D. Bohm, *Wholeness and The Implicate Order.*

16.   See Gell-Mann's (*op. cit.*) interesting chapter, "Quantum Mechanics and Flapdoodle" (pp. 167–175), in which the completeness criterion and its relevant experiments are discussed in greater detail.

CHAPTER 28   THE PERSONALIZED MAGIC OF HEALING: MENDING THE CARTESIAN SPLIT

1.   H. Benson (1975), *The Relaxation Response;* cf. also (1984), *Beyond the Relaxation Response.*

2.   H. Benson (1975), *ibid.,* p. 56.

3.   *Ibid.,* p. 60.

4.   M. LeBrun, "People Wracked with Pain Attracted to Magnet Therapy."

5.   Researcher David Trock of the Section of Rheumatology of the Danbury (Conn.) Hospital treated twenty-seven patients with arthritis of the knee with eighteen half-hour exposures of pulsed electromagnetic fields over a one-month period. He reported an average improvement of 23–61 percent in active treatment over a 2–18 percent improvement in placebo. The decreased pain and improved functional performance of treated patients suggests that this configuration of PEMF has potential as an effective method of improving symptoms in patients with OA. (See D. Trock et al., 1993, "A Double-Blind Trial of the Clinical Effects of Pulsed Electromagnetic Fields in Osteoarthritis.") This method warrants further clinical investigation, Trock concludes (p. 456).

6.   M. LeBrun, *op. cit.*

7.   These figures and the stories/comments on Rolfing that follow are from N. Brodeen, "Rolfing's Resurgence Really Rolling."

8.   R. Cavendish, *The Black Arts,* p. 1587.

9.   R. Guiley, *op. cit.,* pp. 67–70.

10.   O. Friedrich, *op. cit.,* p. 64.

CHAPTER 29   YOU ARE WHAT YOU EAT

1.   ". . . then the lord God formed man of dust from the ground, and breathed into his nostrils the breath of life" (Gen 2:7).

2.   D. Tedlock, *Popol Vuh,* p. 164.

3.   Technically, fajitas may be a bad example. In the past generation the commercially manufactured flour tortilla called for in the recipe has begun to replace the classic corn tortilla consumed since antiquity throughout Mayaland. But then the *fajita* too is a contemporary concoction!

4.   W. Shumaker, *Natural Magic and Modern Science, Four Treatises 1590–1657,* pp. 103–4.

5. G. Seldes, *op. cit.*, pp. 301–2.

6. E.g., E. Gibbons, *Stalking the Wild Asparagus.*

7. N. Cousins, *Anatomy of an Illness as Perceived by the Patient, Reflections on Healing and Regeneration.*

8. See, e.g., R. Cavendish, *Man, Myth and Magic,* p. 191.

CHAPTER 30   COME FLY WITH ME: UFO ABDUCTIONS

1. Ezekiel 1:1–21.

2. There are many "visions" reported in the Bible. I find it interesting that where religion is involved and the observation is personal, such an experience is called a "vision." But it is an "apparition" if the matter is secular or if it is observed by the masses. Apparitions at the popular level have included epidemics of moving or weeping statues and images of Christ or the Virgin Mary on objects as diverse as tortillas and tree trunks. For example, there was a recent wave of reportage on "Jesus trees" in southern New England (see E. Clark, "Every Once in a While Something Happens . . ."). The definition of apparition— "The experience of seeing something which is not present in the same way as ordinary physical objects are"—(R. Cavendish, *Man, Myth and Magic,* p. 2960), if contrasted with the accepted definition of UFO (see below in text), squarely places the two in the same category as far as I am concerned.

3. A glowing light accompanied by crackling sounds caused by electrical discharges during thunderstorms, often seen on the masts of ships at sea.

4. Quoted in J. Grasset, *The Marvels of Science,* pp. 165–7.

5. *Ibid.,* p. 177, my brackets.

6. Defined as "the stimulus for a report of something seen in the sky which the observer could not identify as having an ordinary natural origin. . . ." E. Condon and D. Gillmor, *Scientific Study of Unidentified Flying Objects,* p. 9. See also C. Sagan and T. Page (ed.), *The UFO Experience: A Scientific Inquiry,* p. 10.

7. *Ibid.,* Condon and Gillmor.

8. P. Grim, "Selected Cases from the Condon Report." One skeptic was so confident of this conclusion that in the closing chapter of a book in which he debunked UFOs he offered to buy back every copy of it at list price (Have we heard this before?) if physical evidence of any spaceship could be turned up and pronounced by the U.S. National Academy of Science to be an authentic extraterrestrial manufactured item (p. 255).

9. See, e.g., the six-part series, *Cosmic Conspiracy,* "Six Decades of Government UFO Cover-ups" in *Omni* magazine, 1994.

10. J. McDonald, "Science in Default: 22 Years of Inadequate UFO Investigations."

11. F. Drake and D. Sobel, *Is Anyone Out There? The Scientific Search for Extraterrestrial Intelligence.*

12. See, e.g., E. von Däniken, *Chariots of the Gods.*

13. See R. Story, *The Space-Gods Revealed,* for a critique of von Däniken's ideas, which he views as pseudoscience; and P. Schievella (1982), "Science, Proof and the Ancient Astronaut Hypothesis," for a rebut in which the author argues that one shouldn't judge new ideas only by scientific criteria.

14. Does von Däniken's explanation really make sense? What reason have we to assume that extraterrestrial beings in possession of a technology that renders them capable of emigrating across thousands of light-years of interstellar space would need runways on which to land once they arrive at their destination, or, for that matter, would even possess a countenance that would need to be inserted into a globular screw-top cover to ward off a noxious atmosphere?

15. Cf. T. Good, *Alien Contact: Top Secret Files Revealed.*

16. J. Mack, *Abduction: Human Encounters with Aliens.*

17. H. T. Buckner, "The Flying Saucerians: An Open Door Cult."

18. B. Eadie with C. Taylor, *Embraced by the Light,* and D. Brinkley with P. Perry, *Saved by the Light.* For a medical antidote, see S. Nuland (1994), *How We Die*—also in the top ten but only for a while.

CHAPTER 31   LIFE AFTER LIFE

1. R. Moody, *Life After Life.*

2. C. Zaleski, *Otherworld Journeys,* p. 125.

3. *Ibid.,* p. 175.

CHAPTER 32   CRYSTALS: WHO'S SCRYING NOW?

1. G. Lawrence, "Crystals."

2. J. Page, "Supreme Quartz."

3. *Time,* 7 Dec. 1987, p. 64.

4. G. Lawrence, *op. cit.,* pp. 398–9, gives a concise and clear (as crystal!) explanation of their properties.

5. Page, *op. cit.,* p. 100.

6. For example, if you double its height, divide that into the length of its perimeter you get a close approximation to 3.1416, the value of pi. To boot, the pyramid was oriented precisely to the cardinal points of the compass, and sighted to within minutes of the 30th degree of latitude; moreover, it was believed to be situated on that parallel of longitude that encompassed the greatest land surface of the earth.

7. See the two popular 1970s books by Peter Tompkins—*Secrets of the Great Pyramid* and *Mysteries of the Mexican Pyramids*—for a laborious synthesis including all the glorious (if somewhat misleading) mathematical details. Tompkins incidentally also authored, with C. Bird, *The Secret Life of Plants.*

CHAPTER 33   GEOMANCY: FROM SAWS TO SAUSAGES

1.   N. Pennick, *The Ancient Science of Geomancy, Living in Harmony with the Earth.*

2.   R. Hyman and E. Vogt, "Water Witching: Magical Ritual in Contemporary U.S." See also E. Vogt and R. Hyman, *Water Witching USA.*

3.   From the widespread colloquialism "to devise a sail," which means to lower sail, an apt description of the dipping action of the diviner's rod: D. Rawcliffe, *Occult and Supernatural Phenomena,* p. 334.

4.   Hyman and Vogt, *op. cit.,* pp. 37–8.

5.   *Ibid.,* p. 39.

6.   The art still survives and scarcely does planting time pass without an article attesting to its praxis; see, e.g., most recently, B. Logan, "Searching for Water the Intuitive Way."

7.   *Ibid.*

8.   Pennick, *op. cit.,* p. 90.

9.   This was the contention of A. Michel in *Flying Saucers and the Straight-Line Mystery.*

10.   E.g., C. Ruggles, "The Stone Alignments of Argyll and Mull: A Perspective on the Statistical Approach in Archaeoastronomy."

11.   Cf. A. Aveni and H. Silverman, "Between the Lines."

12.   I discuss several examples of astronomical orientation of ancient architecture in my *Skywatchers of Ancient Mexico,* Ch. V. For a full report by the investigative team at Nazca see also A. Aveni (ed.), *The Lines of Nazca.*

13.   A. Aveni, *Conversing with the Planets,* pp. 214–216.

14.   J. Lovelock, *The Age of Gaia, a Biography of Our Living Earth.*

15.   R. Guiley, *op. cit.,* p. 450. P. Russell, *The Global Brain: Speculations on the Evolutionary Leap to Planetary Consciousness.*

CHAPTER 34   SUMMARY: ON SHIFTING GROUND

1.   S. Geddes, *The Art of Astrology,* p. 16.

2.   E.g., Titus Burckhardt, *Alchemy.*

CHAPTER 35   IS MAGIC A RELIGION?

1.   W. Moyers, *Healing and the Mind,* pp. 179–180.

2.   M. Lings, "Signs of the Times."

3.   The rift continues in academic circles: Recently there was a huge uproar in the Cambridge community over the appointment of a theologian-philosopher to a distinguished lectureship to explore the complementary nature of science and religion. Of religion, one Cambridge don remarked, "What has [it] ever said that is of the smallest use to anybody?" *Gazette,* 7 Aug. 1994, Schenectady, New York, Sunday, p. F7, (Orig. *Christian Science Monitor*).

4. M. Eliade, *Occultism Witchcraft and Cultural Fashions, Essays in Comparative Religion,* p. 63.

5. E. Heenan (ed.), *Mystery, Magic, and Miracle in a Post-Aquarian Age,* p. 18.

6. *Ibid.,* p. 55.

7. "Lazaris Through Jack Pursel," *Sedona,* 4(2), Feb. 1994, pp. 37–8.

8. *Ibid.,* pp. 46–7.

9. *Ibid.,* p. 48.

10. *New Age Sourcebook,* p. 105.

11. J. Needleman, *The New Religions,* pp. 35, 143–4.

12. C. Zaleski, *Otherworld Journeys,* p. 191.

CHAPTER 36   MAGIC AND SCIENCE: J.Z. AND THE RAMSTERS MEET ARCH DEBUNKER

1. I owe this clever term to F. Varela, E. Thompson, and E. Rosch, *The Embodied Mind,* p. 133.

2. R. Leighton, *Principles of Modern Physics,* p. 65.

3. J. Bronowski, *Magic, Science and Civilization,* p. 22.

4. P. Davies, "A Window Into Science."

5. P. Davies, *ibid.,* p. 71.

6. S. Coles, "Science, Myth and Cosmos"—like Morrison's statement, another comment made in a review of one of my books.

7. "Objections to Astrology," *The Humanist,* 35(5), Oct. 1975, pp. 4–6.

8. D. Hess, *Science in the New Age, the Paranormal, Its Defenders and Debunkers and American Culture,* pp. 3–16. His book also was reviewed (negatively) in *SI* (see L. Loevinger, 1994, "Science in the New Age," *Skeptical Inquirer* 18(4), pp. 413–16).

9. M. Gardner, *The New Age: Notes of a Fringe Watcher,* p. 68.

10. M. Gardner, *ibid.,* p. 204.

11. D. Hess, *op. cit.,* pp. 85–89.

12. J. Randi, *Flim Flam!,* p. 3.

13. D. Overbye, *Time,* 26 Apr. 1993.

14. R. Nicholson (1993), "Postmodernism."

15. A. Aveni, *Conversing with the Planets,* Ch. 7.

16. Historian Richard Tarnas defines postmodernism as "an open-ended indeterminate set of attitudes that has been shaped by a great diversity of cultural currents, among them pragmatism, Marxism, feminism and many other 'isms'." R. Tarnas, *The Passion of the Western Mind,* p. 395.

17. Hess, *op. cit.,* p. 37.

18. E. M. Pattison, "Psychosocial Interpretations of Exorcism."

19. M. Gutzwiller, "Letters to the Editor."

20. Paul Davies and John Gribbin, *The Matter Myth.*

21. Davies' and Gribbin's words on Tipler, *ibid.,* p. 308. The second quote is from A. Dressler, *Voyage to the Great Attractor,* p. 3351.

22.   *Ibid.,* p. 43.

23.   M. O'Hara, "A New Age Reflection in the Magic Mirror of Science."

CHAPTER 37   ANTHROPOLOGISTS ENCOUNTER THE OCCULT

1.   E. Evans-Pritchard, *The Azande: History and Political Institutions.*

2.   S. Tambiah, "Form and Meaning in Magical Arts: A Point of View."

3.   That walnuts are brainfood is also a widely held folk myth in parts of the Rocky Mountains. See, e.g., W. Hand, "Folk Medical Magic and Symbolism in the West."

4.   W. Pietz, "The Problem of the Fetish II."

5.   J. R. Fox, (1967), "Witchcraft and Clanship in Cochiti Therapy."

6.   Not the same as our four compass directions but rather the NE, NW, SE, and SW west sides of rectangular space to which, as in most of ancient Mexico, are added an up and a down direction to make a total of six.

7.   E. Mendonsa, "Characteristics of Sisala Diviners."

8.   R. Cavendish, *Man, Myth and Magic,* pp. 211–13.

9.   M. Peletz, "Knowledge, Power and Personal Misfortune in a Malay Context."

10.   M. Douglas, *op. cit.,* pp. 52–3.

11.   This theory, too, has been criticized as being too centered in our own Western gauge for judging all social theories—materialism. See, e.g., M. Taussig, *The Devil and Commodity Fetishism,* pp. 14–18.

12.   See, e.g., A. Métraux, *Voodoo in Haiti.*

13.   E. Durkheim, *The Elementary Forms of the Religious Life.*

14.   See M. and R. Wax, "The Notion of Magic," for a good discussion of this point of view. Also, cf. E. B. Tylor, *Primitive Culture.*

15.   For example, this is what B. Malinowski, *Magic Science and Religion,* had to say about magic.

16.   J. Beattie, "Ritual and Social Change."

17.   S. Tambiah, *Magic, Science, Religion and the Scope of Rationality,* p. 113–114.

CHAPTER 38   SUMMARY: CROSSING CURVES IN AN AGE OF INTERCONNECTEDNESS

1.   M. Truzzi, "The Occult Revival as Popular Culture: Some Observations on the Old and the Nouveau Witch"; M. Truzzi, "Definition & Dimensions of the Occult: Towards a Sociological Perspective"; E. Tiryakian, "Toward the Sociology of Esoteric Culture."

2.   Truzzi, "The Occult . . .", *op. cit.,* p. 411.

3.   M. Murray, *The Witch-Cult in Western Europe.* See also J. Baroja, *The World of Witches,* and R. Robins, *Witchcraft.*

4.   M. G. Marwick in R. Cavendish, *Man, Myth and Magic,* p. 3046.

5. There are an estimated two to five thousand cults in the U.S. today consisting of three to five million members, warns an article in the chief publication of the American Association of Retired Persons, and they have shifted their attention from disillusioned youth to you. C. Collins and D. Frantz, "Let Us Prey."

6. E.g., feature-length all-age-oriented cartoon fantasies like *Beauty and the Beast* and *The Lion King* along with films like *Lorenzo's Oil* and *The House of the Spirits;* and novels like Paul Theroux's *Millroy the Magician* and Leslie Marmon Silko's *Alamanac of the Dead* and *Sacred Water: Narratives and Pictures.*

7. See the front-page article in *The New York Times* by M. O'Neill: "As Life's Questions Get Harder, Magic Casts a Wider Spell." J. Randi's *Conjuring* says pretty much the same thing.

8. Even the book makers have begun to flee the "woo-woo" fringe elements like alchemy and UFOs. *Cf.* M. Jones, "New Age on the Brink."

9. *Ibid.*

10. To mention a few more very recent publications: J.-P. Changeux and A. Connes (1995), *Conversations on Mind, Matter, and Mathematics* (Princeton: Princeton Univ. Press) predicts we will create pure intelligence out of matter; A. Goswami with R. Reed and M. Goswami (1993), *The Self-Aware Universe* (NY: Putnam) contends that consciousness itself creates the physical world, which is already collectively self-aware. Others on the religious side include the Fortress Press' series on *Theology and the Sciences* (begun 1993), which has produced four volumes at this writing; H. Ross (1993), *The Creator and the Cosmos* (Colorado Springs: Hav Press); and N. Pearcey and C. Thaxton (1993), *The Soul of Science: Christian Faith and Natural Philosophy* (Wheaton, Illinois: Crossway). And on the science side of the dialogue: J. Polkinhorne (1994), *The Faith of a Physicist* (Princeton: Princeton Univ. Press); F. Capra and D. Steindl-Rast (1991), *Belonging to the Universe: Explorations on the Frontiers of Science and Spirituality* (San Francisco: Harper); M. Kaku (1994), *Hyperspace* (Oxford: Oxford Univ. Press); and J. Barrow (1995), *The Origin of the Universe* (New York: Basic Books).

11. By his own admission: "Unfortunately for even the expert, the science in this *Appendix for Scientists* is extremely interdisciplinary. To comprehend it at all without reference to a library would require Ph.D.'s in at least three disparate fields: (1) global general relativity, (2) theoretical particle physics, and (3) computer complexity theory. My own Ph.D. is in (1) and I myself can understand (2) and (3) without the Ph.D.'s only because I've spent the past fifteen years teaching myself these two fields. I've done it, so you can do it" (p. 395). Who is "you"? one wonders.

EPILOGUE   OF BACON AND BLACK HOLES

1. E. Abbott, *Flatland.*

BIBLIOGRAPHY

Abbott, E. 1991, *Flatland* (Princeton: Princeton Univ. Press).

Abusch, T. 1989, "The Demonic Image of the Witch in Standard Babylonian Literature: The Reworking of Popular Conceptions by Learned Exorcists" in *Religion, Science and Magic in Concert and in Conflict*, ed. J. Neusner, E. Frerichs, and P. Flesher (New York: Oxford Univ. Press), pp. 27–60.

Ali Shah, S. Ikbal 1993, *Occultism: Its Theory and Practice* (New York: Dorset).

Andrews, C. 1994, *Amulets of Ancient Egypt* (London: British Museum).

Anonymous 1853, *The Rappers or the Mysteries, Fallacies and Absurdities of Spirit Rapping, Table Tipping and Entrancement* (New York: H. Long and Bro.).

Ashmole, E. 1967 [1652] *Theatrum Chemicum Brittanicum* (New York: Johnson Reprint).

Aveni, A. 1980, *Skywatchers of Ancient Mexico* (Austin: Univ. of Texas Press).

——— 1989, *Empires of Time* (New York: Basic Books).

——— 1990, *The Lines of Nazca* (Philadelphia: American Philosophical Society).

——— 1992, *Conversing with the Planets* (New York: Times Books).

Aveni, A., and H. Silverman 1991, "Between the Lines," *The Sciences* 31 (4), pp. 36–42.

Baroja, J. 1964, *The World of the Witches*, tr. O.N.V. Glendinning (Chicago: Univ. of Chicago Press).

Beattie, J. 1966, "Ritual and Social Change" in *Man 1*, pp. 60–74.

Beer, A. 1975, "Kepler's Astrology and Mysticism" in *Kepler: 400 Years*, ed. A. and P. Beer (Oxford: Pergamon), pp. 399–426.

Benson, H. 1975, *The Relaxation Response* (New York: Morrow).

Benson, H., with William Proctor 1984, *Beyond the Relaxation Response* (New York: Times Books).

Bevir, M. 1994, "The West Turns Eastward, Madame Blavatsky and the Transformation of the Occult Tradition" in *Journal of the American Academy of Religion* 62 (3): 747–767.

Blacker, C., and M. Loewe (ed.) 1975, *Ancient Cosmologies* (London: Allen and Unwin).

Blavatsky, H. P. 1877, *Isis Unveiled: A Master Key to the Mysteries of Ancient and Modern Science and Theology* (London: The Theosophical Publishing House).

Block, M. 1932, *The New Church in the New World* (New York: Holt).

Bohm, D. 1980, *Wholeness and the Implicate Order* (London: Routledge & Kegan Paul).

Brandon, R. 1983, *The Spiritualists* (New York: Knopf).

378						BIBLIOGRAPHY

•

Brandon, R. 1993, *The Life and Many Deaths of Harry Houdini* (New York: Random House).

Brasch, R. 1966, *How Did It Begin? Customs and Superstitions and Their Romantic Origins* (New York: D. McKay Co.).

Braude, S. 1986, *The Limits of Influence, Psychokinesis and the Philosophy of Science* (London: Routledge & Kegan Paul).

Brill, J., and A. Reder, 1992, *Investing from the Heart* (New York: Crown).

Brinkley, D., with P. Perry 1994, *Saved by the Light* (New York: Villard).

Broad, C. D. 1962, *Lectures on Psychical Research* (London: Routledge & Kegan Paul).

Brodeen, N. 1994, "Rolfing's Resurgence Really Rolling" *Arizona Daily Star* (21 Jan.), p. D21.

Bronowski, J. 1978, *Magic, Science and Civilization* (New York: Columbia Univ. Press).

Brown, S. 1970, *The Heyday of Spiritualism* (New York: Hawthorn).

Browning, Robert, *Robert Browning: The Poems,* (2 vols.), ed. J. Pettigrew 1981 (New Haven and London: Yale Univ. Press).

Bruce, H. A. 1908, *Historic Ghosts and Ghost Hunters* (New York: Moffat, Yard & Co.).

Buckner, H. T. 1968, "The Flying Saucerians: An Open Door Cult" in *Sociology and Everyday Life,* ed. M. Truzzi (Englewood Cliffs: Prentice Hall), pp. 223–230.

Budge, E. A. Wallis 1972, *The Mummy* (New York: Collier).

Buonanno, M. 1985, "Becoming White: Notes on an Italian-American Explanation of Evil Eye" in *Magic, Witchcraft and Religion,* ed. A. Lehmann and J. Myers (Mountain View, Calif.: Mayfield), pp. 239–246.

Burckhardt, T. 1967, *Alchemy* (Longmead: Element).

Burkert, W. 1987, *Ancient Mystery Cults* (Cambridge, Mass.: Harvard Univ. Press).

Butler, J. 1983, "The Dark Ages of American Occultism 1760–1848" in *The Occult in America: New Historical Perspectives,* ed. H. Kerr and C. Crow (Urbana: Univ. of Illinois Press).

Capron, E. 1855, *Modern Spiritualism, Its Facts and Fanaticisms, Its Consistencies and Contradictions* (New York: Partridge and Brittan).

Carcopino, J. 1991, *Daily Life in Ancient Rome,* tr. E. O. Lorimer (New York: Penguin).

Cardanus, H. 1648, *La Metoposcopié* (Paris: Aux Amateurs de Livres).

Cavendish, R. 1967, *The Black Arts* (New York: Putnam).

Cavendish, R. (ed.) 1983, *Man, Myth and Magic: The Illustrated Encyclopedia of Mythology, Religion and the Unknown* (12 vols.) (N. Bellmore, New York: Marshall Cavendish) (Rev. 1995).

Christopher, M. 1969, *Houdini: The Untold Story* (New York: Crowell).

Clark, E. 1994, "Every Once in a While Something Happens . . ." *Yankee* (June), pp. 88–93, 132–136.

Collins, C., and D. Frantz 1994, "Let Us Prey," *Modern Maturity* (June), pp. 24–32.

Combe, G. 1857, *The Constitution of Man Considered in Relation to External Objects* (Boston: Ticknor and Fields).

Condon, E., and D. Gillmor 1969, *Final Report of the Scientific Study of Unidentified Flying Objects* (New York: Bantam).

Conquest, R. 1993, "History, Humanity, and Truth," *National Review* 44 (11) (7 June), pp. 28–35.

Cooter, R. 1980, "Deploying Pseudoscience" in *Science, Pseudoscience and Society*, ed. M. Hanen, M. Osler, and R. Weyant (Waterloo, Ont.: Calgary Institute of Humanities and Wilfrid Laurier Press).

Crabtree, A. 1988, *Animal Magnetism, Early Hypnotism and Psychical Research 1760–1925: An Annotated Bibliography* (New York: Kraus).

Cranston, S. 1993, *HPB: The Extraordinary Life and Influence of Helena Blavatsky, Founder of the Modern Theosophical Movement* (New York: J. P. Tarcher/Putnam).

Crehan, J. 1970, "Exorcism" in *Man, Myth and Magic: The Illustrated Encyclopedia of Mythology, Religion and the Unknown*, ed. R. Cavendish (New York: Marshall Cavendish), vol. 7, p. 873.

Cross, W. R. 1950, *The Burned-Over District, the Social and Intellectual History of Enthusiastic Religion in Western New York 1800–1850* (Ithaca: Cornell Univ. Press).

Crowley, A. 1991, *Magick in Theory and Practice* (Secaucus: Castle).

Däniken, E. von 1971, *Chariots of the Gods* (New York: Bantam).

Dante Alighieri, *Dante's Inferno,* with notes and commentary by M. Musa, 1971 (Bloomington: Indiana Univ. Press).

Davies, J. 1955, *Phrenology: Fad and Science; A 19th-Century American Crusade* (New Haven: Yale Univ. Press).

Davies, P. 1993, "A Window Into Science" in *Natural History* 102 (7), pp. 67–68.

Davies, P., and J. Gribbin 1992, *The Matter Myth* (New York: Simon & Schuster).

Descartes, R. 1664, *Principia Philosophiae* (Amsterdam: Elzevir).

Dibble, C., and A. Anderson (ed. and tr.) 1954, *Florentine Codex, General History of the Things of New Spain* (12 vols.) (Salt Lake City and Santa Fe: Univ. of Utah and School of American Research).

Dilke, O.A.W. 1971, *The Roman Land Surveyors* (Newton Abbot: David and Charles).

——— 1986, *Mathematics and Measurement* (London: British Museum).

Dillon, K. 1993, "Facilitated Communication, Autism and Ouija" in *Skeptical Inquirer* 17 (3), pp. 281–287.

Dodds, E. 1965, *Pagan and Christian in an Age of Anxiety* (Cambridge: Cambridge Univ. Press).

Douglas, M. 1970, *Natural Symbols* (New York: Pantheon).

Drake, F., and D. Sobel, 1992, *Is Anyone Out There? The Scientific Search for Extraterrestrial Intelligence* (New York: Delacorte).

Dressler, A. 1994, *Voyage to the Great Attractor* (New York: Knopf).

Dunninger, J. 1935, *Inside the Medium's Cabinet* (New York: Kemp).

Duquesne, M. n.d., *A New Voyage to the E. Indies in the Years 1690–1691.*

Duran, D. (*see* F. Horcasitas and D. Heyden 1971).

Durkheim, E. 1965 [1915], *The Elementary Forms of the Religious Life* (New York: Free Press).

Duster, T. 1992, "Genetics, Race and Crime: Recurring Seduction to a False Precision" in *DNA on Trial, Genetic Identification and Criminal Justice,* ed. P. Billings (Cold Spring Harbor: Cold Spring Harbor Press), pp. 129–140.

Eadie, B., with C. Taylor, 1992, *Embraced by the Light* (New York: Gold Leaf).

Ebon, M. 1974, *The Devil's Bride: Exorcism, Past and Present* (New York: Harper).

Edwardes, M. 1977, *The Dark Side of History* (New York: Stein & Day).

Eisenbud, J. 1967, *The World of Ted Serios* (New York: Morrow).

Éliade, M. 1956, *The Forge and the Crucible, The Origins and Structures of Alchemy* (New York: Harper).

———— 1976, *Occultism Witchcraft and Cultural Fashions, Essays in Comparative Religion,* tr. Stephen Corrin (Chicago: Univ. of Chicago Press).

Ellwood Jr., R. 1983, "The American Theosophical Synthesis" in *The Occult in America,* ed. H. Kerr and C. Crow (Urbana: Univ. of Illinois Press), pp. 111–134.

Emerson, E. W. 1865, *Essays by Ralph Waldo Emerson, First Series* (Boston: Houghton and Mifflin).

Evans-Pritchard, E. 1971, *The Azande History and Political Institutions* (Oxford: Clarendon).

Faivre, A. 1992, "Introduction" in *Modern Esoteric Spirituality,* ed. A. Faivre and J. Needleman (New York: Crossroad), pp. xv–xx.

Feola, J. 1978, "Parapsychology Today" in *Gnostica* 47, pp. 56–59.

Feynman, R., with Ralph Leighton 1985, *Surely You're Joking, Mr. Feynman!: Adventures of a Curious Character* (New York: Norton).

Fludd, R. 1617, *History of the Macrocosm and Microcosm* (Oppenheim: J. Theodore de Bry).

Fox, J. R. 1967, "Witchcraft and Clanship in Cochiti Therapy" in *Magic, Witchcraft and Curing,* ed. J. Middleton (Garden City: Natural History Press), pp. 255–284; rite on pp. 266–267.

Frazer, R. M. (tr.) 1983, *The Poems of Hesiod* (Norman: Univ. of Oklahoma Press).

Freidel, D., and L. Schele 1993, *Maya Cosmos* (New York: Morrow).

Friedrich, O. 1987, "New Age Harmonies" in *Time* (7 Sept.), pp. 62–72.

Fullam, F. (n.d.) 1984, "Contemporary Belief in Astrology," MA Thesis, Department of Sociology, Univ. of Chicago.

Fuller, C. 1974, "Dr. Jule Eisenbud and the Amazing Randi" in *Fate* (Aug.), pp. 65–74.

Gager, J. 1992, *Curse Tablets and Binding Spells from the Ancient World* (Oxford: Oxford Univ. Press).

Gale, G. 1981, "The Anthropic Principle" in *Scientific American* 245 (6), pp. 154–171.

Galileo, *Galileo, Dialogue Concerning the Two Chief World Systems, Ptolemaic and Copernican,* tr. S. Drake 1967 (Berkeley: Univ. of California at Berkeley Press).

Gardner, M. 1957, *Fads and Fallacies in the Name of Science* (New York: Dover).

——— 1988, *The New Age: Notes of a Fringe Watcher* (Buffalo: Prometheus Books).

Gauld, A. 1968, *The Founders of Psychical Research* (London: Routledge & Kegan Paul).

Gay, P. 1988, *Freud* (New York: W. W. Norton).

Geertz, H. 1975, "An Anthropology of Religion and Magic I" in *Journal of Interdisciplinary History VI* (1), pp. 71–89.

Gell-Mann, M. 1994, *The Quark and the Jaguar* (New York: W. H. Freeman).

Gibbons, E. 1962, *Stalking the Wild Asparagus* (New York: D. McKay).

Gibson, W. 1976, *The Original Houdini Scrapbook* (New York: Corwin Sterling).

Ginzburg, C. 1983, *The Night Battles: Witchcraft and Agrarian Cults in the Sixteenth and Seventeenth Centuries,* tr. John and Anne C. Tedeschi (London: Routledge & Kegan Paul).

Gleason, J. 1968, *The New Britton and Brown Illustrated Flora of the Northeastern United States and Adjacent Canada* (3 vols.) (New York and London: Hafner).

Gleick, J. 1992, *Genius: The Life and Science of Richard Feynman* (New York: Pantheon).

Gmelch, G. 1989, "Baseball Magic" in *Magic, Witchcraft and Religion,* ed. A. Lehmann and J. Myers (Mountain View, Calif.: Mayfield), pp. 295–301.

Godwin, J. 1979, *Robert Fludd, Hermetic Philosopher and Surveyor of Two Worlds* (London: Thames & Hudson).

Good, T. 1993, *Alien Contact: Top-Secret UFO Files Revealed* (New York: Morrow).

Goodman, F. 1988, *How About Demons? Possession and Exorcism in the Modern World* (Indiana: Indiana Univ. Press).

Goody, J. 1977, *The Domestication of the Savage Mind* (Cambridge: Cambridge Univ. Press).

Gordon, J. 1994, *New York Times Book Review* (1 May), pp. 13–14.

Grant, R. M. 1961, *Gnosticism* (New York: Harper).

Grasset, J. 1910, *The Marvels Beyond Science, Being a Record of Progress Made in the Reduction of Occult Phenomena to a Scientific Basis* (New York: Funk and Wagnalls).

Graubard, M. 1953, *Astrology and Alchemy, Two Fossil Sciences* (New York: Philosophical Library).

Gresham, W. 1959, *Houdini, the Man Who Walked Through Walls* (New York: Holt, Rinehart and Wilson).

Grim, P. 1982, "Selected Cases from the Condon Report" in *Philosophy of Science and the Occult,* ed. P. Grim (Albany: SUNY Albany), pp. 234–246.

Guiley, R. 1991, *Harper's Encyclopedia of Mystical and Paranormal Experience* (New York: HarperCollins).

Gutzwiller, M. 1994, "Letters to the Editor" in *Physics Today* 47 (8), part I, p. 9.

Hall, T. 1984, *The Enigma of Daniel Home, Medium or Fraud?* (Buffalo: Prometheus).

Hamon, L. 1900, *Cheiro's Language of the Hand* (London: Nichols).

Hand, W. 1985, "Folk Medical Magic and Symbolism in the West" in *Magic, Witchcraft and Religion,* ed. A. Lehmann and J. Myers (Mountain View, Calif.: Mayfield), pp. 192–198.

Hanen, M. et al. 1980, *Science, Pseudoscience and Society* (Calgary: Calgary Institute of Humanities and Wilfrid Laurier Press).

Harbage, A. (ed.) 1969, *The Complete Pelican Shakespeare* (Baltimore: Penguin).

Heenan, E. (ed.) 1973, *Mystery Magic and Miracle: Religion in a Post-Aquarian Age* (Englewood Cliffs, N.J.: Prentice-Hall).

Heidel, A. 1951, *The Babylonian Genesis* (Chicago: Univ. of Chicago Press).

Hess, D. 1993, *Science in the New Age, the Paranormal, Its Defenders and Debunkers and American Culture* (Madison: Univ. of Wisconsin Press).

Heyden, D. (n.d.), *Wood in Life and Death* (ms. in press).

——— "El Arbol en el Mito y el Simbolo" in *Estudios de Cultura Nahuatl* 23:201–220, 1993.

Home, D. D. 1868, *Incidents in My Life* (London: Longmans).

Homer, *The Odyssey of Homer,* tr. R. Lattimore 1967, *The Odyssey of Homer* (New York: Harper Perennial).

Horcasitas, F., and D. Heyden (tr. and ed.) 1971, *Fray Diego Duran, Book of the Gods and Rites and Ancient Calendars* (Norman: Univ. of Oklahoma Press).

Hoskins, J. 1993, *The Play of Time: Kodi Perspectives on Calendars, History and Exchange* (Berkeley: Univ. of California Press).

Houdini, H. 1924, *A Magician Among the Spirits* (New York: Harper).

Howells, W. 1962, *The Heathens* (Garden City: Doubleday).

Hutchison, K. 1982, "What Happened to Occult Qualities in the Scientific Revolution?" in *Isis* 73:233–253.

Hyman, R. and E. Vogt 1967, "Water Witching: Magical Ritual in Contemporary U.S." in *Psychology Today,* 1, pp. 35–42.

Isaacs, E. 1983, "The Fox Sisters and American Spiritualism" in *The Occult in America, New Historical Perspectives,* ed. H. Kerr and C. Crow (Urbana and Chicago: Univ. of Illinois Press), pp. 79–110.

Jacobsen, T. 1957, "Enuma Elish—The Babylonian Genesis" in *Theories of the Universe,* ed. M. Munitz (New York: Free Press), pp. 8–20.

Jahoda, G. 1969, *The Psychology of Superstition* (Middlesex: Penguin).

Jarvie, I., and J. Agassi 1967, "The Problem of the Rationality of Magic" in *British Journal of Sociology* 18, pp. 55–74.

Jay, R. 1994, *The Magic Magic Book* (New York: Library Fellows of the Whitney Museum of American Art).

Jenkins, E. 1982, *The Shadow and the Light, A Defense of Daniel Dunglas Home, the Medium* (London: Hamish Hamilton).

Jeyes, U. 1989, *Old Babylonian Extispicy* (Istanbul: Netherlands Archaeological Institute).

Jones, M. 1989, "New Age on the Brink" in *Publishers Weekly* (3 Nov.), pp. 14–18, quote on p. 14.

Kaplan, S. 1978, *The Encyclopedia of Tarot*, 2 vols. (New York: U.S. Games Systems).

Koestler, A. 1960, *The Watershed: A Biography of Johannes Kepler* (New York: Doubleday Anchor).

Kunz, G. 1913, *The Curious Lore of Precious Stones* (Philadelphia: Lippincott).

Lambert, W. G. 1975, "The Cosmology of Summer and Babylon" in *Ancient Cosmologies*, ed. C. Blacker and M. Loewe (London: Allen and Unwin), pp. 42–65.

Lang, A. 1894, *Cock Lane and Common-Sense* (London: Longmans Green & Co.).

Laurant, J. P. 1992, "The Primitive Characteristics of 19th-Century Esotericism" in *Modern Esoteric Spirituality*, ed. A. Faivre and J. Needleman (New York: Crossroad), pp. 277–287.

Lawrence, D. H. 1985, *Etruscan Places* (New York: Penguin).

Lawrence, G. 1989, "Crystals" in *Skeptical Inquirer* 13 (4), pp. 397–400.

LeBrun, M. 1994, "People Wracked with Pain Attracted to Magnet Therapy" in *Syracuse Herald Journal* (27 Feb.), p. BB4.

Lehmann, A. 1985, "Eyes of the Hgangas, Ethnomedicine and Power in Central African Republic" in *Magic, Witchcraft and Religion*, ed. A. Lehmann and J. Myers (Mountain View, Calif.: Mayfield), pp. 151–159.

Lehmann, A. and J. Myers 1989, *Magic, Witchcraft and Religion* (Mountain View, Calif.: Mayfield).

Leighton, R. 1959, *Principles of Modern Physics* (New York: McGraw–Hill).

Lerner, M. 1980, "Foreword" in M. Ferguson *The Aquarian Conspiracy* (New York: J. P. Tarcher).

Lessa, W. 1958, "Somatomancy: Precursor of the Science of Human Constitution" in *Reader in Comparative Religion; An Anthropological Approach*, ed. W. Lessa and E. Vogt (Evanston and White Plains: Row, Peterson), pp. 314–326.

Levitt, E. 1952, "Superstitions: Twenty Five Years Ago and Today" in *American Journal of Psychology*, vol. 65, pp. 443–9.

Lindberg, D. 1992, *The Beginnings of Western Science* (Chicago: Univ. of Chicago Press).

Lings, M. 1974, "Sings of the Times" in *The Sword of Gnosis, Metaphysics, Cosmology, Tradition, Symbolism*, ed. J. Needleman (New York: Penguin), pp. 109–121.

Lloyd, G. 1979, *Magic, Reason and Experience: Studies in the Origin and Development of Greek Science* (Cambridge: Cambridge Univ. Press).

Lodge, Sir O. 1932, *Past Years* (New York: Scribner's).

Löfgren, B. 1968, "Psychoanalytic Theory of Affects" in *Journal of the American Psychoanalytic Association,* 16, pp. 638–650.

Logan, B. 1994, "Searching for Water the Intuitive Way" in *The New York Times* (26 June), p. 41.

Lovelock, J. 1988, *The Age of Gaia, a Biography of Our Living Earth* (New York: Norton).

Lowry, K. 1987, "Channelers" in *Omni* (Oct.), pp. 47–50.

Lucretius, *On the Nature of the Universe,* tr. R. D. Latham 1951 (New York: Penguin).

Lys, C. de 1948, *A Treasury of American Superstitions* (New York: Philosophical Library).

Mack, John E. 1994, *Abduction: Human Encounters with Aliens* (New York: Charles Scribner's Sons).

Malinowski, B. 1948, *Magic, Science and Religion* (Beacon: Boston).

Maloney, C. (ed.) 1976, *The Evil Eye* (New York: Columbia Univ. Press).

Marett, R. (ed.) 1908, *Anthropology and the Classics* (Oxford: Clarendon).

Marwick, M., "Witchcraft" in R. Cavendish (ed.) *Man, Myth and Magic: The Illustrated Encyclopedia of Mythology, Religion and the Unknown* (N. Bellmore, New York: Marshall Cavendish), pp. 3041–3046.

Mauss, M. 1972, *A General Theory of Magic,* tr. Robert Brain (London: Routledge & Kegan Paul).

McDonald, J. 1972, "Science in Default: 22 Years of Inadequate UFO Investigations" in *UFO's—A Scientific Debate,* ed. C. Sagan and T. Page (Ithaca: Cornell Univ. Press), pp. 52–122.

Melton, J. G. 1992, *Magic, Witchcraft and Paganism in America: A Bibliography,* 2nd ed. (New York: Garland).

Mendonsa, E. 1989, "Characteristics of Sisala Diviners" in *Magic, Witchcraft and Religion,* ed. A. Lehmann and J. Myers (Mountain View, Calif.: Mayfield), pp. 278–288.

Menzel, D. 1975, "UFO's—the Modern Myth" in *UFO's—A Scientific Debate,* ed. C. Sagan and T. Page (Ithaca: Cornell Univ. Press), pp. 123–182.

Métraux, A. 1972, *Voodoo in Haiti,* tr. Hugo Charteris (New York: Schocken Books).

Meyer, I. (tr.) 1970, *The Zohar in Qabbalah, the Philosophic Writings of Solomon Ben Yehuda Ibn Gebirol or Avicebron* (New York: Ktav), p. 109.

Michel, A. 1958, *Flying Saucers and the Straight-Line Mystery* (New York: Criterion).

Milne, A. A. 1924, *When We Were Very Young* (Toronto: McClelland and Stewart).

Moody, R. 1975, *Life After Life* (New York: Bantam).

Morrison, P. 1993, "What We Seek in the Sky" in *Scientific American* (Aug.), p. 127.

Moyers, W. 1993, *Healing and the Mind* (New York: Doubleday).

Mulick, J., J. Jacobson, and F. Kobe 1993, "Anguished Silence and Helping Hands: Autism and Facilitated Communication" in *Skeptical Inquirer* 17 (3), pp. 270–281.

Munitz, M. 1965, *Theories of the Universe* (New York: Free Press).

Murray, M. 1921, *The Witch-Cult in Western Europe* (London: Peter Smith).

Needleman, J. 1970, *The New Religions* (New York: Doubleday).

Neusner, J., et al. (ed.) 1989, *Religion, Science and Magic* (New York: Oxford Univ. Press).

Nicholson, R. 1993, "Postmodernism" in *Science* 261, p. 1439.

Nisbet, R. 1980, *History of the Idea of Progress* (New York: Basic Books).

Nuland, S. 1994, *How We Die* (New York: Knopf).

O'Hara, M. 1989, "A New Age Reflection in the Magic Mirror of Science" in *Skeptical Inquirer* 13 (4), p. 370.

Olcott, H. S. 1895, *Old Diary Leaves, The History of the Theosophical Society* (Madras: Theosophical Publishing House).

Oldfather, W. H. 1933 (tr., ed.), *Diodorus of Sicily* (Cambridge, Mass.: Harvard Univ. Press).

O'Neill, M. 1994, "As Life's Questions Get Harder, Magic Casts a Wider Spell" in *The New York Times* (13 Jan.), p. A1.

Opie, I., and P. Opie 1959, *The Lore and Language of Schoolchildren* (Oxford: Oxford Univ. Press).

Opie, I., and M. Tatem (eds.) 1989, *Dictionary of Superstitions* (Oxford: Oxford Univ. Press).

Overbye, D. 1993, *Time* 141 (26 Apr.), p. 74.

Page, J. 1987, "Supreme Quartz" in *Omni* 10 (1), pp. 95–100.

Parker, D., and J. Parker 1992, *The Power of Magic* (London: Beazley).

Pattison, E. M. 1985, "Psychosocial Interpretations of Exorcism" in *Magic Witchcraft and Religion,* ed. A. Lehmann & J. Myers (Mayfield, Calif.: Mountain View), pp. 264–277.

Peletz, M. 1993, "Knowledge, Power and Personal Misfortune in a Malay Context" in *Understanding Witchcraft and Sorcery in SE Asia,* ed. C. Watson and R. Ellen (Honolulu: Univ. of Hawaii Press), pp. 149–177, quote on p. 168.

Pennick, N. 1979, *The Ancient Science of Geomancy, Living in Harmony with the Earth* (London: Thames and Hudson).

Pietz, W. 1987, "The Problem of the Fetish II" in *Res* 13, pp. 23–45, quote on p. 26.

Plato, *Five Dialogues,* tr. G.M.A. Grube, 1981 (Indianapolis: Hackett).

——— *Plato's Republic,* tr. G.M.A. Grube, 1974 (Indianapolis: Hackett).

Pliny, *Natural History,* tr. W.H.S. Jones 1963 (Cambridge, Mass.: Harvard Univ. Press).

Podmore, F. 1963, *Mediums of the 19th Century* (New Hyde Park: University Books).

Price, G. 1955, "Science and the Supernatural" in *Science* 122 (3165), pp. 359–367.

Price, S. 1985, "Delphi and Divination" in *Greek Religion and Society,* ed. P. E. Easterling and J.V. Muir (Cambridge: Cambridge Univ. Press), p. 147.

Puthoff, H. and R. Targ 1974, "Information Transmission Under Conditions of Sensory Shielding" in *Nature* 251, pp. 602–607.

Randi, J. 1982, *Flim Flam!* (Buffalo: Prometheus).

——— 1992, *Conjuring* (New York: St. Martin's Press).

Rawcliffe, D. H. 1987, *Occult and Supernatural Phenomena* (New York: Dover).

Read, C. 1920, *The Origin of Man and His Superstitions* (Cambridge: Cambridge Univ. Press).

Reed, G. 1989, "The Psychology of Channeling" in *Skeptical Inquirer* 13 (4), pp. 385–396.

Reminick, R. 1976, "The Evil Eye Belief Among the Amhara" in *The Evil Eye,* ed. C. Maloney (New York: Columbia Univ. Press), pp. 85–101.

Roberts, J. 1976, *The Coming of Seth* (New York: Pocket Books).

Robins, R. 1978, *Witchcraft* (New York: Kraus International).

Roquemore, K. 1975, *It's All in Your Numbers: The Secret of Numerology* (New York: Harper & Row).

Ruggles, C. 1988, "The Stone Alignments of Argyll and Mull: A Perspective on the Statistical Approach in Archaeoastronomy" in *Records in Stone,* ed. C. Ruggles (Cambridge: Cambridge Univ. Press), pp. 232–250.

Russell, J. B. 1985, "Witchcraft" in *Magic, Witchcraft and Religion: An Anthropological Study of the Supernatural,* ed. A. Lehmann and J. Myers (Mountain View, Calif.: Mayfield), pp. 203–212.

Russell, P. 1983, *The Global Brain: Speculations on the Evolutionary Leap to Planetary Consciousness* (Los Angeles: J. P. Tarcher).

Sagan, C., and T. Page (ed.), 1972, *UFO's: A Scientific Debate* (Ithaca: Cornell Univ. Press).

Sahagun, B. de (*see* Dibble and Anderson).

Salzberg, H. 1991, *From Caveman to Chemist* (Washington, D.C.: American Chemical Society).

Sandstrom, J. 1937, *Palmystery* (New York: Kemp).

Schievella, P. 1982, "Science, Proof and the Ancient Astronaut Hypothesis" in *Philosophy of Science and the Occult,* ed. P. Grim (Albany: SUNY Albany), pp. 267–277.

Schipperges, H. 1992, "Paracelsus and His Followers" in *Modern Esoteric Spirituality,* ed. A. Faivre and J. Needleman (New York: Crossroad), pp. 173–174.

Schrenck-Notzing, Baron von 1920, *Phenomena of Materialisation* (London: Kegan Paul, Treach & Trubner).

Seldes, G. 1927, *The Stammering Century* (New York: John Day).

Seligmann, K. 1948, *The History of Magic and the Occult* (New York: Harmony).

Sellon, E., and R. Weber, 1992, "Theosophy and the Theosophical Society" in *Modern Esoteric Spirituality,* ed. A. Faivre and J. Needleman (New York: Crossroad), p. 318.

Seznec, J. 1953, *Survival of the Pagan Gods* (Princeton: Princeton Univ. Press).

Shore, L. 1989, "New Light on the New Age" in *Skeptical Inquirer* 13 (3), pp. 226–240.

Shumaker, W. 1972, *The Occult Sciences in the Renaissance* (Berkeley: Univ. of California Press).

——— 1989, *Natural Magic and Modern Science, Four Treatises, 1590–1657* (Binghamton, N.Y.: Center for Medieval and Early Renaissance Studies).

Siegel, B. 1986, *Love, Medicine and Miracles* (New York: Harper & Row).

Silko, L. M. 1991, *Almanac of the Dead* (New York: Simon & Schuster).

——— 1993, *Sacred Water: Narratives and Pictures* (Tucson: Flood Plain).

Smith, R. F. 1975, *Prelude to Science: An Exploration of Magic and Divination* (New York: Scribner's).

Spangler, D. 1976, *Revelation: The Birth of a New Age* (Findhorn Bay: Findhorn Foundation).

Spangler, D., and W. Thompson 1991, *Reimagination of the World: A Critique of the New Age, Science, and Popular Culture* (Santa Fe: Bear & Co.).

Stein, G. 1993, *The Sorcerer of Kings: The Case of Daniel Dunglas Home and William Crookes* (Buffalo: Prometheus).

Story, R. 1976, *The Space Gods Revealed* (New York: Harper & Row).

Tambiah, S. 1973, "Form and Meaning in Magical Acts: A Point of View" in *Modes of Thought,* ed. R. Horton and R. Finnegan (London: Faber and Faber), pp. 199–224.

Tambiah, S. 1990, *Magic, Science, Religion, and the Scope of Rationality* (Cambridge: Cambridge Univ. Press).

Tarnas, R. 1991, *The Passion of the Western Mind* (New York: Harmony).

Taussig, M. 1980, *The Devil and Commodity Fetishism* (Chapel Hill: Univ. of North Carolina Press).

Tedlock, B. 1982, *Time and the Highland Maya* (Albuquerque: Univ. of. New Mexico Press).

Tedlock, D. 1985, *Popol Vuh, The Definitive Edition of the Mayan Book of the Dawn of Life* (New York: Simon & Schuster).

Teitelbaum, J. 1976, "The Leer and the Loom—Social Controls in Handloom Weavers" in *The Evil Eye,* ed. C. Maloney (New York: Columbia Univ. Press), pp. 63–75.

Tester, S. J. 1987, *History of Western Astrology* (Wolfboro, New Hampshire: Boydell).

Theroux, P. 1994, *Millroy the Magician* (New York: Random House).

Thomas, K. 1971, *Religion and the Decline of Magic* (New York: Scribner's).

Thompson, E. P. 1972, "Anthropology and the Discipline of Historical Context" in *Midland History* 3, pp. 41–55.

Thompson, J.E.S. 1972, *Commentary on the Dresden Codex, a Maya Picture Book* (Philadelphia: Am. Phil. Soc.).

Thompson, R. 1900, *Reports of Magicians and Astrologers of Nineveh and Babylon in the British Museum* (London: Luzac).

Thompson, S. G. 1989, " 'Entities' in the Linguistic Minefield" in *Skeptical Inquirer* 13 (4), pp. 391–396.

Thorndike, L. 1923, *A History of Magic and Experimental Science* (New York: Macmillan).

Thulin, C. 1913 [1971], *Corpus Agrimensorum Romanorum H. Gromaticus* (Stuttgart: Teubner).

Tiryakian, E. 1972, "Toward the Sociology of Esoteric Culture" in *American Journal of Sociology* 78, pp. 491–512.

Tompkins, P. 1971, *Secrets of the Great Pyramid* (New York: Harper & Row).

——— 1976, *Mysteries of the Mexican Pyramids* (New York: Harper & Row).

Tompkins, P., and C. Bird 1973, *The Secret Life of Plants* (New York: Harper & Row).

Trock, D., et al. 1993, "A Double-Blind Trial of the Clinical Effects of Pulsed Electromagnetic Fields in Osteoarthritis" in *Journal of Rheumatology* 20 (3), pp. 456–460.

Truzzi, M. 1971, "Definition and Dimensions of the Occult: Towards a Sociological Perspective" in *Journal of Popular Culture* 5, pp. 635–646.

——— 1972, "The Occult Revival as Popular Culture: Some Observations on the Old and the Nouveau Witch" in *Sociological Quarterly* 13, pp. 16–36.

Tylor, Sir E. B. 1903, *Primitive Culture, Researches into the Development of Mythology, Philosophy, Religion, Language, Art and Custom* (2 vols.) (London: John Murray).

Underhill, E. 1911, *Mysticism* (New York: Dutton).

Varela, F., E. Thompson, and E. Rosch, 1991, *The Embodied Mind* (Cambridge: MIT Press).

Vega, Garcilaso de la 1970 [1616], *Royal Commentaries of the Incas and a General History of Peru* (2 vols.), tr. H. Livermore (Austin: Univ. of Texas Press).

Vetter, G. 1958, *Magic and Religion, Their Psychological Nature, Origin, and Function* (New York: Philosophical Library).

Veyne, P. 1987, *A History of Private Life I: From Pagan Rome to Byzantium* (Cambridge, Mass.: Harvard Univ. Press).

Vogt, E., and R. Hyman 1959, *Water Witching, U.S.A.* (Chicago: Univ. of Chicago Press).

Walker, E. H. 1984, "A Review of Criticisms of the Quantum Mechanical Theory of Psi Phenomena" in *Journal of Parapsychology* 48, pp. 277–332.

Waterman, P. F. 1929, *The Story of Superstition* (New York: Knopf).

Wax, M. and R. Wax. 1963, "The Notion of Magic" in *Current Anthropology* 4(5), pp. 495–518.

Wehr, G. 1992, "C. G. Jung in the Context of Christian Esotericism and Cultural History" in *Modern Esoteric Spirituality,* ed. A. Faivre and J. Needleman (New York: Crossroad), pp. 381–399.

Weiner, H. 1969, *9½ Mystics: The Kabbala Today* (New York: Collier Books).

Weyant, R. 1980, "Metaphors and Animal Magnetism," in *Science, Pseudoscience and Society,* ed. M. Hanen, M. Osler, and J. Weyant (Waterloo, Ont.: Calgary Inst. of Humanities and Wilfred Laurier Press).

Wilson, C. 1971, *The Occult: A History* (New York: Random House).

Yates, F. H. 1964, *Giordano Bruno and the Hermetic Tradition* (Chicago: Univ. of Chicago Press).

Zaleski, C. 1987, *Otherworld Journeys: Accounts of Near-death Experience in Medieval and Modern Times* (New York: Oxford Univ. Press).

Zweig, S. 1932, *Mental Healers: Franz Anton Mesino, Mary Baker Eddy, Sigmund Freud* (New York: Viking).

INDEX

Abracadabra, 66–67, 355n. 8
Abulafia, Abraham ben Samuel, 83
acupuncture, 270
adaptive response, 297
adepts, 191
Adventism, 54
afterlife
    communication with (*see* channeling)
    Swedenborg's description, 175–176
Agrippa, 83–87
air, in Hebrew tradition, 356n. 3
alchemy, 99–111
    Chinese, 104
    origin of, 38–39
    processes of, 103
    spiritual element of, 108
    theory of, 101
    women, in movement, 100
aliens, 279–280
    on Mars, 281

allegorical thought, in Medieval times, 106–107, 119
altered states, and magic conjurations, 210
American folk remedies, 45
American occult movement
    Blavatsky, Helena Petrovna, 191–200
    Home, Daniel Dunglas, 179–190
    Mesmer, Franz, 169–174
    the Rochester rapping, 152–162
    Swedenborg, Emmanuel, 175–177
    See also spiritualism
amulets, 355n. 9
    fetishes, 326–328
    good luck charms, 3–5
    scarab beetles, 16–17
anagrams, 61, 355n. 2
animal magnetism, 170
    and phrenology, 219–220
    See also mesmerism
animals, moral standards of, 45–46

anthropology
    history of, 334–338
    magic, view of, 335–336
anthropometry, 212
aphrodisiacs, 136–137, 277
Aquarian Conspiracy, The, 341
Arabic writers, translation of Classi-
    cal knowledge, 79
Aristotle, 25–26
"as above, so below" priniciple, 26
    on Emerald Tablet, 58
ascendance of the soul
    in Kabbalistic terms, 60–61
    and Tarot cards, 89
Association, Principle of, 87–88,
    92–93, 356n. 7
Astrological Principles, 118–119
astrology
    of Babylonians, 28
    belief in, surveys of, 246–248
    and body divination, 213–216
    in Classical Greece, 26–32
    credibility, loss of, 121–122
    and medicine, in Classical
        Greece, 32–34
    in Medieval times, 117–122
    and mesmerism, 170
    during the Renaissance, 95–96
    See also planetary influences
Atlantis, 195
    and terrestrial geometry, 300–301
Azande tribepeople, magic of, 324,
    330

Babylonians
    astrology of, 28
    creation myth, 17–18
    exorcists, 18–19
    and hepatoscopy, 20–23

Baptists, 54
baru (seer), 20–21
beast, number of, 65–66, 355n. 6
Bell, John, and Rochester rappings,
    153–154
Benson, Herbert, and relaxation
    therapy, 265–266
biofeedback, 265–267
Blavatsky, Helena Petrovna. See
    HPB
body divination
    and metoposcopy, 212–223
    palmistry, 220–221
    phrenology, 216–220
    during the Renaissance,
        213–216
body octaves, 92–93
body topology, and spiritualism,
    212–223
Bohm, David, and the "Implicate
    Order," 262
Braude, Stephen, and theory of PK,
    261
Brewster, Sir David, explanation of
    rappings, 187
Browning, Elizabeth Barrett, and
    DDH, 182–185
Browning, Robert, and DDH,
    182–185
bubonic plague, 138
Buckner, H. T., and "open door"
    attitudes, 287
Burned-Over District, New York,
    151–152, 165, 167

C., Eva
    and ectoplasm, 204–207
    Houdini's explanation of, 235
Cabbala. See Kabbalah

Calvinists, and communication with dead, 159

Campanella, Tommasso, and diet, 275

Capron, E. W., and Rochester rapping, 155–156

Cardan, Jerome, and body divination, 213–216

Cardano
  and body divination, 213–216
  and metoposcopy, 214–216

cards, playing, 88–89

Carrière, Eva
  and ectoplasm, 204–207
  Houdini's explanation of, 235

Cartesian physicists, 144

Cavendish, Richard, and the Tarot, 89

channeling, 252–255, 368n. 7
  and crystals, 292–293
  as mass hypnosis, 254–255
  and reincarnation, 254

de Chardin, Pierre Teilhard, and directed evolution, 302

charms, 7
  for good luck, 3–5
  for healing, 66–67
  See also amulets

chemistry and alchemy, 110

Chhiu Yen Han, and *feng-shui*, 295

Chinese alchemy, 104

chiromancy, 220–221

chiropractic, 270

Christianity
  and alchemy, 100
  astrology, appropriation of, 117–118
  history of, 76
  magical customs, absorption of, 53, 78
  and numeracy, theories of, 82–83

and witchcraft, 136–138

Zoroaster's cosmology, similarity to, 34–35

Christian Kabbalism, beginnings of, 79–83

Christian Science doctrine, 220

Church of New Jerusalem, in America, 176

cibation, 103

Circe, the sorceress, 36

clairvoyance, 115–116

Cochiti rite, 326–327

coincidences, development of the concept, 145

Combe, George, 222

Committee for the Scientific Investigation of Claims of the Paranormal. *See* CSICOP

common sense, cultural definition of, 6

complexity theory, 262

Comte, Auguste, and faith in scientific progress, 146

Condon, Edward, and UFOs, 283

conjunction, 103

consciousness, in HPB's terms, 194

consciousness, universal, 272
  and de Chardin, Pierre Teilhard, 302

Constantine, 53
  divination, banishment of, 78

Copernicus, 121
  universe of, compared to Dante, 141–142

Copperfield, David, magician, 237

corpses
  alchemical preservation, 105
  Egyptian mortuary practices, 15–16

Coulomb, Mrs., and HPB, 198

Cousins, Norman, and homeopathy, 276–277

cranioscopy. *See* phrenology

creation myths
of Greek colonies, sixth-century B.C., 24–25
Maya Indian, 274–275
and time cycles, 195–196

Crookes, Sir William, and supernatural phenomena, 186–187, 364n. 2

Crowley, Aleister, 207–211
Devil, invocation of, 209–210, 364n. 15 (Chap. 20), 365n. 16
downfall of, 210–211
Hermetic Order of the Golden Dawn, 207–208

crystals, 291–294

CSICOP (Committee for the Scientific Investigation of Claims of the Paranormal), 249, 368–369n. 4, 369n. 6
beginnings of, 317
and crystal healing, 292
and Randi, James, 258

cults, 54, 344, 375n. 5 (Chap. 38)
and Christianity, rise of, 78

curses, 36, 67
evil, expellation of, 131
evil eye, 134–135
voodoo, 333–334

Dante
hell, description of, 128–129
universe of, compared to Copernicus, 141–142

Dark Ages, 75–76

d'Ascoli, Cecco, and *Astrological Principles,* 118–119

Davenport brothers, stage performers, 202–203

Davies, Paul, and purposive science, 321

DDH (Daniel Dunglas Home), 179–190
and the Browning incident, 182–185
European performances, 185–186
Houdini's explanation of, 235
levitation, 180–182, 362n. 9

dead, communication with the, 152–162
in Ghana, 329–330
methods, 162

death
in Christian Kabbalistic thought, 81
in HPB's terms, 198

defixions, 67

demons, 123–124
in early Christian times, 70
in Medieval times, 129

Descartes, René, and the mechanical universe, 144–145

determinism, of astrology, 122

Devil, the, 123–126
appearance, 123, 125, 358n. 1 (Chap. 13)
in Cartesian terms, 145
conjuration of, by Crowley, 209–210, 364n. 15 (Chap. 20), 365n. 16
fall from grace, 126, 359n. 4 (Chap. 13)
and fetishes, 328
pacts with, 129–130
and witches, 133

Devil Himself. *See* Crowley, Aleister

divination techniques
  geomancy, 295–302
  hepatoscopy, 20–23
  involuntary, 19 (*see also* astrology;
    exorcism)
  voluntary, 19, 356n. 4 (*see also*
    hepatoscopy)
divine proportions, of physical ob-
    jects, 91–93
dowsing, 295–298
Drake, Frank, and SETI, 284–285
Dressler, Allen, and *Voyage to the*
    Great Attractor, 322
Drummer of Tedworth, 164
Dunninger, Joseph, magician,
    236–237

Earth
  and Copernicus' discoveries,
    121
  See also geomancy
Eastern religions, appeal of,
    309–310
ecofeminism, 342
ectoplasm, 203–207, 364n. 4
Eddy, Mary Baker, and Christian
    Science doctrine, 220
Egypt
  beginnings of magic, 15–17
  mortuary practices, 15–16
Eisenbud, Jule, and thoughtography,
    259–261
elemental qualities, 101
elements, basic, 25–26
Eleusinian cult, 191, 363n. 1
Emerald tablet, 58–59
  and the philosopher's stone, 101
emotions and music, association,
    93

empiricists, separation of celestial
    from terrestrial, 120–121
energy field, of human body, 267,
    270
  See also mesmerism
envy, and the evil eye, 135
epilepsy, 32–34
Episcopalian, 54
esoteric movement. *See* frauds;
    spiritualism; theosophy
ESP (extrasensory perception), 256
ether, 197
Etruscans, and hepatoscopy, 20–23
evil
  human forms of, in Medieval
    times, 131–132
  polarization with good, 126
evil eye, 134–135
  and social relations, 135
  and witches, 134
  See also psychokinesis
evolution
  directed, 302
  in HPB's terms, 194–195
  and machines, intelligent,
    321–322
exorcism, 130–131
  in ancient Nineveh, 18
  in West Malaysia, 330–332
exorcists
  involuntary divination of, 19
  and witches, 133–134
experimental strategy, during the
    Renaissance, 142–146
extrasensory perception (ESP),
    256
extraterrestrial contact, in Book of
    Ezekiel, 279–280
Ezekiel, Book of, and UFOs,
    279–280, 371n. 2

faith, in scientific progress, 146
Faraday, Michael, 169
    rappings, opinion of, 186–187
Fascinus, the Roman god, 134–135
Faustus, and pacts with the Devil,
    129–130
feng-shui, 295
fetishes, 7, 326–328
Feynman, Richard, 238–244
    and Houdini, Harry, comparison
        of, 243–244
    numerological tricks, 239–240
    science and the occult, ideas on,
        241–242
    and space shuttle *Challenger* in-
        vestigation, 238–239
fig, sign of, 134
finger crossing, 4
Fish, Leah, and Rochester rappings,
    154–155
Fludd, Sir Robert, 92–93, 357n. 1
    (Chap. 9)
    History of Both Worlds, 95
fluids, basic, 31–32
flying saucers, 282. *See also* UFOs
food
    aphrodisiacs, 277
    attitudes toward, 275–276
Forms, Platonic, 39–40
Fox, J. R., and the Cochiti rite,
    326–327
Fox, Margaret, and the Rochester
    rappings, 152–162
Fox sisters, 152–162
    Houdini's explanation of, 235
    as sensitives, 161
fraternities, roots of, 208
frauds, 201–202
    C., Eva, 204–207
    Crowley, Aleister, 207–211

Davenport brothers, 202–203
Koonses' Spirit Room, 202
Palladino, Eva, 203–204
Frazer, James G., 225–226
    Golden Bough, The, 225
free will and astrology, 122
Freud, Sigmund, and the uncon-
    scious, 256–257
future, predictions of
    by Nostradamus, 112–116
    by the Oracle of Delphi, 36–38

Gaia hypothesis, 301–302
Galen, combining magic and sci-
    ence, 49–51
Galileo, numerology, thoughts on,
    95–97
Gall, Franz Joseph, and phrenology,
    216–217
Gardner, Martin, and debunking
    frauds, 318–319
Geller, Uri, and psychokinesis,
    257–259
Gell-Mann, Murray, and order and
    disorder, 262
gematria, 63–66
geomancy, 295–302
    and the Gaia hypothesis, 301–302
Gnosticism, 55–57
    rationality of, 68–69
God
    HPB's concept of, 195
    name of, 355n. 5
    and science, 322–323
Golden Bough, The, 225
good
    human forms in Medieval times,
        131
    polarization with evil, 126

good luck charms, contemporary,
    3–5
Great Enlightenment, 145–147
Greek cosmology, 25–26
    alchemy, 38–39
    creation myth, 24–25
    oracles, 36–38
    planetary influences, 29
    soul, treatment of, 39
Greeley, Horace, and the Rochester
    rappings, 156–157
Gribbin, John, and purposive sci-
    ence, 321

Hahnemann, Samuel, and home-
    opathy, 276
harmonic chords
    of body parts, 92–93
    between planets, 94
Harmonic Law of planetary mo-
    tion, 94
haruspex (seer), 21
haunted houses, 152–162
healing techniques
    acupuncture, 270
    biofeedback, 265–267
    with charms, 66–67
    chiropractic, 270
    and crystals, 291–292
    and fetishes, 326–328
    food, use of, 276–278
    with herbs, 43
    homeopathy, 276–278
    kundalini, 271
    massage therapy, 268–269
    and music, 93
    and numerology, 85
    with the philosopher's stone,
        101–102

phrenomagnetism, 220
placebo effect, 264–265
    and pulsed electromagnetic
        fields, 268, 370n. 5
    pyramid power, 293–294
    Rolfing, 269–270
    Tai Chi, 270–271
    therapeutic touch, 267, 272–273
    yoga, 265
heaven
    in spiritualist terms, 168
    in Swedenborgian terms, 176
hell
    in Cartesian terms, 145
    Dante's description of, 128–129
    first mention of, 126–127
    in Medieval times, 127
    in Swedenborgian terms, 176
Helvetius, 102
hepatoscopy, 20–23, 352n. 2 (Chap. 2)
herbs
    in medicine and astrology, 32
    and Medieval astrology, 118–119
Hermes, 57–59, 354n. 4
Hermes Trismegistus, 75, 354nn. 4, 5
Hermetic Age, 107
Hermetic doctrine, 57–59
Hermetic Order of the Golden
    Dawn, 207–208, 364n. 13
hidden variable, 262
Higginson, Thomas Wentworth, and
    mediums, 168
History of Both Worlds, 95
Home, Daniel Dunglas. See DDH
homeopathy, 276–278
Hopkins, Matthew, witchhunter,
    139–140
horn, sign of, 134
horoscope, 27–28
horseshoes, 4

Houdini, Harry, 203
    and C., Eva, conclusions on,
        206–207
    and Feynman, Richard, compari-
        son to, 243–244
    Spirit Truths Committee, advisor
        to, 234–236
    tricks of, 231–234
HPB (Helena Petrovna Blavatsky),
        191–200
    downfall of, 198–199
    evolution, theory of, 194–197
    god, concept of, 195
    Isis Unveiled, 191–200, 363n. 6
    monosubstance, 196–197
    Secret Doctrine, The, 199
humors, 31–32
Hutchison, Keith, and materialism,
        144
Hydesville, New York, and haunted
        houses, 152
hypnotism, and animal magnetism,
        173
hysterical illness, link to sexuality,
        173

ideoplasts, 206. See also ectoplasm
immortality, elixirs for, 101,
        357–358n. 7
"Implicate Order," 262
impression management, and
        Crowley's invocations,
        209–210
Inferno, 128–129
internal organs, divining by, 22–23
    hepatoscopy, 20–23, 352n. 2
        (Chap. 2)
interstellar communication,
        284–285. See also UFOs

involuntary divination, 19. See also
        astrology; exorcism
Ionian philosophers, 25
Isis Unveiled, 191–200

Jay, Ricky, magician, 237
Jews, and the Kabbalah, spread of,
        79
John Paul II, and exorcism, 130
Jupiter, astrological traits of, 29

Kabbalah, 57, 60
    during age of Christianity, 78–79
    and the Hermetic Order of the
        Golden Dawn, 208
Kabbalism
    Christian, 79–83
    and gematria, 63–66
    and playing cards, 88–89
karma, 254
Kepler, Johannes, 93–95, 357n. 3
        (Chap. 9)
Knight, J. Z., 252–253
    and Gardner, Martin, 318
knowledge, ancient, reverence for,
        75–76
Koonses' Spirit Room, 202
kundalini, 271

Law of Similars, 276
Lemuria, 195
de Léon, Moses, 83
Lerner, Max, and The Aquarian
        Conspiracy, 341
levitation
    of Home, Daniel Dunglas,
        178–179

Houdini's explanation of, 235–236
and HPB, 192
See also psychokinesis
Lévy-Bruhl, Lucien, and evolution
    of magic, 337–338
Life After Life, 289
"like cures like" concept, 277, 325
    in American folk remedies, 45
    and defixions, 67
    for love potions, 136
    in Plinian cures, 44
livers. *See* hepatoscopy
love
    in Middle Ages, 119
    potions for, 136
love potions, 136
Luther, Martin, 54
Lutheranism, 54

machines, intelligent, 321–322
Mack, John, and UFO abductions,
    286
MacLaine, Shirley, and channeling,
    253, 368n. 3 (Chap. 26)
macrocosm, synthesizing with
    microcosm, 93
magic, 7–9
    over the ages, 246
    Agrippa's survey of, 83
    and altered states of conscious-
        ness, 210
    black, and the Devil, 129–130
    and Christianity, rise of, 53
    derivation of, 9
    in Egypt, 15–17
    evolution of, 173–174
    evolution of, according to Frazer,
        James G., 225–226
    imitative, 42–51

invoking, 8
metaphors of, 325–326
as pseudo-science, 224–225
public perception of, 344
puzzles, 61–67
and reality, 349–350
as a religion, 307–310
during the Renaissance, 141–147
revival in the 1990s, 345–347
rites, 328–329
in Roman Empire, 42–51
and the Romantic movement,
    165 166
and science compared, 314–323
sociology of, 340–342
surveys of superstitious beliefs,
    246–248, 367n. 8 (Chap. 25)
sympathetic, 42–51
in the twentieth century, 231–251
    (*see also* channeling; crystals;
    geomancy; healing techniques;
    NDE; PK; UFOs)
universality of, 324–338
magic, principles of
    "as above, so below," 26, 58
    "association equals participation,"
        275
    "like cures like" (*see* "like cures
        like" concept)
    transfer principle, 46–48
magic squares, 61
magic wands, 35–36
Magi tribe, 35
magnetism, influence in America,
    174
Maharishi Mahesh Yogi, 265–266
maledictions, 67
Mars
    astrological traits of, 29, 31
    inhabitants of, 281

Mary the Jewess, 100, 357n. 6
mass hypnosis, and channeling,
     254–255
materialism, 144–145
mathematical laws, 144–145
Mathers, Samuel Liddell, and the
     Hermetic Order of the
     Golden Dawn, 208
Maxwell, James Clerk, 169
McDonald, James, and UFOs, 284
meditation and healing, 265–266
mediums and communication with
     the dead, 162, 361n. 8
Mercury
     allegorical imagery of, 119
     astrological traits of, 27, 29, 31
Mesmer, Franz, 169–174
     and hysterical illness, 173
     investigation of, 172–173
mesmerism, 169–174
     and healing, 266
Mesopotamia, and the beginnings
     of magic, 15, 17–19
metallurgy, 101. See also alchemy
Methodists, 54
metoposcopy, 212–223
microcosm, synthesis with macro-
     cosm, 93
Middle Ages, 75–76
     spiritual orientation of, 76–77
Miller, William, and Romanticism,
     166, 361n. 3
"Mister Sludge." See DDH
Modern Spiritualism, 188–190
monomyth of nineteenth century,
     194, 196–197
monosubstance
     HPB's idea, 196–197
     phlogiston, 140, 197
     search for, 197

Moody, Raymond, and Near-Death
     Experiences, 289–290
Moon
     astrological traits of, 29, 31–32
     and virtue, 118, 358n. 2 (Chap. 12)
Mormonism, 54
mortuary practices, of Egypt,
     15–16
music
     body parts, association to, 92–93
     and healing, 93
     mathematical relationships of,
     68

Nakagawa, Kyoichi, and magnetic
     fields, 267–268
Natural History, 43–49
natural law
     Aristotle's, 25–26
     subjection to, 142–146
Nazca plains, 299–300
NDE (Near-Death Experiences),
     288–290
     medical explanations of, 290
Near-Death Experiences (NDE),
     288–290
Neoplatonists, 69–71
New Age movement, 249–251,
     310–311
     body work, 265–273
     dangers of, 311–312
     and HPB, 191
     philosophy of, 303–304
     and postmodernism, 320
     Wicca, 342–343
New Thought movement,
     226–227
noosphere, 302
Nostradamus, 112–116, 367n. 14

nuclear fusion, 98–99, 357n. 1
numbers, power of, 355n. 11
    and Pythagoras, 67–68
    See also numerology
numerology, 63–66
    and Christianity, 82–83, 355n. 6
    Galileo's thoughts on, 95–97
    and the Kabbalah, 85

occult
    in American history (*see*
        spiritualism)
    beginnings of, 77
    contemporary (*see* New Age
        movement)
    during Renaissance, 141–147
Olcott, Henry Steel, and HPB,
    192–193
Old Straight Track Club, 298
Omega point, 302, 321
On the Greek Medical Corpus, 50–51
On the Occult Philosophy, 83
Oracle of Delphi, 36–38
    and channeling, 253
order of universe
    hierarchical, 28–32
    logical, 67–68
ouija board, 162, 360–361n. 19

Palladino, Eusapia, and ectoplasm,
    203–204
palmistry, 220–221
Paracelsus. *See* Von Hohenheim,
    Philippus Aureolus Theophras-
    tus Bombast
paranoia, and the evil eye, 135
parapsychology, 256–263, 367n. 7
    ESP, 256

psychokinesis, 257–263
    and UFOs, 287
Paris, France, and occultists,
    171–172
Peletz, Michael, and West Malaysia
    exorcisms, 330–332
PEMF (pulsed electromagnetic
    fields), for healing, 268, 370n. 5
pentagrams, 85–86
personality, and physical body
    shape, 213
Philosopher's Egg, 105
philosopher's stone, 39, 101–103
    modern-day, 347
phlogiston, 140, 197, 363n. 9
phrenology, 216–220, 223
    and animal magnetism, 219–220
    and Combe, George, 222
phrenomagnetism, 219–220
physical forces, 87–88
Physics of Immortality, The, 321
physiognomy, 216
Pietz, William, and fetishes, 328
PK (psychokinesis), 255, 257–263,
    368nn. 2, 3
    fraud, 260–261
    tests of, 258
Planck, Max, and quantum energy,
    315
planetary influences, 29
    in Medieval times, 118
    and metoposcopy, 214–216
    questioning of, by empiricists,
        120–121
planetary motion, Harmonic Law
    of, 94
planets, 354n. 3 (Chap. 5)
    association with four humors,
        31–32
playing cards, 88–89

Pliny (The Elder)
  classification of magic principles,
    43–49
  and fetishes, 326
Plotinus, 69–71
Podmore, Frank, and *Modern Spiri-*
    tualism, 188–190
politics and occult behavior, 174
poltergeists, 164
Porta, Giambattista della, and phys-
    iognomy, 216
postmodernism, 319–320, 374n. 16
power centers, 298–301
predetermination, 213. *See also* body
    divination
Principle of Association, 87–88,
    356n. 7
  and body octaves, 92–93
Principles of Philosophy, 144
Project Blue Book, and UFOs,
    283
prophecies of the future
  and Nostradamus, 112–116
  and the Oracle of Delphi,
    36–38
Protestantism, 54
  alchemy, rejection of, 110
psychokinesis (PK), 255, 257–263,
    368nn. 2, 3
Ptolemaeus, Claudius (Ptolemy),
    28
pulsed electromagnetic fields, for
    healing, 268, 370n. 5
Pursel, Jack, channeler, 253
putrefaction, 103–104
puzzles, and power of numbers and
    words, 61–63, 355n. 4
pyramid power, 293–294, 372nn. 6,
    7
Pythagoras, 67–68

quantum mechanics, and PK, 262
Quarterly Journal of Science, 187–188
quintessence, 25

rabbits' feet, 4–5
racism, and physiognomy, 216
Randi, James, 258–259
  and CSICOP, 319
  and Serios, Ted, 260–261
rapping, 169, 360n. 3, 361n. 21, 366n.
    5 (Chap. 23)
  Podmore's conclusions, 188–189
  See also Rochester rapping
Reformation, religious, 77,
    138–139
Reformists, 138–139
reincarnation, 254
relaxation therapy, 265–266
religion
  dissatisfaction with, 308–309
  nineteenth-century crisis of,
    166–167
  profusion of, in early Christian
    era, 52–56
  and science, and Swedenborg,
    175
religions, ancient
  effect on future, 195 (*see also*
    theosophy)
  and magic, 312
Renaissance, 77
  and body divination, 213–216
  and magic, shifting of thought,
    141–147
Richet, Charles-Robert, investiga-
    tion of Palladino, Eusapia, 204,
    364n. 2
rituals, move away from, 138–139
Roberts, Jane, and Seth, 253–254

Rochester rappings, 152–162
  cause of, 160–161
  examination and investigation of
    Fox girls, 157–159
  Houdini's explanation of, 235
  and Shakerism, 168
Rolfing, 269–270
Roman Catholicism, 54
Romans
  magic in early times, 42–51
  secret doctrines, 52–59
Romanticism, decline of, 227
Romantic movement, 165–166
Rosicrucian order, 208, 364n. 13

Saturn, astrological traits of, 27, 29,
    31
scarab beetles, 16–17
science
  over the ages, 245–246
  anti-science attitude, 319–320
  and God, 322–323
  internal problems, 320–321
  and magic, compared, 314–323
  and magic, condemnation of,
    143–147
  and magic, convergence with,
    346–347
  metaphors of, 325–326
  method of, 77, 313–316
  public perception of, 344
  purposive, theories on, 321
  and religion, and Swedenborg,
    175
  universe of, 317, 321–322, 369n.
    12
Scientific American, and the Spirit
    Truths Committee, 234–236
scientific progress, faith in, 146

scrying, 113–114, 291–294
séances
  fraudulent, 202–211
  with the Rochester rapper,
    155–157
  sexual liberalism of, 170,
    203–207, 361n. 8
Search for Extraterrestrial Intelli-
    gence (SETI), 284
Secret Doctrine, The, 199
Sefer Yezira (Book of Creation),
    60–61
senses, relying on, 142–143
sephiroth, 79–83
Serios, Ted, and thoughtography,
    259–261, 369n. 8
Seth, 253–254
SETI (Search for Extraterrestrial
    Intelligence), 284
sex and magic, 210, 365n. 18. See also
    séances, sexual liberalism of
Shakers, 167–168
sickness
  exorcising with words, 18
  in Tetrabiblos, 31
  See also healing techniques
Simon the Magician, 55–56
Sisala divining, 329–330
Smith, Helen, communicating from
    Mars, 281
Smith, Joseph, 54
sneezes, 5
social climate
  of fifteenth and sixteenth cen-
    turies, 137–140
  of nineteenth century, 165–169
  of seventeenth century, 140
social reform, and spiritualism,
    174–175
social sciences, creation of, 145

Society for Psychic Research
    (SPR), 163
soul
    ascent of, 79–82
    idea of, 39
    and Platonic forms, 40
    progression of, according to
        HPB, 199
    progression of, and reincarnation,
        254
    of the world, 69–70
spiritual forces, 87–88
spiritualism, 177–178
    analysis of, 188–190
    automatisms of, 164
    in the Burned-Over District,
        167–169
    and Mesmer, Franz, 169–174
    and metoposcopy, 212–223
    Modern Spiritualism, 188–190
    the movement, 166–169
    phrenology, 216–220
    revival, and the Rochester rap-
        pings, 152–162
    Shakerism, 167–168
    and social reform, 174–175
    Swedenborg, Emmanuel,
        175–177
    See also New Age movement
SPR (Society for Psychic
    Research), 163
stars
    energy for transmutations, 117
    See also astrology
statistics, beginnings of, 145
stress management, 266
sublimation, 104
Sun, astrological traits of, 29, 31
supernatural phenomena, in late
    nineteenth century, 163–164

superstition, 5–8
    belief in, 246–248, 367n. 8
        (Chap. 25)
    held over from childhood, 3–5
    See also magic
Surely You're Joking, Mr. Feynman!,
    241
Swedenborg, Emmanuel, 175–177
    and channeling, 253–254
Swedenborgianism, 177. See also
    Swedenborg, Emmanuel

Tacitus, 49
Tai Chi, 270–271
Tarot cards, 88–90
telescope, technology of, 95, 357n. 4
terrestrial geometry, 298–301
    and UFOs, 299–301
Tetrabiblos, 28, 31
theories on everything (TOEs), 321
Theosophical Society, 191–200
    charter of, 194
    and Isis Unveiled, 194
    Sunrise, 199
theosophy, 191–200
    laws of, 197
therapeutic touch (TT) therapy,
    267, 272–273
theurgy, 70
thought transference, in theosophi-
    cal terms, 197
time, linear, 116
Tipler, Frank, and The Physics of
    Immortality, 321
Tiryakian, Edward, and sociology of
    magic, 340–342
TOEs (theories on everything), 321
Transcendental Meditation (TM),
    265–266

transfer principle, 46–47
transmutation of matter, 99, 357n. 3
    and elemental qualities, 101
    modern, 111
    See also alchemy
tree of life, 77–82
    Tarot cards, relation to, 89
tree worship, 4, 351n. 3
Truzzi, Marcello, and sociology of
        magic, 340–342
TT (therapeutic touch) therapy,
        267
Tunisia, and the evil eye, 135

UFOs, 371n. 8
    abductions, 286
    in Book of Ezekiel, 279–280,
        371n. 2
    and interstellar communication,
        284–285
    messages of, 282–283, 286–287
    past visitations, 285–286
    and Project Blue Book, 283
    sightings of, 282–284
    and terrestrial geometry, 299–301
Uncertainty Principle, 245
unconscious, collective, and UFO
        sightings, 287
unconscious, and Freud, Sigmund,
        256–257

Venus
    allegorical imagery of, 119
    astrological traits of, 27, 29, 31
voluntary divination, 19. *See also*
        hepatoscopy
von Däniken, Erich, and UFOs,
        285–286, 371–372nn. 13, 14

Von Hohenheim, Philippus Aureo-
        lus Theophrastus Bombast
        (pseud. Paracelsus), 107–109
Von Nettesheim, Heinrich Cor-
        nelius Agrippa. *See* Agrippa
voodoo, 333–334
voodoo dolls, 36
Voyage to the Great Attractor, 322

water witching, 295–298
    devices, 296–297
    and geologists, 297–298
    and the Nazca plains, 299–300
Watkins, Alfred, and geomancy,
        298–299
Weiss, Ehrich. *See* Houdini, Harry
Wesley, John, 54
West Malaysia, and exorcisms,
        330–332
Weston, William, and exorcism, 130
Wicca, 342–343
witchcraft, 133–140
    and Christianity, polarization
        from, 136–138
    contemporary, 342–343
witches
    appearance, 133
    and the Devil, 133
    and love potions, 136
    persecution of, 136–140
    powers of, 133–134
    women as, 135–136
witchhunting, 136
women
    and alchemy, 100
    as mediums, 203–207, 253–254,
        361n. 8
    and witchcraft, 135–136, 342–343
wood knocking, 4

word puzzles, 61–63, 355n. 4
words of power, 6–7, 18
    Abracadabra, 66–67, 355n. 8
    for exorcism, 18–19, 130–131
World Soul
    in Agrippa's writings, 83, 85
    and the philosopher's stone, 102

Yeats, William Butler, and the Hermetic Order of the Golden Dawn, 208
yoga, 265, 272

Zaleski, Carol
    conclusions of, 312
    and Life After Life, 289–290
Zarathustra. See Zoroaster
Zen Buddhism
    appeal of, 309–310
    and relaxation therapy, 265–266
zodiac, 27, 352–353nn. 2, 3, 4, 5, 8
    body part associations, 92–93
    signs of, 29–30
Zohar, 79, 83
Zoroaster, 34–35
Zosimus, 100

ABOUT THE AUTHOR

Anthony Aveni, author of *Empires of Time, Ancient Astronomers,* and *Conversing with the Planets,* was featured in *Rolling Stone* magazine's 1991 list of the ten best university professors in the country. Aveni was also voted the 1982 Professor of the Year by the Council for the Advancement and Support of Education, the highest national teaching award. He has lectured on astronomy for the Learning Channel. He lives in Hamilton, New York and teaches at Colgate University.